Fostered Adult Children Together

Fostered Adult Children Together

On The Bridge To Healing

Will we ever get over it?

**Former Foster Children
Share Their Stories**

Ten Stepping Stones

For Adult Survivors of Foster Care

CAROL LUCAS

Library of Congress Control Number: 2019921077

HARDBACK: 978-1-951461-99-7
PAPERBACK: 978-1-951461-98-0
EBOOK: 978-1-952155-00-0

Ordering Information:

For orders and inquiries, please contact:
1-888-404-1388
www.goldtouchpress.com
book.orders@goldtouchpress.com

Printed in the United States of America

Contents

Part One
Our Stories

Part Two
Documents for FACT Support Group

Acknowledgements

The One who deserves the most gratitude for helping me with this book is God, as I believe it was ultimately Him who gave me the courage, strength, perseverance, and grace to do it. I did this book on a wing and a prayer, going with the flow of faith. It was His hand that guided mine.

During the course of doing this book, it never ceased to amaze me how things worked out. When I first embarked on this venture I wasn't even sure where to begin, so I began praying about it and was led back to the place where it all began, my childhood. I was in Illinois visiting some family and decided to visit ISSCS, the children's home I was put in, and while visiting there I was informed of a book about the home, and it was through ordering the book from Jill Vernon, a woman who was involved in doing the book, that my stories began, as she gave me the phone number for another woman involved in the ISSCS book, Yvonne Yorkland, who sent me the ISSCS reunion list, which I used for the first fifteen stories in the book. I want to thank both of them for being so helpful and encouraging.

I want to thank all of the former foster children who shared their stories, not just for taking the time in this busy world, but for having the courage to talk about a past they'd just soon forget. I know myself that it isn't easy to talk about a painful childhood, so I commend all of the people who did this. It was no small task, not for them or for me, but the fact that we share the same past eased the stress. It required trusting me to listen to them without judgment or rejection, which for people who have trust issues, can be very difficult. It also required me to listen to their traumatic stories without internalizing them, which was no easy thing for me to do since I am by nature very sensitive and empathetic.

I want to give a special thank you for my sister Donna, who was my only sibling who shared a story. It meant a lot to me for her to do this.

One particular former foster child I am very thankful for is John Dunn, who is a contributing founder to FACT. I have a lot of admiration and respect for John and he has been and continues to be a great inspiration to me.

I also want to thank my brother Glen Woodard, who is also a contributing founder to FACT, for all of his help in the beginning. Although we had our share of disagreements about the literature, in the end we both got our way, as FACT eventually evolved into the 10 Stepping Stones, which is based on a 12-step format. God in His infinite wisdom worked it all out. Last but not least I am especially thankful for the awesome spiritual document he wrote and allowing me to use it in the book.

I also want to thank all of the countless other former foster children who sent me emails throughout the years, for every one of them reminded me why I do this work. One in particular email has stuck with me, from a woman who had no family and was suffering from depression that stemmed from her isolation and loneliness. She was so happy to hear from me, saying "Thank you, Thank you, Thank you, for being an ear. It's a small break in the midst of this heavy silence and pain." Another woman said, "I am very grateful for all your hard work in preparing this resource for the benefit of many. What a blessing you are."

There were others who thanked me for forming FACT and I am SO grateful for theirs, as it gave me the inspiration I needed at times to remain motivated.

I also want to thank Kim Hughes for supporting me through the rough times, and encouraging me to forge ahead when I felt like giving up. You're a Godsend, Kim!

I thank IUniverse in the original publication of my book and Gold Press for the final publication.

And last, but not least, I want to thank my husband Larry, for always being so supportive and respectful of my work. Without him the book was only a dream. He is the one who made my dream a reality. He is the one who gave me the idea of having excerpts in the foreword and he is the one who paid for the publication. When I began regressing back into my traumatic past he was the one who stopped me from jumping off the same bridge I was supposed to be crossing. No words can express my deep gratitude for the love he showed me. Thank you, sweetheart! I will always love you!

Foreword

FOSTERED ADULT CHILDREN TOGETHER

FACT is a support group for former foster children. This book provides all of the basic information needed for former foster children who are interested in forming FACT meetings, including the literature and directions on getting started.

I wanted to express a moving foreword, and decided rather than writing a long and eloquent one about what compelled me to write this book, it would be more moving to allow other former foster children to express their compelling thoughts. If after reading these you are still wondering what drove me to write this book, then perhaps you will be compelled to read past the foreword.........

Moving Forward from the Past...

In reading these, it may appear we are only dwelling on the past, but in reality, a step backward is a step forward in healing from our foster care experience. Foster kids have been silent long enough. It is time for us to share our experience, strength, and hope with each other. *My wish is that this book will be an inspiration for all foster children---past, present, and future.*

The Stories

The bulk of these stories were written by Carol Lucas as ghost writer for the various contributors, gathering information over the phone and/or internet. There is no particular style for these stories. Each story expresses the individual's personality and experience. Adam Robe, Brent Matthews,

Doreen Oechle, Guy Dufour, Jason Murphy, Jeff Campus, Kristina R., Pamela Jane, and Therese NG's stories were written by themselves and were only edited by Carol where needed. Barbara Richards, Ron Huber, and Testimony Iyore's stories were written from their books.

I want everyone reading this book to be aware that I was admonished by the publisher to make numerous revisions, deleting explicit material relevant to the stories to avoid a possible libel lawsuit in the future. It's a shame that the stories had to be watered down so far to protect the perpetrators that we couldn't express in actuality what really happened to us---we can't name the abusers, locations, or anything that links the abused to the abuser. Any readers who have been in the foster care system pretty much know what these issues are and should be able to fill the blanks in for themselves, where the material isn't lost, it's just hidden.

There are sixty-one stories in this book, but there could be millions more.

What Is It Like Being a Foster Child?

"Being ripped away from my family and placed in foster care left me with emotional scars that have been very difficult to heal, especially strong fears of abandonment. Although I certainly never considered my past a blessing while living it, I do consider it a blessing to be able to connect with others who have walked in my shoes and understand that painful past. I do believe my experience made me a stronger, wiser, and more compassionate person than I would have been otherwise. My biggest blessing is the love of my Heavenly Father, who will never ever abandon me."

Carol Lucas (p. 3)

"I never wanted to be in foster care, but I probably would have ended up on drugs and/or alcohol if I hadn't been taken away from my parents. I always had a backward relationship with my mom, with me feeling like I was mothering her, and my two younger siblings. It still hurts me and I am still longing for my mother. I just wish we could be a family. The only way I've gotten through the hurt is with prayers and humor. I use humor a lot."

Jennifer Powell (p. 45)

"I realize my dysfunctional home life with my mom and being put in foster care was passed on to me largely due to her own similar past, but I am determined NOT to follow in my parents footsteps! I have chosen not to be a victim of my past. I want and need stability more than anything else."

Charlie Powell (p. 86)

"I was in seven foster homes altogether and foster care wasn't always 'rainbows and sunshine' for me, but when I finally found my 'home,' the healing began. I don't want any contact with my birth parents. I consider my foster parents my parents now."

Heather Storm (p. 48)

"My entire experience of living in foster care for sixteen years, being moved thirteen times, and having been physically and emotionally abused and neglected, had a profound effect on my adult life. Like some unfortunate infants, I feel that I effectively 'failed to thrive' as an adult because of my subsequent crippling low self-esteem and total lack of any positive outlook on life, or even any ambition to challenge myself to do or try anything new because I just didn't think I could ever be successful at it. Nobody that I can recall during my childhood in care encouraged me to do anything, or get involved in anything challenging. I basically felt as if I was warehoused rather than cared for. Foster care is necessary; however, it is also necessary that it be provided in a way which respects the rights and wishes of the children it is intended to serve. This means that foster care services need to be provided in a transparent and accountable manner."
www.afterfostercare.com

John Dunn (p. 51)

"Foster care is like a double edged sword. On the one side it can provide a child with protection and safety from abuse and neglect, while the other side can cut away the very essence of who he or she is. It is a lot like a river. There are times when it is smooth and all is well and other times when the water becomes turbulent and difficult to navigate. Foster care is supposed to empower people to change, but instead it creates a sense of powerlessness and hopelessness for children and families."

Adam Robe (p. 62)

"Being in the ISSCS children's home was the only home I knew. I have a lot of happy memories from there and I made a lot of friends. If I had it to do all over again I would go back."

Alice Elston (p. 69)

"They took me away from the children's home to put me in a psychiatric hospital on an adult ward, where my companions were drug addicts, schizophrenic people, sex offenders, people with anger issues, lobotomized people, etc. As bad as it was there, it was as if I had escaped from Hell to be taken from that children's home to be put into that place. I felt like I had escaped from a very dark, frightening place to a place that was a lot less frightening. I think that I should tell anyone what they need to know about how bad those so called children's "homes" are."

B.R. (p. 76)

"I felt scared in my foster care home, but the children's home was a better experience. I was traumatized at first because I was separated from my sister, but I accepted my circumstances there and all of the children were in the same boat, so at least I didn't feel alone."

Anonymous (p. 84)

"I am a child of the system, a system which I believe needs to justify its needs for the huge social bureaucracy that is being created. It is in their best interest to create, or at the minimum, to perpetuate the social ills that create dysfunction, whether they realize it or not. Then they can all spend countless tax dollars on research and debate about what is going wrong with society. The irony of this is that it is a problem, which if solved, would put a lot of people out of a job."

Brent Matthews (p. 87)

"My experience as a crown ward in the CAS has left an indelible imprint that follows me throughout all the years of my life, so that at 55 years old, I still seek the connection and community, at Christmas, at birthdays, and times of crisis, that will never be mine. I remain---staring into the home of others and walking the mean streets alone."

Cheryl Smith (Peacock) (p. 96)

"I have those memories of foster care in a box, and there they sit in the corner of my mind, visited only when I need to draw upon them as a source of strength. That is how I choose to look at my childhood, because to see it in any other way would devour me, and I refuse to be a willing victim."

Debra Cruz (p. 107)

"Foster care, no matter where you are or where you live, can mess you up on the inside. I feel lonely, distant, depressed. I feel like there is an entire chapter missing in the book of my life."

Dexter Dugan (p. 116)

"Being in foster care helped me to realize that there are people out there who really do care. I was fortunate to have had such good, loving foster parents at such a young age. Despite being in foster care, I feel that I have led an abundant life."

Donna White (p. 123)

"I struggle with abandonment issues, both physical abandonment and emotional abandonment. Relationships are difficult and I have yet to find one that I am not recreating my dysfunctional relationships with the parental figures in my life. I never have felt like I belonged anywhere; I feel as I have been aimlessly roaming. I never felt loved, both in the foster homes and in my adopted home. I have always felt as if I was a burden to everyone, that they **had** to take care of me, but no one knew how to love me. This is the most painful legacy of the trauma and a very deep seated one. I believe that as foster children, our roots are ripped out from underneath us, but yet parental figures and society in general expects no ramifications from those roots being destroyed. I believe we former foster children need to tell our stories and to help each other."

Doreen Oechle (p. 127)

"I was moved around a lot in foster care. I didn't like it because I'd get used to a new environment, school, and friends, etc. and then I'd have to make a change. I think I would've been better off if I'd been put in a children's home like ISSCS, where I would have had more stability. Having so much instability as a child affected me as an adult. I don't like changes today unless it is for the best."

Anonymous (p. 130)

"Being a foster kid was not a good experience for me. I felt as though I was herded around like cattle and used for a paycheck."

Anonymous (p. 132)

"If I had a choice I would never have gone into foster care. It isn't normal to be separated from your family and it affects you all your life because you and your siblings tend to be rather estranged. "One positive thing about my experience is that I missed the Great Depression because I was in an orphanage. I had a sheltered life there, but I didn't like the regimentation and I wanted to be with my parents."

Edward Heavey (p. 135)

"It seems people have become detached from the sobering realities of how all abuse and neglect can deeply impact a child's life. I have been very affected by my foster care experiences. All too often I find myself looking over my shoulder and worried about a decision I have made, wondering when someone will learn of it, waiting for my impending doom to hit and trigger those events where I see the streets. I don't intend for it to happen and I certainly don't want it to; however, I can't escape the feeling that it's going to happen, as though it was fore planned in my life. I often feel isolated from everyone as a result of problems due to family and friends and then rush to their side when I'm about to lose them. You never really get over something like this. It takes at least 20-30 years before you can begin to fully fix and cope with the issues. I chose to write my story to speak on behalf of those who couldn't. I consider myself lucky; my life is simple compared to others who can't speak for themselves. Too many find themselves homeless, scrubbing the bins for food, incarcerated, on drugs, in gangs, or in body bags."

Edward Phillips (p. 138)

"If I had a choice I would never have gone into foster care. It isn't normal to be separated from your family and it affects you all your life because you and your siblings tend to be rather estranged. All I ever felt like was a case number, and as a black child back then I didn't feel cared for fairly. I didn't have any respect for foster care then and I don't have any now. I think the foster care system is all screwed up and I give it a big F!"

Emmitt Sorrell (p. 167)

"Foster kids need to grow from learned helplessness to hopefulness and learn to endeavor to persevere.

Greg Crosby (p. 170)

"Because of my past in foster care, I always ended up trusting the wrong people and my life became a mess because of this. I have dug a hole so deep that it is impossible to climb out of it unless I would get some help. I need God to help me. I need a miracle."

Guy (p. 175)

"I was luckier than most foster children and I don't feel that I was deeply affected by foster care, largely due to the fact that our family kept in tact, and for the most part, still does today. But I realize that others aren't always so fortunate. Siblings often lose contact with each other. There needs to be more done in the foster care system. Foster kids are already vulnerable; they shouldn't have to be subjected to further abuse and/or neglect. Foster kids deserve love like everybody else."

Harley Joe Carnes (p. 189)

"Although my memories are scattered and not very vivid, there are some things I do recall. One thing I am completely clear on is that family has and always will be very important to me. Nothing can remove the love and connection I feel with my family."

Heather Milne (p. 193)

"Being in foster care was like living with a wolf outside your window."

Janette McCrary (p. 197)

"My life as a foster kid was anything but boring. In the past I felt worthless and thought I might as well 'off' myself and be off the face of the earth, but in reality, I think my experience only made me a stronger and better person. I still live with a fear of abandonment and am afraid of getting too close to people for fear of them leaving me, but I believe God has always been there for me and loves me unconditionally. I think foster kids are amazing. We are so resilient. Maybe other people don't know how to be there for us, but foster kids need to stick together; otherwise we're screwed."

Jasmine Utsey (p. 210)

"Being moved around to about 40-50 homes, my emotions became like a switch. I became cold and distant, not letting anyone into my world. I felt so alone in this world. I just wanted to fit in and belong. Instead I hated waking up and facing another day. My paper bag was packed again, me dreading the next place they found for me. I still see the problems in today's foster care system as it was thirty years ago when I was a permanent ward. There are so many stories that describe in vivid detail what is wrong with the system, but a lot of people choose to ignore it and continue this disturbing cycle of mismanagement. I hope to one day see drastic changes in protecting these children better. Children don't choose to be in foster care, but are as a result of incapable parenting. May teaching parents to be better parents might be a piece of the puzzle? Hmmmm…"

Jason Murphy (p. 215)

"As for my foster care experience……I was a tender sprout cast out to the elements before I took root---cold, needing sunlight and nourishment, but getting mostly darkness, trampled on and with marring scars. Foster care has malformed me. The enemy meant it for evil, but the Lord meant it for good (Romans 8:28). In other words, a horrific beginning to a perfect child's life could have a horrific ending, but I am here to tell you that this child's horrific beginning is now her greatest gift. So at this point, the Lord is gifting for this to be my most purposeful life work."

Jeannie Lynch (p. 219)

"It was difficult growing up in this type of environment, and it's harder to explain it. I can't really say it all in a nutshell, but we all wind up on very different paths as we travel through life, even though we sometimes walk hand in hand. Although being in a children's home is different from the perceived "normalcy" of the nuclear family, one simply makes the best (or worst) of their situation in order to move on. We either learn and grow from our experiences, which are quite unique, or we get stuck in the vicious cycle of blaming "the hand we were dealt." Although it is comforting to sometimes dwell in the past, it's not helpful to wallow in it. We must make the decision to move forward. God bless all of you who have made it this far and also to those of you who are still working at it."

Jeff Campus (p. 224)

"I like to think that everything I went through wasn't my fault, but the truth is, I still do. All these things are what make aging out so hard. However, there is a message in all this. It is, no matter how hard life is, no matter how much you think you hate someone, the truth is, you can change your life, and you can love the person you thought you hated. You can be free in your heart and in your mind, if you just do something about it. SO STAND UP! You have to stand up and be strong; otherwise, you will fall down in the rubble of your past and get lost."

Jeremy Brown (p. 228)

"Foster children need to know we aren't alone. Because of my fear of abandonment I was always looking for love in all the wrong places. I hated being alone, and spent so many years trying to find somewhere to belong and someone to turn to, not realizing that there is only one being I needed to turn to and that was God. What an enlightening, wonderful wake-up call! We have to have faith in Him and His wondrous, unconditional love."

Anonymous (p. 237)

"Growing up in foster care was a very tough and grueling experience that I would never want to live again, but it made me who I am today, and I'm very proud of myself. I am a survivor."

Kelli Schoen (p. 239)

"My foster care experience has left me with emotional wounds that have been difficult to heal. I am terrified of abandonment and I struggle with low self-esteem and trust issues. I still sometimes feel those familiar feelings of being invisible, and not cared for. My personal relationships have been rocky at best. I still have the ache of wanting a 'family unit' of my own, one with a mother and a father. What has helped ease my pain is praying and meditating on Bible verses, such as this one: "Though my father and mother forsake me, the LORD will receive me." Psalm 27:10.

Kristina R. (p. 245)

"My life as a foster child was very abnormal. Aging out and trying to move on with my life has not been easy. I don't think other people realize just how abnormal our lives really are. If they did they would realized how hard our lives are compared to others."

Lisamarie Kerr (p. 259)

"I was fortunate, considering my circumstances, but many other foster kids aren't today. I believe my tough childhood made me tougher and more resilient. Growing up in foster care, without your parents, you feel like you have to take care of yourself. You have to be strong."

Loraine Mink (p. 261)

"I grew up feeling very confused and confused about being confused, and I still am. I was always running away from confusion, only to run right smack dab into it again, which only caused more confusion. I'll probably die confused. I don't know who I am."

Lu (p. 263)

"I'm thankful that I've chosen not to let bitterness take over because of the bad circumstances of my life. God is able to help us rise above it all and to live a victorious future."

Margaret Raycroft (p. 266)

"My foster care experience had a happy ending, but I know that many others don't. I want to say this to all the foster kids out there: 'There is hope. Just keep the faith. Don't let your past beat you down. And know that you have choices. Rise up against it, no matter what."

Martin Kenneth Hollingsworth (p. 271)

"Foster care didn't make my life safe. It wasn't until I was an adult that I realized all the abuse I suffered wasn't my secret; it was theirs. I can't change my past, but with the right support I can change my future. Everything will be all right for me, but I have to wonder about all the other displaced children throughout the world."

Nikki Daniels (p. 274)

"I have always felt so alone in my experiences as a foster child. There have been times that it has just been too much and I haven't been able to cope with all the memories and feeling of worthlessness that my childhood experiences have left me with. It is sad to admit that on more than several occasions as a young adult, I made attempts to take my life because I felt so insignificant and I had no self-worth. The scars that remain on my arms from my years of self-harm bare testament to the emotional pain that I was in. When you grow up with no stability, with no sense of belonging, with the constant feeling of being 'unwanted' and never knowing real love, is it any wonder? But I have learned not to let my past define me and I find strength from the fact that I survived. I am worthy of love. I have also learned to forgive, because it is the only way for me to let go of all the negative emotions I harbored inside me against those who wronged me. I wrote a poem called *My Guardian Angel*, which is in my story that best expresses how I felt going through foster care."

Pamela Jane (p. 284)

"My foster care experience was like heaven compared to my foster care friend who was in a foster care home from hell. I think foster care homes should be checked into more thoroughly."

Paul Kannenberg (p. 304)

"Foster care was hell."

Ray Reese (p. 306)

"It wasn't easy for me growing up in foster care. I had a lot of anger about it and it took me a long, long time to get past my anger, but I finally did, and got on with my life. I am comfortable with myself today and don't have any ghosts or gremlins to dwell on."

Richard Powell (p. 307)

"Being in foster care has made me more aware of negative people and my surroundings. I am more guarded than I think I would have been had I not been in foster care, but it has also made me a stronger person and a better mother."

Roberta Manning (p. 310)

"Whatever or how bad our childhood was like we must believe in ourselves because if we feel good about ourselves it doesn't matter what the world thinks. It is all between us and God."

Ron Huber (p 316)

"Foster care was like a nightmare for me. My thoughts are best expressed in my story/poem."

S.S. (p. 323)

"Being bounced around in foster care made me feel very abandoned, and I always felt like I was a puzzle piece that didn't fit in the puzzle anywhere. I had a lot of anger, resentment, and shame about being in foster care, and I grabbed onto everything I could to try to overcome my past, which often wasn't good for me. I tried so hard to fit into the puzzle, but it seemed to no avail, was another fail, until I finally surrendered my life to God, Who will never abandon me."

Jeremiah29:11

"For I know the plans I have for you, says the Lord, plans for good and not for evil, plans to give you a hope and future. He is awesome and Mighty to save."

Anonymous (p. 327)

"People need to know the horrors that some foster children have endured while being "cared" for in orphanages. Unfortunately, I experienced many horrors myself, and fortunately lived to tell my story, but many didn't. The evil ones who "cared" for us in the name of God or religion were eventually found out and in the name of God or religion, paid the price. I pay the price every day.

Sebastian DeCarss (p. 329)

"This reflects what is in my heart: Foster children represent the remnants of divorce and broken families. They are like lost sheep taken from their shepherd. They are placed in houses that really aren't home and cared for by those who are called to be detached from them emotionally. In many cases, they are the one of many to be cared for and the only real bonds they have are with the other children. Foster children feel abandoned and often believe that their circumstances are their fault. Most foster children live in a lonely world without any concrete refuge. Many are shifted from one foster home to another, which only serves to add to their confusion of who they are. I was one of the lucky few, who had loving foster parents; however, I still questioned why my parents left me and was often lonely. As an adult, I am still without a total feeling of wholeness. However, through faith in God and knowing I have purpose on this earth, I have overcome many of the demons from my past. For all of us who have been foster children, for those who are now, and for those who will be---we must remember that these trials produce perseverance, and perseverance produces character, and character produces hope. And hope does not fail."

Steve Woodard

"What it is like being in foster care: you feel like you are on an abandoned ship with survivors who have been cast aside in a war---neglected, rejected, fighting for their life. You are confused, baffled, walking around with open wounds, for all to see. At the same time you feel a comradery with your fellow shipmates, who are the only ones who understand what you are going through. You don't understand what you did wrong to get there and you feel like your abuser is the one who is living free, that they are the ones walking around breathing freely, with no consequences whatsoever, as you pay for their crime."

Terri Rimmer (p. 332)

"As an abandoned child, it is a world of its own, a world where everybody tends to be one's family, and yet their presence in most cases make you feel further depressed and abandoned. It is a world where our hobby is always trying to please and satisfy everybody, all because we desperately seek who could call us his friend, a world where the only thought that occupies the mind is not wanting to live. There is just so much about the abandoned child. We only hope to join the younger and yet to come abandoned children sing a better song."

Testimony Iyore (p. 344)

"My childhood horrors silenced me. I didn't have a voice and I didn't dare talk about my feelings. My journal entry on my 18th birthday read: "Happy birthday me, I'm turning 18. Honestly, I am freaking…scared to death!" I felt so alone and finding other foster kids is like trying to find a needle in a haystack, but through the grace of God, I was connected with the Foster Care Alumni of America and I finally have a voice!"

Therese N.G. (p. 355)

"I don't even know why I was put in foster care and I don't remember much of my time while there, except that I know I was abused, both physically and sexually. I've managed to do all right in my adult life, but I never married and had a family."

Thomas Bryson (p. 368)

"Being a foster child almost instantly catapulted me into a life of horrific abuse in many forms, hidden from social services and the world very strategically. Foster care was a legalized way to throw me to the wolves of society. To this day no one has ever been held accountable for the heinous abuse the system that was designed to protect me inadvertently forced me to endure."

Tianna Marie Hartford (p. 371)

"Foster care is like a rose, a bittersweet experience. In a way it's beautiful; it's a way to help a person become strong, resourceful, and possibly successful. However, the thorns are what nip us in the butt---the moving around, changing schools, lack of permanency, etc. However, in the end, transitioning from foster care to the adult world is like your own personal garden. Will it be successful or unsuccessful?"

Tobias Michael Rogan (p. 378)

"Being a foster kid makes one insecure. You do not belong anyplace or to anybody and all you want is to please people so that you fit in. It created chaos and sadness of never measuring up….life long insecurities."

Toni Liebezeit (p. 382)

"My childhood….They couldn't beat it out of me. They couldn't lock me up long enough. Merle Haggard sang a song about me, _The Running Kind._"

_Ty (p. 392)_

"I felt like I was being used as a hired hand in my foster home. Being in foster care left me with a feeling of mistrust."

Wanda Frisbee (p. 399)

"Upon arrival at this foreboding, unfamiliar place (ISSCS Children Home), my brother, sister, and I were naturally fearful. After a week of various checkups and observations, we began another frightening adventure that seemingly would continue for an unknown number period of time. Fortunately, after a short time, we fit snugly into our new existence, and actually enjoyed it. Years later, reflecting on those years, we felt good about having experienced them, for they added a beneficial dimension to our lives."

William Cass (p. 404)

"I have no family, which a hard concept for people to consider. I know I somehow have to resolve both the reality of my childhood, and the degree of abuse and neglect, and the consequential isolation now as an adult; I just don't know where to begin. I think the isolation now is a reminder, a daily and loud reminder of the absolute abandonment of myself as a human being by those who were the ones who were expected to care for me. And although I am learning to love myself, I still seem unworthy to all others to love as well. There is heavy silence and pain. The loneliness is overwhelming."

Anonymous (p. 408)

"To me foster care is just a motel room with an adult posing as a chaperone. I felt very abandoned as a young adult, which sent me over the edge. I realized that no one cared and no one would ever care and I could not trust anyone with my feelings ever again in my life. I was always let down...no more room for hope. I hit the streets. I didn't care what happened to me. I spiraled deeper into a rabbit hole and did not know how or even want for that matter to get out. I carried hatred around with me like a cloak for a very, very, very long time. But let me tell you, the strong arm of God pulled me out and today I am a mother, grandmother, business woman, and author. I still have emotional hurdles, but I take it one day at a time."

Cynthia Stephens (p. 412)

"Even though I have overcome so many obstacles through my faith in God, and I have a good marriage today, I still feel very needy at times, wanting the love and support of a family I never had. I find myself looking for that someone who would take me under their wing, still in need of that shoulder to cry on when the going gets tough, and I still need a mother and even find myself searching for a mother figure."

Mandy (p. 416)

If the excerpts move you to read the stories, then the stories should move you to read the rest of the book.

FACT Dedication to the Woodard Family

FACT IS dedicated to Carol Lucas' family, the Woodard family, that suffered through a tragedy no family should ever have to endure. Shattered, the family fragments left are only a loud reminder of a past that can't be repaired.

...FACT IS...

We are the forsaken children of the world. Although we come from various ethnic and religious backgrounds and seemingly have little in common...*fact is*...there is a common thread woven through us. As children we stood by and watched helplessly as our worlds crumbled apart, depending on strangers to come to our rescue and decide our fate, a fate which many times was worse than what we were delivered from. We have a variety of stories to tell---some of appreciation for the caring people who took us into their homes, some of seeming indifference to our circumstances, and some of hatred toward foster parents who cared not for us, but only for the monetary and personal gain. Even though some of us were fortunate enough to have been placed in a better environment...*fact is*...many of us were placed in homes with people who simply were not equipped to deal with our special emotional needs stemming from the trauma we suffered from having been ripped away from our homes and families, however abusive and neglectful they may have been. Though our experiences are diverse, we share the same basic feelings of loss, isolation, shame, and pain. Our childhood wounds have left us feeling stigmatized. Many of us feel as though we have been nothing but a burden---unwanted by our parents and dumped off on society's doorstep to be still a further burden. Though we may strive mightily to belong in life's mainstream...*fact is*...we find ourselves more often on the fringes of life---homeless, incarcerated, and generally bankrupt. It may appear we walk the same roads as everyone else, but our shoes show the difference. Try as we may to find our way in this world, the search has often seemed futile. It is this search that has drawn us toward another path, a path of our own choosing...... We are tired of being angry, ashamed, and alone. We want to end our isolation. **FACT** brings us together to share our experiences, face our past, and walk a new path that will build a bridge to healing.

Where Does Foster Care Lead To?
Sadly, Often Nowhere

FACT

o   There are 2 million foster children in the world. However, the actual number is probably higher since the estimate is based only on data coming from registered institutions.

o   There are approximately 500,000 foster children in the United States. More than half of the children in foster care live in nine states: California (100,000), Florida, Illinois, Indiana, Michigan, New York, Ohio, Pennsylvania, and Texas. Of these foster children 40% are White, 30% are Black/Non-Hispanic, 20% are Hispanic, and 10 are other races or multiracial.

o   There are approximately 57,000 foster children in the United Kingdom.

o   There are approximately 36,000 foster children in Australia.

o   There are an estimated 3.7 million orphans in South Africa and 150,000 children are believed to be living in child-headed households. Close to half a million children are in formal, court-ordered foster care. About 80% of these children are placed with relatives. Adoption is modest and in decline. Statistics on children in institutional care are not complete, but it is known that there are 345 registered children's homes there, looking after some 21,000 children. There is no support system for children once they reach the age of 18 and leave formal care.

o   UNICEF estimates there are between 140-190 million orphans in the world and out of these orphans an estimated 15,000 children die every day from hunger related causes. Approximately 7% of these orphans are stolen and forced into prostitution.

o   There are approximately 3,000,000 reports of child abuse or neglect made every year in the United States, which is about 60,000 per week, with nearly 900,000 confirmed victims. Approximately 500,000 end up in foster care, which is double the number from 1987. Approximately 800,000 children every year come in contact with the foster care system.

o   Between 80-90% of foster care placements can be traced to substance abuse.

o   Approximately 63% of children in foster care are re-abused. The foster care system is taking kids away from parents who abuse them and handing them to people who abuse them and they are being paid. Some foster parents care more about the money they will earn from being a foster parent than the foster child themselves. Recent studies in the U.S. suggest that foster care placements are more detrimental to a child than remaining in a troubled home.

o   Approximately 40,000 infants are placed in foster care every year.

o   Children who experience child abuse or neglect are 59%

o   more likely to be arrested as a juvenile, 28% more likely to be arrested as an adult, and 30% more likely to commit a violent crime.

o   Approximately 32% of these foster children are between the ages of 0-5, 28% are between the ages of 6-12, and 40% are between the ages of 13-21. The average age is 10.

o   Over 2 million children live with their grandparents or other relatives because their parents can not care for them.

o   Approximately 70,000 children living in foster care have had their biological parental rights permanently terminated. Approximately 57,000 of these children were adopted.

o   The average length of stay in foster care is three years.

o   The average number of foster care placements is three, but it is not uncommon for children to be in 20-30 different homes.

o   Approximately 48% of foster children live in non-relative foster homes, 24% live in relative foster homes, 18% live in group homes or institutions, 45 live in pre-adoptive foster homes, and 6% live in other placement types.

o   Approximately 250,000 foster children are waiting to be reunited with their birth parents.

o   Approximately 127,000 foster children are waiting to be adopted.

o   Nearly 50% of all foster children suffer from chronic health conditions such as asthma, visual and auditory problems, dental decay, and malnutrition.

o   Foster children have a higher probability of having ADHD (Attention Deficit Hyperactivity Disorder).

o   Children in foster care are more prone to becoming overweight and obese. Bulimia Nervosa is seven times more prevalent among foster children than in the general population.

o   Children in foster care are 3-6 times more likely than children in the general population to have emotional, behavioral, and developmental problems, including conduct disorders, depression, school difficulties, and impaired social relationships. Up to 80% have serious emotional problems.

o   Children die as a result of abuse while in foster care approximately 5 times more often than children in the general population. Children in foster care have an overall higher mortality rate than in the general population.

o   More than 20,000 children each year never leave the foster care system---they remain in foster care until they "age out."

o   Approximately 20,000 foster children "age out" each year or emancipate each year.

o   In many states the "age out" for a foster child is 18. On the day of their birthday before midnight, they must leave foster care.

o   Up to 50% of former foster youth become homeless within the first 18 months of emancipation.

o   Approximately 5,000 homeless youth die every year from violence, illness, or suicide.

o   Former foster youth have a higher rate of suicide than youth in the general population.

o   Former foster children have double the incidence of depression compared to the general population.

o   Approximately 40% of former foster youth aging out will experience alcohol or drug abuse.

o   Approximately 37% of former foster children have some type of mental disorder due to experiences within the foster care system.

o   Approximately 30% of the homeless population spent time in foster care.

o   A history of foster care correlates with becoming homeless at an earlier age and remaining homeless for a longer period of time.

o   Approximately 60 of all young adults using federally funded youth shelters have previously been in foster care.

o   Approximately 65% of youth leaving foster care need immediate housing upon release.

o   Approximately 1/3 of the foster youth have incomes at or below $6,000 per year, which is substantially below the federal poverty level. Foster youths get a median of $5,000 in public support after aging out of care and most kids don't get anything.

o   Youth transitioning from foster care have disproportionately high rates of physical, developmental, and mental health problems.

o   Former foster youth are found to suffer from PTSD (Post Traumatic Stress Disorder) at two times the level of US War Veterans. Approximately 60% of foster children who had experienced sexual abuse and 42% who had been physically abused suffered from PTSD and approximately 18% of foster children with PTSD were not abused.

o   Approximately 33% of all foster care alumni have no form of health insurance.

o   Foster youth with multiple placements are 5-10 times more likely to become involved with the juvenile justice system than youth in the general population.

o   50% of emancipated foster youth experience high rates of unemployment within 5 years of emancipation. Less than half of former foster youth are employed 2-4 years after leaving foster care, and only 38% have maintained employment for at least one year.

o   Youth in foster care are 44% less likely to graduate from high school and after emancipation, 40-50% never complete high school. 70% of foster care youth who emancipate want to attend college, but fewer than 10% enroll in college and of these only about 1% graduate.

o   Females in care are six times more likely to give birth before the age of 21 than those in the general population.

o   Parents with a history of foster care are almost twice as likely as parents with no such history to see their own children placed in foster care or become homeless.

o   Case workers in the foster care system burn out and leave the profession in very high numbers. The annual turnover rate in child welfare is more than 20%. The recommended number of cases for social workers is seventeen, but in some states the number is 3-4 times that number.

o   United States taxpayers spend $22 billion a year ($40,000 per child) on foster care programs.

o   Approximately 80% of prison inmates have been through the foster care system.

o   If Nothing Changes….

o   By the Year 2020:

o   22,500 children in the United States will die of abuse or neglect, most before their 5th birthday.

o   More than 10.5 million children will spend some time in foster care.

o   More than 300,000 children will age out of the foster care system, some in poor health and many unprepared for success in higher education, technical college, or the workforce.

o   75,000 former foster youth who age out of the foster care system will experience homelessness.

o   There will be more than 200 million orphaned children around the globe---over 2.8% of the world's population.

www.Abcnews.go.com/Primetime/FosterCare
www.aif.gov.au
www.azhope.com/about/foster-care-statistics.php
www.cba.ca/news/canada/story/foster-care
www.child-adoption-matters.com/foster- care-statistics
www.childrensrights.org
www.faithbridgescare.org

www.fostercarealumni.org
www.fosterclub.com/article/foster-care-statistics
www.heysf.org
www.mojuproject.com/about/orphans/
www.news.change.org/homeless-youth
www.onthemovebayarea.org
www.prairieguy.wordpress.com/the-basic-foster-care-facts
www.thefca.co.uk/foster-care-statistics
www.unicef.org/southafrica/protection
www.zerafoundation.org/html/facts
www.en.wikipedia.org/wiki/Foster_care

On pages 515-516 is a list of suggested resources for former foster children---books and self-help support groups that could be helpful during recovery from various issues mentioned here.

FACT Founder

Carol Lucas

I am Carol Lucas, the founder of FACT. I am a former foster child and due to my own emotional issues stemming from my foster care experience, I felt a need for a support group, but when I went in search for one, discovered there weren't any, so decided to form one myself. One would suppose that with all the support groups available, there would be one for former foster children, especially since there are so many of us (currently about 500,000 in the U.S in the foster care system) and we have such strong issues, but somehow we have remained hidden.

Foster care, which was intended to be a bridge to carry foster children over the troubled waters until they could safely and soundly stand on their own two feet as adults, is often instead a bridge with only a dead end, with many children getting to the end of it only to find themselves dreadfully unprepared for what they find on the other side.

As the …FACT IS …document states, "many of us feel as though we have been nothing but a burden---unwanted by our parents and dumped on society's doorstep to be still a further burden" and "though we may strive mightily to belong in life's mainstream…fact is…we find ourselves more often living on the fringes of life." The pain and shame that should have been relieved on the foster care bridge as children is sadly often instead being relived as adults.

It is my hope that we can come out of hiding and face our shameful past so that instead of walking a bridge to nowhere we can "walk a bridge to healing." It was my own pain of witnessing the long-term effects in my family that motivated me to form FACT, raise awareness, and advocate for foster children. After having worked through much anger and hurt, by the grace of God I am "walking the bridge to healing" and want to invite other former foster children to join me. "We" can do it "together."

Contributing Founder to FACT

John Dunn

I am John Dunn, a contributing founder of FACT. I am a former foster  child and due to my own emotional issues stemming from my foster care experience (I was in 13 homes), I felt a need for a support group and was pleasantly surprised to find FACT. I contacted Carol, requesting permission to use some of her literature, and at that time, wanting to disregard the more spiritual material, but she resisted the idea of us being divided and suggested we collaborate on FACT. I suggested using a 12-step format and since her brother Glen had also previously urged this idea after the two of them and another woman had composed the original 7 stones, Carol decided to revise the original material into the 10 Stepping Stones and the Bridge to Healing.

Initially I resisted using any mention of God in the FACT material, but today I am grateful to her for persisting with me on this issue, because as time went on I realized that in my own life, spirituality was robbed from me and I was made angry about it. Today I am more accepting of spirituality and realize that it was certain people who had hurt me, not God.

I am also the founder of the Foster Care Council of Canada, advocating on behalf of the approximately 88,000 foster children in Canada. It is my hope that through advocacy, future foster children will be spared the pain that thousands of foster children, including my brother and me, have had to endure. I am honored to introduce FACT to Canada and help others "walk a bridge to healing," through the grace of a Higher Power that I am beginning to become more familiar with and believe in.

Contributing Founder to FACT

Glen Woodard

I am Glen Woodard, a contributing founder of FACT. In October, 1999, while visiting with my sister Carol Ann, we sat down one night with another person to simply talk about FACT and what would be needed as a working foundation for a support group for people who as children were subjected to the trauma of separation from their birth family and the further trauma of their experiences while in foster care. Although Carol already had begun working on FACT in 1988 and had even pursued meetings, the ideas she had weren't fixed in stone.

That evening we hardly expected what happened. In the course of about six hours, the Statements of Belief and the seven of the final ten Stepping Stones to Healing were written. This original material has remained virtually unchanged. Thus was FACT as we know it today was born on that momentous evening.

All was not harmonious in the following months. At first I recommend that FACT not be a 12-step program, to which she agreed, but as a member of a 12 Step program I began to lobby for a similar program tailored to the needs of former foster children. Carol would not yield to this suggestion. For some time we both could only agree to disagree.

As founder, Carol has of course done most of the work of writing and assembling all of the materials which now appear on the FACT web site, and has gathered all of the stories for this book. I am simply glad to have been present at the birth of FACT and for my part in its inception.

While I consider my own experiences to be light compared to those of so many others who were in foster care, my experiences were traumatic and most certainly affected my life. I have worked and continue to work on issues concerning my childhood. My message is that there is hope for all of us and the promise of recovery is real.

It is true that I wrote the spiritual document in the back of this book, but in reality it was simply given to me by God, words of comfort for all. I am grateful that my pen did not falter in the writing.

Part One

Our Stories

*"For while the tale of how we
suffer, and how we are delighted, and how we may
triumph is never new, it always must be heard.
There isn't any other tale to tell;
it's the only light we have in all this darkness."*
James Baldwin

Carol Lucas

FACT Founder
Stepping Forward

Be Real to Heal

I am sharing my story, not just because I am the founder of FACT and it is expected of me, but because like all of the other stories in this book, it needs to be heard. If it can help other foster child, it is well worth telling. I will be as real in the telling as I possibly can, as I believe that revealing, and feeling, is healing, that only by being real can we begin to heal. I will reveal even the most shameful parts of my story because along with freeing me from shame, it frees others to share their shame. Shame, by its very nature wants to remain comfortably hidden, but I know from experience that it will continue to follow us around like a shadow that we are afraid of until we face it, that only by freeing it from the dark can we begin to live in the light. Out of respect for my siblings and other family members I am only sharing the truth about me. And the truth is I had a very traumatic childhood, one that led to further trauma as an adult. I have been raped three times, almost murdered once, homeless for a month, and living much of my youth "living on the fringes of life," not really sure of who I was, or what I wanted to do, mostly preferring to stay drunk or high, which I did quite well for seven years. I have been suicidal, almost succeeding three times, and I have been in and out of therapy so many times I can't count them, preferring mostly to run from the therapists than to them in my early years, as the truth was just too painful. I have also been a frequent visitor to AA, ACA, and other support groups. I have also been a frequent visitor to grocery stores, looking for boxes to help me pack my belonging in because I was moving, again.

It has been a long, hard journey in healing from my past, one that was wrought with many, many anguished tears, tears that left me feeling very vulnerable and alone, so much so that I decided to form a support group for former foster children. I poured my whole heart and soul into forming FACT and I pray it will touch the many lives that need it, as I have seen the healing in my own life, and wish it for others. As I look over my shoulder it is clear to me that God has been steering me toward truth all along. And the truth is He was able to take me, a broken child, and mend me. It is with this truth that I share my story.

In the Beginning was Innocence

My story begins in Mattoon, Illinois on July 24, 1955. I am the seventh born of a Catholic family that would eventually have ten children, seven girls and three boys. According to what I was told, right after my birth our family moved from the country into the small town of Mattoon, where we remained until our family broke up. I only have a few vague memories of my young years---sitting outside in a washtub wearing a little sun suit my mom had made for me, making mud pies and eating them, being chased by a big dog once and running like crazy to jump over our fence to safety, getting my arm caught in a wringer washer, and there was an incident when my sister as playing with matches and caught my hair on fire, and my retarded older sister beat my head with a broom, but luckily my brother knew what to do and threw water over my head. I remember being very upset that my beautiful, long, curly hair had to be cut off some because of the frizzled ends. I don't remember having a lot of toys, but we managed to entertain ourselves with a little red wagon, of course fighting over who got to steer and who got to push. My sisters and I only had one doll buggy, and maybe a few dolls that we had to share, but I don't remember bickering over them. I have pictures of our family that show a television, so we no doubt entertained ourselves with that, but I don't remember. One very pleasant memory I have is of the ice cream truck coming down our street during the summer, and the anticipation of possibly having an ice cream treat.

From what I have gathered from family members and old photos, some of which fate brought my way after my mom's death in 1992 (my sister found an old roll of film in a box of belongings, which was old family photos, and some of them were of me as a young child, which I'd never saw before), apparently at one time we were a big, happy family, perhaps a big dysfunctional family, but nevertheless, a happy one, with birthday parties and such. I was especially close with my next youngest sister and we used to share birthday parties because we were only born one year and one day apart.

Me on second from right

One big happy family, me in front

A Chaotic Home

I was told by relatives that we were all wanted children, that my parents agreed on a large family, and I believe that is true, but unfortunate circumstances came our way when my dad was drafted into WW11, and he was left to deal with not only the physical aftermath of the war (malaria), but also the war within himself, spending many years in a VA hospital. I'm sure it didn't help his mental and emotional state either dealing with his wife's affair with his own brother while he was away at war, and I can only imagine the burden he was carrying about his children. I only have a couple of memories of my dad when I was young. I was no doubt conceived on one his visits home from the VA hospital. I remember him coming home one time and getting very angry at my mom for not feeding us properly and him making us hamburgers. I can also remember him spanking me once and then immediately giving me some candy because I was crying, but other than that I have no other early memories of him. Due to my dad's absence my mom was forced into employment, which left our family vulnerable to every kind of dysfunction imaginable. Needless to say, we were a very poor family, depending on whatever means we could to get by. My mother turned to our godfather, relatives, and church charity for help and would have also accepted help from others had there not been sexual motive behind their offering. My siblings and I were left on our own most of the time, without adult supervision, the older children doing their best to care for the younger ones. My brother told me that he and my other brother used to steal hotdogs and other food from the grocery store to help feed the family. My sister Mary, who is 4 years older than me, was my caretaker more than my mom. Well, if you think things were chaotic before, you can only imagine how much more dysfunctional it became now. It was total chaos. I recall my oldest sister, Jeannie, having an epileptic fit while my mom was gone, and all of us being frantic, not understanding what was happening or what to do. I can also remember standing on a stool by our stove in the kitchen, trying to make my own oatmeal, feeling very hungry and frustrated. I remember rats (or maybe they were mice) running around in our house, and holes in our walls. I remember some inappropriate and hostile behavior that took place with me that made me feel very vulnerable and unsafe. I can remember walking the streets barefooted and hungry, and having my dad's previous co-workers at the Coca-Cola Company in Mattoon give us all free cokes when we walked by. Here comes the Woodard clan again...

A Child's Trust Destroyed

When I was about the age of 4, when my mom was no longer around much to look after me, our family fell prey to an unsuspecting "friend" of my mom's, a sexual pervert who took advantage of me, molesting me in exchange for food and clothing. I have no memory of the sexual abuse; I only know by what is stated in my file. What I do recall is being very frightened of a man who came to our house one day and me hiding behind the couch to feel safe. I would like to think the sexual abuse never happened, and aside from the fact that the doctor's confirmation proved it, my gut intuition and my reactions in the past to older men leaves little doubt in my mind that it did happen. Often in the past whenever I was around older men I would feel anxious and angry. My file states "To what extent Carol has been damaged by the sexual perversion of the older man it is difficult to state. Carol does not mention these incidents and it is unknown to what extent Carol was molested." I had so much rage at this man that years later, when I was beginning therapy, I felt like the Incredible Hulk. I wanted to sue the state of Illinois for not prosecuting the SOB and if he had been alive at this time I for sure would have made a special trip to Illinois to give him a piece of my mind! I have hated this man like I never hated before and have tried to work on forgiveness, but it is hard to come by. I have even tried excusing him by saying that maybe he was abused himself, but still, I have no mercy for child molesters. God will have to continue to help me with that one. He will also have to help me forgive my mother, who I have had a very difficult time forgiving.*

*As a Christian I wrestled with unforgiveness and felt uneasy, so I decided to ask God to help me forgive all the people in my past who hurt me, which although was not easy, I was able to do through a process called *Healing of the Memories*. I know no longer want the burden of unforgiveness. *Healing of the Memories* didn't take away the memories, but I no longer feel like the memories are hurting me the way they used to. I feel a lot freer from the past.

My relatives were aware of how dysfunctional our home was and how neglected we were, and we did receive some help from them, but the final straw came when two of my siblings were caught by my uncle , behaving inappropriately with each other, and our family was turned into social services. I have questioned if his motive for turning us in was completely pure, but anyway, this is how it all began, my entry into foster care…

Foster Care Trauma

The day I entered foster care is a total blank to me. I have absolutely no memory of it; I guess it was so traumatic that I just blocked it out. Years later when I asked my mom about it she told me that I was hysterical, and my aunt told me that we all looked a pitiful sight, each one of us clutching a paper bag of clothes. According to my file I entered "care" on August 3, 1961, shortly after my 6th birthday. Knowing how sensitive I am, I'm sure I was not only very confused, but terrified beyond words. All I recall is a vague sense of being in a home for a short time, only a few days and I remember eating at a breakfast nook. According to my state file, I was placed at the Jess Tinch home in Mattoon with my older sister Debbie and my baby brother Steve for about one week, but we were all removed due to the "over activity and unadjustment of the the baby, Steven." My file states that "on the day of this placement Carol was seemingly unafraid and in fact, talked to her sister Debbie in order to alleviate fears she had in going from the home." Supposedly, I was a very cheerful child and my file states that "Of all the children she seemed to take the separation from the family in better spirits and tried to cheer the other children."

The reason I seemed to be in good spirits probably was due to the fact that I thought my mom loved me, and therefore I never thought she would abandon me to some strange home. My file states that "Carol seems to be very secure in the knowledge that she was wanted by her mother and speaks of returning to her mother. Supposedly I was favored by my mother, and although my file states that "This favoritism was known to

Carol and the rest of the siblings," while working through my childhood issues in therapy years later, my therapist reassured me I would not have know I was favored, that I was just a young child wanting love from her mother like any other child would. I say this because as an adult I struggled with some guilt over this and I had to come to terms with the fact that it wasn't my fault she favored me. I have also had to come to terms with the fact that certain family members still may resent me for this (sibling rivalry doesn't always end with childhood unfortunately!). I am sure as a child I felt some love from my mother and she told me we were bonded when I was very young, but her favoritism affected me in a very negative way. In a Diagnostic Statement in my file it states that "In placement for Carol we should take into consideration the extreme social and physical deprivation that was present in the home. However, Carol's emotional neglect was of a different sort than the other children. Her needs were met by her mother, but this in turn antagonized the other children against Carol. However, this favoritism of her mother gained her a great deal of ill will from her siblings and due to the fact that the mother left the children almost entirely in the care of the oldest child, and was gone a great deal of the day, and most of the night Carol probably suffered because of this favoritism," and under Social and Emotional Adjustment in my file it states that "The adjustment within the natural family was aided or thwarted by the attitude of the mother who considered Carol one of her favorites." Years later I asked my mom about this, and she said she didn't love me any more than any of the other children, that I was just a very sweet and sensitive child who seemed to need more attention, and she tried to give it to me, but whenever she did give me the attention my siblings gave me a hard time, which only created a vicious cycle of harassment by my siblings, and over protectiveness by my mother. The sibling war was on and I was in the right in the middle of it! I was totally innocent. I loved all of my siblings, and all I wanted was to be accepted by them. It doesn't really matter how she felt about me though, as it didn't change the fact that she didn't come to visit me while I was in foster care, and she never apologized to me for it later in life when I was reunited with her. She also voluntarily gave up two children that she had with another man after her and my dad got divorced, which inclines me to think she didn't really the responsibility of any of us.

Foster Home Number Two

I went from the foster home in Mattoon to one on a farm, with three of my siblings, and there were also five other children there. I might have been all right at the first foster home, and thinking I would be back with my mom, but I don't think I was ok with this one at all. My file states that "Carol did not seem to be too happy in this home. She was very quiet and shy on the days the worker visited." Why would I be happy in a home away from my mother, and especially one where I was neglected? The foster home was awful, and what it made it even worse was that as a young child, I had absolutely no way to make sense out of what was happening to me, and there wasn't anybody to help me through the trauma, to console me, and reassure me I would be all right. The four of us who went there all had to sleep in the same bed, and at 4:00 A.M., we were all yanked out of bed, without any breakfast, and forced to go outside and feed farm animals, and do farm chores. I remember being chased by a pig one time. You never saw a little girl run so fast! It scared the hell out of me! All I remember eating there was rice and white bread, and I don't recall any interaction with the foster parents. We were not allowed to go to church, or school, and I remember my two older brothers fighting with the foster parent's boys. What stands out in my memory the most, is how afraid I was when I was thrown outside in the dark to do the farm chores, and looking up at the stars, thinking how pretty they were, somehow detaching myself from the ugly situation. Years later, when I was in therapy (a lot of us foster kids end up in there), my therapist called what I did "disassociation," and said that being a bright child, it would have been the likely thing for me to do, since I was the age when children are very imaginative. If the foster home had been decent, and the parents warm and understanding, I'm sure it wouldn't have been so traumatic, but the foster parents obviously only took us in for the money, because they sure didn't seem to care about us. Talk about jumping from the frying pan into the fire! In my file it stated that the court declared all ten of us "neglected" children. So tell me, what kind of sense does it make to take children out of one neglectful situation, and put them into another one that is even worse? If we had stayed in our original home and been neglected by our mother, at least we would have had each other, instead of being separated, and put in strange homes. But still, I hate to ponder how much worse things could have gotten if we hadn't been put into foster care…

Luckily, fate was on my side and God was watching over me. This home was only a temporary placement until a permanent one could be found. I was only there about a month, but it seemed like longer. I remember the day I left Rose Hill, and was taken to court, where our parents (I think), and other extended family members, were also awaiting the decision of where we would all go. I was VERY CONFUSED, not understanding what this courtroom was, or what was happening, but I had some kind of sense of something important happening that involved our family. I don't recall leaving the courthouse and making the trip to my next placement, but I do recall arriving there. As a matter of fact, I can't recall any of my transitions from one home to another. I am assuming that it was so traumatic for me that I blocked it out.

A Family Shattered and Scattered

Well, I was right about the courtroom involving something important about our family. On September 12, 1961, my siblings and I were all declared "neglected children" and made wards of the state of Illinois. Although I only remember going to ISSCS with my two older brothers, according to my file, I was also there with three of my older sisters, where we spent several months in the receiving cottage. According to my file I was "Eneuretic for the first time since removal from her home," and that "On the days the worker came to take her sister on pre-placement and placement, Carol seemed to ignore the worker to a great extent, perhaps fearing the day she would have to go, or feeling hurt that she was not the first one chosen for placement." Man, did they ever have this wrong! I am sure the reason I was peeing the bed then was because my sister was my caretaker at home, and I missed her when she left. My file states that "Carol took the separation from her sisters very hard." As a young adult I always turned to my sister when I needed help and I spent a lot of time with her. Having to come to terms with the fact that my sister who took care of me as a child, isn't capable of even taking care of herself, let alone the six children she had and lost, has been a very sad, and difficult to face. I love her very much and pray for her.

Wood Cottage

Another Strange Place

I entered ISSCS on September 12 of 1961 and left there on June 12 of 1963. Overall it was a decent, caring children's home that really tried to provide some normalcy for me and all the other children there, but I still didn't want to be there. I wanted to be in my own home with my mom and siblings. I missed my family terribly. I can remember praying for my whole family, one by one, every night when I knelt down by my bedside to say my prayers. For the first six months we weren't allowed any visits with relatives, and then we started visiting with extended family members, which was real nice. I felt more secure then, but I hated going back to the home after spending time with my family. I remember one time spending the night with my grandma (dad's mom) all by myself, and her tucking me into her feather bed and saying prayers with me. I could have stayed with her forever; it was pure heaven. I also visited my Aunt Norma and Uncle George, who fostered me when I left ISSCS. I felt very insecure at ISSCS and I was very shy. I remember wetting the bed a lot and having to hang my sheets that I had rinsed out myself on the clothesline, even in the winter when the sheets got stiff. I had a very difficult time in school because I was so emotionally distraught that I couldn't concentrate and was always daydreaming. My file states that "Carol has a slight speech difficulty," and I was "inattentive, had difficulty in concentrating, and daydreams." In my file it stated that "Carol's innate intelligence is higher than her present test scores indicate. This was due to her emotional deprivation. She uses withdrawal as a defense. She is considered a sick little girl. Carol would not see any of the men who planned to interview and test her. She needs affection, love, and support. She has suffered much deprivation during the first six years. It was felt she has the ability to relate, but she is afraid of men because of her past experiences. If Carol is left at ISSCS she will probably become more withdrawn. She is at present emotionally emaciated. It would be difficult to find a mother for Carol who could be too protective. The foster father would need to be a quiet, in the background type. Since Carol is disturbed, she needs to be treated for the disturbance. This would not mean custodial care. Therapy will be to find her a good foster mother." I remember visiting a foster home and according to my file, on January 4, 1962, I was taken to a home in Decatur, but I don't think I wanted to stay there, because I wanted to be with my family, and I think I believed in my heart of hearts that I would be back with my mom. I remember playing a lot at the home. I bicycled, played jump rope, hopscotch, golfed, played on swings, slides, monkey bars, etc on playground, and every chance I got I went swimming in the pool there, but the most memorable of all was playing on the maypole. I loved swinging around on that! I think playing all the time helped me cope. One particular fond memory of the home was Legionnaire's Day, otherwise known as *Children's Day*, when we were all treated very special. One of my happiest days was the day my sister returned to ISSCS. According to my file she returned to ISSCS in February, 1962. I remember I was sitting on the floor in the cottage watching the movie "The Wizard of Oz" when she came walking in the front door. I went up to her and said, "Aren't you my sister?" and she said "Yes," and of course I was thrilled to have a sister with me again, and I didn't feel so alone. My file states that "Carol seems quite dependent upon her sister. They are very close." My brother, Glen, and I used to ride our bikes over to visit with each other also, so there was at least some sibling connection. My two brothers and sister all rode the bus to the Catholic Church, and I remember me and my running around in the church aisles, talking with people, because we didn't understand Latin. I remember one time on the way home from church they all said they were going to get to leave, but I had to stay there alone. They were only teasing me, but at first I thought they were serious. Talk about a young girl getting hysterical! I started crying and screaming "You guys can't leave me here all alone; please don't leave me here all alone!" I just remember how afraid I was of the prospect of being left there all by myself. I had very strong fears of abandonment, and that is something I will probably always struggle with somewhat. I am terrified of abandonment.

I was so upset over this picture. They cut my beautiful, long hair, and it's apparent I don't trust, as I can't make eye contact.

I never went back to visit ISSCS after I left, until the summer of 2009. The home closed in 1979, but many of the buildings are still there and are used for businesses. The cottage (Wood) I had lived in was torn down, but I got to see the one cottage (Lincoln) left standing, which was identical to Wood cottage. Walking along the grounds felt very strange, surreal you might say. It had been so many years since I had lived there. When I first started walking down the sidewalk I started to feel sad and tears came to my eyes, but I immediately shut them off, which I realized was the same reaction I had there as a child, of being sad (and angry!) and wanting to cry, but feeling frozen and unable to. In retrospect, I had to be a strong little girl, so there was no time for tears. I still have a hard time crying to this day. Walking down the sidewalks, I remembered walking them as a child, staring at the cracks as I walked along, stopping and saying "Step on a crack, you break your mother's back." I don't recall ever stepping on a crack, but I do recall wanting to, and having a lot of ambivalence about it. I was very angry, sad, and confused about my mom, and didn't understand why I wasn't with her. I was hospitalized with whooping cough while I was there, and wanted so much to have her there with me, but she was nowhere to be found. I felt like she just dumped me off there and forgot all about me. To say I've had anger at my mom is a huge understatement; in fact, I'm not even sure rage would be an adequate word. Years later, when I was working through my childhood issues in therapy I was overwhelmed by the amount of anger I had about her, and of course behind all the rage was hurt. DEEP HURT. I mean really, how could a mother just abandon her children? According to my file "The mother has stated that she doubts very much whether she will be able to visit due to the fact that she works on Sundays, and has no transportation facilities" Too busy???! While in the beginning my file states that "Of all the children she seemed to take the from the family in better spirits and tried to cheer the other children," it certainly didn't express that later on, after I no doubt began to realize my mom was not going to come and get me. Instead I was very troubled and withdrawn.

And Here I Go Again…

What did happen after being at ISSCS for almost two years is that I went to live with an aunt and uncle, right before my 8th birthday, along with my brother. Even though I was happier to be there than at ISSCS, it was a difficult adjustment for me, especially school. I remember the first day of school as being very traumatic, so much so that the teacher had to take me by the hand and walk me into the new classroom, with me crying. I think I was sort of the teacher's pet for awhile, because she knew my situation, and took special care of me. I am very thankful for that teacher today, as she made a very traumatic time for me less scary. Being at my aunt and uncle's home was ok, but I definitely knew I was only being fostered, and my brother and I weren't treated as well as our cousins. I knew I was "different." Then when I was about 9 there was something inappropriate that happened to me. It was around this time that I started having dizzy spells real bad, which I wonder might have been brought on by emotional trauma. Sometime while I was living here my aunt forced me to go visit my mom once, which I remember telling her I DID NOT want to do! By this point I had pretty much written her off. I was angry that she had abandoned me, and here I have to go see her?! Why didn't SHE come see ME? I remember me and my brother visiting her for a short time, and her giving us some candy. I was very shy around her, and still confused somewhat about what had happened, but one thing I knew for sure is that she abandoned me, and then there I was again, on the sidewalks…….

This is a picture of me and my brother while we were living with our aunt and uncle.

My DAD!

When I was about 9 years, old my dad began visiting me, and he gave me a bicycle for my birthday. What a gift that was! I loved that bicycle! And I didn't just love it for the sake of it being a bicycle, but because my DAD gave it to me! Up to this time my dad was basically a stranger to me, so although I felt a bit shy about his sudden interest in me, I was also thrilled. I'll never forget the day he came to pick me up to take me shopping for clothes to wear at ,his upcoming wedding and how thrilled I was to have a beautiful new pair of patent leather shoes. It was the first time I ever had my dad's undivided attention, and I LOVED it!

Not long after this I attended my dad and step mom's wedding, which was very happy and memorable.

I am on the far left, wearing the outfit my dad bought for me.

My DAD for GOOD!

A few months after my dad remarried, and right before my 10th birthday, I went to live with my dad, along with my brother, who actually set the whole thing in motion by acting up one day at my aunt and uncle's. My brother had been acting up and my aunt threatened to send him to our dad's if he acted up again, and one day he started throwing stuff around her porch, so he told him to pack his bags to go to his dad's. I was too shy to come right out and tell her I wanted to go with him, so I kept following her around all day, until finally she came right out and asked me if I wanted to go with Glen to our dad's, to which of course I replied "yes." I not only wanted to be with my dad; I also didn't want to be separated from my brother, as we had always been together in our homes.

MY HAPPIEST DAY!

The day I went to live with my dad was indescribably the happiest day of my childhood. Where once I had felt lost and insecure, I now had the love and security of my dad. I remember him making me a name tag shortly after I arrived there, with MY NAME on it, which gave me a sense of identity for the first time.

I no longer felt like just an unwanted kid. My dad made me feel very special. We were financially poor, but somehow he always managed to find money to put under my pillow from the tooth fairy, and have a real Christmas tree with presents from Santa Claus, and birthday parties for all of us.

Me on right

Me in front on right

My dad didn't show any favoritism; he seemed to love us all. I remember being sick with tonsillitis, and having him nurse me all day, which was such a comfort, especially since I had such a traumatic experience in the hospital when I was at ISSCS. My dad helped me with my homework, and was very proud of me in junior high school for being on the honor roll, and when I wanted to be a cheerleader in 8th grade, he somehow managed to scrape the money together for my cheerleading outfit. My dad was the light in my dark childhood. I have some very happy memories with my dad, which I treasure.

Me of left of my dad, touching his shoulder

Unfortunately, the woman he married, my step-mom, wasn't always so nice, and was very physically and emotionally abusive. One time when I was about 15 years old, she came up to my bedroom like a crazy woman, and yanked me off my bed by the brush rollers in my hair, and dragged me over to the hallway and into another bedroom, where she proceeded to beat the crap out of me, and call me all kinds of obscene names, to which I responded to by yelling at her to leave me alone, then went downstairs and yelled at my dad to do something about "that crazy bitch!" I found out years later that she was an alcoholic, and also bi-polar, which explained her erratic behavior and frequent trips to the psych ward. Back then it was "hush, hush," so were left in the dark about her illness. The only real issue I have had with my dad is that he didn't do more to protect me from my step-mom, but I now realize he was just trying to cope, and was not only afraid of the abuse escalating with us, but also toward him. I remember her throwing hot irons at him and cursing. One day when I was about 15 years old, my dad greeted me at the back door on my return from school, and ordered me to spend the night with my sister who lived close by, because my step-mom had threatened to kill me and him both. I think she was real jealous of my close relationship with my dad. Every day before I went to school, and every night before I went to bed, I kissed my dad goodnight on the cheek, but the unfortunate day came when I could no longer do that...

Another Cruel Blow

Fate dealt me another cruel blow when I was 16 years old, and lost my dad to heart failure. To say I was a little sad and depressed would be a huge understatement. I felt like my world had turned upside down again, just like it did when I was taken away from my mom and put in foster care, except this time it was worse in a way, because I knew he was gone for good, and there was no chance of every seeing him again, whereas with my mom, there was a chance, because she was still alive, and I kept hoping and wondering if I would ever see her again. I became so depressed after his death that I was barely able to function, but somehow I managed to make it out of bed every morning and go to school. My English liked me a lot and knew my situation, and was always gently bringing me back in the classroom because I was daydreaming again, something I resorted to as a young child because reality was too painful. Not only was I grieving my dad's loss, but I was also struggling with guilt, some of what belonged to me, but mostly from what my step-mom was dumping on me, telling me I caused his death by giving him so much stress, running around with boys, and even running away once. My step-sister tried talking me into running away with her again, but somehow my dad found out, and with tears in his eyes, begged me not to, telling me how hard he tried getting us kids back and how much he loved us, so of course I didn't run away. Looking back, I think it's incredible that my dad was able to get the fortitude and strength to get custody of most of his children, especially since he was a DAV with PTSD and physical disabilities. He got actual custody of all but three of his children, and two of them he had access to because they lived with my uncle, so the only one he didn't see was Julie, and he was in the process of getting custody of her when he died. I won't say he was perfect, because no father is, but I am so grateful I was able to live with him for almost 7 years, unlike so many foster kids today who never even know who their parents are, let alone see them. When I was in Illinois in 2009, I went to his grave, and was a bit surprised at my reaction. Right after his death I started getting therapy and was diagnosed with depression, stemming from guilt and anger about his death, feeling like he had abandoned me again, but the only thing I felt when I was at his gravesite, was sadness, and a deep love for him, because I realize (after working through my anger in therapy years later) how much he did for me, and how hard he tried to make up to me for my traumatic childhood. My dad had our whole family in family therapy at one point, so I'm sure he understood all the family dynamics, and how screwed up we all were. I still miss my dad, and would give anything to have even one more day with him, to give him one more peck on the cheek and tell him I love him.

Another Change

About six months after my dad's death I was moved again, because my step-mom couldn't afford the house we were living in, so that fall I had to attend a different high school, something that although I didn't complain about or even talk about, I didn't like. The shell I had managed to crawl out of when I was living with my dad, began to look more appealing to me than the strange environment I was now forced into, so that is where I retreated back into, my safe shell. Not only did I miss my dad, but I also missed my old friends, my old house, and all the things that were familiar to me. I hated the change and was having a hard time coping with it. I was extremely shy at this new school, so much so that I couldn't/wouldn't make new friends, even when peers were friendly toward me. I remember girls trying to be friends with me, but I was so shy that I wouldn't talk. I was a loner, and I daydreamed in class even more than I had before, just wanting to escape from it all. I remember walking home from school all alone, with my head down, sad, depressed, and lonely, feeling like I was carrying the weight of the world on my shoulders, with nobody who cared about me, or understood me, and I sure didn't understand myself. Since I was the oldest of the three siblings left at home I felt responsible for my younger sister and brother, but in all reality, not only was I not responsible, I didn't have a clue how to be.

I could hardly even take care of myself emotionally, and here I was trying to hold them up. I had the opportunity to be adopted by a by my 8th grade best friend's family, and sometimes I wish I had let them, as I think my life would have been smoother.

Things wouldn't have been as bad after my dad's death, had my step-mom been more loving and supportive, but she wasn't; in fact, her drinking and bi-polar episodes only got worse, as did my depression. She was very mean to me, telling me I'd never amount to anything, and nobody would ever want me, and I believed her. My self-esteem was so low you couldn't scrape it off a sidewalk. Not only did I not have a father, but I didn't really have a mother either, and I wanted one. I felt SO abandoned, but I didn't know it. All I knew was that I was very unhappy and depressed. I shuffled through my days, feeling more like an old woman than the young girl I was. I wasn't a typical teenage girl at all. The things normal teenage girls want to do, like go to proms, football games, etc, didn't appeal to me. I remember coming home from school and reading the Bible, searching for life's meaning. I became very serious, and became a "seeker," developing a strong urge for God. I tried to be a typical teenager, and even took a night job as a waitress at a truck stop, but it only lasted a short time, because I was so shy about truckers flirting with me that I asked to wash dishes instead, and then I just quit due to the lack of sleep. I really felt like a stranger in a strange land, and nothing made me happy. Nothing. I felt like I wanted to be in another world, and started drinking, and smoking pot some to escape. I had a boyfriend my step-mom didn't like, and I came home one day to find my whole room a shambles, my clothes and everything thrown everywhere, which seemed to match the state of my mind and my whole life. I just felt like giving up.

Copping Out

In January 1973, during mid-term of my junior year in high school, I decided I just couldn't take it anymore, and didn't care about school, so I quit, just like that. The school counselor tried changing my mind, but to no avail. I had made up my mind that I just didn't give a shit anymore about anything, and that was that. I decided to leave home, as I just couldn't take my step-mom's abuse anymore, so I went to live with my brother. I was going through a very severe depression, and suffering from anxiety real bad. I felt like I was losing it, going off the deep end, with nobody to rescue me. It was a very scary time for me, and for some reason (guilt?) I thought I was going to die soon. It was at this time that I got involved with my brother's roommate, who had just left his ex-wife, and was also feeling very vulnerable. Looking back, we were like two people adrift at sea on a life boat, and although it wasn't the healthiest relationship in the world, at the time it suited us. I knew he was a junkie, but I didn't give it much thought, because I figured he was all I had. Strange, how when you are that needy, you lose all your common sense. He and I were both foster kids, and had abandonment issues with our mothers, and came into the relationship with tons of unresolved emotional baggage, and we left the relationship the same way, but I am still grateful that he was there for me; at least I wasn't alone. I missed my dad terribly, and I think the fact that he was ten years my junior appealed to me, because in my mind he was more mature and fatherly than a guy my own age.

Reunited with my Biological Mom

Right after I turned 18 years old, I started having an urge to meet my real mom, my biological mom, I think mostly because I had this strange idea of my impending death, and thought I should meet her, so I began praying to meet her, and God answered my prayers. This meeting came about not by her pursuing me, but by me finding out her whereabouts from my sister, whose boyfriend's aunt was acquainted with my mom, then me contacting her. Unlike the day I was removed from her, I vividly recall the day I met her again. I was alone in my apartment, when I heard a knock on the door, and I opened it up, looked at this woman, and just said, "Hi, Mom," and then we hugged, as if it had been twelve days since we had last seen each other instead of twelve years. It was strange, really. She was probably more nervous than me, chain-smoking as she sat on the edge of the chair. I don't remember what all we talked about, but I don't think it had much to do with the past; it seemed more like idle chatter to me, and then she gave me an old family photo album and left, after about a two hour visit. She was hoping to see my brother that evening also, but he was off working and didn't return in time, and she had to leave, so I believe, if my memory serves me correctly, she returned the next day to see him, and we all three visited.

But, be careful what you pray for; you might get it! As much as I thought I wanted to meet my mom, and I really did, what I wasn't prepared for was all the ambivalent feelings I had toward her. And I sure wasn't prepared for all the ANGER that was bubbling under the surface, ready to erupt like a hot volcano whenever I was around her. Somewhere inside of me was a very ANGRY and HURT child who didn't know how to handle this SO emotional situation. Shortly after meeting her, I ended up in the hospital for 10 days with hepatitis and she came to visit me, unlike the time I was sick with whooping cough in the hospital at ISSCS and she was nowhere to be found. At this point I didn't feel angry, only comfort that she was back in my life, but even though my anger and hurt had seemed to fade with her memory, the feelings were always there, just hidden. And it seemed like I was back on the sidewalks again...

A Girl Interrupted

Not long after my bout with hepatitis, my ex-husband decided he wanted to move out to Montana where some friends were, so we loaded up our '55 Chevy and off we went, to Big Sky Country, God's Country. I won't go into great detail, only to say I had a profound spiritual experience upon my arrival that lasted a whole week, the most blessed week of my life, which changed me forever; unfortunately, after having experienced such bliss, I felt rather disconnected and disinterested in this world, and became very depressed, to the point where I thought it best to get some help. I won't say I was suicidal, but I felt like I wanted to die, so I got some professional help. I remember the psychologist asking me what my childhood was like, to which I replied, "I don't want to talk about it, and I don't see what that has to do with who I am now, anyway." HA! She probably thought, "Here's a keeper!" My childhood had EVERYTHING to do with it, but you know how 18 year olds are…..little miss know-it-all was deep in denial.

After I came back to Illinois I continued therapy and went to vocational rehab, both of which I detested. The therapist I was seeing immediately took me off meds, explaining to me that I wasn't psychotic, just depressed, with unresolved childhood issues, which I persistently denied. I remember her telling me I had problems stemming from my childhood, and me just refusing to listen. I could say it went in one ear and out the other, but I don't think it even got as far as my ears to even bounce off. I just wouldn't/ couldn't hear it, period. It was too painful for me. I wasn't going there. Where I did go to was the bottle.

Battle with the Bottle

The bottle and I had been acquainted in times past, but now we became best friends. I still remember the night I had this amazing revelation about booze. My first husband and I had taken off for Florida for a short visit with his sister before "settling" into an old hotel somewhere in Alabama, and I woke him up one night, and excitedly said, "I know what the answer is for me; it's drinking!" And so drinking it was for me, every chance I got. We lived like gypsies for awhile, moving from Alabama to Santa Fe where my brother lived, then back to Illinois, up to Delaware, and back to Alabama, all within less than a year's time. It was during a separation we had in the summer of 1975 that I came to my half senses and told him I couldn't/wouldn't live like Bonnie and Clyde anymore, and high tailed it out of Alabama on a bus to live with my sister back in Illinois, that my drinking really escalated. I celebrated my 20th birthday with 20 Valiums and beer, landing in a ditch that night with my sister. Some friends happened to come by and find us, thank God, or I don't know what might have happened, as I was so messed up that my knees were like rubber, and I could barely walk, or talk. When I think back on that incident, I wonder what the heck I was trying to do, and the only rational conclusion I have come up with is that I was suicidal. It just doesn't make sense that I would do that if I wasn't.

UnHappily Ever After

Shortly after my 20th birthday, my first husband and I reunited and got married, but unfortunately "happily ever after" turned into "unhappily shortly after," when he decided he wanted "free love," so along with the infidelities came more booze, and one day while he was off having an affair in Florida, I overdosed on booze and sleeping pills, and landed in a psych ward with my stomach pumped, deciding it best I get sober, which I managed to do, until my husband decided he wanted me more than the other woman and came back, but he was right back into all his old ways again, and so was I. "If you can't beat 'em, join 'em," I guess. The truth is, I was terrified of abandonment, even if it meant staying with somebody totally dysfunctional, which he was, but I didn't recognize it at the time.

My fears of abandonment put me on another bus, this time to follow him down to Florida, where I made a last ditch effort to save our "marriage," to no avail. His wild ways got wilder, and I got crazier. I was drinking more than ever, and taking valiums and sleeping pills, anything to numb out. One night while I was drinking in a bar, somebody gave me some pills, which I thought were valiums, but was something else, and I started feeling weird, and asked somebody to give me a ride home, and I must have blacked out, because the next thing I know, it is almost a day later, and my ex-husband told me he thinks I got raped, because I was freaking out, screaming and everything, when I came home, and I tend to agree, especially since I figure I was trying to escape the trauma by sleeping. Our marriage came to a head one day, when he introduced me to his new lover and her husband, and I was introduced to husband number two, Jim, who was also a foster kid, and was wandering around on the road, and happened to wander into the bar/restaurant I waitressed at. It's amazing how dysfunctional people find each other, gravitating to each other like flies to shit. I still remember the day my first husband and I broke up. He took off and left the restaurant, leaving me to cook and waitress all by myself, so I put the "closed" sign on the door, and proceeded to get good and drunk, along with my new man, who happened to wander in right at that time.

So I was "in love" again, and I started living with him down the road on Sanibel Island, until we went to his home state of Michigan, and then back to Illinois, where I got my divorce, and we lived for awhile, then back to Florida and back up to Illinois, stopping in New Orleans for a bout of homelessness, which was a nightmare. I woke up in junk yard one morning all hung over and bruised up from my second husband beating me, feeling lower than scum, just wanting to die. In AA they talk about bottoms---well, I couldn't get any lower than this. I found my way out of that mess, but it wasn't easy.

Home began to take on a new meaning after being without one. Settling down and having some security began to look more appealing to me than living like a gypsy, but I still didn't have a clue as to how to accomplish this, and although part of me wanted sobriety, or at least knew I needed it, I still didn't want it more than drinking, so when I started attending AA in Illinois in the beginning of 1981, I just couldn't get sober. It gets darkest right before the dawn, though, and I was about to see some light. I had managed to quit my cigarette addiction the year before and had acquired a food addiction, one that gave me a pretty hefty shape, and one night while drinking and doing some pain pills I got from a neighbor lady I cared for who had cancer, I smoked up the apartment so bad that my ex-husband became thoroughly disgusted with me and took off. We had always gotten into fights while drinking, and he'd pack his bags and leave, then come staggering back later, so I wasn't too worried at first, but after a few days, I realized he was really gone this time, and decided to go on a drinking binge, a "beer diet." There had been a rare family reunion at this time, which I didn't go to, so my brother came to visit me, and ended up rescuing me, helping me move out of my apartment and in with my sister for a few days until my ex-husband came to take me to Michigan.

A Fresh Start

Although I resisted leaving my home state, I was happy to make a fresh start in Michigan. I was happy to have my normal body back, but I was still drinking, and where drinking was, trouble was sure to follow. After a few months in Michigan my second husband and I were about to be homeless again, and I remember thinking "I can't go through THAT again!" And God must have thought so too, because when he and I went over to see his long lost dad, he told us we were welcome to live with him, as long as we kept the house clean and mowed the lawn, etc. At first I thought it was great, a drinker's paradise, since his dad was also alcoholic, and bought us booze all the time, but after about six months of continual weekend binges, along with some "controlled" drinking during the week (maybe a six-pack instead of a case!) I began getting "sick tired of tired of being sick and tired" and started rethinking sobriety. In March 1982, my ex-husband and I had gone over to an old neighbor's apartment we'd lived next door to when we had first moved to Michigan, for a weekend of partying, and things got out of hand when a friend of theirs took a shine to me while I was dancing, and next thing I know I was being forced into a room where he attempted to rape me. Luckily, he was too drunk to do really do anything, but it was a terrifying experience, compounded by the fact that our "friends" encouraged their friend to rape me, and holding Jim back when he tried intervening. It was a horrible experience, but a blessing in disguise, because it was after this incident that I decided I really wanted to get sober, which I managed to do somewhat by myself for about seven months, but I kept slipping, so on October 1, 1982, I went through the AA doors a third time, this time to stay. They say AA will work if you work it, and I was ready this time. I wanted a better life for myself, so I continued going to AA meetings, and other than a few minor relapses, I stayed sober. In September 1986, my ex-husband and I had gone to Illinois to live, and he took off on me, "abandoned" me, and I got good and drunk, which was my last drunk, and have remained sober ever since. They say if you don't remember your last drunk, you haven't had it; well, I definitely remember that drunk, because I wanted to die. After coming back to Michigan, I really worked the AA Third Step, and surrendered my life to God, as I knew my life was a mess, and wouldn't get better unless I did. I also started attending church at this time.

The Turning Point

It began to dawn on me not long after this that I had deeper issues than besides drinking, and I suspected that those issues had something to do with my childhood, but I honestly didn't know how to deal with them, nor did I honestly care to. I had already had some alcoholic therapy early on in sobriety, but that only addressed the alcohol addiction, and then I tried a regular therapist a few times, who told me I was having a hard time growing up because of my childhood, but it could still be done, and I remember thinking, "OK, so I need to grow up," but that still didn't address my childhood crap. Then there was the therapist who just wanted to "fix" me by encouraging me to get a good education and be successful, which is fine, and I was already pursuing that, but there was still this "stuff" inside me that seemed on the verge of boiling over, that I knew I needed to resolve, but didn't know how to. After my ex-husband and I reunited in early 1987, I decided to see another therapist, who wanted to do the "real" therapy, and after one visit I decided I didn't really have any childhood issues after all, and left as anxiously as I came. During this time my marriage was rapidly falling apart, and I didn't feel emotionally ready to face that, which only made facing my childhood issues all the more difficult. I was on emotional overload. I knew I had to leave, because I was living in a very unhealthy environment that threatened my sobriety and sanity, but even though I knew in my head the necessity of parting, emotionally I was all entangled, not just with the aspect of saying good-bye to someone I'd shared eleven years of my life with, but also with the idea of change, of having to uproot myself, and having my world turn upside down again. It was like my childhood all over again, and even though I was 33 years old at the time, I felt more like 3---insecure, scared, vulnerable, alone, and abandoned.

The Dawning of FACT

It was during this time, around September 1988, at the time when I began contemplating divorce, that I began to feel the need for a support group for my childhood "stuff" and went in search of a support group for former foster children, only to find out there was none, so I decided to attempt to form one myself. I had become acquainted with another former foster child in AA, who also felt the need for extra support and encouraged me to form a support group, so I started praying about it, as far as what to do, what to name it, the format, etc. The name came about quickly, through an ACT mouthwash on TV. I remember thinking, "AH HA! THAT'S IT! Fostered Abandoned Children Together!" (The word Abandoned was changed to Adult years later). I started formulating ideas for FACT and ways to have meetings at the perfect time, as when I left Jim a few months later (Jan. '89), I began to really feel the need for support, so my AA friend, and one other person had meetings for a short time, only about a month or so, then when my friend left for a lengthy vacation, it got postponed, and then my life just got so busy with work, school, and just basic survival, that I didn't have time for it, but occasionally I would get fired up about the idea, only to get frustrated with the lack of time, resources, response, etc, and I felt like I was banging my head up against a brick wall, but I never really gave up on the idea, I only surrendered it to God and figured when the time was right it would happen.

Therapy for Real

Shortly after getting divorced, I realized I needed some therapy, so I started seeing Frank, a therapist who was recommended to me by a very good AA friend. I was ready for real therapy this time (or at least as ready as I was ever going to get!), as I definitely didn't want to see divorce number three! It was very scary facing all my feelings, and Frank suggested I go to ACOA (Adult Children Of Alcoholics), so I figured since my step-mom was alcoholic, and I definitely came from a dysfunctional background, it was worth a try, but I remember telling Frank that I didn't seem to fit in there, that the people didn't seem to understand my foster care issues, to which he replied, "I wanted you to go to ACOA so you would see that your issues are different, that the abandonment you experienced was more severe," and then he went on to explain how a young child being taken away from parents is the worst thing that can happen to a child, and he highly encouraged me to form FACT. He also told me he thought I was very strong, and a uniquely loving woman, which made me feel good. He also thought I was real bright, and encouraged me to pursue college, which I did. He retired not longer after I stopped seeing him, but we remained friends through phone, emails, and occasional visits. The last time we talked was on his birthday in 2009, shortly after my visit to Illinois and ISSCS, and before his death. I told him about visiting ISSCS, and said,

"You know, Frank, you never really get over your childhood," to which he replied, "No, you don't ever get over it, but you CAN get beyond it, which I believe you have." I told him about writing a book, which he was highly encouraging about. I miss Frank a lot, as he was a father figure to me.

A Family Tragedy

It was during my time in therapy with Frank that a terrible tragedy struck my family, one that was very difficult for me to handle. Thankfully I was in therapy and got the support I needed and was able to pull through it. That saying "what doesn't kill you will only make you stronger" certainly applied here.

Hanging in There

I really believed God knew the right time for me to be married again, but I didn't really believe it when I was freshly single. More than anything, I hated being alone, as it seemed like a constant reminder of my childhood abandonment, so when this nice looking guy came along, I got involved with him without even considering the fact that he didn't have a pot to piss in, letting him live with me, then when financial problems forced me out of my apartment and we went our separate ways for a few months, I was begging God for his return. Be careful what you pray for; you might get it! My prayers were answered MY way and we got back together, and moved into a small house. Luckily, I had enough sense (and enough therapy) to quickly realize the mistake I had made, and asked him to leave; unfortunately he didn't have anywhere to go, and me being the good hearted person I am, I let him stay with me until he found another place, which ended up being a year later. In retrospect, I realize how terrified of abandonment I was, and of course I knew WHY, but I still didn't know how to conquer my fears. How do you just get over childhood abandonment fears that are so deeply rooted? I really believed I had surrendered my life to God, but I think I still help back some control, just in case God forgot about me or something, because deep down I didn't really believe He would be there for me. I had a very traumatic experience in 1992 that increased my faith in God (I was almost murdered in Detroit), and I was beginning to see that God wouldn't abandon me, yet when it came to being alone, I still had a difficult time and resisted it. But then a miracle happened, and I can't really say exactly when or how this happened, but I began to feel more comfortable within myself, and more independent, not so needy and afraid, and after my boyfriend finally moved out, I realized that I actually LIKED being alone. Maybe it was having to put up with him and his sloppy ways for so long, or maybe I was really growing, probably both, but I finally felt freer, more whole.

A Miracle Marriage

Not long after I was free from this guy, a friend told me about the Little Rose Chapel, where miracles happened, and I became a frequent visitor there, enjoying the peace, and praying, but not specifically for a man, only for peace, and a stronger relationship with God. I had decided that I was ok with being alone, and living my life for God. I was finally ready to truly surrender, without giving God any instructions. After about a month of visiting the Little Rose Chapel, I met my current husband, through a woman I was working for. She told me her brother was a real nice Christian gentleman, and I figured what the heck, I might as well at least start dating, so we started talking on the phone a lot, and dating. His sister later told me that the ad I responded to for her work was the only advertisement she'd ever put out, and I was the only person who responded to the ad. Sounds like a God thing to me! I am still utterly amazed at the God and how He works these miracles in our lives, when we step out of the way and quit trying to run the show ourselves. It is always when I give a simple "I surrender to God" that see the most awesome things unfold in my life, not when I am saying long, fancy prayers and verses.

Well, you might think I went rushing into my knight-in-shining-armor's arms, living happily ever after, but it wasn't quite that simple, mostly because I was too complicated. Early on in our relationship, I told him I was afraid of him and he said, "Why? I'm not going to hurt you," to which I replied, "I know. That's why I'm afraid of you. I'm not used to normal men." But I took a leap of faith, trusting and believing God had put him there for me, and about six months later we were married. It ended up being the best decision I ever made. I always say "I put my head first and let the heart follow." It must have worked, because we're still together 17 years as of 2012, and our love just keeps growing and getting stronger. He recently had a serious health crisis, and being faced with the possibility without him not only made me come face to face with my childhood demons again, but it also made me realize how precious he is to me, and how deeply I love him. He is my best friend, and we have a real love, a commitment, one that is grounded in spiritual values. God worked miracles with his health, and he's fine now, but I don't ever want to take him for granted. I want to appreciate every day we share together. But I still have my moments. My demons still try to haunt me at times, and I can still be sensitive about my childhood hurts, but as my therapist in the past said when I told him you don't ever really get over it, "No, you don't ever get over it, but you can get beyond it." For all of you foster kids who read my story, I want to say the same thing to you. If *I* can get beyond my childhood, so can you. There is always hope.

How Foster Care Affected Me,

It is obvious from having gone through what I did, that I was affected by foster care. Anybody who reads my story can see that I wasn't all together. They have a saying in AA, "I'm here, because I'm not all there." Well, that is why "I'm here in FACT, because I'm not all there." And as I continue peeling the onion of recovery, I see more deeply into the core of why I'm not all there, which largely has to do with my traumatic childhood. Foster kids are so used to the dysfunction that we often don't see beyond that.

I have grown so accustomed to trauma, that when I was severely beaten, raped (it was attempted rape), and almost murdered, instead of going to the hospital to get checked out, like the police suggested, I went home, and the next day, I went to my scheduled Gynecologist appointment, of all things!

I remember the doctor asking me what happened, because my face was all bruised up, and me telling him I got attacked, responding to him in a tone of voice I would use if someone asked me what I did last night, or what I ate for supper. The doctor has me checked out for a concussion, and I was fine (by the way, my definition of 'fine,' is 'f'd up, insecure, neurotic, and emotionally unstable.') That fits me just fine. I was in a Child Psychology course at College at the time, and when I went into school the very next day, my professor asked me what happened, and I calmly told him I was attacked. He asked me if I was getting any therapy, and I said, "No, but I have talked with a woman over the phone," and he highly suggested that I get some therapy, which I did not do. Seriously, most people would not have responded to that trauma the way I did. I just kept on going, and put it out of my mind, at least my conscious mind. But years later, it came out of my unconscious mind, and into my conscious mind, and almost drove me out of my mind! When I finally did seek help years later, my therapist said that most people wouldn't have handled it as well as I did, and that the fact that I was used to trauma is probably why. Well, that's the up side to being a survivor of foster care, and God only knows what else. I'm a survivor, as we former foster kids all are. If you take somebody from a Beaver Cleaver family (if there is one!), and put them into a traumatic situation like I was in when I was almost murdered, and that person would probably end up in psych ward, but not me, not us; we're strong. We just keep on going, because it's all we know; we have to be strong. To this day, I find it difficult to cry. I'm afraid if I cry, I will be weak, and fall apart, that I won't survive.

As I mentioned in my story, I shut down emotionally when I was in foster care. It isn't safe to feel, and be vulnerable, when you know you have to be strong to survive. There wasn't any one who comforted me, or nurtured me, told me I was safe, that I was loved, I was going to cared for, that I was worth something, and that it wasn't my fault. It wasn't until years later that I found out in therapy that a big reason we blame ourselves as children, is because we need to feel that the adults are ok, that they will take care of us. Children so badly want to feel safe, that they'll try everything to be good, so the caretakers will take care of them. What a huge revelation it was for me to finally realize that none of it was my fault, and then when I started working through my anger at the ones whose fault it was, instead of internalizing it all and taking it out on myself in self-destructive ways, I ended up with some true self-worth.

I know for sure I have Post Traumatic Stress Disorder (I'm afraid of my own shadow! Really!), and I also know I have strong issues with relationships, due to my intense fears of abandonment. Depending on what age you went into care, you might feel like you're dying. I found that out in therapy, also. It was explained to me that as a 6 year old child, I felt like I wouldn't survive without my mother. I thought I would die. It was very traumatic, very frightening. Most people don't understand what it is like to be taken away from their parents and put in strange homes, and often in strange home where the foster parents are strange, also, meaning they either don't know how to care for us, or they don't care to care. We have been taken out of our natural homes because there are issues, and now we are in homes with even bigger issues. It is a never ending trauma, and we all find our ways of coping. I coped by withdrawing; I just went into my shell, where I felt safe. Still today, if somebody hurts me, (and it doesn't take much for me to be hurt), I will crawl into my shell, and I won't come out until I am good and ready, and even then, it will be at a slow pace.

Did I mention that I have struggled with depression and anxiety? It has gotten much, much better over the years. I think a lot of my depression was due to suppressed/repressed anger, and some physical issues (I am hypoglycemic), but once I worked through a lot of my anger, and started taking care of myself better, both physically and emotionally, my depression is practically non-existent. I have my moments of anxiety, but they don't last long, and I able to work through it, without going into a full-blown anxiety attack.

I just can't take rejection! Can I say that again? I just can't take rejection! You would think with all the therapy I've had, and all the support groups I've gone to for support, along with a very loving husband who loves me so much, that I would get over my fear of rejection, but it's still there. I know everyone has some fears of rejection, but foster children really have a lot, and it's no wonder. I especially have a strong fear of rejection when it comes to women, because of my mother abandoning me. I just can't seem to get past it, no matter how much I work on myself. It's there for the rest of my life. It doesn't take much for me to go running the other way when I feel like a woman doesn't like me for some reason. I am very skeptical of female relationships because of my issue with my mother, but I do have some good female friends I trust. When I wrote the document, Our Unique Issues, I was speaking from personal experience. I seem to vacillate between desperately wanting relationships with people and being real clingy with them, to being afraid of them, and being super independent. But that, too, has gotten much better. I am learning to have a more balanced attitude toward people and relationships, not to be so desperate and clingy, or afraid to the point where I won't let people in at all.

I still have a fear of going hungry, because as a young child, we were very poor, and I didn't eat well. I tend to be rather frail, and I think it is mostly due to that. And I love my home; in fact, I love it so much, that I really don't like to travel much. Traveling is unsettling for me, due to my childhood. One of the women who shared her story in this book, Nikki Daniels, talked about the very same thing. I feel safe at home. I'm adventurous enough that I like to get out, and I walk everyday, and I enjoy going away for a day or two, if it somewhere where I know somebody, but to just out traveling all over the place, and staying in strange hotel rooms, does not appeal to me at all. I could travel with my husband because I feel safe with him, but I would never want to travel alone. I have to feel very safe. I am like the Hobbit, who likes to stay in his cozy little home.

Another way I was affected by foster care was being a mother. When I was younger, I didn't want children, even though I love them, and I didn't know why until I started working through my issues. Then when I got married to my current husband, I thought I would try to have a child, even though I still wasn't sure if I really did, but I was already 40, and after a few years, I just gave up. I finally came to the conclusion that deep down, there was still a lot of ambivalence and uncertainty about being a mother, and I was better off not having one. It gave me more stress than joy whenever I thought about it. And I was going to school and forming FACT, so I was very busy. There is a Psalm in the Bible that says "God will give you the desires of your heart," and I have come to find out, especially since I did this book, that reaching out to other former foster children, is the desire of my heart. It truly is, and it is amazing to me that God knew this, even before I did. I feel like I am mother to the motherless, and if there is any way that I can help a former foster child, to nurture them, then I am doing God's will in my life. I truly love and care for them. Foster children have gone through so much. They need other former foster children who understand them, mentor, and nurture them. I want to be one of those people.

Oh, and did I mention all the moving around I did when I was younger? I lived like a gypsy. I was so unsettled at times that I didn't even bother unpacking my bags! I got tired of it as I got older, and finally settled down with my third husband. Now I'm so settled it's hard to get me far from home. I LOVE my home. But it appears I will be making another move in the near future, but it is a good one. It is one I am looking forward to.

I could go on, and on, about all these issues.......You gets the idea....... "I'm here, because I'm not all there.".......But I'm getting there!.......

One positive way that foster care affected me is that I am a survivor and I persevere, in spite of obstacles in my path.

I graduated from the University of Michigan with High Honors, which seems nothing short of a miracle when I think back on my childhood. I am proud of myself for achieving this, and so is my husband. And I know my dad would be very proud, also. He told me he thought I had the intelligence and ambition to go to college, and encouraged me to do so.

I am also proud of myself for forming FACT and writing this book. It was SO much work, but it also brought me SO much satisfaction. And most importantly, I believe God is proud of me.

The University of Michigan-Dearborn

As a Mark of High Academic Achievement

Carol Ann Lucas

is hereby designated a

Graduate with High Distinction

In recognition thereof, this Certificate is awarded

this first day of May, two thousand ten

Daniel Little, Chancellor   Catherine Davy, Provost

There is hope for all of us.......

A Glimmer of Hope for our Family?

My family, which in the past 30 years has only had sporadic contact, has been communicating some. At least there is some hope, or so I thought. In the past I have often felt sad about our family. I think a lot of that sadness came from remembering the happy times we had at one time---the birthday parties, the locomotion, playing together, fighting over our little red wagon, and then the happy times when my dad got custody of us, only to have the family togetherness come to an end again after his death. Due to some emotional turmoil within our family and within myself last year, I am much more at peace about this, because I am more at peace within myself. It no longer has a hold on me. My life belongs to the present, not the past. I realized that our family is what it is, and there has been too much damage for us to truly be a family again. I wish everyone in my family well, but I refuse to be strangled by them, or the past. I love them all though and continue to pray for them. I just know my boundaries better today.

Post Traumatic FACT Disorder
And now for the closing chapter of my story…

When I first embarked on the writing of this book I went about everything in a very orderly and organized manner---managing my time, having a daily calendar to write down dates for contacting people sharing their stories, having all the paper work neatly stacked, emailing people, saving everything on a zip drive, etc., but upon near completion of the book I was feeling very disorderly, and began to suffer from Post Traumatic FACT. Disorder, which led me to seek professional help again, this time with a very excellent Christian therapist, who has reassured me that I am not crazy, that I had an "avalanche of crap" hit me (my husband almost dying, an upsetting situation with a foster boy we were going to adopt, health problems, writing the FACT stories, which triggered my childhood traumas, losing my beloved dog Trucker, family problems, with one brother stirring up trouble about my story that led to another family member threatening to sue me over some assumed content in my story, feeling stalked by a man on the Internet, which triggered off feelings about my near murder incident that happened years ago, etc.), which is enough to drive anybody over the edge, and with somebody like myself who has had so much trauma, it is no wonder I began to feel emotionally overwhelmed to the point of regressing into areas of my childhood of not feeling safe. That is the last place I wanted to be! I am learning a lot about boundaries from this therapist and how to take care of myself better, as I realize now that although I loved being passionate about the book, I was driven to the point where I wasn't loving myself enough to take good care of myself. I almost drove myself crazy to the point where I even felt like giving up on FACT, but aside from the fact that it would have been hard to walk away from something I had put so much work into and had always been very determined to do this, and felt I had a responsibility to do it, I knew I had a calling from God to do FACT and I couldn't just turn my back on God, which was ultimately why I chose to forge ahead. I also realize that although I love everybody in my family and am happy to be reconnected with them, there are so many unhealthy family dynamics that it is mind boggling, and downright disturbing, and so for the sake of my own sanity I need to have strong boundaries. This is not to say that I don't want to have a relationship with my family, just that I need to have firm boundaries. What I have come to realize is that our family still has a lot of healing to do, and that I am not responsible for any of my family members healing, nor am I responsible for my mother favoring me, something which I carried guilt about for years (sibling rivalry never really goes away). Another realization that came about my family is that although I am part of my original family and I love them, they are only a small part of the family of God. How freeing it is to finally come to these realizations! So here I am in therapy again, peeling another layer in this onion they call "recovery." Will I ever get over it? Probably not! But I can get beyond it, which I believe I am doing, by the grace of God and support from loving people. So for all of you foster kids who are struggling, my heartfelt message to you is this: "There is always hope for healing. If I can get beyond it, so can you." Thank you, God!

New Beginnings……….

Me and Holden

Upon the republication of this book, I have my own answer to the question "will we ever get over it." The answer is "no!" not completely. My husband, the love of my life, the one who changed my life, passed away and I am sadly reminded that my past abandonment will haunt me until the day I die. I will get completely over my past when I cross the bridge from this earth to Heaven to join the Lord and my husband.

Carol Lucas and Her Extended Family

Another Generation of Foster Care

The last thing I wanted in our family was to see history repeat itself, as I did not want to see my own dear and innocent nieces and nephews suffer the way my siblings and I did, but unfortunately the thing I feared most happened. Due to my sister's poverty and alcoholism and her husband's absence (he was in prison), my sister's three children were horribly neglected and eventually ended up in foster care. I know my sister and don't believe for an instant she would intentionally harm them; it's just that her addiction to alcohol was stronger than her love for her children. Sadly, this is not unusual, for foster care to be carried on to the next generation. I was hoping it would end with our generation, but the bad news is that it didn't. The good news though is that it appears it will end with the next generation. My nieces and nephews were initially in some bad foster homes, but they all three eventually ended up in good, loving Christian homes that offered them love and stability, something they were so lacking with my sister. Although they have scars from their early years and some of the foster homes they were in, the love and dedication they finally received has made a huge impact on their lives and all three of them are doing well. Considering what they went through, this is nothing short of a miracle.

When I asked Jennifer, Charlie, and Heather if they would like to share a story in my book, they all three were happy to do it, even though they hardly know me. They each have their own unique story. I have always felt bad I wasn't there to help them in the past, but since I was here in Michigan and they were in Illinois, I wasn't even contacted. I have wondered why the rest of the family in Illinois wasn't contacted, but given how disconnected our family has been through the years, it shouldn't surprise me. Anyway, I am happy they took the opportunity to share their stories, as it can offer hope to others, and I am especially happy to have the opportunity to have them in my life again.

Jennifer Powell...
Hurting and Longing for Mom

When my Aunt Carol asked me if I would like to share a story in her book for foster kids, I decided I would if it would help others to see how foster care is handed down from generation to generation. I never knew my mom was in foster care until my aunt told me. She told me she thought it might help me to at least understand my mom better and why she was such a neglectful mom, and it does, but it still doesn't take the hurt away.

A big reason for my hurt is due to the fact that I am the oldest of me and the two siblings, Charlie and Heather and was the caretaker because my mom was drunk most of the time and was very neglectful. I feel that as the oldest sibling it is my role to make the family stay together, even today. My earliest memories of my mom, family, and home life aren't that great. I never had a regular relationship with my mom. It was always backward. I feel like I am the mother and my mom is the daughter.

I was raised with my mom until I was about age 15. I was 14 ½ when I was put into foster care, Charlie was 10, and Heather was 8. My mom didn't pick us up from school like she was supposed to and she was very neglectful in other ways also. She was more interested in drinking than caring for her children.

If it hadn't been for foster care I probably would've ended up on drugs and alcohol, so I am grateful for foster care in a way, but still, I did not want to be in care. I wanted to be with my family. I was not happy in care. When I emailed my Aunt Carol and said "If you want to know if what I went through messed me up," I said "honestly, yes and no." The "yes" part is that I didn't grow up with Charlie and Heather in care like a normal family. Instead I went to sibling visits at McDonalds, see my dad in prison, and see my mom (when she was sober at DCFS offices. The "no" part is if it weren't for God I would be in a huge mess, but because I started going to church, things went ok for me while I was in foster care, but I wasn't happy, so I developed an eating disorder (bulimia) just to get out of the foster home. Then I ran away and ended up on the sixth floor at Sara Busch for an eating disorder and I spent my 16th birthday at a park pavilion because I ran away. I did not like my case worker! All I wanted was to be with my mom and be a family again, which never happened because my mom called my case worker drunk and said she couldn't make it that day. My mom refused alcoholic assessment and classes that DCFS asking her to comply with. My dad was locked up in prison when he found out we were in foster care, so he couldn't do anything. My dad watched me grow up in pictures. He sent me money and letters from prison.

I know my God above was watching over me while I was in care. Right after I got saved and baptized in church at age 17 I got hit by a car, but no harm was done! I was in the Children Home's van on my way to a visit with my siblings and we flipped in the ditch in Effingham three times, upside down, and all I got was some minor abrasions. That was an act of God! I graduated at age 18 in May of 1997 and I moved back with my mom in

Garrett where she was living at that time, until she met her new husband, who for valid reasons I did not like and get along with. He never hurt me, but I never felt comfortable with him. I saw her wearing sunglasses in the house at noon, saying she had 'pink eye.' I can't get this out of my head! I told my Aunt Carol, "You have no idea what pain is until you witness this."

I still love my mom, and I may look a lot like her, but I am not anything like her, nor do I care to be. I don't want to be like either one of my parents. I was very confused and lost years ago, but I'm doing much better now. I don't smoke, drink, or do drugs, and I have a steady job at a motel. I am also no longer bulimic. I walked away from an abusive relationship I had for six years and have been in a stable, loving relationship for the past three years. Even though I wish it had been different, I'm not holding a grudge against either one of my parents.

I'm pretty close to my dad today, but I don't like the way he expects me to be there for him, when he wasn't for me for so many years. I'm trying very hard to wash my hands of my mom, and I have moved on, but it still hurts. I only live fifteen minutes away from my mom, but I haven't seen her in almost three years. She has a husband who is a lot like her and I've tried so many times to help her, but never got through to her. Sadly, Charlie and Heather won't go see her. I convinced Charlie to see her three years ago, but Heather won't see her. She hasn't seen our mom since 1993, when she lost us. Heather was only 8 years old at the time. It hurts me because she was up to visit me and never wanted to go visit our mom. It would make me SOSOSO happy if she would!! I can't stand the thought that my sister doesn't even want to reunite with our mom. I told Aunt Carol, "Please pray for me to get over this because it's killing me." My mom told me, "This marriage will be the end of me." Is she trying to hurt herself? My mom looks totally miserable. One time she started crying when she looked in the mirror at herself. She was so pretty at one time and now she won't even put makeup on or wear clothes.

Back in 2006 or 2007 my mom was sober for two months and I got to meet a mom I never met before. I wish it would stay that way, but unfortunately it didn't. What has been the hardest thing is seeing her look so bad. It's breaking my heart and I can't get it out of my head, so much so that I dwell on my mom at night repeatedly.

It still hurts me. I just wish we could be a family. The only way I've gotten through my hurt is with prayers and humor. I use humor a lot.

Charlie Powell

Longing for Stability

I want to share my story along with my siblings to show how even though foster care was passed on to me by my mom who spent time in foster care. I have chosen not to be a victim of my past. I am determined not to follow in my parents footsteps! I am hoping that by sharing my story it will give other foster kids hope and inspiration for a better life than what was handed down to them by their dysfunctional parents.

I don't remember much of my early childhood and what I do recall isn't good. My early home life was very dysfunctional. My dad was gone, so I was left at home with my alcoholic mom, who apparently cared more about her addiction than she did her own three children. We lived in a trailer park that was filled with roaches and I can remember walking to the store to get groceries and to a friend of my mom's to get cigarettes. The truth is I never really had a mother. I love my real mom to death, but she wasn't a mother the way she should have been.

I was put in foster care in 1992 at the age of 10, when it was discovered how dysfunctional our home was, and I was moved around constantly (I think I was in five homes) before I finally got settled in a stable home.

I didn't like my first foster home and luckily I wasn't there long because social services found out that me and my siblings weren't being properly treated there and removed us. My sister Heather wasn't happy there at all. They weren't caring foster parents and were obviously only in it for the money.

My second home was with a teacher for a short while, a month maybe, along with my sisters. It was just a temporary placement until a better home could be found.

The third home was also with my sisters and we only stayed there 2-3 weeks before we were removed because it was discovered we were not being treated properly there. I felt powerless to help my sister.

My fourth home was with my sisters again, and again the foster parents weren't very nice. I remember being hand-cuffed to the bed. The home was rather dirty and at the time we were removed the home was shut down.

I was in my fifth home for 6-8 months. My sisters were there with me for some time and then at some point I was alone. It was a nice Christian home, so I don't know why I was removed.

My sixth home was a group home with a lot of boys and girls, where I stayed for about six months. Then in 1994 I went to visit a foster home, and then I went back to the previous home for a week, and then was moved permanently to my last foster home, where I still remain today. It is a very nice Christian home. There were fourteen boys there in the beginning of my stay, but now I'm the only one there. My foster dad died three years ago, but I have a very close relationship with my foster mom and enjoy being there with her.

I can see how God is putting things together in my life and I have a lot of connection. I have had a good job for seven years building towers for hospitals, etc. I got out of a three year relationship because my ex-girlfriend tried to keep me away from my family. About two months ago I met a Christian girl on Facebook, and am hoping it might be a long-term stable relationship.

I would not have had to be put in foster care if my real mom had gotten it together, but she didn't. In a way though I'm glad I ended up in care because I wouldn't be who I am now if I hadn't. I probably would have ended up an alcoholic if I hadn't been put in care. I feel very grateful that I ended up in a Christian home, which was nothing like my real mom's home.

I talk with my sister Jennifer occasionally and regularly with my sister Heather. I saw my real mom about four years ago, and at that time she was very sick and alcoholic looking, and living with man who didn't seem very nice. I see my real dad sometimes when he invites me to, but I have so much anger built up inside of me about the past, as he has never even apologized for everything me and my siblings went through. He wanted $500 from me awhile back, which made me angry. I feel as though he should have been helping me when I was a growing up and today if I needed it, but instead it is the other way around. He also tells me I should leave my foster home and be out on my own since I am a grown man of age 29, but I feel like I might as well stay here with my foster mom until I get married. I have stability here, which I never had in my childhood. I want and need stability.

Heather Storm

Survival

Jennifer is in back, Charlie, and Heather (me) in front

When asked by my aunt Carol if I would like to share a story in her book for foster kids, I decided that to help others realize that they can come through difficulties it takes people who are willing to tell share their histories, good and bad. Although I am Charlie and Jennifer Powell's sister and we shared similar experiences, they weren't identical and each of our memories is different from one another.

My earliest memories of my home life and my real mom are very dysfunctional. I remember going hungry a lot because I was afraid of eating the food she prepared. We lived in a trailer that was roach infested and many times these critters would end up in our meals. I also remember walking to get food with food stamps and going out to the street to get cigarette butts for my mom to smoke. There was no running water at times, so I got made fun of for being dirty and having unkempt hair. Charlie and I used to feed horses across from our trailer court and sleep in a horse stall with a horse named "Little Kid." The horse's owner was an older couple who gave us some food and other items. I remember Jennifer getting violent and throwing chairs and tables. I remember her having many issues and outbursts where she would also be violent with us. I even remember her putting a cat in the freezer once when she was mad at me.

I was in a total of seven foster homes. The first time I went into foster care was at the age of 5, due to medical neglect. I had pneumonia and my mom didn't take me to the hospital like she should have. I was hospitalized for several days, possibly weeks. I do not have a sharp memory of this time in my life. I was placed in a foster home. I am unsure if my siblings were also placed in foster care at this time.

I went back to live with my mom and I'm not sure how much time lapsed between my return to her and my second entry into foster care. I think I went back home twice to my mom, each time for about a year. One night my mom's boyfriend kicked us all out in the cold around Christmas time and we went to a homeless shelter, and it was at this time that all three of us went into foster care together.

I don't recall a lot about my second foster home, except that it was trashy like my mom's home. I remember being removed due to missing school and having head lice that went untreated. The third home wasn't so great either. I remember a guy running around in his underwear and I remember going to the state fair and not being allowed to ride any rides. The foster parents wouldn't even let me and brother see each other, although we lived in the same home.

The fourth home was only for a short stay and I don't remember anything about it. I believe that it is what they would call a "respite" home. The fifth foster home I was in was with an older couple in a subdivision. They were nice most of the time, except when I was forced to eat thing things that I did not like, such as sauerkraut. I remember them having a convertible car and having a nice home. I was also attacked by a dog at the neighbor's house. I never felt comfortable in their home and due to some behavior issues on my part, I was moved.

The sixth home was when I was around 10 years old. I remember loving this home very much. They had two Dalmatian dogs that I loved very much and I remember having many nice things, which I had never had before. It was here that I started counseling to work on some of the issues that I had been having. I remember wanting to live the rest of my childhood there and having some very close friends there. I remember wanting to be adopted by them and even writing a letter to my caseworker telling her what my wishes were. It was shortly after writing this letter that I was moved to my final home. I was moved due to not being an adoptable child.

I then went to my seventh and final foster home. I resided there from 5th grade until I graduated high school. I consider this family as my biological family. They live in a great log home on the lake with a ton of space. They also had horses, which I loved and I had my own horse. I showed horses in 4-H and did many outdoor activities throughout my time there. I graduated from OV high school and then got a scholarship from the Department of Children and Family Services. I graduated with a Bachelor Degree in Social Work. I got married my senior year of college and today I am a case worker for Lutheran Child and Family Services. I love my job and what I do and feel that I am able to help the children through the process because I have been there!

I married my husband in October of 2006. We dated from my senior year in High School until my senior year in college, when he proposed. We now reside 15 minutes from the last placement I had. I have no contact with my biological mother and limited contact with my father. My father has since started a family with another woman and they have two small twin boys together. I have dealt with the issues of abandonment with my parents and have forgiven them in the best way I can. It is hard to forget what someone has done to you, especially when it affects the rest of your life. Foster care was not always "rainbows and sunshine" for me, but when I finally found my "home," the healing began. If it were not for foster care, I am not sure where I would be. It is hard to say if I would have been successful or if I would have ended up living a next generation of family poverty. The cycle has to end with someone, and it has ended, at least on my part, with me. People ask me if I have regrets about not having my biological parents in my life and some may even think it is a bit cruel. I say why have something in your life if it only brings you down and causes more harm than good? Everyone has their own way of dealing with difficulties in life and my way might not work for everyone, but each person has to figure out what works best for him or her and go with it. I did. No turning back.

John Dunn

Founder of the Foster Care Council of Canada
Contributing Founder of FACT
Life in Foster Care is Like a Subway Ride

My name is John Dunn. I was born on November 16, 1970 in Toronto, Canada into a family which consisted of my mother, my older brother, and my two older sisters. My brother is four years older than myself, and my two sisters are both approximately ten years older. At the time, my mother was an alcoholic who also suffered from Bi-Polar Disorder, known back then as Manic Depression. From what my sisters have told me, when I was about 18 months old, my mother was gone a lot and my two older sisters took care of me and my brother. I was told that one day my mother attempted to jump off the roof of a two-story house when she was going through an episode of depression. I was 2 years old at the time. The Child Welfare authorities were notified after this incident and this is when my sixteen year career as a foster child began.

For the first thirteen years of my life I was moved through foster homes with my brother. Some of the homes were good, some were abusive, and some were just short term. Many of my memories of these foster homes are not good. I remember having pliers applied to my penis as a threat to crush it, should I keep on wetting the bed. I also had my head forced into and flushed down a toilet that was filled with feces and urine right after it had just flooded due to a large bowel movement I just had. I also remember my brother and I being forced to cut the throats of cute little rabbits, then bleeding them and skinning them. We were also made to cut off the heads of chickens. I would hold the chicken on the block and my brother would swing the axe. Less disgusting, but still emotionally traumatizing, was always being the new kid in school and having to make friends quickly, and then lose them just as quickly, when we were moved to a new home.

Johnny Dunn (Front - Little Brother)
Ronnie Dunn (Behind - Big Brother)
(Separated by Catholic C.A.S. Toronto)

John Dunn (Founder / Ottawa)
Ron Dunn (Co-Founder / Toronto)
(Reunited By Luck)

At the age of 4 I was reunited with my brother at a foster home, but much of the time I spent in foster care was without him, which was very tough for me. I was almost adopted at one home in Trout Creek, Ontario, but due to the physical abuse in the home, the plans fell through.

When I was 10 years old, my brother and I finally got a chance to meet my mom, and later that year, my older sisters. I still remember one time shortly before getting to meet her, when I talked to my brother about us finally getting to meet her and him saying he did not want to meet her at this time because he wanted me to ask her one thing first. He wanted me to ask our mom if she was "mad at him." I guess the whole time we were in foster care my brother thought it was somehow his fault that our family was destroyed. Then, the day finally came when I met my mother at the Catholic Children's Aid Society (CCAS) in Toronto. I still remember it clearly and it is amazing. I walked into what used to be the waiting area (before they renovated it) of the CCAS, on the second floor, and sat on the chairs near a lady who also appeared to be waiting for someone. This woman kept looking over at my 10 year old self with this look I did not quite understand. Then, after a few awkward minutes, my worker came around the corner and said, "I see you two have already met!" That was it! The woman next to me, who had been looking at me the whole time, completely lost her composure and started crying, and as I call it today, "attacked" me with flailing arms and Kleenex balls flying out of her sleeves as she hugged me like nobody has ever hugged me before. It was kind of scary, but deep down inside, it felt great to know that someone really, really LOVED ME. We were then taken into a private room to the left, and we sat. She cried, and cried, and talked, while looking at me up and down with such a deep, penetrating look that seemed to touch my very soul. I now understand that this was the look that only a loving mother could give to her own child, and it felt good, really good. It just felt…right, and sadly, foreign to me. Eventually my brother decided to meet our mom, after I told him that she was definitely not mad at him, and we spent the next few years having visits with each other.

When I was 13 years old, my brother and I were separated and I continued moving through foster homes on my own. I moved a total of thirteen times by the time I was 18 years of age and I suffered physical and emotional abuse in two of the places where I stayed the longest. By the time I was 18, I was tired of moving around and tired of people watching everything I did, so I decided to leave the system. I spent the rest of my life getting jobs, losing jobs, moving between apartments, and town, or cities, and eventually becoming homeless at times. Somehow I managed to stay away from drugs, but I led a very unstable life at this time.

Then my mother, "Mickey," as she was known to her friends, whom I had developed an incredible relationship with over the years, eventually lost her mental health doctor because he moved to the United States to teach, and who was great at keeping her fairly stable when it came to her Bi-Polar experiences, the doctor who while he was caring for her was able to help her maintain years of full-time employment helping homeless and troubled women at Toronto, called Rendu House, got a "by-the-book doctor," who did not medicate her as she was used to, and eventually her episodes of mania and depression spiked drastically again, turning her back to drinking after years of sobriety, which ultimately led her to commit suicide by an intentional overdose on October 6, 1998. I was 28 years old at this time. This was a heavy blow to my brother, who was very close with our mom all of his life, both before we went into foster care and after we met her again. I was also very close with mom, but somehow I was not immediately impacted by her death. For me, it was a delayed reaction. I attended her funeral and did cry, and missed her very much; however, since she only had a pine box covered in white cloth, I was not even aware that her body was in the room. This was something I learned later. I just thought it was a table with pictures on it. I guess in my state of sadness I just did not realize that she would naturally be at the funeral. There were a lot of people there to remember mom, since she had touched so many people's lives in both the circles of AA, NA, and in her life of helping others who had also gone through what she knew all too well.

In 2001, three years after her death, her death finally hit me. I had an emotional breakdown. It all started when I wanted to ask the CCAS for my foster care records so I could look over them and try to put the pieces of my life together in my head, to make some kind of connection with my past, but to my surprise and dismay, the CCAS refused to allow me to have copies of my files. I initiated a complaint about this and ended up speaking to the disclosure worker's supervisor, then to the Executive Director, Mary McConville, for a three hour meeting with her flanked by her chief legal counsel at the time, Alex Duncan, and my disclosure worker, Barbara Myland. I eventually made my way up to the Board of Directors level of the complaint, which merely supported McConville's decision to deny me copies of my files. The only excuse ever given to me for not letting me have copies of my own life records was that "they might fall into the wrong hands." If I had simply been given copies of my files back then, I probably would have put them into a life book and may never have contacted them again. As a matter of fact, I probably would have never embarked on any of my advocacy work at all, but since they denied me copies of my life records, I was driven to find out why they were so militant in keeping them a secret.

I was so frustrated with them withholding my records that I became very angry, and eventually, as a method of venting some of that frustration, I created a radio documentary for CBC's OUTFRONT, titled "Too Many Stops," which takes you on a virtual, thirteen minute subway ride through my life in foster care. That story is available on-line at my website shown at the end of this story.

After exhausting all possible avenues of complaint with the Society regarding my files, I was further driven to protest sealed CAS records by walking from Toronto to Prince Edward Island with a sign on my back which said, "Former Foster Child Walks for Open Records." During the walk, while alone for weeks on end, I finally began to fully and properly mourn the death of my mother, and at that point, I dedicated the rest of my life to working for improved quality of services and accountability in child welfare across Canada.

Upon arriving in PEI, I was interviewed by a local CBC Radio show in Charlottetown, I stayed at a shelter called Harvest House Ministries, and I got a night job stocking shelves at Walmart. After staying in PEI for about six months, I began returning to Toronto, and a good friend and advocate, Jane Scharf, offered me a place to stay in Ottawa with her so I could take a break and just relax for a bit. I gladly took her up on the offer. I originally met Jane before the protest walk to PEI. Jane had worked in a group home near Ottawa where she reported excessive restraints being used improperly as punishment instead of for safety reasons against children in the home, and because of our related on-line activities, we became aware of each other. Jane supported me emotionally and financially whenever she could during my walk by periodically wiring me greatly appreciated donations as I walked. She could barely afford donations, as she was conducting a hunger strike to end small child restraints, which lasted 38 days during the same time I was walking out east. Her website, which is still up and which celebrates her victory on the issue, can be found at http:// endchildrestraints.tripod.com.

After staying with Jane for a couple of months in 2003, I ended up on my own, became homeless once again, moved into a rooming house, and have since remained in Ottawa, where I continue to advocate for improved quality and accountability of child welfare services through a non-profit organization I started called The Foster Care Council of Canada. The Council is an organization that is made up of both current and former child welfare clients. This organization is not an anti-CAS organization, as it has been labeled by some; however, its mandate includes advocating for improved quality of services and accountability in child welfare services. Over the past few years, the Council has made various submissions to committees of the Legislative Assembly of Ontario regarding child welfare related Bills, advocated for changes to child welfare practices and policies through the Ministry of Children and Youth Services, assisted former wards in becoming aware of, and filing claims with the Criminal Injuries Compensation Board for abuse suffered both in and before foster care, and has shown them how to obtain access to their foster care records. I personally have laid provincial offence charges under the Corporations Act against the Children's Aid Society of Ottawa and its Executive Director, Barbara MacKinnon, for failing to furnish a list of their members in their attempts to block me from advocating for kids in foster care to become non-voting members of their own Society, and we continue to do more actions and raise more awareness as time goes on. We are currently attempting to get more people informed of and involved in advocating for changes through the political process, and have appeared in the media several times regarding child welfare related issues. We hope more people will come and visit us at http://www.afterfostercare.ca to learn how they too can get involved and possibly help us out as well!

Unnecessary Litigation, Wasted Value for Money, and Lack of Accountability in Child Welfare

I am currently aware of at least two provincial offence charges against two different Children's Aid Societies in Ontario, three citizens in Ontario, who were forced to initiate what are known as "private prosecutions" against Children's Aid Societies in Ontario. A "private prosecution" is when a regular citizen presses charges against a person or corporation without the assistance of the police or the Crown, but instead swears what is called an "Information" to a Justice of the Peace to initiate the entire procedure. In these cases, the charges were provincial offenses, not criminal offences, the details of which can be found on our website.

Life as a foster child is not easy and does leave lasting scars. It was through my search for recovery than I ran across the FACT website for former foster children and connected with the founder, Carol Lucas. I became a contributing founder by collaborating with her about some changes. Even though I still struggle with God and spirituality, which FACT supports, I have great respect for it and I believe very much in its cause, to provide healing for former foster children.

Life in Foster Care is Like a Subway Ride

Life in care starts at Union Station
You start on a train
It takes you on a trip
The path is dark, isolated, and confusing
As you travel, you wonder what the next station will look like

Every station is completely different, yet serves the same purpose
It is exciting to try and guess what the next station will look like
After awhile you get used to the dark tunnels between stops
You no longer see the tunnels as long and dark, but rather just a short
period of time
As you go on through this journey, (northbound)
You get to Bloor
A MAJOR CROSSROAD IN LIFE
You now have a choice to make (Like at 18 years in care)
Do you stay underground in the "SYSTEM" by transferring and going
along Bloor, or do you keep heading north where it takes you above
ground, where you can see the sky, the clouds, and all the freedom all
around? Even though the ride along Bloor will be longer, familiar, and
safe, I cannot help but want to taste the freedom of the open sky, to see a
change of scenery from the dark lonely tunnels of restrictions. I go north,
on a one way ticket to freedom.

John Dunn/February 20, 2001

Who Am I?

I am John
John Dunn
John Francis Dunn
Also Known As:
John Holluski
John Rick
John LeBreton
John Dunn
John LeBreton (again)
John Kennedy
John Baker
John Gooley
John (Rob/Corley)
John Francis Dunn

My Monsters

My monsters don't exist in a closet
Or underneath my bed
I can't hide under the covers
And just play I'm dead.

No, my monsters once lived inside me
And they gnawed at me all day.
They taunted m with their insults
Cause I was their fated prey.

They danced inside my mind
And they lingered in my heart
They knew my innermost secrets
And my innocence they tore apart.
No, my monsters once lived inside me
And they told me not to tell
They told me if I did
That I would go to hell.

They whipped me with their fresh scars
Of fear and terror and pain
They induced me with guilt pills
So I could not bear the shame.

Now my monsters live in tall buildings
Behind bullet proof vanes
My monsters live in houses
With socially approved names.

My monsters live in courthouses
Where your life is ironed on papers
My monsters live in mansions
Discussing their latest capers.

My monsters live with children
Causing them more grief.
I killed my own monsters
But there is still no relief.

Yes, my monsters may be
Faded fragments of my past
But I still have my toy sword
Against its sinister grasp.

And with it I will wield
A monster of revenge
Against your faulty perception
Of being justice's friend.

After foster care…What is my purpose? Afterfostercare/ the Foster Care Council of Canada

Deep down inside, I feel the whole reason I was put throughthis life of torture and pain, and why I have been kind of "reserved" from normal society, is so that I would learn all of the feelings that are caused by being involved in the foster care industry, and to one day use that "weakness" of empathy as a strength to help others who are going through the same thing.

As of 2012 I have a Crown Ward Newsletter for the Foster Care Council of Canada.

John Dunn Afterfostercare.ca , Foster Care Council of Canada

From the album:
"Queen's Park" by Bv

Children's Aid Society of Ottawa Membership

Mission: The Children's Aid Society of Ottawa is committed to protecting the children and youth of our community from all forms of abuse and neglect. We work to keep them safe and secure, both within their families and the communities in which they live.

Being a member of the Society provides you with an opportunity to be involved and support the Society's mission, help raise community awareness of the important work being undertaken by the CAS and help promote the notion that the well-being of children and youth is the responsibility of the whole community.

The Society bylaw defines 'regular member' of the membership year as: any person eighteen (18) years of age or over residing or carrying on business in the territorial jurisdiction of the Society; or corporation having its head office or carrying on business in the territorial jurisdiction of the Society; and has, in the opinion of the Board of Directors, a genuine interest in the objectives of the Society. Please note membership dues for 2009-2010 are set at no cost.

Name _John Dunn_   E-mail _Johndunn @afterfostercare.ca_

Address _12-1160 Meadowlands Drive E_   Postal Code _K2E 6J2_ Telephone _613-270-1039_

The following information will be helpful in assisting the Board of Directors in determining membership. Potential members may also be contacted for more information.

Why are you interested in becoming a member?
I wish to become a member in order to be able to advocate for improvements in child welfare services, to be afforded the same rights other members enjoy under the Societies By-laws and the Corporations Act and to run to become a Board Member.

What is your experience, background or interest that is pertinent to the Society's mission?
I grew up in foster care for sixteen years as a crown ward and have an interest in advocating to keep children and youth safe and happy in their communities, including those living in foster care and to advocate for increased transparency and accountability of the children's aid society in an appropriate way through proper channels.

How did you learn about the Society's membership?
The society does not advertise memberships on their site, I learned about it via LAW CLERK Cou

How would you like to contribute to the work of the Society?
I would like to educate the public of the good work being done by the society, get them involved in with the society and its committees, panels and consultations, and to teach them how to better work with the society through appropriate channels.

Signature _[signature]_   Date _Nov 14, 2009_

Thank you for your interest!

Adam Robe

Unwritten Future

I was abandoned at age 5 and found myself in the foster care system, without a clue as to what was happening to me, as so many others have experienced. I hope that by sharing my story other foster kids will realize that they aren't alone, that there are many others who share the same feelings.

I was placed on a bus with my 6 year old brother and 4 year old sister by my mother, where we traveled to live with my grandparents. When we arrived, no one was there to pick us up. Apparently, in her haste to get us out the door, my mother *forgot* to tell my grandparents we were coming. Thankfully, she was forward-thinking enough to put a note on my brother's shirt with the contact information for my grandparents. The police were sharp enough to pick up on this and called them. When they arrived, they instantly stated that they were having no part of raising three children. The police tried to contact my mother, but they were not able to reach her. Thus, I began my journey in foster care.

My first night in foster care was very difficult for me. Although I was with my brother and sister, I still had no idea what was happening to me. My foster parents tried to help me feel more comfortable, but I was in a state of shock. How do you tell a 5 year old child that his whole life has changed---overnight?!

As the days went by and I realized that my mother wasn't coming back for me, I felt pure dread. I couldn't understand why she didn't come for us and I cried at night when no one was around. At times, I was very angry with her and deeply hurt. How could she do this to me?!!! I didn't know it at the time, but I was becoming depressed and withdrawn. Because I didn't have the words for what was happening to me, it wouldn't be until much later in my life that I would fully understand that I was going through the stages of grief and loss. I don't know exactly how much time had passed since we had been thrust into the foster care system, before we were moved again. My sister and I were placed in a home together, and my brother was placed somewhere else. Not only had I lost my mother, friends, neighborhood, and way of life, but I suddenly found myself without my protector---my brother. I felt powerless and afraid. I hid my fear and pain by putting an invisible barrier around myself.

As a child in foster care, several things became clear to me right away:

o   Being ***bad*** can mean that you could be moved. This doesn't mean that someone told me this; just the simple act of seeing children come in and out of the foster home after an *incident* was enough to make the ground rules clear.

o   The impression is given that everyone wants to hear that you are doing great and that you are happy to have been rescued from your abusive parents…so, don't share what you are really thinking or feeling because it could lead to more therapy or more medication.

o   Don't get attached to people because they may not be there for you

o   I found that people treated me differently when I was in foster care. My peers at school were leery of me and it was difficult for me to make friends.

o   I pushed my own "self" away and became someone else, in order to protect myself and to be accepted by others. Relationships became superficial and short-lived.

o   I walked around not having a clear understanding of who I was and what life held in store for me.

Christmas day in care was always a difficult time for me. My sister and I (both in the same placement) would race to the tree to see if Santa brought us everything we wanted. After we demolished the living room, I would look around and see everyone laughing and having a good time, but inside, I felt that I wasn't really a part of this family and all I wanted was to be at home with my mom. I would head to my room, wondering what my mom and brother were doing. Were they thinking of me? Would I ever see them again? Sadly, no one in my foster home knew (or publicly acknowledged) that I was struggling with these feelings. My foster parents never talked to me about my biological family, nor did they ask me how I used to celebrate the holidays with my family. I believe those conversations were never held because the professionals in my life feared what could come of them. Would I start misbehaving? Would it make me sad? On the other hand, starting this conversation with me could have opened the door to a more meaningful relationship. It may have helped me to open up about how I was feeling inside.

After three years in foster care, I was placed in an adoptive home with my sister. I remember having a few visits with my parents prior to being placed in their home, but what really stands out for me is the day that I was leaving my foster home. My foster mother sat me down and told me that I would be leaving to live with this new family and that they were going to adopt me. She asked me how I felt about that, and I remember shrugging and saying that it was fine. What else was I going to say? She went on to explain that if this family hadn't come forward, they were thinking of adopting me and my sister. At the time, that didn't mean much to me, but over the years I thought, "You had three years; how much more time did you need to decide that another family wasn't coming forward?"

In my new home, I continued the practice of keeping myself protected from my new parents and extended family, and even now, after all the years of social work training and self-reflection, I am still opening doors in myself that were closed long ago.

Unfortunately, after several months in my adoptive placement, I came home to find that my sister was no longer living with us. She had been moved earlier that day, while at school. My potential adoptive parents sat me down and explained that because of my sister's behaviors, they were not going to be able to adopt her. They explained that this was a very difficult decision for them because they loved her very much, but the stress she was causing them was too much. They asked me if I wanted to stay with them and I responded that I did. I found out later that my sister was placed in a family about an hour away and that they were going to adopt her. On my adoption day, I was surprised to see my brother and sister at the court house as well. All three of us were being adopted that day, but into different families. This was the third time I had seen my brother in four years. To say the least, I no longer knew him, but I was glad to see him. After my adoption, my brother, sister, and I got together often for visits. Our adoptive parents thought that it would be a good idea for us to see each other so that we could continue to have a relationship. In a time when this concept was rare, I was able to get to know my brother again, as well as continue to be a part of my sibling's lives.

Like so many children in care, I had a desire to discover why my biological mother never came back for me, and when I turned 18 years old, my brother and I began the process of tracking her down. My adoptive parents were very supportive of me doing this and provided me with the paperwork they had received about my family when I was adopted. Because I had a unique last name and we basically knew the last place we had lived, we were able to find her within an afternoon of making phone calls.

Before talking to her, we had found out that our biological father had died of heart disease when I was 8 years old. He was no angel and we discovered that he had married three times (and had not divorced any of his wives), and that we had at least four or five half brothers and sisters from his relationships.

Once we worked up the nerve, my brother called our biological mother and spoke with her on the phone for about thirty minutes. I did not have the desire to speak with her then, but through my brother's conversation with her, discovered that she had remarried and had another child with her second husband. She was still living in the same area and she told him that she thought about us often. Even though the initial conversation my brother had with her didn't really answer any questions, I didn't really feel the need to talk with her again until years later. I called her when my first child was born and talked with her for quite awhile. I was 32 years old and this was the first time I had heard my mother's voice since I was 5 years old. I didn't feel any anger or resentment towards her, but more a feeling of acceptance of what had happened. I was happy with my life, and although there were things that I wish I could have changed, I didn't have any feelings one way or another about my biological mother.

That being said, I guess I still had a desire to see her in person, and then years later, I decided to make a trip to visit with her and my half sister. I hadn't spoken with her prior to my visiting because I didn't have a good working phone number for her and I wasn't even sure if she still lived in the area. I went to the last known address for her and was surprised to find that she did still live there. When I first saw her, my original thought was, ok, well, she looks a lot older than I thought she would (she was 63 years old). Her reaction to me was one of shock. I think she wondered why, after all these years, did I come to her home, and she was a little leery of why I was there. We visited for a couple of hours and I met my half sister and her four children. My biological mother didn't open up with me at all and was very "forgetful" about the events that surrounded us leaving her home. She wouldn't say my biological father's name, nor would she discuss anything about him. I ended up visiting with them the next day as well, but no other information was provided then, either.

When I left, I didn't know what to think. Part of me was angry because she wouldn't talk to me, but I also knew that she was protecting herself as well. I came back home and spoke with my brother and sister about my visit and received several different reactions. My brother was indifferent and although he was interested in what she said, he said he had no interest in visiting with her or talking with her again. My sister, on the other hand, was very angry and resentful that I went to see her. She didn't want to hear about the visit and was upset that I told her that I went.

To my surprise, several weeks later my brother called me and said that he would be interested in going to see her with me if I would be going again. We planned a trip for later that month and I contacted my biological mother to plan the trip. This visit ended up being more productive, in part because my brother could remember some of the events of our childhood and used those memories to spur conversation with our biological mother. The conversation was more open and she shared more about what had happened. She wouldn't take any personal responsibility for what had happened, but we learned more about our childhoods and the life we were living (from her perspective). We visited our old neighborhood and one of the schools we had attended.

Since leaving the visit, I can say that I am glad that I saw her, but I am not sure what type of relationship we will have in the future. She has called me one time since our visit, but other than that, there has been no other contact. I have never held any fantasies about what life would have been like with her, and I am grateful that I was adopted and well taken care of. If I would have grown up with my biological mother, I am not sure what direction my life would have taken me, but I do know that my experiences taught me a great deal.

I mentioned earlier what foster care taught me, but I would like to add to that list. Foster care also helped me to develop some of the healthier traits that I have today. The first one is my dedication to my children. I know how it can be for a child if they do not feel loved, wanted, or needed. Every day, I do all I can to make sure that they feel loved and a part of a family.

Another lesson that foster care gave me was the ability to adapt and accept all people, regardless of their backgrounds. I can easily blend in with folks from all walks of life and I find that I am able to communicate effectively with all groups of people. This has given me the ability to see things from different sides and to take them into consideration before making a decision. I also have a calm outer shell that helps others feel calm, even in situations that may become heated or stressful.

Finally, I learned that there are a number of fantastic people out there who are willing to open their arms and homes to children. Although we hear about the "negative" incidents that occur in the foster care system, I believe that the majority are involved because they want to help children. There are very few people involved in the foster care system that deliberately do things that are not in a child's best interests, but like all walks of life, the few that do make it difficult for the others. The foster care system is not perfect, and yes, it does need a major overhaul, but for now, we need to do all we can to make sure that the negative effects on children are minimized.

My physical journey through the foster care system is over, and although my mental journey is still underway, I strive to continue to learn from my past and to help other children and professionals make a difference in their lives and practice.

Later in life, as a young man working in the world of retail management, I heard about CASA's (Court Appointed Special Advocates for Children) and knew I had to become involved. I began volunteering for CASA and quickly found my calling in social work; however, although I had the compassion, firsthand experience with the system, and a knack for getting through to children, I lacked the academic training and the professional experience to make a living by helping others.

Now, with more than a dozen years in the social work field, I have helped hundreds of foster children and their families adjust to tough life changes. My experiences range from working as a family-centered service worker in the Children's Division, to supervising CASA's, to directing foster care programs, to serving as a regional director of an adoption and child welfare agency. I have authored five books for children in foster care and child welfare professionals (Robbie the Rabbit). The website address is: www.robbiethe rabbit.com.

As I gained more experience in the field, I recognized that there was a huge gap in the system; primarily, a lack of services and support for children who have "aged out" of foster care. In 2008, I became connected with the Foster Care Alumni of America (FCAA). I eagerly jumped at the opportunity to be a part of a great group of people, to help write <u>Flux</u>, a book that would help this population during their transition from foster care to a life after foster care. I am proud to be a part of an organization that works to help the foster care alumni.

Alice Elston

I Was a Homer

I want to share my story in the hope that other foster children, who perhaps didn't have it as well as me, will read it and realize that there are good homes out there. I know this to be true because I was in one of them. I am fortunate that I didn't go through the severe trauma that so many other foster kids have gone through; there are so many children who are lost and don't have any place to go. I just wish they could have had my experience and been offered the stability I got, as I couldn't have a better home to live in than ISSCS. With that said, I will now share my story.

I was born the youngest of four children in 1937. I don't remember the first five years of my life, except for what I have dreamed or had others tell me of them, which is common when children have young trauma in their lives. All I know is that my mom was very ill (with diphtheria and scarlet fever and back then there was no cure), and she also had a nervous breakdown. My dad couldn't handle taking care of us by himself, so he placed us with an aunt and uncle, but they already had six children of their own and didn't want the responsibility of any more. My dad died while we were here (he had been badly gassed in WW1 and I think it contributed to him being Bi-Polar), and my mom had another nervous breakdown, and this was when my aunt and uncle contacted Child and Family Services, who placed us in ISSCS (Illinois Soldiers and Sailors Children School) as wards of the state. At the time we were placed there they had about 800 children, ranging from ages 5 years old to high school senior age. We were first placed in a receiving cottage for incoming children due to health reasons, where we stayed for two weeks. My sister being the eldest, she went to Girl's Row, and we three younger ones were placed in the Gingerbread Village. I was put in the Betsy Ross cottage with boys and girls my age, my younger brother went in Roth cottage, and my eldest sibling went in Bennett cottage. We had a permanent house mother and many helpers to work with her in keeping us maintained and structured. We had an outside playroom and playground beside our house. The building next to it was used as our kindergarten classroom, and the outside was used for games and reading. We had a place where we could sit while reading and we had a table with all kinds of books on it for us to read.

If we had parents that were living they were allowed to come and visit us on Sundays or for special occasions. There was a motel across from highway 66 that they could stay overnight at.

I never really felt abandoned by my mom because I visited her during summertime and on holidays, and we also kept in touch through letters. She died when I was 20 years old from a heart attack due to her scarlet fever.

All of the children marched two by two to church, or to the free movies we were allowed to watch on Fridays, Tuesdays, or during the summer, or anytime we went to get shots, physicals, clothing, shoes, etc. Breakfast was a bowl of cereal or fried mush, eggs and toast, and milk. They were very strict about giving us vitamins, and we had to take cod liver oil in the morning and castor oil at night. Our food was delivered to each house by a truck. After we had consumed our meal and washed the containers, they were set out to be picked up and taken back to the kitchen to be refilled for supper. I remember that for Thanksgiving and Christmas of 1942 and 1945 we were marched to the main dining room and fed a gigantic meal served by the older girls and boys before marching back home for the day.

Once I was moved up to Girls Row, I lived in Lincoln cottage, which was one of the eight cottages, and I didn't have. I had to march everywhere I needed to go. The Home was self-contained, with our school, auditorium for church, movies, or plays we put on, band or orchestra, practice, meetings, and shows put on by local groups. We had our own hospital, sewing center, clothing store, shoe shop, fire department, bakery, dairy shop, and maintenance section, which once a year would paint walls, do outside house repairs, fix beds, and whatever else that was broken. I can remember that once a year, our house mother would get all her ingredients together to make candy, cookies, stuffed dates, cakes, and homemade fruit cakes; we girls had the honor of cracking nuts by the ton, or so it seemed. We would put newspaper down on the bathroom floor, have hammers to pound the nuts carefully, so as not to smash them, and then we would pick out the meats from the shells. The bakery would be for the house mother to use for one whole day, and the smell was heavenly. She was of the old school of cooking; not once did I see her use a measuring cup or spoon, and her angel cakes were out of this world. She knew that was my favorite and would use fifteen eggs in it to make it extra fluffy.

We had two adjoining farms that supplied our many needs, and we also had the local farmers in the area supplying us. I remember going to the yard beside the tennis courts where they had picnic tables set up, and we would use them to snap beans, shell peas and lima beans, shuck corn, and whatever else that needed to be done. We would sing songs, tell jokes, and throw stuff around, but it was all in fun. We were allowed to burn small stuff in a burning barrel away from the houses. I always liked that job, as it got me outside a lot. For burning large boxes, etc., we would carry them up to the same area where we cleaned the vegetables, where they had a large outside container to throw them in for burning later. During the summer we had swimming, hiking, and bicycle riding around the grounds. We had a large recreation building that had pool tables, a sewing/craft center, and a television room, where we could go for privileges when we were good; if not, we had to stay home "bored out of our gourds," so we all tried our best to be good at all times, but it wasn't easy with 20-30 girls in one cottage.

Our cottage consisted of a huge living room, dining room, side room where we could do puzzles, type letters, read, play games, and there was a huge bathroom with sinks, toilets, and an open shower area. Beside the back door there was a room in which to store our boots, hats, toys, and along the hall wall were hooks for coats or sweaters, and beside it was the kitchen. In the hall beside the bathroom was a cabinet for towels, washrags, scouring powder, and such? Up the stairs was a huge dormitory in which our beds were, plus the closets. We each had one dresser, and there was a side room for sewing, storage room, extra sheets, blankets, pillows, and a private room for the permanent house mother, with her own bathroom, and in the hall there was another storage case for dress shoes, shoe paste, show strings, etc. Upstairs on the attic landing was an ironing board. I didn't like going up there much, as I didn't like the dark or spooky areas too much, so I would usually talk someone into going up there with me, to read a book while I ironed. (During the war, we would have total blackouts, with no lights anywhere and it was too spooky for me, so I've always had a fear of the dark.) We never locked up doors or windows because we had a night watchman, in military dress, who walked the perimeters of the Home.

We went on trips to Starve Rock, Museum of Science and Industry in Chicago, etc., and I even went to the American Boys Camp the first year they allowed girls in as an experiment. That was the best time, outside of going to Girl Scout Camp overnight.

We all had chores to do in the morning, once we awoke, made up our beds, and got dressed. Usually we had breakfast, did our jobs, and then headed off to school. It was very cold on the flat lands and we wore snow suits and galoshes with hooks to stay warm. I remember the snow coming over the top of my boots and having wet feet during school. We didn't get much time off for snow storms, what with having our school right there on the grounds.

In order to leave the Home we had to have a permission slip signed by the house mother, the dean of girls, and the superintendent, and woe to anyone who lost their permission slip, as we had to turn them back in. We had to work hard to earn that privilege, "the right of freedom!"

On "Children's Day," or "Legion Day," as we called it, the American Legion Chapters brought meats, salads, desserts, breads, drinks, and gifts of cereal, cool-aid, cookies, etc. They would also bring trains on wheels, cars that stood on end, ponies to ride, and my all time favorite, clowns who did magic tricks and such. We would have to go to church first, then come home and eat, clean up, and then we had time to play before they had the big parade where we could all participate before we headed back to our homes. What fun we had! It happened in June, and it was better than Christmas, Thanksgiving, and Easter all rolled in one.

Below: Photo from an inidentified newspaper clipping dated 1949 of Legionnaires from Macomb, Ill. at ISSCS on Legion Day. (Courtesy ISSCSHPS Archives.)

Once, when I was 10 or 11 years old, it was right before Christmas and I couldn't sleep, so I softly crept down the stairs (I had remembered which ones creaked, or groaned, or moaned) and went into the living room to admire the presents that were all underneath the tree. We weren't allowed into the living room without permission, so one didn't want to get caught. I went through every single present that was under the tree to see how many I had---the grand total was sixteen---then I had the job of putting everything back underneath the tree, all mixed up. The next morning, when asked who had moved the presents, it was always with the innocent look of "not me!" They would have men come for breakfast, feed them, get them dressed, and they would come marching down the steps to go to the individual houses (cottages). Of course, we were all told the real Santa was too busy, so these were his helpers. It took me a long time before I didn't believe him. We would have to sing songs and be on ten pins before he would finally begin to call out names and hand the presents out. One of the girls came down with polio in her back, and we were all quarantined for what seemed like forever, and we had to have the Salk vaccine, which was in the experimental format at that time.

The high school girls were situated in the last cottage on Girls Row and were caught sneaking into the dormitory, so they were switched into our cottage to better watch over them, and we were sent to the last cottage, as we weren't that much trouble. It was quieter away from the administration building. Besides the play house, we had a recreation area within sight of the houses, where they had basketball courts, swings, slides, and merry-go-rounds. I can remember sitting on the basketball court while they were building the new water tower. The high school girls were up near the edge shouting questions to the workers, but we weren't allowed to step over the boundary of it, to get close to them.

We had our own power house that burned coal, to create steam heat to warm all the buildings with, and electricity. We also had our own laundromat, where beddings, clothes, etc. were sent to be cleaned, dried, and ironed before being sent back to the individual cottage. I was the one who always had to teach the new girls how to make a hospital bed, with special folded corners, and how to darn holes in socks, as it was hard to replace socks in those days. If you didn't do it good, they would cut it out and make you do I over again, so I learned fast how to do it right. The high school was a mile from the Home and we were bused to and from school. Me, I always tried to miss the bus so I would have to walk to school, or walk home. I liked being by myself, but I had to stop and look at the flowers, the trees, or the cats and dogs along the way. There was a quiet little park that I would stop and relax in before finally heading home. I was always in trouble; that was my middle name.

I had an insatiable desire to read and would read anything and everything I could get my hands on--- my books, or other people's books; I didn't care what I read, as long as I could read. I would also volunteer to help in the library and could usually read the new books before anyone else had a chance to. At one time I even thought of becoming a librarian, just so I could read, read, and read some more.

We had a victory garden one year and grew our own vegetables and even had our picture in the local newspaper. I was a Brownie Scout when I was younger, then a Girl Scout the rest of the time I was there, and even came back to help our scout leader with the younger girls after I left the home.

Moving out of ISSCS was very hard for me because I had been so sheltered there that I didn't know how to handle the real world. It was a big adjustment for me. I loved the Home so much that I would have lived there forever if I could have.

B.R.

A "Nutter"

I would love to share my story because all my life I have felt gagged by it and it is a very healing thing to be able to be heard. For decades I felt so guilty about what happened to me and blamed myself, but now I realize that I was just a child, a victim of horrible circumstances, that the real monsters are the ones who were supposedly my "caregivers." They are the ones who are guilty and should be blamed, not me, and by exposing the truth about it I am freeing myself. Although I wasn't a foster kid in the sense of being moved around a lot, I know what it is like to be taken away from my parents, placed in a strange situation where I was dependent on strangers to care for me, only to be further abused and let down.

I am a survivor of the "pindown scandal." Ever since I was a young girl I have been treated like a "nutter," with all the indignity that goes with such a term, but defying the odds, I have turned myself into a nuisance, contacting everyone I can in order to be acknowledged. I just can't let it go. I am determined to be heard and I will find little serenity until the system that nearly destroyed me is rebuilt from the ground up, all the memories thus expunged.

As for the memories…

I suffered sexual abuse when I was a pre-pubescent child. Being so young, I didn't know what it was he was doing; I just knew I didn't want him doing it, but I felt I couldn't tell my father about it. After passing for my local Grammar School and showing a talent for music, the traumas of my childhood helped bring on a total breakdown at the age of 13. There was an obvious dysfunction in my parental situation, although I find it difficult to or talk about; all I know is that my parents could no longer cope with it and so at age 14 I was placed in a children's home.

While I was in the home I was severely abused. I was punched by a man in charge, for crying during the night, and put in a cell, where I was left alone day and night with the lights continually on so that I became confused, which I believe is a psychological torture used by the CIA. Nobody even made an attempt to find out why I had been crying; they were just dead cruel to me. When they finally released me from the cell I went straight up to the bathroom and jumped out of the window on the first floor to escape, but when I ran down the road, the man chasing me got two workmen to catch me, then threw me on the pavement and twisted my arms behind my back to return me to the home. According to another girl's suicide letter, they were letting people come into the "home" to have sex with her against her will (the word for that is RAPE!). I thought if I just smeared snot and shit all over the place they wouldn't bother me, but instead they thought I was a mental case and placed me in a psychiatric hospital in, where I was subjected to further abuse and neglect, repeatedly sexually harassed by a male nurse, and receiving no school for at least a year. The psychiatrist there told me there was nothing wrong with me and that I was only there as a "place of safety." It seems like a strange place to keep a 14 year old girl safe, on an adult mixed sex ward where there are drug addicts, sex offenders, and people with serious mental health issues.

After a year in there I was sent back home to my parents, but my home circumstances still weren't the greatest, my father suffering from Asperger's Syndrome and the family financially desperate, and despite my good school grades, even after changing schools twice to avoid "you're a nutter" bullying, I was forced, or at least felt forced, into employment. Not only was our family financially desperate; it was also desperate to put on a happy face to the community and deny the fact of our family dysfunction, for even though I was no longer being sexually abused, I was suffering from physical abuse. As I wrote in my book TIP, "After coming home, I suffer terribly from bad nerves, but nobody knows this, as I'm afraid if I tell, I'll be thought of as 'mental'. I feel I have to touch things all the time, over and over, in groups of four; even numbers are good, odd numbers are bad, and the worst number is thirteen, but three is nearly as bad. My mum is superstitious of the number thirteen, but she doesn't do that. I don't think anybody in the world does what I do. I don't want to do this touching ritual all the time, but if I don't do it, something terrible might happen to me. I think about the bad stuff a lot, but I don't hate my brother for what happened; in fact, I feel sad and pity him, because I don't think things are right inside his head. As for me, I wake up sweating and have to do my secret, stupid things to calm me down. The person I want to blame most is myself, and I can't do that. It's a big fight to stop myself doing that though. Actually, it's the hardest fight of the lot."

I got a job at an agricultural firm, which I hated and was rubbish pay. I felt like rubbish most of the time, and although I applied for other jobs, no one wanted to hire me because of me being in the psychiatric hospital. Where I come from there is still employment prejudice about mental health issues; it isn't considered a criminal offense like sexism, ageism, and racism are.

When you come from a traumatic past you tend to be vulnerable and many times naïve. I somehow got sucked into a religious Jesus People cult, but left because they were a bunch of bullying control freaks, constantly telling us we would go to hell if we so much as breathed wrong. After I escaped from them I got married to a man who said he was a Christian, but turned out to be another bully and also a heroin addict, which was terrifying. Of course I wouldn't have married him had I known this beforehand, and I ended up leaving him 14 years ago and tried divorcing him, but the court won't allow it for some reason. I don't know if the court is doing it to be purposely malicious and my solicitor doesn't understand it either. She got the bailiffs to serve the court order to file for divorce at his address, but he wouldn't answer the door, so an advertisement was put out to try to find him. I don't even know if he is still alive. I am not able to divorce a man who threatened to kill me and who I have not seen for 14 years.

I met a wonderful man and we had a few dates and he wanted to take the relationship further, but I was too traumatized by what had happened with my husband and someone else, molesting me and raping me, which was brought on by my fragile mental state and low self-esteem from having had a decade of abuse behind me. My son was conceived as a result of the rape. I didn't report the rape at the time because I didn't realize I had been raped at that point. I had been abused so many times that I didn't know what the definition of rape was, thinking a rapist had to be violent, with a gun or knife or something, not realizing saying "no" or "please don't" counted as rape. Nor did I know anything about predatory grooming. I was being treated for mental illness at the time of the rape because I was always crying, and people were always calling me a "nutter" because of that, but I was crying because I was suffering from PTSD (Post Traumatic Stress Disorder) due to all my past happenings (traumas). A man I knew who was supposedly a friend, was fully aware of my mental state and pretended to help, and then raped me. My boyfriend knew something was wrong with me, but I didn't have the nerve to tell him the whole truth, that H. used emotional blackmail and threatened suicide as a way to keep me in his grip. He was also getting me to masturbate him, which I only did to keep him off my back for a week or so. I felt so ashamed about what was happening that I just stopped my new relationship, and once he was off the scene, my dad's friend came around a lot and molested me, often in front of my family. My sister was disgusted and asked me why didn't I stop it, but I didn't know what to do because of the emotional blackmail.

I ended up going to the doctor to get antidepressants and sleeping pills, but instead of taking them as prescribed I saved them up and took them along with a bottle of wine, because I had just had enough. I ended up the hospital and was so afraid of being mistreated there that I escaped, and the police found me in my nightie and brought me home. I didn't trust the policeman at first and was shouting at him, but he was very kind and said he didn't know anything about what I was saying and what I was shouting about happened a long time ago, so I let him take me home, and I agreed to let the police send somebody for me to talk to about the incident, but when the policewoman came to my house the next day I was too scared to talk to her. After this incident my friend treated me in a despicable way, telling me "I needed help." I didn't go the police, but when I found out my son had Asperger's Syndrome, the clinic that diagnosed my son sent a community nurse to my house to help support me. She was very kind; she let me cry on her shoulder as I rambled on, telling her everything, and it was like something inside of me snapped. I screamed at Haswell and told him that never again would he lay a finger on me, but he took me to court and lied, telling everyone that I had stopped him from seeing his son, and when I tried telling everyone the truth no one would listen. I even tried to get the community nurse to tell them, but it was like everyone closed ranks. I think that my friend, because he was a freemason, or at least his father was, had everyone join ranks against me.

I started seeing my boyfriend again when my son was 4 years old, about the time I won the court case against my friend, and we have been together and dating ever since, and want to get married, but can't because I can't get a divorce. The same court that allowed me to suffer CIA style psychological torture has refused to grant me a divorce, even though I haven't seen my husband for 15 years!

And another thing. The employment agency keep sending me for interviews at their office, which is a stone's throw from the psychiatric hospital where I was put as a child, even though I have begged them to please not make me go near that place, to let me have it near my home or in my home. So they sent me on a job bus, which was bad as well, because I was trying to explain why I wasn't working and all the things that had happened and they left the door open and other people could hear everything and I started crying. The woman was really not nice and this went on for a half hour and people were snickering about me crying. I have to do this every six months, tell them all about the abuse, the rape, the court, everything, and I feel really sick whenever it is time to do all this again. I don't understand why they are so desperate to send me to this place, when I tell them that is where they put me as a child. I think they are doing it on purpose, to grind me down. It is malicious.

After many years of a relatively normal life I eventually managed to get a mature perspective of my past and this is when I started my persistent campaign to reveal the rampant abuse apparently taking place in most forms of social and mental care, but I didn't want revenge because I'm a Christian. I just wanted justice, and I still do. I just felt the truth had to be revealed.

To my dismay though, I realized very quickly that there were many who DID NOT want the truth to be revealed. I went so far as to enlist the help and support of someone in a high position. My MP eventually told me he had been involved in the Pindown investigation, but that there had been no conspiracy, but as a prosecuted survivor I am sure that is simply not true.

In 2004 there was another tragic incident that was reported, when an 11 year old care child died as a result of pindown style abuse, revealing how little or nothing had changed since my ordeal years ago. I suspect there was a cover up.

In 1999 I asked a Human Rights Lawyer to help me after I was picked up by the police for a failed suicide attempt and put in a hospital, discharging myself because when I woke up I was afraid they'd shout at me and force me to serve tea to patients, as had happened before at age 16 after a suicide attempt. He sensed something sinister and was trying to help me fight the people involved, but then he died. I am still fighting the unbelievable injustices that me and hundreds of others who have been traumatized by the care system and sometimes I feel alone in this, but in recent years the mainstream media have zeroed in on the appalling controlling behavior of care staff, social workers, and court solicitors in cases like mine.

It seems like "everything we can" is just a mantra that keeps being repeated, with no reality, and it will remain just that until such time that the diseased social care system is cured.

I wrote my book while I was going through the SFC. I was sent for "therapy" and the stupid nit wit sent psychiatric hospital, one of the places I was abused as a child, and I collapsed in the street after a really traumatic therapy session. They open you up and leave you all exposed. I was taken to a hospital and the A & E were so angry that I was only a panic attack case and not a road accident case (in other words, a time waster), that they threw me off the hospital trolley and left me there, sobbing in front of a waiting room full of other patients. Once you've been abused, you are easy meat for all sorts of other abuse. It's like you have a tattoo on you, saying "VICTIM, PLEASE KICK ME" on your forehead or something. Well, somehow I wrote my book and paid for it myself to have it self-published, thinking that if I got some publicity the court might be more inclined to leave me alone and stop all the malicious, vindictive persecution, which I believe did work, as I eventually won my case, but I am still being bothered.

The Affects on My Family Relationships

What is sad is how this affected my relationship with my family. My family has the old "scapegoat" mindset and can't deal with the truth, leaving me alienated. My dad apologized to me about two weeks before his death, telling me he wished he'd been a better father to me, and my mom is so screwed up inside about it that she just can't deal with it and thinks I will turn on her, I suppose, which isn't so. I forgave my brother decades ago; I don't have one iota of maliciousness in my soul for any of them, but I won't let people talk crap about me, which is why I wrote the book. My family all stood by and did nothing as I was being repeatedly taken to court by my dad's friend, and repeatedly threatened with prison by judges. The only thing my family appears to have done is gossip about me behind my back and try to justify the awful way I was being treated. I hardly see any of my family now and I found out that they have been putting about a story that I seduced my perpetrator, and there was also a tale about being abducted!

They all know it is absolute crap, but they would rather believe it than just face up to the simple truth, because it is too painful.

I remember being in the court, to see if I would be allowed to go home, sitting there feeling like a bank robber or something, the persecutor instead of the victim, having to say I was sorry and promising to be good, as if I had done something wrong! And when I resisted saying it, my mum told me to shut up, which really made me seethe with anger inside! Nobody wanted to tell me what I was supposed to have done wrong, or listen to my side of the story. They just pushed me here, pushed me there, and I was sick of being pushed around all the time. I hadn't hurt anyone and I hadn't stolen anything, yet I was being treated like a criminal. It was the other people who should be saying sorry to me, not me apologizing for something I didn't even do. It was so unfair. I ended up mumbling an apology to the judge, and the judge was satisfied that "justice" had been done. I was now free to go home, but I would almost have rather gone back to the home. When I got out of the courtroom I was so angry that they had forced me to tell a lie, but when my mum explained to me that I wouldn't have been able to come home otherwise, not getting angry at me for getting angry. I suddenly felt like crying and hugging her, but I didn't. We weren't close enough for that.

I am aware that my life history is so ridiculous that it hardly seems possible, but sadly, it is not only all true; I realize now it is being repeated on a grand scale. Since I have been campaigning against the court and child abuse I have come to realize that as bad as my own history seems to be, I am so frigging fortunate, as some people have had even worse injustice!

My friend and his friends would have destroyed me, but my book won me publicity and made it impossible for them to smash me up in secret (they always have to have a shroud of secrecy to do their dirty work). That's the way of these people---darkness---and it's the opposite of God's ways, which are always done in the light. Remember, they took Jesus at night as well; they did not dare arrest him in front of the crowds. The abusers are always so scared of what they have done being displayed publicly because they know they have done wrong. I don't want to hurt anyone at all, but I won't allow people to tell lies about me, and I won't just roll over and die, or disappear like they wanted me to either! This crap needs exposing. No one should have to go through this. The whole lot of them courts needs to bulldozed, every single one, because they are destroying so many people.

This forced adoption industry is making some evil people very rich and they are laughing their heads off because they reckon they are untouchable. As for me, I will keep trudging along in my pursuit for justice, as others advocates do. We all try to shout as hard as we can, in order to make a difference. It is as if that somehow by advocating for others, we are also advocating for ourselves. By voicing ourselves, we aren't just reaching back to the past to complain about it; we are reaching to the future, so others hopefully won't have to suffer as we did, which ultimately helps everyone to heal. It may seem like the helpless helping the helpless, but somehow by helping, we are also helped. I think what we are all doing reminds me of a flock of starlings chasing a cat away from the chicks.

Anonymous

Kinship Care

My story is probably not your typical foster care story; at least I don't see it as one. I never even really thought of myself as a foster child in the real sense of the word because I wasn't in foster care homes like so many children are these days. I was fortunate to be in homes with relatives, what is commonly referred to as kinship care. I'm not saying it wasn't bad or that I wasn't affected; I just don't think I was as seriously affected as other people who were shuffled around from one strange home to another. I also wasn't abused, physically or sexually, as so many others are. My sister told me when we were older that she was sexually abused at the age of 5, by whom she wouldn't tell, but to my knowledge, I wasn't sexually abused.

My mom and dad divorced when I was about 3-4 years old. I'm not real sure why, but it probably had to do with my dad's alcoholism and post-WW11 problems. He was sick with malaria and was in a veteran's hospital recuperating for a long while. My oldest sister was mentally retarded and also suffered from epilepsy, which no doubt created more stress. I'm the youngest of three girls. Between the age of 3 or 4, and 7 I was passed around from my mom's, my dad's, and my aunt and uncle's. There was no stability in my life. I don't remember ever being in a school for more than one year at a time.

My mom remarried a man in New Jersey and my sisters and I moved there, but he wasn't accepting of us and was verbally abusive. I thought we would finally be settled when my mom remarried, but fate dealt us a fatal blow. One day my mom and her husband had been arguing about something and she took off in the car and ended up in fatal accident. I speculate that they had been arguing about us girls being there, as they had words quite often over the issue of us being there. I knew I wasn't wanted there by him, most likely because I didn't belong to him.

Losing my mom at such a young age was very hard, to say the least. I cried a lot when she died. I was happy to see my dad when he came to pick us up in New Jersey after my mom died, but we couldn't depend on our dad to take care of us because of his sickness with malaria and alcoholism. Even though he was alcoholic, my dad wasn't abusive, and I remember him being very nice and affectionate. I believe he tried his best to take care of us, but he just couldn't completely rise to the occasion. We were shuffled back and forth between my dad's and our aunt and uncle's until I was 15 years old, when my dad died of his alcoholism (cirrhosis of the liver). Now I was left without any parents.

When my dad died I felt like the bottom fell out of my life; it was a feeling like having the floor move beneath you---a very scary feeling. Thank God for the goodness of my aunt and uncle. They were both very nice people and truly cared for us, but they had five of their own children to care for, and I think they were just too overwhelmed, especially since my oldest sister was disabled, so they were unable to keep us permanently. I love my aunt and am still close to her, but not having your own parents makes you feel lonely, and I don't know how you ever get over losing your parents when you're so young. I never really thought of myself as an orphan though, because I had my dad until I was 15 years old and I had my aunt and uncle, but I do realize I was affected by the loss of my parents. Growing up without a mother was the hardest part for me. I know my aunt loved us like her own children, but I still missed my mom.

One of the most difficult things about being moved around so much is how it affected my school life. I disassociated a lot by daydreaming and I couldn't learn easily. I had to teach myself to enjoy reading because I was so preoccupied with my situation that I couldn't really enjoy school. School wasn't easy for me because I was always fearful of being moved again, so I couldn't concentrate enough to study. Once you have been moved around some, you learn to expect it and are on edge all the time, just waiting for the next move. With my dad gone and my aunt and uncle unable to care for us any longer, another move was inevitable.

When I was 13 years old I went to ISSCS (Illinois Soldiers and Sailors Children School) in Normal, Illinois. I liked the home all right and was able to make friends there. I can't really say I loved the place, but I didn't hate it, either. I guess my attitude was one of acceptance; you just have to accept what you can't change and you just have to go on. What else can you do? I didn't have anywhere else to go. One nice thing about the place was that we were all in the same boat and were thought of as family.

I don't really think I have any words of comfort or wisdom for foster children. What the kids are going through today probably makes my situation look minor in comparison, but still, I do understand the feelings of loss and abandonment. I was a very emotionally needy young adult because I was so afraid of being alone. I think growing up the way I did and having so many hardships made me more mature for my age. When you don't have a normal childhood you lose your innocence a lot quicker. When I was 18 years old and left ISSCS I became very depressed, feeling all alone, not knowing where to go or what to do; I felt so low, the only way to look was up. It's hard enough for teenagers to venture out on their own, but when you come from an unstable childhood and don't have parents to fall back on, it leaves you feeling vulnerable and scared. I ended up marrying immediately after leaving ISSCS, but the marriage only lasted a short time. I remarried again and had two boys and have only moved three times during my marriage of thirty-nine years. I don't think I am as confident as some people, due to my childhood, and I can see how my past spilled over into my professional life.

I'm not sure why I chose to be anonymous. I guess I figured it wasn't necessary to share my name. I thought the only important thing was the story, but maybe I am a bit guarded. Even though I have had some therapy in the past and shared my experience with a therapist, it isn't as easy sharing it with strangers. We aren't really strangers, though, are we?

Brent Matthews

A Child of the System

Sins of the Parents

My name is Brent Matthews and this is my story. I was born in Edmonton AB with a fraternal twin brother in 1960. Although my father didn't tell me much about his past, his upbringing, he told me it wasn't good and was like something out of a soap opera, so you can only imagine. My father was not well received by his new step mother. I believe he was about 5 years old when he was placed into a boarding school in London, England, and there he was pretty much left until the age of 15. In 1930, during the start of the Great Depression, when my dad was 15 years old, he was sent to Canada to work on a farm. He stayed a short time out east in the Halifax area and worked his way out west by hopping freight trains. He found work on a farm in Mundare, I believe, until the Second World War broke out and he joined the army. He fought the Nazis in Europe, mostly Italy, and returned to Edmonton after the war. Here, he and a friend started a dry cleaners business. It was here that he met and married my mother, who started out as an employee of the cleaners and was sixteen years his junior.

My oldest sister was born, and then my twin brother. I came along six years later. I came out first, and my mother and the doctor were surprised when they found out there were two babies. My twin brother came out five minutes later and was much malnourished. It seemed as though I must have been feeding much better than he, as I was six pounds and my twin was only two pounds, but that quickly changed as we grew up. He surpassed me in stature and I was subject to many brotherly beatings from him. I believe he was somewhat resentful, as I was usually able to acquire all skills, such as walking and schooling, much faster than him. Besides the rivalry, life was good; we were well liked in the community and had many friends. We had a comfortable life and the security of our own home. We also had a holiday trailer, a pleasure fishing boat, and had time for family and friends. There was no indication of any marital strife or any reason to believe that our world would be shattered when I was 11 years old.

It was in the early 1970's when we received the news. My mother sat me down and calmly told me that her and my dad would be separating and would be selling the home we had all grown up in and all the matrimonial property. Further to this, my mother would be moving away from the community and the school we were in would no longer be an option. She said that she had already discussed the matter with my brother and sister and that they had been given a choice who they wished to live with and they chose to stay with her. She said that I could also have the same choice. After many tears and begging that she would reconsider, to no avail, I stated that I would like to stay with my father. She seemed caught off guard by my response and I suspect she was a little angry. She quickly changed her position and told me that that was not an option, that I had to come live with her. My crying prevailed nothing and I soon realized that choices were an illusion.

Things quickly went from bad to worse. We moved into an apartment basement suite. It was here I found the reason for my life being shattered. Again, it was like a soap opera of sorts.

I guess it may have been at that time that I realized how selfish people are. We didn't stay there long, but moved to a rundown and dilapidated old house in the inner city. My brother and I took solace in the fact that we had no rules to obey, as the adults were usually too self-involved to know that we existed.

It was also at this time that I became aware of the lawlessness of the system. My father and mother hadn't been separated long before getting a legal separation, and although they called it a separation, it was effectively a divorce. My father died in the 1980's and the many years of them being apart were only considered a legal separation, but after his death she was entitled to a widow's pension from him, as if they had been married. I also realized at this point that the system was also making my father pay child support for me and my brother, even though they weren't divorced. I guess this must have helped to form the views that helped me to see that dysfunctional behavior is not only condoned, but rewarded by the system.

Well, my brother and I found ourselves in some pretty tough surroundings and I am glad that we fought so much in our earlier years, for it somewhat prepared us for the environment that we now found ourselves in. To gain acceptance in our new surroundings and not be beaten up, we had to be bad. We had to hook up with others like ourselves for protection; it was a self preservation skill that we had learned as a result of our circumstances. You have to survive it and you learn that there are no free rides in this system. That's why many in communities congregate, to find others like themselves. The disenfranchised usually find one anther quite quickly; they usually have many things in common that they can identify within each other---poverty, dysfunctional homes, no rules, or perverted rules at home. If the system sets up some sort of community support, it is usually run by someone so far removed from the reality of the people it is supposed to be serving that they just further the isolation and the alienation, rather than help alleviate the suffering. It wasn't long until we would become further afflicted and alienated by this system. It seemed as though it had chosen us and said, "We need you to show society that we are protecting them from your kind." That was the only message we seemed to be hearing, that we were worthless and without redeemable qualities. I recall the rejection of it and soon began to view the world as "out to get me." This was true to some extent. It penalizes you for the things that it creates in your lives and then if it can deny you your basic living needs, such as food, clothing, shelter, and security, and it can bring one to a state of hopelessness and despair. Once in this state, many will act out in rebellion against the system that has engineered this affliction. It is only normal for alienation to occur and aberrant and destructive behavior to follow. It wasn't long before we were taking things that weren't ours and doing other juvenile delinquent crimes. Everyone wanted to examine us and see if they could figure out why we did such things; some suspected it was the environment, but would do nothing to improve it. They seemed to keep empowering the dysfunction---the adultery, the drunkenness at home, the poverty, and the unhealthy affiliations.

Over the course of my life I have seen the same scenario repeated over and over and can only come to the conclusion that this is by design, since the system cannot sustain itself without creating dysfunction. I also came to know it from the inside. As we continued stealing cars, breaking and entering, and learning how to make keys for the parking meters, the authorities felt we needed to be incarcerated for a period of time in a youth facility. I entered into a diagnostics center, where some friends were already, and new ones were made. Here, we didn't feel inferior, for we were all here because we were outcasts, the rejected ones. So much was abnormal in our lives, I suppose, if we were to compare ourselves to the general population.

Here, though, we could compare ourselves to ourselves and feel good that we were all screwed up. The staff in this facility, as well, was all screwed up. It was 1974/1975 and the trends of the time were the feminist movement and the free love movement; the reengineering of the family was in full swing. The thought of the day from the psychologists, the social workers, and youth workers who were graduating from universities and coming to work at the facility, was that traditional family was antiquated. Regardless that those laws of old were created to protect families from breakdown by penalizing aberrant behavior, such as adultery, this new school of thought by the social workers was going to throw the old book out the window. In a sense, we were the type of experiment to teach this new lawlessness, regarding the family too. The system was going to reengineer the family.

Some of the social workers were on drugs; they felt like this was the way that they could identify with us and show us kids that they weren't so different from us. They didn't seem to care that they were condoning drug use. They basically said to us that we weren't doing anything wrong, other than getting caught. One of the staff used to take us to his house for sleepovers and get us stoned on weed, hash, and opium. He even took us on a mountain hike for ten days where we could get stoned up in the wilderness. Another staff member, who was also a director of one of the units, would consistently google me when I would walk by him. Although I was 14 years old, I was small for my age and looked about 11 or 12. I knew that he was looking at me in a sexual manner and I found him highly repulsive. He was as round as he was tall and must have weighed about 300 lbs. One of my friends who was in his unit would always come and ask me if I wanted to come over to his house with him on the weekends, and I looked at him as if he was crazy. He couldn't convince me, and I suspected he was being molested by him. Later, a staff member from my unit approached me and asked me if I wanted to transfer units; he said that the director had requested my transfer. I became quite terrified and said that I didn't want to and he said he didn't blame me. I think he suspected something was going on as well and told me that he'd let him know that I didn't want to transfer to Unit 2.

Once again the system was taking away my hierarchy of needs; this time it was a need for security. After these instances, I decided that I could be safer on the street and decided to make a break for it. I escaped and found some of the gang. I decided to lash out at the system once again and broke into several businesses. At the time I couldn't see that these businesses were just businesses and that they were possibly families that earned their living at them; to me, they were just part of the world system that was out to destroy me. I felt they were legitimate targets. I also hit the parking meters again. I must have really hurt the city revenue, as they were forced to change all the locks in the city. The system wanted me really bad and decided to assign an extra contingent of police to get me off the street. I am not sure how I was so evasive, but I was. I managed to elude them to the point where it was told to me that a couple of cops got fired because of me. I really didn't think I was so much trouble; I was just in survival mode and doing what was necessary. After about 2 ½ months of being on the run, I was arrested and hand cuffed while I was sleeping. A friend of mine had broken under pressure and led the police to my hideout. They decided to send me to the maximum security section of the youth facility, which was Unit 3. It was safe there in the sense that I was not transferred to Unit 2, where the director of the Unit was trying to get me transferred earlier. It later came out that my suspicions were correct and that he was molesting the boy who had tried to get me come with him for a sleepover at his house with him. It was a scandal of gigantic proportions that the system felt was too damaging to it, so they censored if off the news quickly.

I was now safe in Unit 3. I was off the street and had some time to think about where I was going. I really always wanted a chance to have a life like everyone else. It seemed like so many things were out of my control. Now I decided that I would get as far away from this system as possible, but that I would do it by my rules, whatever it took. I did not want to be a fugitive for the rest of my life and I did not want to be locked up in these lawless institutions. I would do what they said I needed to do to get out, get through school as quickly as possible, and make a good life for myself. I did not realize that I had been marked by the system for life, that the system deals with you by a different standard once you have been in it, and that it deals with you above the law, as I was later to find out. All those things had yet to be discovered, and my goal now was just to get out of Unit 3. While in Unit 3, I was quickly approached by some of the fellow inmates for an escape plan. They had heard about how I escaped from TR in Unit 1. TR was short for the thinking room. Here, the staff could lock down the kids who they felt were displaying non-compliant behavior. The lock-up could be for up to one month. The room was small, with a mattress on the floor. You received a spoon to eat with. There was no washroom and if you had to go to the bathroom, you had to bang on the door, and if the staff heard you they would come and escort you to the washroom. Most of the kids would get tired of waiting and piss down the heat register in the floor. The stench became unbearable and was enough to make one throw up. It wasn't long until I decided that this was not a place to be. I was in there for my first AWOL (Away Without Leave). I decided to use the spoon that I had been given to eat with to take the frame off the observation window of the director's office. It was an unbreakable glass, so that we could be monitored, like a specimen to be studied. The director had gone for the day and I now had access to his office. From here I gained access to the girls dormitory, to the outside fenced grounds, and then off the facility. This was the AWOL that resulted in a 2 ½ month run. It was because of this breakout that I had gained notoriety and I was being requested for break out plan in Unit 3. I had already scoped the place and determined what would be the point of least resistance; now I just needed to test my theory. I didn't really like the guys who approached me, as they seemed to cause a lot of friction in the Unit. I decided it would be nice to see them go, and gave them my plan. They asked me if I was coming, and I declined. They were successful, my plan was successful, and it was now quieter in the Unit. I could concentrate on getting out by complying with regulations of the Unit and rising through the color scheme that was used. Green was the highest color and with green came unescorted absences from the facility. I obtained it with no color drops and asked how I could get into an outside school and be discharged. They said that I would need a place to go, and I asked my mother if I could move back in with her and her boyfriend.

She was still in her adulterous relationship and the social workers seemed to think it was an appropriate solution. There was to be a follow up with an outside social worker that never occurred. It seemed that they were setting me up for failure, but I was determined to make things succeed. I had gained access to an outside school and was doing quite well. I was a year behind where I should have been, and because of the missed school, I had to repeat 8th grade again. I worked extremely hard at my school work and thought that I should be able to do grade 9 work instead of grade 8 that I was in, so I approached the school principal and asked him what I needed to do to get put in the proper grade level for my age, and he suggested I should talk to the school counselor about it. That was one of the worst days of my life, as I was about to find out. After approaching him and explaining that I thought that I could do grade 9 work and would like to be put in that grade if possible, he looked at me rather sternly, as though he was already aware that I was a transfer from the youth facility. He reviewed my marks and stated that there wasn't anything the matter with my marks, and then he further reviewed my file and said, "Oh, I see what the problem is. You were transferred from the detention center." He looked at me and said, "I see what you need," and then he stood up and took the strap out of his drawer and grabbed my arm by the wrist, lifting it up palm facing upward, and then proceeded to strap me. I cannot remember being quite so violated and the incident brought me to tears, once again abused by those in authority over me. A simple "no, you can't go into grade 9" would have sufficed. After that, he must have assumed I was leaving school, as he said, "I really don't think you should go." I guess I took that as my queue that I was kicked out. Now I had to go home and explain the fact that I was not in school to my mother. She assumed it was my fault and berated me accordingly, using the useless, worthless, and a variety of terminology that said I wasn't going to amount to anything.

Well, I was back to going nowhere fast. The follow up from the social worker after being discharged from W never happened for some reason. It also seemed like this incident occurred shortly after the discharge from the other place. I had still been a ward of the province, and though I was staying with my mother and going to school, I was still under the care and control of W. Now, looking back on it, I would have to say that the timing was perfect---discharge him, get no follow up support from the social worker, put him in a dysfunctional environment, and get him kicked out of school at age 15. Hmmm…not much chance of working, since you have to be 16 years old to be legally employed. At least I still had a bunch of troubled friends that would accept me. I would just have to go and look them up again. They would always be looking for a new scam or trouble to find. This is the life that the system decided to give me so I could accommodate it; after all, I was only being compliant. It had socially engineered this catastrophe from the word "go." For some reason, though, it always wanted me to take responsibility, as though I had choices. Next to jumping off a bridge, I didn't see any. Anyway, back to a life of crime on the street I went. Attitudes grew worse and soon I was resigned to the fact that I would always be a wanted fugitive. The police already knew me very well from when they set up their task force to take me off the street after I had escaped from the youth facility. I was already a bad guy as far as they were concerned. A hopeless case. From here I don't think it's hard to see the attitudes that I developed. The funny thing is that those in places of authority who work for this system of abuse have a totally different perspective; to them, the system has been good to us. They have never experienced how it has denied them their basic living needs of food, clothing, shelter, and security. They view life through a different lens. They have been insulated from the reality of its abuse; therefore, it's much easier to look down upon us trouble makers as though we have some mental deficiency. It could never be the system relegating us to a life of crime because it's trying to redefine the family to make it more "inclusive." No, the ones that are in authority have no desire to stop the dysfunction they are perpetrating because they aren't affected from it, except in a positive way. The dysfunction that is created by the system is their security. It is because of this dysfunction that they have there, "Great West Life" insurance policies, dental and medical plans, and all the other securities that remove the desperation from the afflicted ones. Why would they ever want to change such a system to make it more inclusive? Stopping the dysfunction is society would take those things away from them, and besides, there are social aid agencies, charity organization, and the like, to help the less fortunate.

I have come to the conclusion that even the social aid agencies make their living off of this system of abuse. They are only treating the symptoms and not crying out for the cure.

Junkie

Life back on the streets was all about survival. I seemed to be accomplishing many tasks all at the same time. I was revenging myself by getting back at a world that seemed to be out to destroy me. The authorities that were out to get me, I could pay back by doing considerable damage to the businesses and government that were trying to screw me. My mother, who had created my circumstances, I could pay back by showing her how useless and unproductive to society I was. The police, I could pay back by not getting caught in my crimes. Even in my fallen state I seemed to maintain a level of moral code. I would never steal from individuals, unless they were involved in some sort of crime themselves, such as drug dealing. Living off prostitution, in my eyes, was an absolute no no, even though many of the people that I associated myself with felt there was nothing the matter with doing that. I would never seek out a fight, but felt that if the other individual made the first move, I was justified in defending myself and giving him a good beating, if I could. I seldom lost a fight, as I felt that there was a force of good at work helping me when I was morally right. That was some of the moral code that I lived by, even though I was considered a criminal by the system. Some would call it "honor among thieves," but to me it was just a few lines that hadn't been crossed that I intended to keep. Over the years that followed I tried to hang on to the small measure of morality. With the drug addictions and somewhat warped sense of right and wrong that had now been engrained in me from the system of abuse, it was no small task. There was also a criminal code that my associates seemed more than willing to share with me. It was actually mandatory that I know this code, complete with the linguistics. Should the average person be listening in on our conversation, they might think that we were almost speaking some foreign language. Criminal linguistics can also be somewhat intimidating to an average person; it is designed that way for a reason, to control through fear. Blackmail and extortion are common practices and meaner the associations you have--- the better off you are in this world, the more chance you have of surviving, and the more chance you have of not being bothered; however, once you become connected, you become aware of the crimes of others, and in a sense, an accomplice after the fact. You become farther and farther away and alienated from the authority of the system; even if it is a system of abuse, it is a lawful system of abuse. This is the world that was now mine.

Dysfunction

The System must be able to sustain itself, otherwise it would soon become subject to much scrutiny from the public. It must be able to justify its need for the huge social bureaucracy that is being created. It becomes a question of supply and demand. The police, jail, hospitals, judges, lawyers, social workers, etc., all need a supply of outcasts to justify their positions. It is therefore, in their interests to create, or at the minimum, to perpetuate the societal ills that create dysfunction, whether they realize it or not. Then they can all spend countless tax payer dollars on research and debate about what's going wrong with society. The irony of this is that it is a problem, which if solved, would put everyone out of a job.

Cheryl Smith

Surviving Poverty
Peacock Poverty (www.peacockpoverty.org)

Because poverty is such a huge issue surrounding foster care, I decided to elaborate on it in my story by sharing what is on my Peacock Poverty website. I hope this helps those of you who need it.

We know that poverty has many faces, circumstances, and effects here at home. It ranges from the qualified immigrant dentist, of color and gay, to the transgendered, the First Nations people, to refugees, the working poor, the disabled, disenchanted, mentally ill, and the generations of poor that social or public policy has produced.

In my case, I am the third of four generations born into poverty and raised by the state. My mother, her mother before her, myself and my children were all "raised by the state" or were under state care at some point in their lives--- through the "Children's Aid Society," which actually started as the Humane Society, to prevent cruelty towards animals and children. They were one and the same until not so long ago. Sometimes I think we'd be better off if we'd stayed there---people care about animals; but then again, with what's going on at the humane society these days…Still, I think a metaphor works here. There have been deaths in the Children's

Aid Society and there are many ways to "die." It can be a slow and painful road to "recovery"---whatever that means. We seem to measure everything by the worst case scenario; if it's not the worst, it doesn't count. Anything else can and **should** be tolerated. Canada's poverty is measured relative to extreme conditions in so-called third world countries and because we're not falling like flies (some would say we are), we should be grateful. Next to the extreme, people say, "Hey, you got it pretty good here. Quit complaining." That's like healing the heart we pray with and neglecting the knees we pray on.

Each generation, in my case, has had the added challenge of mental health complications; in fact, it was the **point of entry** for the state in my life as a child. Chicken or egg, then, I have to ask. Which came first? Just think about that for a minute---the state controls you and is in charge of your life, in an intimate and basic needs way, until that legal arrangement ends with one full swoop and you are left without family and to your own devices. Social agency becomes the family and government, Big Daddy. See the young child. Think about the horror and trauma that landed her there. I was 4 years old. Can you imagine anything more vulnerable? You get taken to the main offices, get checked out by a strange and frightening doctor (mostly men then) on a cold and clinical table; everybody is a stranger and larger than life. You don't understand what happened or why you're here or where your mommy went. Social workers buzz about you and make decisions that will affect you for the rest of your life. I have been neglected, beaten, and molested as a result of some of those decisions. More importantly, I "learned" who I was, what I was worth, and what my life meant to the larger community through these experiences. On the other hand, we've got Dr. P. on television all over the glove espousing that, ah, "Kids are resilient; everything will be okay"… when the evidence clearly demonstrates that they're not and it will not be ok, if wounds are left to fester. Children need to be treated with care and love, community and connection, and nurturing, because if they're not, they'll end up being the adults that have to visit Dr. P., after a lengthy career in self-destruction and the endless repetition of abuse and trauma, at the very least (at worst, prison/jail). If young wounds aren't cured young, they don't just melt away.

I have pondered long and hard the connection that poverty and mental health "disturbances" share. The only thing I know for sure is that such a connection does exist. It begs the question though, that if the state were doing such a bang-up and "better" job, where are all these generations coming from? Wouldn't the poverty and abuse have been eradicated by now, after four generations of state care? We keep doing the same thing and getting the same results. Some call that insanity. We need a huge paradigm shift and I believe that is now underway. Shape shifting---therein lies my hope.

My Beginnings

Mine is not a unique story. Remember that as I take you back to my beginnings. My mother was/is a brilliant woman, talented in many ways---a model, and worked two jobs trying to raise six kids. Our home was filled with books, music, art, and craft. TV was limited and we were taught to think for ourselves and to use our imaginations. My mother was also quite ill and prone to psychotic breaks. She was violent and brutal, physically and psychologically. She did not like to be touched. I was the primary caretaker of my siblings and even of my mother when she got ill. I love my mother. Her own brutal beginnings were worse than mine. She needed help that she didn't get. She even confessed this brutal beating to the CAS; it's in my records. **She did her best and I'm grateful for what she managed to give me in all that chaos**. I was left in the hospital for almost a month at birth while my mother decided whether or not to bring me home. I guess she had her doubts too. I held that experience emotionally for most of my life. It was a deep black pit without words. **But one has to fight back**. Forget **your** memories. Try and see if you can. When you thrive, memories can carry and guide and comfort you; when you don't, they can surely bury you. Sirens, ambulance, police, stretcher, white jacket, needle---mommy's gone. The empty house, me, that last one left, all my brothers and sisters shipped out, gone already. One here, two there…for another year, two…or three. Over and over again. Receiving centers, institutions, group homes, foster homes…out of eight placements, only one with a sister. I have grieved the loss of my siblings, and did at every single separation. I still do. In fact, I have forever lost my baby brother to suicide. Part of his history included ritual molestation and abuse. He's not the only one. **Still, I accept and embrace my life. One must to find peace.** They put me on anti-psychotics at age 12. Nobody explained to me why I was given the medication. All I knew was that I had these funny feelings like I was floating up in the sky and then people would scurry and bring me medication. I can't remember if I went to sleep then, or what happened. I can't remember that.

I had eight placements in the CAS between the age of 4-15, when my crown wardship was dissolved and with it, all CAS direct services and supports. I was scarred, broken, already an addict, with no clue as to what was possible for me in this life and how to go about creating it. I ran away from home again, from the abuse and dysfunction, and hit the streets of Vancouver at age 15. I was among the walking wounded and smashed into every wall conceivable, re-victimized, traumatized, and brutalized. Addiction, domestic violence, and sexual assaults ensued. Public housing ghettos, social workers, minimum wage service jobs, and welfare lines became a way of life. I was given no information or direction regarding any diagnosis, or any problem for that matter, never mind treatment. When it came time to fight for my own children, I spent two years in court, though I could think of no way to care for them alone and on my own. The psychologist saw me once and deemed that, "though I loved my children, I would **never** be able to care for them," due to her diagnosis of clinical depression. I was offered no support in bringing my family together and keeping it intact. Instead, another generation was lost, or so I felt at the time. The emptiness and shame rested heavy on my heart for most of my life and to this day can still bring tears of loss and sorrow. I remember being on the stand and being questioned by a lawyer. A mere lapse in my memory allowed her to shame me and destroy any credibility I might've had. I remember sitting in the hallway of the courts afterward. I sat stunned and silent, watching a cockroach walk up the wall. I was frozen, in shock, and so in need of **care**.

In my own broken family, my children, two boys in their mid-thirties, have healthy middle-class families and work very hard at dangerous, but well-paying jobs. Both of my boys are the primary shopper and chef in their families. I like that! And both of my boys wouldn't like me calling them boys. They have beautiful families and they have each other. How did they manage this? It was the best in us reaching out and coming down through the generations, until finally, through our own determination and will, they broke through. I bid them well. Both of my children have had brutal beginnings and both of them were cut loose at age 16 by the CAS. They were not in one piece at the time. What they healed and accomplished, they did despite their beginnings and without the aid of the state.

Are the poor then "inferior specimens" of human kind? Are they lazy, stupid, and incompetent? Or are issues of systemic inequity, imbalances, stigma, and racism the players of poverty in a country as rich as Canada? And so the debate continues as does the fragmentation…A lot of the people I work with or have interviewed for Peacock have much the same tale to tell---First Nations bloodlines lost, not families, extended or immediate, mental illness, foster care, trauma and abuse. These are common themes among us that emerge. Four living generations of families that have no contact with each other, no real breathing connection. How did that happen at the hands of a Society and a government that promised to protect us, to keep us intact as their highest goal? If there is no family at the end of it all, then there is not community, or at the least, community will be fragmented, warring and dependent on Big Daddy, without the example of our elders and our children to care for, without the structure and natural flow of life. This cycle of generations of life interrupted creates added dependency on the system. What family support (blood or not) could provide, especially extended, is lost to us all as a community. There were even foster parents (two that I remember), that would've made a beautiful addition to the "family" I had to create. Again, social policy…when both parties desire it, why does the system discourage these relationships from blossoming over a lifetime? I believe it's a precious loss, and costly both socially and economically. I can tell you that personally, before reaching this place in my life, I have felt endless depths of loneliness and filled them with tears. The aching soul that is yours to carry for so long while you heal is overwhelming. Every holiday reminds you…you have no family; you do not belong. A shelter/agency doesn't cut it. We've got to do better. We've got to nip it in the bud. I was also introduced to love along the way. I call it the Light. It always felt the same when I came upon it. Snippets of hope and guidance by those special people everyone (hopefully) has in their life. A teacher, group home worker, a foster parent. I've always looked towards the light I found in bits of my journey. Don't ever think your kindness and humanity for another doesn't have an impact. It can offer such sweet comfort in the memory bank. I am eternally grateful to those people. Don't be afraid to care and to share it, though they teach you to keep those boundaries clear. At age 35, I landed in a hospital and was diagnosed, medicated, and treated. Those twenty years out there were destructive and costly, not only to myself, but the end, to us all. Potential to contribute lay dormant, screaming for actualization. This alone can feel like death. Most people want to contribute, want to belong, and give back. Post-diagnosis has not been much easier, just more manageable. Diagnosis and meds are no panacea; treatment is governed by policy and varies; diagnosis can be many and varied over time, and with doctors, and sometimes were more damaging than not. For better or worse, they provided a context for my life. I have been labeled many things and there was a time when I believed them all.

Memories

Some of my early memories are great. We rented a house---glorious, spacious, and green, safe and connected to community. The zoo was just up the street. I can still smell the days---the hot sun, the camels eating their grass and hay, my brothers and sisters, me the babysitter, around and in the wading pool. Spreading the blanket on the ground under a large tree. We've got lunch---peanut butter sandwiches and kool-aid. And then those beautiful hills in winter, steep and covered in a warm blanket of thick snow. The tobogganing! Look at the area now, how beautiful it is, and expensive, inaccessible to us now. That was my neighborhood. The houses were beaten down and broken, but it didn't matter. The world has changed since then and so have our stomping grounds, over and over again. Gentrification has made of us gypsies, as we move from unaffordable to affordable neighborhoods endlessly throughout the city. In the end, where will we be? Later, we moved. Moving south to the projects brought me down, even as a kid. Everything was concrete, just like they are now, and whatever "land" we did have then for community gardens and such are being lost to re-development and re-vitalization. People are feeling quite powerless and frustrated about this process. They do not see it as a move towards "inclusiveness," but rather as a reduction of their space, freedom, and enjoyment of life. They don't believe the stigma will be reduced, but rather sharpened. Fences will go up to keep us out. There is something about connection to the earth when you are a child, that if you experience it, it can carry you through so much. You can feel disconnected to people sometimes, but you can find solace in feeling your connection to Mother Earth, if you're lucky enough to find an accessible and significant piece of it. It can carry you through. It has me; in fact, She is the Mother in my new family. It is time to bring some spirit to this science, to think in more holistic terms and frames of reference. The social culture of poverty includes broken adults from a broken system among its ranks, and we land in shelters, jails, drop-ins, food banks, ghettos, housing projects, rooming houses, hospitals, and agency after agency. These have been my home, my family. I know them well. We don't really have a welfare state where certain rights would be entrenched. What we have is a social safety net, providing not even the bare essentials (food and clothing) to those who are considered mostly non-deserving. That net is now one big hole and we're falling through it fast.

I live in private market housing. I choose to live outside rooming houses, ghettos, social and supportive housing because that is where I have spent most of my life and life is short. It has been ten years. I treat "diagnosis"---the many I have had---spiritually, physically, emotionally, and with a minimum amount of medication. I thrive in the present community. I am free. At present, I'm spending 75% of ODSP benefits on rent. There is no affordable and adequate housing; there is only either/or. Average rent for adequate housing is between $8-900 per month (for a 1 bedroom in Toronto, Welfare distributes just over $500 per month to its recipients. There is a 12 year waiting list for public housing, if you so choose it. These environments, as I have found with my lengthy experience, can be demoralizing and rob one of all hope and autonomy. Sometimes you can hardly breathe because it gets so constricted with governance and bureaucracy. It breeds aggression (frustration, anger) and dependence. I have seen it. I have felt it. Still, these are the best of times for me. My work is meaningful and I am passionate about it. I am moving at light speed. I have purpose and meaning in my life. I serve the public good through the social enterprise that is Peacock Poverty. Coming from where I did, being in the condition I was in, it is truly a miracle that I'm alive. I am healing and thriving beyond my dreams. It is breathtaking. It has taken me this long to finally claim my voice and begin to heal in a way I's never known before. It's working out beautifully, this tapestry that is my life. I am truly, truly blessed.

Two years ago, I was diagnosed with breast cancer. It saved my life. I still battled the demon of addiction and was in the throes of a lengthy relapse. I would've died, if not for the interruption of cancer. Many factors were in place that readied me for this healing. I received the best medical care by the finest doctors in world renowned hospitals. I was firmly entrenched in a healthy community. They could and did support me. The Voices experience and training had given me a new context with which to view the facts of my life. Pat Capponi still remains one of my mentors. Michael Creek is an impeccable soldier, leader, and agent for change. They continued to welcome me back to the fold over and over again, despite my struggles and challenges. But there was more. Something else happened. I was introduced to services and supports through my cancer diagnosis that are generally out of reach for most poor people, that are outside of the realm of **"normal"** existence. This opened up a whole new world to me. Wellspring is a holistic cancer treatment center and resource free to all cancer patients and their caregivers--- Yoga, energy healing, support groups, art therapy, community, and more. It was here that I found my current self-identified Spiritual mentor (psychotherapist is the title on her card). She is also a nurse, writer, international lecturer, and co-founder of Wellspring. I was allowed to see her for three sessions at Wellspring. This resulted in her inviting me into her private practice for whatever I could afford. It has been a long time since I could afford anything for her. Mary Vachon continues to work with me regardless...

This has meant the difference in my life. No more bandages. **Real healing. Real progress. Real results**. Felt deep down and obvious from without. I wish it for everyone. And so I find myself coming full circle. I'm doing what I've always wanted to do, what I was meant to do all along anyway, just by a different route. I'm a grassroots journalist and publisher, bringing the stories of the poor, the skills, talents, and resilience of this community together for all to see, to re-write the resume of the poor, to fight stigma, to inspire hope and change from within and without. And to give us a place to have our say our way, without agency scripting or agenda. Our voices, our truths, our service to those less fortunate. We did it. Our community. People in drop-ins and food banks, housed, sheltered, and on the street. And we keep on doing it. Passing it forward in gratitude. There are many voices out there. They all matter. All lives have meaning. I trust you to listen to as many as you can.

THE SECRET of the LIGHT (MY LIFE IN FOSTER CARE)

In a time before the Great Changing lived a young girl without a voice. The nest she was born in had a weak foundation and threatened to fall away beneath her feet at any moment. Her name was Hope, and she often hid in closets. In times of darkness, the hole in the floor grew larger and Hope was forced to the edges to keep from falling out. One night a white stork came and plucked her up from where she was sleeping and dropped her down in another nest where the floor was in good condition and where there was Light. After forever, she was again plucked up and returned to her own nest and Hope was happy and scared. Before long, she had a sister, and one time in the darkness, they were both plucked up and dropped in different nests, where they waited until the hole in their own floor could be fixed. Hope came to have five brothers and sisters who were also always plucked up and dropped down in different nests. One day the stork stopped taking them home and they were all lost to each other in this time. Hope had no voice, so all her words were stuck inside. Still, she hid in closets. Some of Hope's new nests had problems of their own and did not shine the Light. But some did, and that struck Faith. It was always familiar, always warm, and ever loving. It didn't matter who it was or where it was, the Light would always feel the same. Hope would not forget. Time passed and Hope was almost fully-grown, but she was still very young inside. She found herself standing before a man who sat up very high behind a large bench. He looked down at her over his glasses and told her that she would return to the nest that she was born in for the very last time. Hope was very happy and scared. So Hope returned to her first nest. She noticed that the floor still had not been fixed. Not only that, but she began to notice the cracks in her own wings, too. She became more frightened and confused. Hope decided to fly away. Soon Hope got lost and grew tired. She flew in circles because she did not have a Plan. The cracks in her wings were sore and were always uppermost in her heart, which was heavy with the words she could not let out. In the distance one day, Hope saw a brilliant Light, more brilliant than she had ever seen. She was drawn to it. She remembered the Light in her past and the Love it held. She kept memories close while she slowly made her way towards it. In her travels, Hope saw glimmers of the Light that guided her. There was the Light of the classroom that strengthened her wings, the Light of the pen and paper where she could write the words that she could not speak, and the Light of kind strangers and friends who helped her to never forget. But there were also places of darkness. Some of these were addictions, abuse, aimlessness, low self-esteem, and poverty. There were more. They appeared as large cracks in the mud that Hope was ill equipped to avoid and that she would fall into from time to time. There was great suffering and damage done in the cracks that Hope would have to someday address. Without her voice, Hope felt powerless. She searched for the Light, but she could not see it. Still she hid in closets. One day a doctor told Hope that she was very sick and that they would have to cut away one of her wings in order to save her. Hope was disturbed because she didn't know how she would ever reach the Light with only one wing. Her remaining wing was carrying the weight of the cracks she had fallen in. Hope was devastated. She did not want to be different than those others she judged herself against. She would be visibly marked for life. Before this, her damage could not be seen. She did not believe she could ever overcome the overwhelming darkness, and because she could not believe, she got stuck. Once in a long sleep, Hope returned to a time before the cracks, before the holes in the nests. She could smell the Innocence of long ago and of her life beginning. She heard music and saw books and paints and dancing and great Beauty in the world around her. She felt her goodness and her passion. Her strength was renewed and her belief restored. She had visited her True Self. And she could now see the Light. Upon waking, Hope saw in the short distance a beautiful lotus flower, grown in the mud, yet untouched by the mud. It was a brilliant purple marvel, and upon reaching it, she climbed up on one of the petals. As the petal began to break away from the flower, Hope began to find her voice. The petal brought her to the shore of the mud, while she sang loudly the song she remembered from her long sleep. Her voice was joyous and powerful: "Forget your perfect offering. There is a crack in everything. That's how the Light gets in. That's how the Light gets in." And Hope vowed to honor her broken wing. Standing on the banks of the mud, Hope reached down and clasped the petal in her palm. The petal told her she was worthy. The petal told her she was loved. Hope saw that like the lotus, her True Self was also untouched by the mud, and she promised to consult her True Self in all her affairs. From that time forward, Hope used the message of the petal to guide her. She looked in her own life for the people, places, and things that grew the Light and reflected the message of the petal. To everything else, she had to say good-bye. And she did, and her joy became great and her misery small. Listening carefully to the dreams of her True Self, she developed a Plan. It was the beginning of the Great Changing, and not perfect, but Hope found the support and guidance she sought. She began to repair the damage, and in so doing, found her own unique power. Because she had lost her own family, she created a new one from special people she encountered who also needed a Sister or Daughter or Mother or Close Friend. She found great freedom in being able to choose and build a Family of her own. She never forgot where she came from and counted all the blessings from all the generations therein. Finding her Home, creating her Family, and executing her Plan was a good deal of joyful and sometimes painful work. Hope became stronger day by day. She asked to be guided by the Light, and she was. She asked to be protected from the dark, and she was. Simply because she was alive, Hope still felt pain and still had fear. Sometimes she got lost. At these times, she would hold the lotus petal in her palm and listen for the Message: "You are worthy. You are loved." She would marvel at the mystery that was Life and count her many and wonderful blessings. In this spirit, she joined the good fight for Great Changing and used her experience to point out the cracks and holes, that others might be saved. She carries to those the message of the petal: "You are worthy. You are loved." And this way, Hope never forgot.

Debra Cruz

What is Life Like as a Foster Child?

We are helpless, afraid, and alone. We are the foster children. For some of us, our lives began in turmoil, and for some, the turmoil started like a menacing fire and burst into a terrible flame. Our childhood is ripped from us. Then comes foster care.

We start out in foster care already broken. Why are the foster parents so amazed when we don't act like normal children? What are they thinking? We have been taken away from everything familiar and thrust toward people we don't know. It was the behavior of adults that caused us to be taken in the first place, and now we are given to another set of adults. What are we supposed to do? We don't trust anyone anymore, and we are given like property to strangers? The fear is unbearable. The loneliness is a black void. The insecurity is a dark cloud that follows us from home to home, from adult to adult. We have no place to call our own, no real beginnings, no hope, we are not loved, and we are so aware of that.

School is difficult. You become aware of how different you are and how hard it was to keep up, after going from school to school. Not only to you have new "parents," a new routine to get used to, new house rules, a new system of punishment, but now a new school. You already feel so insecure, but to have all those eyes stare at the "new kid" makes you want to disappear. Add to this how your education has suffered, and you are not just the "new kid," but the "stupid new kid." It gets worse with every new house you go to, and every new school.

There is no way to describe what it is really like to be a child and have no control of what is happening to you. It is a horror beyond words. You are not alive; you are merely existing. You feel nothing, you become numb, you trust no one, and you completely withdraw from the world. Some children become enraged, some become severely timid, some become dependent on anything that provides any semblance of comfort, and some children are completely destroyed. The few who flourish are those who have had the wise and understanding foster parents who grow to love their foster children and do everything a parent should for their "child." These are the angels in the system, but they are few and far between. Imagine taking a broken child and placing them with foster parents who are abusive; how do they measure their self-worth?

If you are a foster parent, please be good to us. We need to be loved and understood. We need patience and kindness. We are already broken… do not shatter us.

A throw away kid…

This is my story as a foster child. I hope it helps someone understand us, especially the foster parent. I hope it makes the case workers really listen to us. I hope it changes the system, but I'm afraid it won't.

Me, before it all began…innocent, unbroken.

Taken

Don't let me mislead you; I am not a child now, but I remember everything. I remember thoughts and feelings; I remember the looks and attitudes of those around me. I was a watcher, a silent, withdrawn watcher. In a way, I still am. I was taken from a stay in the hospital to the social worker's office. There I met my younger siblings (I was the oldest). I didn't know what was happening, but I don't think I cared at the time. I was already broken at this point. I had already shut down emotionally, a child in a box, detached, going through the motions. I had no memory of the particular incident that put me in the hospital. It had just happened, and my mind protected me from the memory; it still does to this day.

Yes, we should have been taken.

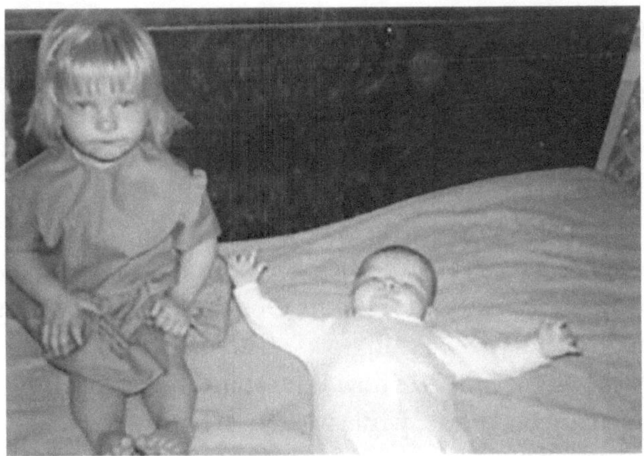

Don't get me wrong; child services were right in getting us out of that home. It was horrible there. After my mother divorced my dad she married a man who wasn't very nice. Even his parents warned my mother to stay away from him. She didn't listen. She moved in with her very young five children. I remember so many horrible moments with that monster. So when I finally ended up in the hospital, it was good that we were immediately taken out of the home, but then came foster care...

How can you expect us to be grateful?

This is to all of the foster parents: we don't like you. You have to earn that right. You have to earn our trust, what little we have left. Oh, and something else. Don't expect us to be grateful for what you are doing for us. What do we have to be grateful for, anyway? We were ripped from everything and everyone we know. We were thrown to you, and you want us to be grateful? We didn't choose you, and we know you will probably never love us. You are strangers, you are dangerous, and you are another set of adults we have to listen to, another set of adults who can hurt us. You have power over us, and we are helpless. Our life lays in pieces around us. We are shattered, damaged, broken. How can you expect us to be grateful?

For who tried, we remember you well.

Of all the foster homes I've been in, one stands out as a shining example above all the others. They *were an older couple. I only remember their last names, and their son* was the local pastor of the church we lived near. This was the first foster home, and I wish we could have stayed, but tragedy struck the family, and then we were gone. I think the foster dad died, which is why we had to go. Let's not focus on that though, but on how great this couple was. First of all, they NEVER hit us. They just talked to us, and tried to teach us. What matters most is they never hit us, or yelled at us. We had routine. Everything was structured, and we knew what to expect every day. Don't you see how important that is to us? No surprises, no chaos, no changes. At least while were with them. I remember regularly eating pancakes for supper and watching Kung Fu on TV. It didn't matter that I didn't understand the TV show that well; it was the *tradition* of it that was comforting. The one thing I loved there was sitting on the porch swing and singing. I rarely talked, rarely smiled, but I would sing. It was freedom! It was expression! My siblings would join in, and you clapped for us! You smiled at us. You made us feel special, and you didn't take our song from us. They NEVER hit us; did I say that already? Yes, it's that important. We know pain; you can't hurt us anymore than we have been hurt already. Does is make you feel better when you make us cry? That is what we've been taught. The Hayes never hurt us or yelled at us. I think they really understood. They were wise and patient. They were good. I truly honor their memory. They were the only ones.

The Worst

We don't like you, and we don't have to. We really don't like you, and we know you don't like us; you just like the dollar sign that comes with us. I won't give their name, because I don't want to hurt their relatives. They ALWAYS hit us. Many times. My brother got the worst of it. He was willful. He was only 6 years old. He was a boy without love. Don't you understand that? Why did you make him work so hard? HE WAS ONLY 6 YEARS OLD! He had to feed all the animals before school. A lot of animals for a 6 year old, even horses. He would get the switch if he missed the bus. He would get the switch if he couldn't feed all the animals. He would get the switch for so many things. You taught him anger. You taught him hate. You broke him, and he stayed that way. I WAS ONLY 8 YEARS OLD! I remember all the work. Washing handprints off the walls. Polishing your silver. Cleaning your oven. Stepping on tiptoes to hang out your laundry. Staying up after you've gone to bed so I could iron your clothes. Washing your dishes. Vacuuming your whole house, upstairs and down. I didn't want to get hit. I still did, and I can't remember why. You made a game of it, jump the switch. We would be lined up; the youngest is 3 years old. Jump the switch while it tore at our ankles and bit into our legs. You enjoyed it. Why else would you do it? You were paid to hurt us. We stayed with you the longest, and we paid for it. As if that weren't enough, you made us sing. Wasn't that so cute, five little kids singing for your guests. You took the one thing that belonged to us, our voices, and made us entertain your friends. We don't like you or your friends. You sold our voices to your friends. All the work, all the pain, all the misery, and we never said anything. We learned it didn't matter. We learned there were consequences when you talk.

It's Grandma!

I remember it being an unusual day to start with. We were going to the store! This didn't happen often, going out. It was thrilling event, and we were somewhat excited, or at least as excited as troubled children can get. We arrived and were on our best behavior. Our eyes scanned the aisles, looking for things children look for. Candy, toys, soda, GRANDMA! It was grandma! Our grandma! She was here! We ran to her screaming her name, which was, of course, *grandma*, and she bent down and scooped us into her arms. We felt love like nothing we've felt before. Our wonderful grandma tried to sneak us out of the store, which was impossible since we made such a ruckus! Instead of being rescued, a man in uniform was called and our grandma was forced to let us go. What started out as a wonderful day became a day of sadness and loss.

Gone

The social worker came today. This means we are leaving, but she didn't take us all. She only wanted two of us, the two little ones. They get in the car and then they are gone. This is something new. Something different. Where are they going? Are they going home? Are they going to Grandma? Why didn't they want the rest of us? Please don't leave us here with these people, please.

The Teacher

Another school. Another teacher. A bunch of kids looking at me. The kids. They are different than me. They are happy when school is over. Not me. I don't want to leave, but I don't say anything. I do what I'm told. My desk is next to the teacher's desk. I like being close to her. She is nice. I was sitting at my desk silently doing my work when a stick of gum was slid to me. I looked up, and it was the teacher! She smiled. I quietly opened the wrapper and popped the gum in my mouth. She didn't give anyone else a piece, only me. She snuck a stick of gum to me every day after that. Every day I thanked her with a smile. Teacher, I wish you knew what you really gave me. To you, it may have been a simple piece of gum, a small token of kindness. To me, it was so much more. It was something all my own, something precious no other kid in room had. That little stick of gum made me feel something I had never felt before…worthy. Some may say you were just giving a stick of gum to a troubled little girl, but I like to think you were listening to God's whisper.

Together Again

The social worker came today. How many of us does she want? Will I be left here alone? I had to pack too, but I'm so scared. What if the next home is worse than this one? What if they leave me here? I'm a good girl.

I have to be good so God can find me. I'll be good if you let me go to Grandma, I promise. We all got into the car, my two other siblings and me. We went to another home, and the two little ones were there. I remember seeing them, but I was so locked within myself that I didn't react to their presence. Just standing there, maybe I said "HI," I don't know. I had to sever the connection to them, because they could leave again. I severed the connection to all my siblings. I existed with them; I didn't live with them. I just stopped *living* altogether. It sounds cold, heartless, selfish, I know. I wish I had been stronger, but I was just a kid. I was the oldest, and they looked to me for strength, but I was so dead inside. Oddly enough, they still looked to me when something different happened, something good, something bad--- anything. They all looked to me for...what? I don't know. Perhaps they saw my detachment as strength, but it wasn't. It was merely survival.

The Visit with Our Real Daddy

We were ushered into the social worker's car. This usually meant that we were going t stay with a different family, a different set of rules, a different lifestyle, everything different. We were taken to grandma's house! What? Can we stay? Is our nightmare over? Do you know what made this better? Daddy was there. Our daddy. Not someone else's daddy, not a fake daddy, not a foster daddy, OUR daddy! He should have gotten custody of us after the divorce. He could afford it; he had a good job; he worked for the Army Corp of Engineers, but we were given to our mother. Big Mistake. It didn't matter now, because it was daddy, and some woman. We stayed a few hours, and the dreaded social worker came back. So gullible we are, so naïve, so young! We wouldn't get in the car, would you? But we were offered a soda. A soda? We were fooled into getting in the car for a soda? Yes. Oh, how young we were.

Going Home For Real This Time

I remember standing outside with my siblings. That woman wanted to take our picture. That woman who is standing with my dad. We didn't know what was going on. We have become completely jaded by now. Never trust anyone again. Never. Adults lie. Adults hurt you. Adults are dangerous. Adults can make you do anything they want. Adults have complete power over you, and you are nothing. Never trust anyone. Ever. We went home, to my dad's house in Titus, Alabama, and that woman lived there too. My dad's new wife. Our step-mom. This will sound cold to those who haven't been there, but for a long time, our new house was like another foster home. Do you understand? Another house, another set of adults, another set of rules. We were not normal children. We were not happy-go-lucky kids. At least not the older three of us. The two youngest don't remember much about foster care, but does that mean they weren't affected?

Rise Above or Fall

It wasn't easy for any of us. Not our father, who had to live with the knowledge of first, losing his children to the ex-wife, and then to foster care. A man denied custody because he was a man, and because he was single (wasn't that ridiculous). Not for our new mom, who had to be a mother to five troubled kids she had never met before. But especially not for us, the kids. This affected us for the rest of our lives. We know that bad things can happen no matter how safe you feel, or how good you are. But you have a choice…rise above and become one heck of a strong person, or fall. No matter what you feel, no matter what people say, no matter what reasons there are, you can rise above. Don't you see? If you fall, if you let this beat you for life, they win, you lose. You are out of there, away from foster care, away from what put you in foster care, but you are still trapped. You are your own prisoner. Refuse to stay locked up. You have the power now. Don't let your past hurt you or turn you into a shadow of a person.

What I've Learned

I've learned not to sweat the small stuff. I really don't even sweat the medium stuff! It takes a lot to get me angry. I am very patient. I can be really compassionate and empathetic, but only to a point. I expect you to help yourself. I expect you to be strong, too. Don't whine on and on about how bad your life is. Is it really that bad? Don't tell everyone your sob story because, let me tell you, someone out there can top it, and they don't go around expecting sympathy from everyone. I am also very logical. It took me some to learn emotions, or rather, how to show emotion. I'm still learning. I still hide my true feelings a lot. It doesn't take much to make me laugh. I can laugh at the simplest things. Allowing myself to laugh was something I had to learn. It was the easiest to learn, probably because I am so *hopeful*, even when it seems there's no reason to be! I can hardly understand why I'm so hopeful, but I know just how bad it can get, and I know I am a survivor. All those other emotions are the ones I still have to work on!

Dexter Dugan

Hope for a Better Legacy

I want to share my story so people know how hard foster care is and what it does to kids, physically and mentally. People may not know this, but most foster kids don't make it out of high school, let alone have good lives. I'm trying to make something of myself so that when I have children, they don't have to go through the same thing as I did, that I don't pass on the legacy that was passed on to me.

I don't remember the exact date, but it was the spring when I was only 4 years old. I was living with my family---mom, dad, three sisters, and one brother. My story started because one day my older sister (she was 13 years old) basically disobeyed my mother, who called ACW (back then it was BCW). ACS calls that "one smack abuse." If that was the case, every parent, especially Latinos like my mom, should have their kids in care. ACS made things appear worse than it actually was. There were other allegations made about my parents, but I don't believe them. They are responsible. We were healthy and always eating, and the house was clean. The whole neighborhood knew us and how we lived, mainly because my mom talks a lot. I loved my parents, and still do. To tell you the truth, I miss that time with them, and every time I think of that I cry, because it makes me wonder what our lives would have been like if ACS hadn't broke our family up.

One late afternoon, I remember someone knocking on the door, and when my 13 year old sister answered it, a group of police walked in and I and my younger siblings ran behind our parents. After that, there was a big fight and the next thing I know, I was being pulled away from my father and carried to a patrol car and we pulled away.......

The sun had set and I don't remember exactly where, but we were in a shelter somewhere in the city. I was very confused and scared. After awhile, we were put in a van and driven to our first foster home, while our older sister stayed somewhere else. This foster mother was one of the good foster mothers that I've had. She was about 50 years old and lived in an apartment, along with her grandson and another foster child, who was a teenager. I don't remember everything about being there at her place, but I do remember we had weekly visits that took place at an agency every Thursday from 4:30-5:30 with our parents, and when we saw them, we ran to them like we hadn't seen them in ages. We had a great time, that was until we had to leave. That's when the tears came out. We walked with our parents to the train, but the only problem was, we weren't going the same direction; their train came first and we waved goodbye. That's how it was every Thursday. There are also a couple of special visitations I can remember. One was Christmas of that year, when we went to my grandmother's house and visited with all of our dad's family, and another one was a day in 1998, when we went to Astroland for a fun time with our family; we stayed until Astroland closed, but then it was sad again as we got on the train to go home. By 1998, our foster mom couldn't really bring us to the visits anymore, so a driver from the agency took us. What I sometimes hated was that instead of taking the BQE to the bridge, he would take another route. The first time he went that way, I got really happy because I saw the train elevated tracks outside and said, "We're going home!" But I was tearing up again, because the parkway begins about seven blocks from our old house. Overall, it was great in that foster home, but in 1999 we were removed for some unknown reason, probably to move us closer to the agency.

Now, I want to get to the interesting part. This happened in my second foster home. By this time my fourth sister was born and my mom told me that as soon as she was born, ACS took her away. That part always makes me mad. If I was able to tell a person's personality by looking at them, like

I can now, I could honestly say that I would've sensed something wrong with this lady, but I was still just a child then. The first night with her, when she asked us what we wanted, we said, "McDonalds," so she let us have that, as she did for about a week, but I guess she only did it for us to let down our guard, because after that, she got mean. Other times, she would make us stand in a corner, and not for ten minutes, but for hours at a time. One time, we were supposed to go to church, but right before that, we went shopping, and she had me bring in all the bags. She told me to hurry up, otherwise she'd leave me, and leave me she did; as soon as I finished, I saw her drive off. Her daughter made me stand in a corner until she got home and I cried until she returned. My feet hurt as if I had walked the half length of the city (and I have done that). On top of all that, before our weekly visits with our parents, she always said, "Don't tell them anything that happened. Remember, you have to come home with me." Since I was scared of her, I complied. I was in a corner, of course. I have a phobia of waterbugs (I get that from my father), and of all things to do, she made me pick up the dead ones and throw them out. I would be there for hours, while she sat there saying, "What are you scared for? It's dead." Eventually, I would pick the dead bug up, literally shaking because I was so scared.

In the winter of 2000, there was a big snowstorm that forced schools to close (a rarity in this city), and my sister and I wanted to stay in the yard, since everyone was going in. When the sun was about to set, we knocked on the door to come back inside, and she opened the door just to tell us that since we wanted to stay out, to stay out, and then she closed the door. We were out there freezing, long after the sun had set, and then she finally let us in the house after all that waiting. But luckily, she messed up in the late winter of 2001. She hit one of my sisters with the house phone, which left a scar, and at the visit, my parents noticed it, which confirmed their suspicions that something was wrong. ACS made a surprise visit to the house and saw what was going on, and removed us a few days later. On the day she was taking us to the agency to be moved, she had the nerve to give us all napkins, as if we were supposed to be sad that we were leaving.

Now, the next home, which was still in the same neighborhood, was just as interesting. The foster mom was odd and I don't think she liked me and my brother, but she treated our sisters like queens. She took them everywhere and gave them everything they wanted, while me and my brother were left home being yelled at all the time by her daughters. She had three or four adopted daughters and the second to youngest was really mean; whenever our foster mom went somewhere with our sisters, we were stuck with her. September 11, 2001 (9-11 event) was one of the few times she wasn't hostile to me. I watched the news as I did my homework, and the only thing she said to me was to do my homework, and she calmly answered my questions about what happened. Then winter came again, and one time, I really got fed up with the way her daughter was treating me, making me stand in the backyard in my pajamas, freezing. Another time, my brother and I got tired of the foster mother not taking us anywhere and convinced her to take us with her, and I forgot where she took us, but we just ended up staying in the car. She never took us anywhere nice, except for an occasional trip to Red Lobster or something; in fact, it was so rare, I think it was only about five times she took us somewhere. She started to renovate the house in the summer of that year, but she never finished, and conditions began to worsen---dishes were piled up in the sink and nothing was cleaned, and it got so bad that my brother almost burned the house down. Luckily though, she was planning on moving out of state, so we were removed from her home. This was the last home that the four of us were together in.

When I was about 10 years old, my brother and I were moved to another foster home on the other side of the neighborhood, while the girls were moved to a home somewhere else, and our younger sister joined them there later. Our older sister was 18 or 19 years old and had signed herself out of foster care by this time. Nothing bad happened in this home. Like the first foster mother, this one did her job, which was to take care of us and make us feel loved. She even had a dog and a son. We were with her until November of 2004, and then my brother and I were placed in my cousin's care. That same month, we switched to a new agency, but it's not over yet...

By 2007, our parents lost their parental rights, which I think is just pure stupidity. I have never gotten an answer as to why their parental rights were terminated, nor have they, and although they tried for three years to regain their parental rights, they were denied. I hold no grudge against my parents, as I feel they were wronged as much as I was. In my opinion, the system failed, not my parents.

October of 2008, my cousin took his girlfriend to Aruba for her birthday and was gone for a week, and I don't know how ACS found out, but they showed up about 9:00 in the evening and took us to our house to get a few days worth of clothes, since it was only supposed to be temporary. I should've thought about it more; if I had, I would've disappeared for awhile. Anyway, my insides were heating up from the building anger. We ended up in a very dangerous neighborhood that I would never touch. Just by looking at the foster mother in that home, something told me it wouldn't go well if we stayed there for a long time. Luckily, my case worker had the same vibe, but we still stayed the night there, though. The foster mother drove us to the station. I do thank her for that, but that entire day at school sucked for me. Now, I hate showing my emotions to people, but this time, I couldn't help but look pissed. During school, I called my case worker to get an update on the situation and she said that she found a new place for us to stay for the weekend. I was relieved, and later that day we went to the agency, where they already had our stuff.

We didn't go far away; we went to a group home for boys. Luckily, I knew most of them there and we stayed there until Monday, and then we were switched to another foster home after our visit with our siblings. This home was in a bad neighborhood I wouldn't go to, and the foster parents were of West Indian descent; as soon as I heard the accent, I knew we were going to have problems in the future. The first month was fine, but then out of nowhere, their 18 year old son started acting up. This kid took Lysol and sprayed me and my brother with it, talking about how we have to hold our farts in or leave the room to fart. Now, I want someone to tell me you can feel anything, let alone a fart, when you're asleep. We were asleep! How can we just feel it, when we are technically unconscious? This went on until we were punished. Another time, he locked us out of the house for two hours. I had keys, but there was a second lock that I didn't have a key to. I was about to go back to MY house. After I called the foster mom, he finally opened the door. Of course, the foster father didn't even get off his butt to open the door. I got into arguments with the foster father because he wanted to be a jerk, talking about how he would do things. We told the agency all of this and they did nothing! On weekends, I would leave at 5:00 in the morning to go to my mother's house and wouldn't come back until Sunday night.

It wasn't until April of that year that we were removed and placed in another foster home. My sister was finally in reach, but she was living in another area, and my two youngest sisters were in another area. This lady had five kids of her own and everything was good for awhile. We could come and go as we pleased, until her cousin came in October. He and I got close and found that we both liked trains. The first time we had a real problem was when I was put on probation in school and I came back with one box not signed, and when the foster mother asked me why it wasn't signed, I told her I forgot. She tried to TELL ME THAT I DIDN'T FORGET, that I just didn't do it, and she tried to do all the talking, but I cut her off by telling her that she can't tell me what goes on in MY head. She asked me what I said, and then told me that she's an adult, that I can't talk back to her because I'm still just a child. Her "husband" tried to tell me to calm down and stop talking back, but I told them that my parents taught me to speak my mind and not let anyone try to tell me different. Then I hit her in the core by saying that she just couldn't handle a contradiction from a thinking 16 year old. I walked away and started putting on my jeans, and I heard yelling in the front yard as I was putting on my shoes. She came to the backyard and confronted me. I got my phone, chargers, mp3, and jacket, and walked out the door, slamming it as I left. I walked to the station and I called my father and tried to tell him what happened, but I could barely get the words out because I was trying not to cry at the train station. I told him that I was going to my old foster mom's house, but I went to a friend's house instead. Now I was technically AWOL. I disappeared until Monday until I had a meeting and told her what happened, including the part about the foster mom trying to chock me. At the meeting, the foster mom skipped that part and then tried to cover herself up by telling them about what I did in school. Reluctantly, I went back with her after the meeting, and everything was fine until one day, like an idiot, I forgot my phone on the couch and she seen some messages. I knew that family was nosy and I had let my guard down. When I came back to get my phone, she told me that if I have anything to say, to tell it to her face. I said, "Whatever," took my phone, and left. The next day, she was still talking about it. The more she talked, the madder I got. To make a long story short, I was spending less and less time there, until I just stopped going back.

ACS counted is as AWOL again and called another meeting, and I told them how I felt. It turned out that I was able to go back to my cousin's place in three days, which was a Monday. That Monday came, and by the time the sun went down, I was home---not parentally home, but still, home. At least I am with family and not strangers. I also get to visit my parents. I have a pretty good relationship with them today. I see my dad more than my mom, but mostly because he lives closer to me than her (they are separated, but not divorced). ACS has been trying to make me change my mind about aging out of the foster care system, to be adopted instead, but I still say, "NO." I've been in foster care since I was 4 years old, so another four years doesn't seem that far away. I am currently living with my cousin and I plan on living here until I age out. I don't need the flawed system of ACS; I have all the support I need at home.

I wish my family had stayed together and I hadn't been put in foster care, but I suppose it could have been worse. I feel very fortunate and am grateful to at least still have some family connection, which many foster kids don't have. The most important thing to me right now is finishing my education and moving forward in my life so that my future family doesn't have to suffer the way I did. My hope is for a better legacy.

Donna White

Moving Forward

I want to share my story to help other foster kids realize that they can reach their full potential in life, no matter what their childhood has been like. I want them to realize they can move forward in life and not be stuck in the past. Despite being in foster care I feel I have led an abundant life. Being in foster care helped me to realize there are people out there who really do care. Although I was fortunate to have had good, loving foster parents in my life at such a young age, my life did not start out so well.

I was put in foster care at the age of 5 because I was being sexually abused and neglected. Sad to say, my first memory of my life is not a pleasant one; it is of being sexually abused by an old man who was supposed to have been a 'friend' of the family.

My first foster home was with my sister. I wasn't there very long and I remember being very upset about being separated from my sister when I was put in a children's home. While I was at the home I became acquainted with some foster parents, John and Roberta Adams and they would come and visit every weekend and I went to their home on holidays and vacations. I never wanted to go back to the home after being with them. They wanted to adopt me, but my biological parents wouldn't let them. I have many good memories of my foster parents. I remember going to a cottage in Wisconsin. They taught me strong family values. I went to church and I remember midnight mass. They were very huggy, affectionate people and they made a big deal out of birthdays and Christmas, giving me a lot of nice gifts.

One night when my foster parents brought me back to the home the staff took the foster parents and me aside and informed us separately that I would be leaving the next day to go live with my natural dad. I don't think it was nice or thoughtful the way the situation was handled. It was very traumatic for me and for the foster parents also. Later on my foster mom told me that nobody would mention my name for six months after this incident, and that she cried for six months. Obviously, the foster parents really loved me and wanted me as their own child. This trauma didn't just affect me; it also affected other people, including extended family and friends who had grown attached to me. I remember crying hysterically because I was so upset about being separated from them. Eventually, once my foster mom realized she wasn't going to be able to adopt me, she adopted another girl, who I consider to be foster sister today.

Although my dad was not a stranger to me, as I had been visiting with him for two years before going to live with him, and once I was with him I was happy, there was still a part of me that mourned my foster parents. I never discussed wanting to talk with my foster parents with my dad. I guess I figured he wouldn't like it, so I didn't, but I did miss them none the less.

I don't remember the day I left the home. I was very traumatized, as I was leaving the only safe environment I knew. I remember the first day I was introduced to my dad and step mom. The social worker told me, "You're going to go into the room to meet your mom," and upon seeing her I said, "That is NOT my mom."

I went to go live with my dad on June 11, 1967. I remember being happy with my dad. I became adjusted to living with my dad largely because I was happy to be with my siblings. One bad memory I have of living with my dad is being spanked because me and my sisters were running around with some black guys and we ran away once to a park and were found on a park bench. The only time I was spanked by my dad was when this happened. This happened when we were living in Decatur, Illinois, when the riots were happening, so naturally he was concerned about our welfare. Not long after this we moved to Hammond, Illinois, a very small town out in the country, where I lived until my dad's death when I was 15 years old.

I took my dad's death very hard. It was very traumatic for me. It didn't help that my step-mom tried laying a guilt trip on me about his death. I can still remember the day she sat me and my sister down and told us that it was our fault our dad died. I wish I could have had a long life with my dad and I still miss him to this day. I sometimes wonder how my life would have been different had he lived longer. After my dad's death I continued to see my older boyfriend, who was not only an escape from my abusive step-mom, but also a father figure for me. Things got pretty rough while living with my alcoholic and abusive step-mom. She was very mentally and emotionally abusive. A week before I turned 18 I moved in with my boyfriend because my step-mom didn't want me living with her anymore. I hadn't been in touch with my foster parents for about five years, so I didn't think about turning to them. At this point I just got totally wrapped up with my boyfriend. He was my life.

I ended up marrying my boyfriend and had a son with him when I was 25. My husband wanted me to abort the baby, but I wouldn't, so we separated. I left him when I was six months pregnant, which took a lot of courage and strength. It was very scary being out on my own, especially with a background like mine. I ended up raising my son on my own until he was 11 years old, when I married my current husband. Life has been good with him.

I ended up contacting my foster parents when I was pregnant and have since kept a close relationship with them, which has been a great blessing in my life. It was a struggle being a single mom, so having them in my life again was a comfort. I didn't feel so alone. Although I love my foster family very much, I still miss having a relationship with my biological family. Sometimes when I'm at my friend's family reunions I sit around and look at the picture of what our family could have been and it makes me sad. I am trying to reestablish some ties with my biological family today and now talk with some of them, which is nice.

I would like to end my story by saying to all you foster kids out there that although being in foster care is not the most ideal way to grow up, a lot of good can come out of it. I don't see foster care as just a negative; it can also be a positive thing. I see myself as a survivor. Experiencing foster care can bring out the good and strong in a person. I feel that being a foster child made me a stronger person and most importantly, it made me a more compassionate person. It has also brought me closer to God and today I am a Christian.

Doreen Oechle

A Painful Legacy

I was born in Canada, into a family with too many mouths to feed. I was the eighth child of a family that would eventually have a total of nice children.

I was taken away from the family by social services at approximately 2 ½ years of age. All nine of us children were taken away and farmed out to family, if they were available, or to foster homes. I do not remember much of the early foster homes. I have a slight memory of a very sweet older couple (I believe this was the first home), of being in their kitchen and watching my younger brother throw a severe temper tantrum. For him, it was the beginning of many temper tantrums. Actually, both of my brothers (social services tried to keep the youngest three together) had the temper tantrums; I was the quiet little mouse in the corner watching and observing, learning what I needed or did not need to do to survive.

I really don't know how many foster homes I was in. I remember the last one the best and unfortunately, they are not good memories. I look back now and feel as if my brothers and I were treated as the family dog that no one wanted and kicked every time they could. It was a matter of survival in this home; no one was going to help you survive, so you did whatever you had to, to survive. I remember not being able to talk unless spoken to, and I remember sitting at the table for dinner, terrified to ask for anything. When I was adopted, just shy of my 8th birthday, I weighed about 50 lbs. I was underfed and remember being hungry quite often; I remember eating food off the ground on my way home from school. Our diet consisted of turnips, beets, carrots, and Bear and Moose, from what I remember. I remember one day wanting a Popsicle when the ice cream truck came around, and begging the foster mother for 10 cents, and she taunted me with the 10 cents for the longest time before she actually threw it across the kitchen floor and I had to go scrambling for it. This was very out of character for me; I believe it is the only thing I ever asked for in that home. Their food was kept down in the basement and I remember sneaking down to eat some crackers one day. Christmas was a time to watch the other children (the foster mother's biological children) open gifts. I was appointed to babysit the foster mother's youngest biological daughter who was around 2 years of age; I remember having to watch this little girl for hours. I was the one who cleaned the house and did the dishes every night. There were no friends to play with, no time to have fun and simply be a child. All the foster children slept in one room (I believe there were about five of altogether) in bunk beds. I can still remember how terrifying this woman could be and I remember being frightened, but at the same time I remember a tenacity and courage about me, as if I was not going to let her get the best of me. That tenacity and courage has been my saving grace at times, and the only thing that has gotten me through some of the toughest times of my life. That home was like a battle field and I was finding cover wherever and however I could.

My two brothers and I were adopted when I was 8 years old. We were taken from a home of poverty to an abundant one, and we each had our own room. The difference in the financial aspects of the two worlds was like night and day; however, the emotional aspect of the change was more similar to the foster homes than not.

The lasting legacy of the trauma that I experienced in the foster homes and the disruption of my original family is what have been the most painful, and what I still struggle to overcome. I have been in therapy for about six years. My therapy was prompted by a panic attack that seemed to last for about six months. I think the battle field finally caught up to me and I was smart enough to get help.

I struggle with abandonment issues, both physical abandonment, as well as emotional abandonment. Relationships are difficult and I have yet to find one that I am not recreating my dysfunctional relationships with the parental figures in my life. I never have felt like I belonged anywhere; I feel as I have been aimlessly roaming. I am realizing that as I heal more and go through my own recovery that I am getting a very small glimpse of what the trauma in my life robbed me of and I am beginning to understand what love means. I never felt loved, both in the foster homes and in my adopted home. I have always felt as if I was a burden to everyone, that they **had** to take care of me, but no one knew how to love me. This is the most painful legacy of the trauma and a very deep-seated one, one that has taken years to recognize, to admit to, and now I need to figure out where to go from here.

I am sharing my story because I believe that as foster children, our roots are ripped out from underneath us, but yet parental figures and society in general expects no ramifications from those roots being destroyed. I believe we (former foster children) need to tell our stories and to help each other.

Anonymous

Foster Care Was All I Ever Knew

I was born in Bloomington, Illinois in 1936, the baby of six children. My family broke up because my dad was an alcoholic and my mother had a nervous breakdown. I'm not sure what mental illness she was diagnosed with or if they even had a name for it back then, but she spent twenty-seven years in a mental hospital and died there. I'm sure at least part of the reason she had a nervous breakdown was due to the stress of trying to raise six children and having an alcoholic husband. She was no doubt very overwhelmed by it all.

I don't remember my early home life because I was just a baby, only 3 months old when I was taken away from my natural home. I went to live with my grandmother on my mom's side, along with my sister who was 5 years older than me. My two older brothers and sisters were able to stay with my dad, but apparently he didn't think he could cope with the two younger ones, especially since I was just a baby, so we had to leave. I lived with my grandmother for nine years, but when she ended up married things didn't go so well anymore because her husband didn't like me being there. When they moved to Joliet, my 14 year old sister rented her own room by herself and finished high school and I went to live with my 18 year old sister in Indianapolis, but that didn't work out either because I got in the way. Not only did she not have room for me, but I also interfered with her personal life and independence, so I had to go live with my other older sister, who was 19 years old and married, with one young son. I spent three years there, but the living arrangement was very crowded, so it didn't work out either. We moved from a two and a half room apartment in Bloomington, to a small trailer, and at one time, when my sister and two brothers were also staying there with us, there were seven people living together, which was way too crowded for all of us. They were a young couple with a child and didn't have the money to take care of me.

At the age of 11 or 12 I left my sister's place and went into my first non-kinship foster care home in Leroy, Illinois, which was all right. I liked the small town school there and the foster mom taught me how to work, which was good training for my future, but when her other foster girl was returned to her mother, the foster mom decided that one girl wouldn't do her any good and let me go also. I guess we were there for her convenience, but she wasn't mean about it.

From this place I went into another foster home in Normal, Illinois, this time with a single woman. My brother was there for a short time and it might be why I was put there. This was a good home for me. She was a very motherly woman and she used to take me to church with her. I stayed at this home for three years, until I graduated from high school, and then I ended up marrying young and having four children.

I never thought I was seriously affected by my foster care experience, but I guess I was affected some, because I don't like moving around, which is why I have stayed at my job for such a long time. I told myself that when I got married and had children I wouldn't move around, that I wanted my kids to have stability. Going through the foster care experience, I didn't know or understand what was happening and just went along with everything. I didn't know anything different and just figured everybody went through this and lived this way, but I came to realize later on that wasn't true. In retrospect, it would have probably been better if I had been put in an orphanage, where I would have had more stability, but I was just a child and had no say in the matter. What is nice about being an adult is that I do have a say in the matter, and I chose not to repeat the past with my own children.

Anonymous

Well, I Survived...

I was born in 1936, in an apartment, not a hospital. I don't know why. I am the oldest of three children, with a younger brother and a baby sister. I have quite a few memories of my early childhood, but they are mostly unpleasant ones. My father was an alcoholic who used to come home drunk and beat my mother, which of course frightened me a lot. We moved around a lot, probably due to evictions because my dad couldn't pay the rent. I have very few memories of my mother and I don't know if she also had a drinking problem or not, but one day, when I was about 7 or 8 years old, she just took off and never came back. In plain language, she abandoned us. I never did see her again. I did try to find her when I was older, but it was as if she just disappeared from the face of the earth. Sad to say, I figured she was probably a Jane Doe in some cemetery somewhere.

I remember being left alone for three days, eating nothing but peanut butter with a spoon out of a jar. A neighbor reported us and the police came to pick us up and took us to some temporary holding place for children, until a suitable home could be found for us. I'm not sure how long we were there---maybe a few weeks or so, and then my brother and I were put into a foster home together, while my sister went somewhere else, but I'm not sure where. We were only at the foster home about two months because the parents couldn't tolerate my brother's bedwetting.

All three of us went to the next foster home, which also included four or five other children, but we didn't stay there very long either, only about six months. I remember very little about the first two foster homes and I don't know why we were removed from the second one. Nobody explained anything to us because we were just young children, but it would have been nice if somebody had at least tried. In my mind, I guess I thought we were just "moving on." It seemed like were moved around like a herd of cattle, feeling unimportant and unloved. I felt like nobody loved me.

The third foster home I do remember, unfortunately. It was not a good home; in fact, it was downright horrible. I was treated like a piece of crap there, very unfairly. The foster parents had two teenage sons who were treated very special, while we were treated very inferiorly. We were always wrong and they were always right. We weren't allowed to eat all the foods their boys could and they used to kick us under the table at mealtime when there were certain foods we weren't supposed to eat. As punishment, we were forced to kneel on bumpy ashtrays for a long time, which was very painful. The boys tried coming into our rooms and bullying us, until one time when I kicked one of them into a door mirror, then after this they didn't bother us much. We were locked into the attic for punishment, sometimes overnight.

The social worker didn't come around much, and when she did everything was "hunky dory," but one day while she was visiting, she asked my brother if he wanted to go to ISSCS (Illinois Soldiers and Sailors Children's School) and he said he did, so he left. About two months later I went to ISSCS. The social worker asked me if I wanted to stay with my brother and I said "yes," of course. My little sister was only about 2 years old at this time, so she couldn't go with us, and I don't know how long she stayed there at the foster home after we were gone. I do know she was adopted, though.

I was about 10 years old when I arrived at ISSCS and stayed there through high school. ISSCS was a lot better than the foster homes, even though I didn't really want to be there, either. I would have much rather been home with my parents, had they been decent parents, but they weren't. My mom never came to visit us and my dad only came to visit us a few times at ISSCS, but he was usually drunk and didn't say much. At the age of 19 I decided I never wanted to see him again, and I never did, even though my brother and sister did and encouraged me to also. A childless couple from Legion's Day at ISSCS, Bill and Virginia Frank, wanted to adopt me, but my dad wouldn't allow it. They even offered him some money, but he said it wasn't enough money, so I wasn't adopted by these people, but I felt very lucky to have them in my life. I called them "mom and dad" and stayed in touch with them until they died.

I also had some very nice house parents at ISSCS, but it wasn't easy leaving there. I was given just $40 and booted out on my own. I felt pretty helpless, but I signed up for the Air Force, where I ended up staying for twenty years. I consider myself successful. I was an air force craft mechanic for about five years, and then I had a desk job as an air craft maintenance scheduling specialist. I met my first wife in Bunker Hill, Indiana and we had one son; unfortunately, they both died young of kidney failure due to Type 1 Diabetes. I feel sad about their loss, but life goes on, and I remarried a woman with four girls. Sad to say, my sister didn't do as well as me and my brother. I didn't meet her until twenty-five years after we were separated. There was a "locator section" of the Air Force Times newspaper, for people interested in searching for lost loved ones, and someone had left a phone number next to my name for me to call, and to my complete surprise, it was my long lost sister. She had known my name as her brother and after sharing our history with each other it became clear, without a shadow of a doubt, that we were indeed siblings. She told me she was adopted by a family who wanted a companion for their daughter, but that she had a miserable life there, living a prison like existence. When their daughter left for college, they were afraid my sister would run away, so they locked her up in a room and only allowed her out to go to the bathroom, and they brought food to her room. She wasn't allowed to attend school and when the school questioned the parents, they said she was sick. This went on for a number of months until she was finally able to get out and get a lawyer, who freed her, since she was now legally of adult age. She never spoke to the parents again after this. She now has three children and is on her third marriage, so things haven't been the best in her adult life either, but she has survived.

How would I describe my experience? Well, I survived also, but not having your own parents leaves a void in your life. The foster homes I was in were terrible, and I don't recommend them for other children. I think people who do have foster children shouldn't have their own children, as there is usually or often favoritism shown for their own kids over the foster kids. If people do decide to foster children, they should do it out of real love and concern, not monetary gain. I was shown much more affection from my ISSCS house parents and the Frank's than I ever was by the foster parents, and it was no doubt their love that saved me.

Edward Heavey

Grateful for the Institute

I was born in 1928. I had four brothers and one sister. My mom died when I was five years old and shortly afterward, my dad was hospitalized, leaving him unable to care for us, so we all became "wards of the state." I went to a Catholic orphanage. What I remember about this place wasn't good; in fact, it was a terrible place. I wasn't allowed to see my brothers, so I snuck out at nighttime to see them. I can remember hiding on the fire escape, talking with my one brother. I recall being wacked on the hands because I was crying about missing my mom. This was only a temporary placement and in the meantime my dad looked around for a suitable place for us and found a children's home.

Boys' Row

I entered the children's home on October 1, 1934 and was put into an isolated receiving cottage for six weeks, due to family illness. Even though I was grateful for this home, as it gave me some stability, education, provided necessities such as food, clothing, along with positive activities, sports, and plenty of playmates, I never considered it my home. I had a family outside the "Institute," as I called it, which came to visit me on a regular basis, and I wanted to be with them. I refused to call my house mother "mom." I think I was very angry about my mom's death and it took me a long time to get over it. My mom must have treated me special and I never felt that way at the Institute. The prevalent attitude there was that "children were to be seen, not heard." All in all, I know it was better for me to have been in there during the Depression because I was well provided for, but I still did not want to be in there. I don't remember any of the kids liking it there. Some of them tried running away and we would talk about it and how we might also like to run away. I thought about running away, perhaps hopping a train, but I never had the guts, and besides, where would I go? I never liked the regimentation at the Institute and the house parents at the Village where I was at for the first five years were very strict disciplinarians, who also had monitors and tattletalers doing their dirty work, such as paddling me, forcing me to duck-waddle, do pushups, lay flat on the floor, and sit in dark, isolated rooms. We weren't allowed back into the cottage after breakfast until lunchtime, and if we tried, we had to lie under our bed. I must have been a troublesome and angry kid because it seemed like I was always getting in trouble. I was moved around some at the Institute and in one cottage I got beaten real badly because I wouldn't get out of bed one morning.

In the summer of 1943 I was sent to a foster home. When I was 14 years old my dad sent me and my sibling's money for train tickets and I moved out to Washington with him. My dad never went to court to get custody of us, so I assume nobody cared that we left, even if we were still supposedly considered wards of the state. I don't remember feeling any particular way about leaving the foster home and going back to live with my dad; I was just going along with life like I always had in the past.

I know my foster care experience affected me, especially in my parenting skills; even though I wasn't abusive, I never really knew how to show love or give guidance to my children. I don't know if things would have been different if I hadn't experienced my upbringing because I have nothing to compare it with; I only have my experience. I was married twice and my second wife and I were married for thirty years. At age 29 I went to law school and became a lawyer, a legislator, and then a superior court judge. I tried my best to avoid juvenile court because due to my past, I became too emotionally involved, but once in a while I was forced to. I heard a few foster care cases and had some impatience with the social workers because I felt that they didn't understand the family dynamics of children and treated them like property instead of human beings. Even though I wasn't fond of the Institute and for years was too ashamed to admit to being there, I still think they should bring orphanages back. Foster homes are a good alternative on an individual basis, but orphanages have a very significant role to play in deciding whether a child gets stability. I feel that because I had the stability of the children's home and the support of my family, my life turned out much better than it would have had I been shuffled around in foster care homes, like so many children are today.

Edward Phillips

Behind Curtains

My Life before Foster Care

My name is Edward Phillips. I find it funny looking back on my life, amazed that I ever made it to where I currently am in life, how even though I have made many dreams and aspirations for myself, they are often completely are out of reach and touch with the reality that I live in. I constantly find myself in a struggle to stay in my current home and the dismay of always finding me near the verge of the streets is always surprising. I chose to share my story with others in order to bring awareness to everyone about the many problems of the *good old system* that no one tells you about. It is quite sad that a 21 year old is speaking on such a topic, something that he should know nothing about. It seems people have become detached from the sobering realities of how all abuse and neglect can deeply impact a child's life. The most bothersome part is how children are overlooked and spoken words are undervalued. The typical reasoning is that "oh he's just a kid; they don't know what they're talking about." Your age really doesn't matter in these circumstances; the beatings won't stop for you, nor will the neglect. People tend to think neglect doesn't harm kids, but quite the contrary; it often leaves kids fending for themselves, and life teaches the values which carry the kids into incarceration. Essentially it is important for foster parents to know not just how to provide, but to properly and efficiently foster a child emotionally. The effects are often life altering, regardless of how small they are, because they carry through at such an age in development. They make a profound impression on the rest of the child's life, continuing into adulthood. Smaller things add up over time and in some cases they are worse, because they cause multiple problems instead of one specific big problem when the kids begin to seek help.

All too often I find myself looking over my shoulder and worried about a decision I have made, wondering when someone will learn of it, waiting for my impending doom to hit and trigger those events where I see the streets. I don't intend for it to happen and I certainly don't want it to; however, I can't escape the feeling that it's going to happen, as though it was fore planned in my life. I often feel isolated from everyone as a result of problems due to family and friends, and then rush to their side when I'm about to lose them.

I am 21 years old. I was 6 when everything started for me. Thinking back I can remember the days before grade school. I was addicted to my mom's affection. I would wake up and run downstairs to see my mom smiling at me. Often times I would sit in her lap, playing with her hair while she watched her favorite show *Touched by an Angel.* Throughout the day she would set out the paint, colored pencils, markers, and crayons, which I would draw pictures with. She was my world then and I couldn't picture a day without her. Later that year we moved into a smaller house and shortly afterward the fighting begun. I often spent much of my time in my room or at school. Many nights I would wake up to loud noises in the house. One night in particular stands out for me. I remember seeing my dad and mom on two sides of the room. My dad had a look of dismay on his face and my mom had a look of shock as they both looked at me. My mom called for my brother to come and bring me back to my room. He ran out and grabbed me by the arm and walked me back to my room.

I fell back to sleep easily. I awoke the next day to find my mother running around the house in a frenzy to gather some belongings. I walked with her into the garage as she shoved a suitcase in our white Trans Am. I asked her where she was going and she replied, "I'm leaving." I asked her, "Can I come with you?" She paused and thought for a while in the garage. "I'm not coming back here" she said, and I replied "I don't care." She then told me to go some clothes really quick. I bolted into my room and opened my dresser and grabbed an arm full of clothes and ran back out to the car. She finished setting the suitcase in the care, then grabbed my clothes and stuffed them into the trunk. We grabbed the cat and left. I remember very little of the trip.

We finally arrived at my grandparents. I loved them to death and enjoyed spending all my time with them. As a child I frequently would run around the house and watch cartoons. During the year I attended school, which was new and strange. It was March and I remember being looked at as strange, as though I didn't belong. After a few months I moved with my mom to somewhere in southwest Iowa with her boyfriend. It was a relief at first to be somewhere new. We were living in a trailer park and we would frequently go up to her boyfriend's property. It was all farm land and I would run all throughout it, scheming new places to explore on each and every new acre. During most of my stay in Iowa I came home at night and went to bed, and in the morning I would wake up to find my mom still gone. Little did I know at the time where she was at.

Before all of this happened there was a time of peace and quiet for me. Between the ages of 5-8 my dad was in the National Guard. When he went to Missouri to drill every month he would drop my brother and I off at my grandma and grandpa's. I can recall the days when I would run around in the pastures circling their house, picking black berries, chasing fireflies, celebrating the 4th of July with fireworks I picked out, making forts, running to the park to play, visiting my aunt and uncle, and feeding the farm animals. I remember going to the store with my grandpa and picking out toys at the dollar store. We went to several rodeos, a monster car event, and sometimes the auction house to bid away animals. It was like any normal childhood should be like.

My Childhood

When I was 6, shortly after the 4th of July my dad came to get me. I was clueless that I was to leave my mom. It registered in my head, but I had no clue what it meant. I came back with my father, which was a day drive. By night I got home and I realized that my mom was gone and nothing could bring her back. I cried the whole night through and got little very little sleep that night. My brother had come in to check on me that night to see if I was sleeping and I faked that I was so he would leave me be. The next day I began to settle into a strange life. I had never known my father, except the lunches at the *Olive Garden* my mother used to take me to on his break.

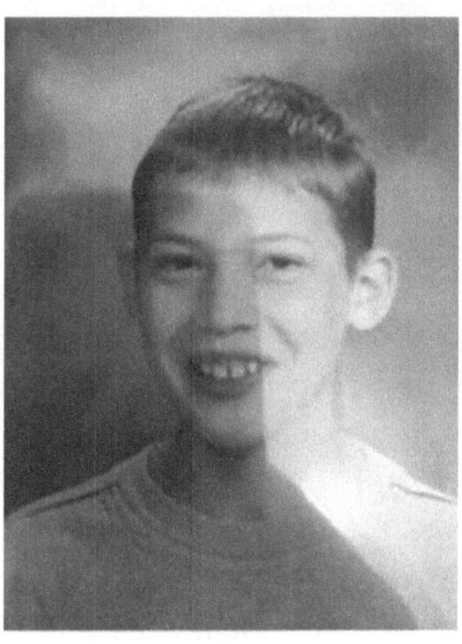

(Age 7)

The whole time that I stayed in the house, as brief as it may have been, was strange to me. My dad was never there and I was always at school, back when I actually enjoyed school. My brother was actually kind to me and looked after me there. Shortly after the year finished up we found out my grandma Tanya was undergoing treatment for chemotherapy. We moved in with my grandpa to help look after her. School was great for a while and I loved going. I was in the first grade when we moved back. I enjoyed being around all the kids. It was much better than all the stress and tension at home. My grandma Leda died the same year from cancer. That lady gave me my childhood. All I knew was she was gone just like my mom. My grandma died about 3 weeks after we got there. I can't remember any funeral. Shorty afterward we moved out to the home my dad had purchased out west. I spent a semester out there with my dad while my brother stayed with my mom. She fought for him, but lost. My dad sold the house and moved to live with my grandpa.

After my dad got my brother things began to change and got twisted into a sick nightmare for me. My father spent most of his time in a room watching TV. On occasion he would play a computer game with me to spend time. My dad had problems with his job. When he told the family they thought he had lost it, I do remember it, although I didn't think much of it.

I began to take the rap for things my brother did. Countless times I can recall sitting down writing the sentence "I will not steal" 100 times, then 500, and 1000 times. As the problems continued my dad would make me write two and three lined sentences. I remember doing them when I was on Christmas vacation. I thought I should be enjoying my break instead of writing them, but kept telling myself the sooner I finished, the sooner I could enjoy it. I was diagnosed with ADHD that year. During the 3rd and 4th grade I was high strung and couldn't sit still or keep my hands to myself. I lost all my friends and began to get special attention and motivation to help me get through school. No one would talk to me there and I was frequently called names, bullied and harassed. I still would have rather went to school if you asked me. My dad was still punishing me.

When I was 8 we moved. I figured it would be a good change. While we stayed at the hotel it was. Then we moved into a duplex. My dad made me watch cop shows and footage of life in prison and told me that was where I was going to be when I grow up, getting raped by big bubba. Not once did I bad mouth my brother. I thought it was what brothers were supposed to do.

My brother and I didn't get along very well. I always hid things well. He would tell me nonsense stories that scared me. I was afraid of the dark until I got into the foster care system. It was these various things that made me happy to be at school, although I was impartial to how I felt. I thought my home life was normal. After that one particular incident my dad threatened to put me in jail. He brought me down and showed me the police station and told me he was going to leave me there if I didn't find the GPS that was lost. My brother ended up showing me where it was at.

It wasn't until after this happened that my dad began to connect two and two together and sent my brother to live with my grandpa. He told me that things were going to be better for me. We moved and stayed with my grandpa, but it wasn't until my brother pulled a knife on a kid at school that he was sent to my mom. It was either that or jail until he turned 18, according to the judge. While we were there he continued doing things and warned me about a lady from the system coming to ask questions. She did come to our house, but my brother had prepped me and I lied to her. After he left I felt better, but I began to miss him. I began to feel miserable at school and had met my best friend Danny I used to go to his house frequently and spend the night. I enjoyed being there. My problems disappeared and I forgot all that was done to me. He had got me hooked on Linkin Park at the time, which was tremendous at the time because I used music at an outlet. But then he moved away to Virginia. To this day I still have not been able to find him.

When I was 9 my dad took a job out west and I moved with him. School was still hell for me. The kids used to harass me so hard there. I frequently spent a lot of time on the road with my dad because we lived in Phoenix. We moved out to Saint Louis shortly after and I was terrorized every day at school. It was the worst I had ever experienced. I remember the principal announcing on the intercom that the Trade Centers had been hit and the TV was turned on. It made me happy because none of the kids were going to mess with me for the next few days.

My Years in Foster Care

My dad decided to move down with my aunt. It was an ok for a time. I was restricted because of my cousin who was 21 at the time. I was only 9. My dad spent much of his time in his room and I spent my time getting into things because I had no toys to preoccupy my time. Eventually my aunt confined me to the dining room. Shortly after my 10th birthday my aunt let a few people with name tags in the house. I thought it was strange because she never had let anyone in the house that looked like that. I saw her talk with them briefly and then bring them into my dad's room and show them around in there. That was also strange, because she never even opened up the door. An hour after the people left she called for me and told come on, that we were going somewhere. I asked her why my stuff was in a basket in the car and she told me we were going shopping. I didn't think anything more of it. Instead she brought me to an office building. We went straight to a room where I met a lady, later to find out she would be my case worker. My aunt talked with her a bit in private and then my case worker came in and my aunt told me that she was going to be back with the rest of my stuff the next week. She didn't say anything further. My caseworker sent me into a room with toys, where I played until she spoke to me and told me that I was going to stay at a home temporarily. At the time I had no idea what was going on. I was only 10 and was still in my innocence. I still remember it as though it happened only two years ago.

When I was 10 I was brought to a house for the weekend. It was my first placement and surprisingly it was one of the best homes I had been in. I think it was due to the fact that there were only girls staying at the home. I became attached to the place within the short time I stayed there and was deeply hurt when yanked from the home. Of course I didn't know it at the time, but after losing my dad I mentally blocked everyone out and it wasn't until later on in my teenage years that it became a problem. After that I was shipped through at least a dozen placements. Most of them were temporary placements, but I do remember a few of them.

One such home I was pulled out of because they thought I was too annoying. They had a baby. I was quiet there and minded my own business and kept to myself, but somehow they still threw me out. Another was a home on a farm. It went quite well there, although none of the kids seemed to like me. I was just exploring their property and the acres when I was on my way back home when I saw a truck that one of the kids my age was driving coming down towards me. I saw the dog lying in the road and tried to drag it out of the dirt road by its paws. Later on the kid went to my foster mom and lied and told her that he saw me beating on the animal and dragging it around. She made be bunk with the same kid and I was to be thrown out of the home the next day. In the middle of the night though I woke up to barking and apparently coyotes were trying to get into the chicken coop, so the lady had the kid fetch the 22 and go out to shoot at them. I wanted to help but dared not to ask, as I didn't want to get into more trouble. I avoided the lady.

The next day my case worker came and got me and lectured me. She asked me what the hell I was doing, beating on a dog. I was sent to yet another place. I was sent to a home filled with foster kids. I thought everything was fine there, but apparently some of the kids spread some lies about me to the parents and they told my caseworker and I remained there for a week in a room to myself until she found another placement for me. This home had fourteen other foster kids in it.

The other placement I had was a miserable experience, perhaps my worst. I was sent to a home with several kids and I shared a room with three other kids. We all bunked in a room that was 8"x10". I was stuck in the room for a week before I was able to move into a separate room because I told the foster parents that the kids bullied me. I had to wait because a girl was staying in the other room. As soon as she left I stayed with some kid that was 17. He gave me no problems. After he left things got worse at school and home. I was bullied here. They would also always talk about me and my family. I was frequently called a bitch, pussy, and told that I should die. One day the kid there cut a thorn vine and started hitting me with it. He chased me around trying to hit me and the other kids followed with sticks and what not trying to hit me. I was digging a hole and became fed up with it so I picked up the shovel and told the kid" I dare you to try." It frightens me to this day because my exact thought at that moment word for word was I'm going to burry this shovel in his skull." I even visualized what it looked like, the shovel coming down on him and planting firmly in his head, a big gash where it went half way through his skull and sat comfortably, blood leaking out right afterward all over the shovel. I told the counselor about it this past year and he told me I had no reason to be concerned, that it was a completely normal reaction. But what kid in his right mind at 10 years old is intent on killing another kid and would carry through with it? This is worse that than shooting someone, because it's not a matter of pulling a trigger. It's scary, and it was at a time when I didn't have video games. There were no gory games at the time that I could play. I didn't see it on TV all the time. Yet I knew exactly what it would look like and the satisfaction I would gain from killing the kid.

At this place I had locked myself in a room and propped my feet against the filing cabinet and back against the door to keep the kids and adults from bothering me, but the kids went and got a progged my ass and leg with it from underneath the door. The kid snitched on me and the parent thought I was delusional. I told her all about it and said that the boy was the problem. She didn't believe me and so the next day had my caseworker come and get me. It wasn't until right before my 18th birthday that I saw the lady. Nearly 7 and ½ years later at court she apologized. She said she felt really guilty and that right after I left the kid started on some new kid that she took in. I told her that everything had worked out for the best somehow, and I still feel that it did to some extent.

Preteen

This outburst landed me into a rehab facility. Initially when I entered the program I had no clue what was going on. Frequently I would try to work the program and watch my friends. At the time I had considered my family get a DC date and graduate out of the program. I struggled in school there. I couldn't grasp the concepts taught in class, particularly in math with decimals and fractions. I frequently would watch the kids on my unit act out and see two big male staff running down the hall and I would watch the kids get put in holds with their faces planted on the floor with rug burns all over their faces from where the staff had shoved their elbow in the back of their necks. One time I watched a good kid struggle with the staff. Afterward I looked and saw blood smeared all over the cell walls and there were blood droplets in the cell and blood was smeared on some of the hallway walls and room doorways. About a month after the incident staff had begun to hassle me because I wasn't working my treatment their way so I became quite accustomed to that cell, along with the hallway where I was isolated from everyone 24/7. They made me get up and eat alone and sit at a desk and do school work until bed time, then sent me off on my way. The remaining six months was like this. I became angered and started shouting and yelling at the staff, so the doctor drugged me up on Seroquel and Depakote. By the time I left treatment I was 5'2" and 150 pounds and was so drugged up that I constantly drooled all day.

I attempted to work my program there for a while; however, I grew tired of losing friends who graduated from the program. Each and every friend that I have made and watched age out of the facility I took as a death because they were a close friend. It didn't stop there by far. It has grown to consume me and so everyone that I lose as a friend or grow distant from I have taken just the same. I grew very cold and distant. It was there I learned that I had apathy issues. Due to good fortune I was placed with a lady, where I stayed for three months, but it was her parents that truly were a blessing to me. The foster dad loved me as the father I never had. He would always play and goof around. I was embarrassed at first due to his birth defect. I soon realized that it didn't matter. I realized that this man cared about me. I became proud to show everyone I met to him. Kay on the other hand was by all definition a mother. She always looked after me and gave me everything I needed. She never kept me from going out and doing anything, she merely encouraged me to do so. She understood the importance of having a childhood and I now understand why she rarely said no. I love that lady like I loved my mother. At the time I began to struggle with school and began to have problems with friends. This was in 6th grade. All was well at home, but school was an entirely different matter. I struggled keeping friends and making friends after a while. I began to reflect on my past, seeking answers for the pain and problems I had experienced. It was at this point I became severely depressed. I became suicidal, even though I had two people who cared about me. I remember imagining the look on peoples face as they discovered my body. It brought me great satisfaction. I was 12 at the time. Unfortunately I was too stupid to know how to do it. I didn't tie myself up high enough with the belt to strangle myself. Instead I woke up a minute later, realizing that it hadn't worked. My depression eventually passed when I found out a girl had a crush on me. I have rarely spoken of this suicide attempt. I had made a promise to myself that I would never try suicide again. Instead I would live each day with no regrets. Later this grew into my personal credo, to live each day with no regrets and to the best of my ability. I saw no point in killing myself, so I figured I would just ride out life until I die. I now of course understand that few people will care if I die, and even fewer will take notice. It's sad, but it's a full truth.

Some Good Memories

Not all was bad. I have amazing memories of spending time with these foster parents, helping them with chores and venturing on their property. I would go down to the pond during the summer and fish, and even though I never could catch anything I enjoyed it. I ran around in the forest like I never got to as a kid, being a typical kid catching crawdads in the creek and poking sticks at bugs and lizards; however, I began to be defiant to my family as a typical teen and was frequently mouthy. One day that cost me my placement. I offended the foster mom and she slapped me and afterward she reported herself. I recently found out that she and her husband were divorced. I can't help but feel responsible for it. I know that somehow I contributed to the situation. A lot of people would tell me that I didn't, but that's not what I want to hear. I know I screwed up their lives and I must accept the fact and make amends to them and seek forgiveness. What tore me apart was that on the way out my foster dad told me "You will always be welcome here son." During my stay there I began to reconnect with my family for the first time. It was strange. It didn't change how I felt toward my foster parents in general. While I stayed there their son, whom I looked up to as a really close friend, died from a heart attack. He was only 40. It was a shame, as he had really turned his life around. He was a great man and I loved him like family. My grandpa on my mom's side came down to try and adopt me, but unfortunately after he went back to home he found out his cancer had come back. It consumed him within a month and he died. I was fortunate to talk to him, even if he didn't know what was going on. My caseworker would have let me go to the funeral, but they had it before I could even make plans to show up.

Young Teen

After this placement I was sent to another foster home. I began to stop caring, even though the parents were kind. Eventually I began sneaking out of the house at night to venture around. In turn I was tired of being constrained and started feeling dead, so I started stealing, mostly petty stuff. I got caught and wound up in and out of jail for a while. This happened about 6-10 times. I stole a bike, and mostly worthless shit out of the car. Looking back at it I see that I did it for the thrill and excitement and it made me feel free. I didn't feel miserable from being boxed up in this house, trying to earn the ladies respect. I would frequently find ways around the alarm systems they put up so that I could sneak out. One time I broke into the elementary school and into the lunch room and stole the lunch money, which was about $110. Juvie didn't bother me much. I eventually grew accustomed to it. They made us get up every morning at 6:00 and took our mats away so we couldn't sleep. They kept the temp at 60 degrees, so we would sit in our cells until it was our rotation out in our jumpsuits on a cold concrete slab. I at one point was told to stay off the top bunk, but I disobeyed. After that they made me eat blended foods for a week, which is the worst thing you could eat. Jail food doesn't taste good anyway and this was a 30 day bid that I did. The next time I got caught out of the house at night I was sent back and my public defender told the judge that the next time I was caught that I was to go to DYS, right as the judge was about to let me off.

I was shipped off somewhere else for a month until a placement opened. While I was there I learned quick to keep my mouth shut and mind my own business. I was one year short of going to the older side and I heard that it was hell. It was a bunk block. A fight broke out at least once a day. A lot of the kids I came across were gang affiliated; there were from 7-15 on my unit, mostly Blood's. I learned a bit of what it was about and the general knowledge about getting your stripes, wearing your flag all the time, things you can and can't do, insults, and even some of the gang signs-- a lot of them repped PIRU. I gained much respect and was lucky I didn't get out because I know I would have set out in search of trying to join a gang and I would have been another body on the street. While I was there I made a good friend. Initially there was a person we both knew from out of state in Indiana. I came to see him as a brother and treated him as nothing less.

The Worst One Yet

I only spent a month there, but the whole duration was unlike anything I had been through before. I never knew when I was going to be jumped on in the showers or a corner or my cell. I recall one kid who had arrived who was very brain dead from all the crack he had snorted. I received my DC date and was sent off somewhere else. I never could seem to work my treatment there. At the time I had become rebellious. I could not seem to get my act together. I can sure say as soon as I got locked up I took to praying to God really quick. They put us to work, saying it was for community service. They had us out with picks, shovels, and wheel barrels, leveling out hills and digging 6'x4'x8' slop holes to throw brush boulders and leftover food in from the pig pin. They made us scrub at the patios with brooms and a hose to clean them and rake the gravel from the edge of the road to the center on the 4 mile stretch road. For six months I would wake up go to school, finish school and then work till dusk with the rest of the kids. On Sunday we were fortunate to take the day off to watch movies and relax for the day. After dusk we would have free time in the chow hall. During the summer we worked from morning to night. I made several enemies there, but I never got into a fight. I was fortunate. Despite the fact I was frequently harassed there. I was told I was fortunate to go there, that there were worse facilities. I had spoken to a guy named there who was in charge of the small engines shop. I had arranged with him that if I worked my treatment he would teach me the trade. I began to get my act together. I was going to get my GED, but then two kids I knew were plotting to go AWAL and I wanted to go with them. I wanted to go to another state with my good friend. I decided to skip out on it because a discharge date that had popped up. We had planned it for the 4th of July and I left shortly after. Three boys got away and the head man of the facility called us all together and dared anyone else to try to escape. He informed us that they escaped, stole a car and made it out of state before the car ran out of gas. One boy ran to his family's place, one was picked up on the road, and the other one was caught running. All of them were sent back to DYS and were going to be held until they turned 21 and were going to be charged as adults for grand theft auto and some other charges. I give them props still after all of it because with all the rednecks out there they could have been shot on sight and disappeared. I was transferred over to another facility.

(Age 15)

I stayed in the group home and was evaluated for about three weeks. The girls got caught sneaking around outside to the boy's room one night. Three girls and two guys, including me had plans that night. Shortly after I got into a fight with a kid and I was transferred to the main facility. At first it was ok. I tried to work the program, but I didn't get along very well with the staff there. I eventually gave up trying to work my treatment because of this. I would occasionally just get pissed and leave, going out into the hall. I spent a lot of my time in the hallway on the cold tile floor. At one point a staff member had pissed me off so much that I walked into my room and started hitting the wall. I messed up my fist pretty bad and had to go to the hospital. I almost broke my hand. Most of the staff was 6' to 6'8" tall. I met a kid there who was from New Jersey. He was a really cool kid and we became pretty good friends. I remember him grabbing the cereal and honey buns off the cart while the kitchen was being remodeled and we shared it. I also met R. there. You never knew what to expect there. One of the kids used to piss on the heater vents in the bathroom. Some of the staff there were cool. While I was there I got in trouble multiple times for writing one of the girls. They would post our letters up. I can recall reaching a point where I thought I was never going to get out of there. While I was in school I pictured myself living out on the streets. I couldn't see myself graduating. I was at a 7th grade level and still struggled in class. I honestly thought I was never going to make it out and that my future was going to be out on the street. I DCed out of the program to a religious program. It was a beautiful place, but I couldn't grasp why they made us do certain things, like only listen to religious music, and wear certain clothing. It was very strict. I became good friends with three of the staff there. I really respected and looked up to one of the men. We were free to do as we pleased during the summer and they held counseling sessions. I had a deep respect for the man who ran the facility. He had discussed how he had reformed his life from a hard drug addiction and turned his life around. I met up with a kid I knew from therapy sessions at the therapeutic home I stayed at previously. I met a kid there who became a good friend of mine. We disputed a lot between the Cowboys and the Colts. That was the year they went to the bowl. Eventually my mouth got the best of me. I was having a conversation with the man I respected so much about how I felt and about all the anger and resentments that had built up in me from being in the system. A girl overheard and apparently it scared her shitless; she thought I was a danger and reported me and so I was kicked out of the program after six months.

Once more I was shipped off to another facility. This place was laid back, but I became angry with the therapist there and gave up on my program for a while. Shortly after I tried to work it again, but failed--- same story as the one in Little Rock. I was obstinate and refused to give into the drama they forced on us. A teacher there began to work with me and I had begun to excel in school. Everything else started to fall in line. It was always interesting because there was always a big incident once a week. There was a kid with a blood disease and whenever he was put in a hold he bled badly. I loved to watch him spit up blood straight into the staff's face, just because of the screwed up things they did. There was an occasional suicide watch.

(Age 16-18)

I became lucky one day in December and got out on the 17th and went to another home. In my honest opinion it was one of the best placements I had ever been in. The foster mother had brought me in her house. And because I was musically talented she spoke to the principal at the high school and got me in a music program, which was fortunate; otherwise I would have never made it through the 2 ½ years I was there. I attended another high school and was one of only ten white kids in the school. Most of the schools were violent. I stayed and shared a room with another kid. He and I got into several fights because he used to steal and break my stuff. I almost choked the kid out on the stairs and couch before her son; a boy came and pulled me off him. I really wanted to kill the kid and if I had a chance I was going to, so I was waiting for the chance to smash his face in, but he was removed from the home. While I was there I struggled to keep up in school. It was named in the top five magnet schools in the United States. Somehow I pulled through and managed to pass my sophomore and junior year. I met several friends, but never got to go out. I spent much of my time at home playing video games as a means to make time pass till I aged out. I really got into music at that time. I got into NJROTC there. I honestly think what got me through it was my three friends. They became family to me. I relied on them for almost everything.

One of the kids that stayed there had aged out of the system, but still stayed there. He and I had gone out mudding one night. We cut it close because the guy had come back and chased us in his truck. We almost rolled the truck down a hill. The guy cornered us and pulled a gun and started shooting at us. We hulled ass down the road and I hopped out and swung the gate open, and we pealed out, ripping the driver's side mirror. I'm still amazed we got out of it in one piece. While I was there I worked for a guy who wound up cheating me out of a few thousand dollars. I started sneaking off and visiting my family. I devised a plan shortly before I aged out. I moved all my stuff out of the house. I left the next day, on my birthday. The night before several people, including my foster mom, tried to convince me not to do it. I had already made up my mind though. I was either moving out on my own or go live with my family. I was tired of the limits the system placed on me. They were going to force me into college and weren't going to let me get my driver's license or a car, so I dipped.

My Years after Care

After I dipped out of the placement I stayed with my grandparents. I was there for about two weeks before I moved up to where my family lived. I flew to get there. At first everything was very busy and close. It hadn't felt like I left. I started up in school, expecting a new start. School there was a new experience. I wasn't left hung out to dry and expected to prove myself. I had fit in well here. My dad had expected me to study, but school had never really sat well with me. I was promised a better school than the one before, which had turned out to be all false. I was given much freedom at first. I got to go out and socialize for the very first time. I struggled through school, with grades just below passing. I managed to pull through just to graduate, due to all of my teachers and the people at school looking out for me. I am still grateful for it.

Things at home, however, had become slowly difficult. At first my dad would complain here and there, telling me that I needed to study, or telling me to go study, but instead I would play a game or write, anything else rather than do school work. As time went on I began to become secluded, annoyed and tired from all of the complaining and arguments. At first I would hide in my room, only to hear about it later, which I would have rather done than hear about it for an hour. It almost seemed endless. He would come home from work and start complaining about dishes, or not eating food, or about cleaning. It was always something. This is the last thing I had expected from moving up to my family.

Eventually I told him why I did some of the things I did. He started to lose trust in me. I would constantly borrow things, and they would disappear to my room and get lost in the clutter I lived in. I began to tell false truths to avoid conflict with him. I would use the spare change to buy gas, just to cover for places me or my brother had gone. It got to a point where I would avoid him and tell him only what he needed to know. Likewise, if I did tell him, I would be forced to sit and listen to him rant for an hour or two, so I would frequently zone out in the middle, and become burnt out and apathetic at the rants. The only thing that had kept me in the room was the threat of kicking me out. With lack of real friends in a secluded, stuck up state, I was liable to find myself out on the street. In the meantime I was thinking of joining the army and was asked to try out college by my brother. I wound up attending for a year, just getting by, but I didn't care enough, nor did I have the patience to bear through it. I wound up dropping out, but I screwed up when I forgot to withdraw from my second semester the second year. Luckily my financial aid went through and paid for it. I had taken up smoking, so the college fines were overwhelming and I didn't have the money to pay it off and start back at school.

(Age 19)

My brother and I got along some days and other days we fought. At the time I began to mess with heroin. There was one day with my brother that I won't forget. I didn't realize until months later that I could have lost him that day. I still feel like a worthless piece of shit for it. He may have forgiven me, but I don't think I will ever forgive myself for it. If only my dad had known the full extent of what had went on. My brother eventually got stuck in a situation with the courts where he had to turn his life around, and he completely has now. I'm not grateful enough for it.

(Age 20)

Later on I started working, with no school. My dad had agreed to let me work. He and I had got into an argument and I walked out on him. I was on the street for about a week. My ex had let me stay the night at her place, until her mom caught me one morning. Somehow my brother had talked my dad into letting me come back, since I had gotten two jobs that week, one of which one I still work at. I had also gotten into an argument once again after that and walked out yet again about five months later. I lied to my brother, telling him that I was staying with some woman, just so he wouldn't try to talk my dad into letting me come back. I feared going to that place and still do to this day. It brings back too many familiar feelings. While I was on the street a friend, let me stay at his place and I am extremely grateful for this, to both him and his dad. I recently got in trouble with the cops for shoplifting and having master keys to my apartment complex. I wound up staying in NJ much longer than I intended. I am now in debt to my dad for bailing me out of jail and paying for a lawyer. I have my last upcoming court date in a week. My dad has become more understanding in the time I have been away and we have stopped arguing so much. I can only hope that he realized that it drives me away.

(Age 20-21) I moved out for much of my own personal reasons. I couldn't allow myself to be held back anymore, nor could I bear to argue with my family. I have been through enough problems without adding to them.

I also want to note that I have been frequently sexually abused. I do not wish to speak of it further than that.

Plans and Goals for my Future

Though I moved out I still am not by far done. I had begun speaking to Carol Lucas about two months ago. She so generously asked me to share my story in her book. Within a month I plan to move to Little Rock, Arkansas and shortly after join the army and tour overseas for a year. Afterward I plan to come back and finish school. I want to continue my service in ROTC and major in Music Education and Music Composition. I plan to write real music as such from the Romantic Era. I then would like to go back and major in Quantum Physics. I hope to teach music at the wonderful high school, Parkview, in Little Rock, and wish to live there as well. I also intend to expand and contribute to the FACT support group. I want to start a chapter out in Little Rock. I think the most important thing is becoming a teacher. I would rather educate kids in music and give them a skill and talent that will keep them off the street, and help them make it through any problems they may face, during which I can teach them a dying art. Studio music is something anyone with a good high school education can do, and sometimes that isn't needed. Specifically I find my calling is to help kids who have been through the system and provide advice on how to make it through current situations, and how to amend and move from the past, and start living for themselves. If I can do this, rather than fixing a broken system, I can reduce the number of kids that continue to suffer. I would be giving not just one person a dream, but many.

Broken Notes

As my decision to write my story, I wanted to try and fill in as much as I could to serve whatever purpose to help, and in doing so I had to sift through some of the papers I had kept all these years and the paperwork in my file. I would have submitted it in full, in original form, but seeing how big my file is, most of it would be too long.

At one of the facilities, I had apparently written a number of things. In one instance I was writing to vent my frustration. I was 14 at the time. Here's a fragment of what I wrote: "No more, I'm through, I'm done. I'm going to let it fester and suffocate. I'm through with this bullshit. No more. I've tried so hard, but all I've been getting is shit. Mr. F. is always bitching at me, pressuring me into religion and all. I'm tired of all this shit and the way he treats me. I'm going Goth. I'm sick of this shit, not me, Mr. F., dudes a bitch. Fuck this shit. I'm through with it, I'm done. I've tried and never get far and where the fuck is god anyway. I'm going Goth, maybe satanic and do drugs, maybe fuck up my life. Hay why not? Some staff already has in this bitch. I have no future. No. And I'm through and I'm ready to start clowning and acting out and doing what the fuck I want."

I had also made a list while here. On one I noted to be patient with the meds they had me on. I had wanted to get off. I was on three meds, two of which I didn't need when entering (Strattera-ADHD, Symbax-mood, and Cogentin had side effects and I took all of them once a day) and upon leaving I was on six meds (Clonidine 3 times a day- ADHD, Prozac once a day-depression, Seroquel 200mg in the morning for psychosis and 400mg at night, Bentriopine 2x a day for side effects, and Topamax 2x a day for migraine prevention). Of all of them the only one I needed was the ADHD meds. I frequently asked to be taken off the meds, but Dr. H. refused. Later, after I left the last facility, the final doctor I had seen said that he saw no need for me to be on any of the medications. I actually had him write a recommendation for me to join the service at this facility, as though the seven months I was locked up hadn't been enough. They continued to press and made my incident with the theft charges a part of my treatment, and prescribed some of the medications for it. They had made an issue of me helping people and told me that if I kept doing it I would not be allowed to discharge from the facility. Often they wrote that I had been at the bottom of the point system due to arguing with staff. Frequently they expected you to talk in therapy sessions and when you did they wrote that you were defiant if they didn't hear what they wanted. I refused to talk and they still wrote up a bad report. They wrote of me writing and reading as stress relieving techniques, but they were more of a means to pass time and a way to help me get out of and through the drama. Throughout the whole six months the staff frequently did a lot of word play; they would twist your words around on you in reports. One such one they wrote that I had said "I ain't doing shit! I don't have to because I'm going to court and the judge is going to get me the fuck out of here!" I remember that I had told that staff that when I went to court, I was going to tell the judge what was going on and beg him not to send me back, and instead place me somewhere else.

Also in my treatment plan was the fact that I had carved a swastika in my hand. There is a very faint scar now. When I was 14, being young and dumb, I tried to impress some skin head. He was a good kid, despite his views. I carved it and tried to scar it over with ice and salt. I wound up getting caught and was punished. I can't say enough how happy I was when I left this place.

In one of my documents (age 10), there was a note of neglect and a mention of PTSD. They claimed that I was extremely violent and got into fights and it said that I denied being suicidal. One of the teachers had requested that I be removed off of the Abilify 30mg and Depakote 500mg. There was a note of the mental illness that the state clamed my father having, may have been misdiagnosed.

The most I have on what my aunt had wrote was the fact that my dad did something bad, which I cannot speak of.

It bothers me a little to find a whole packet specifically written to cater and comfort the foster parent, but there was none for how to handle and raise the foster kids. It kind of makes me wonder what they honestly teach the parents when they send them to the classes. What's more irritating are the idiots in the system. I don't understand where they're getting their degrees. Half the shit they do and ignore is probably illegal.

I did come across several grievances that I had written about some of the staff. On most of them I had signatures from about 10-15 kids, so not all was ill spent. I do have some certificates from doing well in school from one of the facilities. One woman there was one of the people that I all too well forgot had helped me so much more than I know. I have the feeling that she is part of the reason I was discharged into my last foster home.

During my time while locked up I thought pretty much as though I was locked up. I spent a lot of time writing poems, something I'm terrible at, letters, and I kept a journal of my dreams. I wrote a lot of letters to girls, but hung on to all of them, seeing how that could throw back my discharge date. A majority of them were addressed about what was going on, my plans, and what I was to do when I saw them, addressed "To Baby Girl" "From your Baby Boy." I did write a letter to my mom and brother, but I never did send it. I wrote to my mom. I now know I didn't know what I was talking about. To my brother I just briefly explained what was going on while I was at one facility. I did keep a journal at a point in time. I still have it. Most of it reflected around some girl. I can't believe how over protective I actually was back then. Most of the journal was written in 2007. I do find it a little much to share, just as some of the next one. This one was recent and was mostly centered on my last ex, which completely ended when she had decided to use. Now I refrain from any contact from her. I wrote on multiple occasions of how she had hurt me. One such one I had wrote about how she brought back old feelings for me and I actually had felt suicidal. I wrote about how I wanted to make a noose and tie it around the balcony, and jump over and watch my body sway in the wind. I also had written about how I wanted to shove a big kitchen knife into my heart with my own hands. I could honestly say that this was the only person I had ever fallen in love with. This was someone who I had walked to see, sometimes on a daily basis. It was about a three mile walk there and I had done this in rain, snow, and fog in the middle of the night during January. It was about this time that I had a dream that I could actually call a nightmare. I will go ahead and share it to give an idea of the kind of dreams I have.

I wrote, "I had the most god awful nightmare. Thank God it was only a dream. I was with a good friend and we went to some place to hang out. He had to run an errand and we stopped in a place I had something to do, so I went to take care of it. I saw my ex there. She and I were going to hang out. I came back and was thrown in a cell block, where I saw her happy. Then I knew something wasn't right. We were locked in, so my roomie and I broke out somehow. We ran to his place to get something so we could come back and get everyone else. I had been looking for my ex-girlfriend before that, but couldn't find her. We came back and got someone released. Come to find out, the place was a cryogenic place. They murdered people. I came in there to find that out, but found a friend's head. I couldn't see if her head was in a plastic container, so I ran out and came back to double check. I ran back out and a dude was chasing us. I snapped a doctor's neck and ran. I was trying to get my shit. I did, and then I started looking for evidence. I found my friend's phones, which had finger prints, and a bag with stuff that had recorded the events. I grabbed the stuff and came back out, only to find two guards who chased us. My friend was caught. I struggled to snap one of the guy's necks. I couldn't, but I stabbed the other guy to death and started to leave. I left and got the shit out. I ran back in looking for more, and looking for my ex-girlfriend's body. Two of the doctors started to chase me. I got out and broke a glass door on the way out. I got locked out. I broke back in through more glass. I snuck around and found something, then started arguing with the doctors. I found out they were both my mom and dad. I remember I was going to go to the FBI to make sure nothing like this would ever happen again. They settled down. I was deranged, depressed, and pissed. I had lost her and told them that they couldn't do shit to me. I previously saw the doctor's cell phone that I stole from him. I asked to see her belongings, only to find out that she was murdered. I grabbed her belongings. I was crying and depressed, so in exchange to get my mind off of confronting the authorities, they offered to tell me how she died to ease my mind. I was completely deranged at this point. I remember I was coming to terms with my new reality, and I was not happy about that. I had lost my one love. Then I woke up. Thank God it was only a dream. I was about to murder all the doctors over her, then kill myself over the loss of her. Thank God she is still here." Other than that I had a few things I had written---ideas for science and hypothesis. Hopefully one day I can share them only as the one who came up with the ideas. I wrote some music as well. In addition I have my awards from my one program I was in.

Thoughts and Feelings

Both my dad and brother are wonderful people I never really clarified much throughout my story, so don't let it deceive you. My brother, after cleaning up his act, has been the best I could ask for. The most important of it, I personally feel, is that he has been most understanding. He doesn't agree with my decision to move or join the military, because I have something good where I'm at, but he none the less has minded and respected my decision; in fact, he has argued my point to my dad. My father too has taken care of me and he let me drive his car even after I have wrecked it. He bailed me out of jail and got me a lawyer. He is paying for me to go to NYC and to the shore, even though he hasn't the money to do either. My dad, even when I was a child, was still doing right by me. It may appear the contrary, but he did the best he could do and only what any other loving father would do in his situation. There was nothing more that he could do, and he neither had the knowledge or experience at the time to handle the situation. I don't hold my mother responsible, either, for any misfortunes that I have had. It was just the same for her. I later found out that she had fought tooth and nail with my case worker just to gain the ability to speak to me. In the end she never was able to reach me until after a long period of me asking, and my caseworker presenting it to the judge. Often times we forget what it means to be young. We live through the eyes of our parents and can do no wrong. Kids really are the most precious thing in the universe and there isn't a thing that will ever match them. So kids can't be held to expectations or restrictions, nor can they be expected to understand everything. Often times you would have to go through strenuous lengths just to see them, to understand by merely explaining the reasons. It's something you can't force on the kid; they have to understand on their own. If they don't, then it's not their fault, nor only the parents. It is the community that they interact with as a whole. For that matter, there are a lot of people who would blame people for their actions or accuse one of parenting the wrong way, so typically we forget what it's like to be constrained with no help, something that they understand that we may not. As I said, everyone does things to the best of their abilities, no matter if you're a criminal or an upstanding citizen. That's not to say people can't change, but the kind of change for those kinds of people with unstable foundations from childhood take the kind of change that an addict faces or anyone who you ever have met that undergoes rehabilitation. The mind is complex and can't be understood so clearly. It only stands to reason. I project that me getting over what happened to me may take nearly half my lifetime, and that's even with a FACT support group to back it. It's because of these kinds of things that we have seen that we will never quite get over it, something that wakes us up in the middle of the night to a life and death nightmare, night after night for months. I fear that I block mine out. The ones that I have had are deranged or completely sick and twisted, consisting of murder and butchered limbs. All of the dreams are some sort of taboo and that's only to start. I am always stuck in some sort of high tension high stress situation, sometimes in a high stress environment, and there's always the lingering thought that something really isn't right, that something bad has to happen. Even so, you would never know this if you knew me. None of my friends could believe the extent of my life. Instead, the typical responses I get are "Oh, or Wow," and occasionally I get an understanding person to an extent, where I'm told I'm smart, or been through a lot, or even that I'm lucky, but the truth is, I'm lucky to even be alive. I'm privileged to be going strong still, blessed to still have dreams and inspirations, to be so kind, and try so hard. I'm only the one out of two hundred or so who make it. I never will be able to experience the torments that the other kids have been through.

Kids are the eyes watching, yet unable to speak because they don't know how to communicate on an adult's level. It seems more and more that kids are treated unjustly, and there has always been that discrimination, but lately it appears to be the new thing. We need more advocates for kids, more people to speak up for them, and people to hear kids out. People base how they raise their kids off of balance of structure, and freedom, and try to promote peaceful solutions, but that still isn't enough. It takes communication, patience, and respect. All of these are a two way street. You can't expect and demand respect, nor can they. It's both a give and take, but you give more than you would anyone else to see them grow right. If you invest this in them, then you are less likely to have problems.

It is obvious that I have mixed feeling about the system and everything as a whole; however, I do have very strong opinions about some things. I do not agree at all with the system. It is broken and widely covered up. Many people think it is a great thing, but it for the most part has been misconstrued. Despite the fact, it isn't just the system that is broke; it is society as a whole. We make things illegal, only to make kids want something more that they can't have. We idealize ourselves and call ourselves authority, yet we have much to learn. We constantly look down on kids, thinking that they either know nothing or are confused about what their talking about. Often I have been looked at this way, but I guarantee that I have been through more than most people will experience in their life.

Society has a problem with raising kids. They do this often for convenience or because children are cute, for whatever reason it shouldn't be. Raising kids should be put off until an individual is responsible and patient enough to handle a kid. I see many parents either neglecting their kids or yelling at their kids, then wondering why they turn out the way they do or do the things they do. We're only breeding a worse society. Someone has to listen to these kids. Single parenting just doesn't cut it, either. Many frown on addicts, homeless, criminals, and people with psychological disorders. Of these I assure you that a majority of them are former foster children or kids who have come from broken homes. Something has to be done and someone has to speak up to address this problem. The government isn't going to fix anything. It fixed my life just fine. I also like the fact that we often miss interpret free will. Some may have the luxury, but for the criminals and everyone else, it's at the mercy of what you learned growing up. Some people are just doing the best they know how to do at each time a problem happens, just as I have done. You really never get over something like this. It takes at least a good 20-30 years before you can begin to fully fix and cope with the issues.

A lot of people tend to think that age is what makes you an adult; others believe that it's your actions and responsibilities you handle. Honestly, I don't think either is quite it. Age is just a number. I've come across kids that act like adults. What makes an adult is also the way they handle other people. Are they open minded? Do they listen, or give willingly to a stranger they know nothing about? How do they take care of the people they know? How do they take care of their family? It isn't something that can simply be measured and all people have different expectations. Responsibility does have to do with it; however, I think it has more to do with social skills and how you care for others. I have come across people older than me of all ages, most of which don't act mature. They don't act like adults. Some of it I can tell just by the way their kids behaves or the things they say. Then I have also seen kids 14 and younger trying to bring money home for their family. They understand the concept of money and they are accepting. They treat you like family, something most people wouldn't do to someone even who is a friend.

I chose to write my story to speak on behalf of those who couldn't. There are millions of kids who don't even get the chance for college or a future, and those who do like me don't know what to do with it when we get there. I consider myself lucky, but I know my life is simple compared to the others who can't speak for themselves. Too many find themselves homeless, scrubbing the bins for food, incarcerated, on drugs, in gangs, or in body bags. I finally have found my purpose and realize that I have become way too content on being free from my torment. I realize that I shouldn't be alive right now, that I shouldn't still be here where I am. I should have been one of the ones who didn't make it so many times. It truly is a blessing that I have made it this far and I will continue to treat it as such. The only thing I can ask is that others speak up and make a difference for the ones who can't. Life is too short to waste and the innocent youth is all we have left to treasure in this world. What they say is true; life is sacred and the mind is a terrible thing to waste.

I wanted to clarify a point. Most people look at social work as something wonderful and it is; however, your efforts are better spent elsewhere helping others out. Caseworkers are constantly overworked and underpaid. My caseworker had sixty kids and I believe that is about the average caseload. A kid's life shouldn't be handled under these circumstances. Often time the caseworkers take shortcuts in doing things, like investigating what really goes on. Caseworkers also have a tendency to say things that may later come to harm a kid, or make rash decisions, such as placements that impact the kid just the same as the previous placement.

I had hoped to pull up the report that my case worker had typed up. It was sick to see words twisted so, and I had hoped to share it to help give people an understanding. I do plan to start a chapter of FACT in the near future. I don't expect anyone to really ever understand; it's something you have to just live. Most of this was not just meant for the general population; it's for the kids who are struggling through this right now. Hang in there. There is hope.

Two stories I recommend are *Go Ask Alice* and *A Child Called It*.

I give my thanks to my family. I love you guys. My friends, I love you too. You guys are my family. Also, I give thanks to all who were named in my story and all those unnamed who helped me get where I am. I wouldn't be here without you. Thank you, Carol, for giving me the opportunity to share and giving me a chance to do something wonderful. If anyone has any questions or comments, feel free to email me. Danny, I know your still out there somewhere. If you ever stumble across this, then hit me up. behindcurtains21@yahoo.com

Emmitt Sorrell

A Rebellious Boy

I was born into a large, African-America family, the second born out of seven children, six boys and one girl. My mother and father separated because my mom was interested in another man. She also had a gambling addiction, one that she was very good at and prospered quite well from. I had a very large, extended family and neighborhood families who helped me and my siblings at times, including an aunt (my dad's sister), who decided to turn our family into Child and Family Services; why, I don't know. My dad was so angry at her for breaking our family up that he jumped her and chastised her.

I was 9 years old when I was taken away from my parents and placed in foster care and 17 years old when I left my eighth and final placement. The first place I went, along with all of my siblings, was a children's home. We weren't there very long, only a few months, thank goodness. They weren't nice to me there. They were very prejudiced toward us and we were forbidden to mix with the white children; I even got beat up real bad once for talking with a white girl. I never understood why I should have gotten in trouble for that; I was just a kid being nice to another kid. My mom and dad visited us a few times while we were there, but there wasn't any mention of them getting us back.

From this children's home, the seven of us went into two separate foster homes, four into one and three into another. I went to live in a good foster home, and although they were very nice foster parents, I became quite rebellious, always running off anytime I pleased, to see my family, and they eventually got tired of me, and so I ended up in another foster home that was right down the street from them.

The Bymun's were also very good foster parents, and African-American like the Chapel's, and they welcomed me into their home; in fact, since they were unable to have any of their own children, I could have been the very best thing that ever happened to them, but again, I became rebellious and they couldn't handle me, so I left this foster home also, after about one year. From here I went to live with the Coley's, another very nice foster home, but it was the same old scenario, with me being rebellious.

I really just wanted to be with my family and was determined to see them, no matter what. I would walk or take the bus and go visit my mom, grandma, dad, and cousins, anytime I wanted to. I'm not sure how long I was there at the Coley's, but I think it was only for a few months, and then I went into a mental institution. I believe I was put there because there was nowhere else for me to go. There were black attendants there, who were real nice to me, but I was mixed in with mentally ill adults, not children. I was the youngest one there. I remember doing leather work in their craft shop.

I was only there for a few months also, then I went to another mental institution, but there was a boy's cottage there, so it was better than the one in Alton. It was mixed (black and white), but I got treated well there. I was only there for a short time also, a few months, and then in January, 1960, I went into a children's home. I wasn't as well received as the white children; they didn't roll out the red carpet for me. They were very prejudiced toward me there. I was the first African-American boy in that cottage there and the cottage father told me, "This was built for our (white) kids." He came right out and said he didn't want any black boys there. His demeanor was very poor and his treatment of me was even worse. I was stuck doing all their hard, dirty jobs, such as shoveling snow. According to another cottage boy, one time when I was late coming back to the cottage for supper, I was given a dinner out of the garbage. I didn't deserve the treatment I got there. They should have been looking out for me there and instead I was treated badly and made to feel inferior to the other boys. I only spent nine months there, but it was nine months too long.

Going through the foster care system, I always felt like I was just a number on a piece of paper, not a real human being, but the two children's homes were the worst places because they were so prejudiced toward me; at least in all the foster homes I had African-American foster parents who welcomed me and were very nice to me.

I left the children's home in September, 1960 and went into my final placement, another real nice foster home. They really made me feel like I was part of their family and since I was 17 years old by then, I was allowed the freedom to come and go as I wanted. I was told I could go home and live with my dad if I chose to, which I did for a short time, but he was remarried with more children and I wasn't interested in being a babysitter like he expected me to be, so it didn't work out and I left there. By age 18 I was on my own.

My parents are both gone now and I don't resent them for what happened, even though I wish it wouldn't have happened. If I was going to resent anybody, it would be my aunt, as I felt she had no business meddling with my family and breaking us up the way she did, but regardless, I still love her and she never even found out I knew she did it. I wish things could have been different and I know my experience influenced my decision not to ever be married; even though I have eleven children from seven different women, but I was not willing to risk going through what my family did.

Greg Crosby

Stranger in a Strange Land

Hello, my fellow foster kin. I probably wouldn't share my story with just anyone, but I feel comfortable with you all because I know you understand where I'm coming from. I don't take any great pleasure in saying that I'm another "refuse" of society, but it's true. Foster children are damaged goods, the outcasts of society, and feel stigmatized as such. We come from broken, destroyed families, and although I realize that broken, dysfunctional families are a by-product and symptom of a sick world, it still doesn't make me feel any better about my own situation; it brings me no great comfort, because when I look at the big picture, I still wonder what it could have been like, not just what it is.

What it is, in reality, is a tragedy and it's a very hard thing to recover from. You take this stuff to your grave. Gravestones often say "Rest in Peace," but I want to "Live in Peace." Unfortunately, with the issues and problems in my life today, living in peace hasn't been easy. As I look around at my 1 ½ acres of land, where my burned up house used to stand, I feel like I'm having labor pains, trying to birth a new situation, which is bringing back memories from my childhood. I was in labor pains as a child, when I was forced to leave one situation and birth another one. When you suffer loss as a child, later losses in life seem more amplified. I not only lost my home, but I am also grieving the loss of my beloved pets, three cats and one dog, my companions who loved me unconditionally, which is something you can't get from any people, not even your own parents.

I'm sure my parents loved us as much as they knew how, but I came from a very dysfunctional home, what little I remember of it, and as a result, my family fell apart. I don't have a lot of memories from my young years, but I know for sure about one incident when I got burned by a radiator, as I still bear the scars. My father was a Vermont farmer, trying to provide for a family of eight (I'm the 6th out of seven children). He was also a womanizing alcoholic. My mother was a devout Catholic, who ended up having a nervous breakdown, no doubt from all the stress and strain. We were very poor and my father couldn't care for us properly, so when I was about 4 years old, I was put in an orphanage, along with my siblings. I'm not sure how long I was there, but my dad ended up coming to the orphanage and picking all but the youngest one up and taking us out of state, where he could pursue a living, along with his new wife he'd snaked, who just happened to be the nurse who took care of my mom in the hospital when she had a nervous breakdown.

My mom ended up having another nervous breakdown when she lost her six children, whose whereabouts she was in the dark about. Imagine what it would be like to wake up one day and finding out your children are missing, how devastating it must have felt to her. My dad left the baby with my mom, so she raised him, but in the meantime, he'd had another child with his new wife, who was brought to Illinois along with the rest of us. My dad and step-mom were only together for about two years before things fell apart. They were both alcoholic, and it was a fight for survival in that home. My step-mom was not a nice woman; she was very abusive. My step-sister got treated well, while my siblings and I were treated as an imposition to her. My sisters had to fix breakfast for my dad, step-mom, and her daughter, while the rest of us were forced outside, then when they were finished eating, we were allowed back in. We would be so hungry that we'd be scurrying around the kitchen trying to find any morsel left over that we could, which was usually just the bacon grease, but if we got lucky there might be some bread that we could dip in the bacon grease. I can remember being so hungry that I would claw at the ground, trying to get some grass to eat. I also remember sneaking around one time and eating some raw bacon, which later gave me worms. One time, when I got in trouble for eating some pecan pies, my step-mom punished me by dragging me to the corner of an animal bin in the barn, where she proceeded to force hot peppers in my mouth and smear them all over my face; I thought I was bleeding when I seen all the red juice coming out of my mouth. My dad was gone most of the time working, so he was largely unaware of what was happening and how abusive and neglectful she was, but when he did sometimes discover how bad her behavior was toward us, he would beat her. I don't have a lot of memories of him, but I do recall him bouncing me around on his knee and tickling me when I was young, so I do believe he loved me, it's just that he was caught up in his own world of alcoholism and trying to survive his marriage to her.

We ended up living in a trailer next to a farm house and it was at this time that my dad just took off and abandoned us, never to be seen again. I have no idea what happened to him, but I heard that he died, probably from alcoholism. God must have been watching over our family because luckily, there was a foster mother living in the farmhouse and she took me and my siblings in for four years. She may have saved my life, as by the time I got to this foster farm house, I looked like an Ethiopian child because I was so malnourished. Unfortunately, the social worker involved with her other foster kids found out we were living there and had to take us out of the home because there was a limit to the number of foster kids allowed in one home, and this foster mom was way over the limit. This woman was a very nurturing woman and was very sensitive to human needs---a real angel. She never even received any money from the state for us; she just took us in from the kindness of her heart. There should be more foster parents like her. She ended up fostering thirty-five children throughout her life. I'm 54 years old now and still need nurturing, and am fortunate to at least have her in my life still. (She just turned 100).

I was 8 years old (1966) when the state got involved and my five siblings and I became wards of the state (dependents upon the state). This is when I was placed in ISSCS (Illinois Soldiers and Sailors Children School) and I remained there until the age of 17. It was a good place to grow up in, considering my circumstances. I was given all the necessities---food, clothing, shelter, education, and all the playmates a child could want. I had no real complaints about the place, but do you think I'd rather have a loving mother and father, and siblings, a regular family? You bet! I wish

I could have had a normal family, but I didn't; there was separation and pain in my family instead, even though I'm at peace with them now. My oldest brother was so debilitated by the whole situation that he had to be placed in a mental institution, which is where he remains today.

Will we ever get over our childhoods? I doubt it, at least not completely. Some wounds are so deep that you can't have complete closure; you just learn to live with the wound. The loss of my mother was one of those wounds; it was a wound of the vacuum of missing her. She just couldn't quite repair the damage that had been done. I had started writing her when I was about 10 years old. My mom and her sister hired a lawyer to help find us, so she knew of our whereabouts by this time, but I only sporadically wrote her. You need affinity for relationships, and time had pulled me and my mom away from each other. She periodically contacted me at ISSCS, but she was too poor to visit us, as she was in Vermont and we were in Illinois. When I was 36 years old I went to Vermont to visit her and I remember reading a letter to her that my older brother had written to me, sharing things about our past, and in the middle of reading the letter I had a "catharsis," and started crying uncontrollably like a baby. My mom made amends to me, in so far as she admitted that our family was too dysfunctional to provide the love, empathy, and compassion I needed.

I still need mothering and it seems like I keep on trying to prove myself to a parent that doesn't exist. The loneliness comes upon you and even though you don't want to be lonely, you're always waiting to be abandoned. People can look at you and not see your emotional pain. I have been severely depressed, trying to pull myself up out of poverty, and get on with my life ever since I lost my home, and I have sometimes turned to alcohol and cigarettes as a way to self-medicate and ease the emotional pain. I know it's wrong to escape in the bottle, but my emotional pain won't leave me alone. God gives me a certain amount of grace to deal with my emotional pain and He has continually come to my rescue, but I have been so depressed, that if I had a bottle of anti-depressants ten feet away from me, I couldn't or wouldn't walk over to get them. I have feelings about death, but it takes more courage to die than to live.

I guess you could say I have been educated by life, which isn't a bad thing; in fact, it can be a good thing, but sometimes it seems so unfair. I know one thing---I have been humbled in my life. I am struggling with poverty today, which is a big part of my depression. I have been accused of being a part-time philosopher, and as a result, it seems to me that "life" is a series of problem-solving events, and as soon as you get over one problem, you have to solve another one. I realize we all have misfortune and suffering is universal, but foster kids get way more than their share. I will persevere in spite of my misfortune though, and have faith in God, because I know that is where my real hope lies, and even though I feel like a stranger in a strange land, I am no stranger to God.

As Emerson wrote, "What is important is not what lies behind us, and not even what lies in front of us, but what lies within us." If only we foster kids didn't compare ourselves to others in the world, and know that what lies within us is just as good as what lies within others, we wouldn't feel so much like the "refuges" of society, because in God's eyes, we truly aren't. I want to share my short poem with you:

But Do You Know Why

Why? Why sometimes we cry
It's like a wound healing, that our mind is feeling
But because of God's love and creation, we sometimes cry in elation,
For all the love we feel, now I know our minds will finally heal

Guy

My Childhood Story…Persevering

I am writing my story to explain how the Children's Aid Society has affected my life, both in the past, and in the present.

I was born in Canada in 1970 and lived there for the first five years of my life with my mother, father, and five older siblings. In November of 1975, an event happened that changed the course of my life forever. My mother was killed in a car accident that also involved some of the children, including me. I was in traction from a broken leg and therefore, was unable to attend my mother's funeral. The next several months were extremely difficult on my father, as he had just lost his wife, had to take care of funeral arrangements, two sons were in the hospital, another son was grieving his fiancée (she was driving the car), and he had to make medical decisions for his only daughter who was in critical condition. My dad started drinking heavily due to the stress and pressure, to help ease the pain, yet despite this, he spent the next five years in court trying to get compensation for his kids who were involved in the accident (the car had hit a slow-moving truck that was in the road without lights on, during foggy weather), and finally settled on a relatively small amount because he couldn't afford lawyer fees.

My brother and I went back home to live with our father after leaving the hospital. My father was left alone to care for us, our sister in the hospital, and work. Since he was working, he planned on hiring someone to care for us; however, my older brother made a complaint to the CAS about him being unable to care for us, so they just came and took Don and me into "Protective Custody," without even giving my dad a chance to tell them that he was going to hire a nanny to help out. There was no discussion, and no help offered by the CAS; they simply showed up one day and took us away. Fortunately, for me, the first place they took me was to my dad's sister's house. My aunt and uncle had wanted to adopt two children, so I was placed with them, and although they wanted to adopt me, they felt it might create too much trouble down the road, so they placed me back in the hands of the CAS after two months.

After I left there, I went to another small town a half hour away, and was reunited with my brother. We were placed in a foster home where there were about 15 foster kids at any given time. This is where I first started school and made some new friends. I remember my father coming to visit me there and trying to take me and my brother home with him, but these attempts only led to his arrest by the police. After some months there, the CAS acknowledged that there were too many children in this small house, so they moved us back to H., to another town and another school.

This foster home was a good home; the foster parents were kind, but they were older and found it difficult to keep up with us, so we weren't there long. My brother and I were moved again, but this time we were separated.

My next home was back in M., and although I didn't know it at the time, I found out years later that the foster parents had been waiting to adopt two boys; however, CAS never told them about my brother. They were going to adopt me, but my father wouldn't consent. I was happy in that home. I remember them taking me to the lake, going fishing, and getting a lot of attention and love. About three months later they informed me they were going to adopt another boy, and when they brought the baby home I totally changed. I was frustrated that I had been there for a few months and I thought they hadn't even considered adopting me, so I started acting out at home and in school because I didn't feel special anymore, and even though the family tried explaining to me in detail that I was still their little boy, that I was still special, and that they still loved me, I was still very confused and told them I wanted to be a "single child" in the family, and didn't want to live there anymore. The foster mom told me she didn't want me unhappy, so she called CAS about the situation, and with no questions asked, and no counseling offer, they told her to pack my bags, and they were on the doorstep within an hour. Because I was taken away again on such short notice, CAS placed me back in H. with the same family again, until they found another home for me. Again, I was only there for a short time, and in a new school again.

After that, CAS had no place to put me or Don, so they asked my father to take us back. His reaction was normal in my eyes---he told them that they had taken us away from him before, and he wouldn't take us back, just to have us yanked away from him as soon as they found someone else to take us; it wouldn't be fair to us, or him. From there, I was put in another home, and started in a different school again. The foster parents had two of their own kids, my new "brother and sister," and we all got along just fine. I went on trips often with this family and felt like this family was finally the one I could stay with forever. Even though I had an occasional temper tantrum, they still considered me to be, and treated me like one of their own kids. In school I didn't have bad grades, but there were always comments from the teachers that I was smart, but I was a daydreamer, and couldn't pay attention (I wonder why!). I stayed there almost a year, and then one of my older brothers approached CAS and told them he wanted to adopt me, and since my dad agreed to the adoption, the foster parents felt that the proper thing to would be to let me be with my real family, even though they wanted to keep me with them.

So I moved to live with my big brother and his girlfriend. I really enjoyed being with my brother. I remember he showed me how to water-ski, took me snowmobiling, and taught me the construction trade. The most important thing to me though, was meeting a lot of my relatives for the first time. I was there for several months and they were the best in my life up to that time; then, one day my brother told me he had decided against adopting me because my being there was causing problems between him and his girlfriend. I was crushed because I knew I would be heading back to the CAS and another family.

To this day, I don't understand why, after my return to H., why I didn't go back to live with the previous foster family. I loved being there, and they loved me staying with them, so I don't know why CAS didn't ask them to take me again. Instead, I was placed in another home, with three new "sisters." I HATED living there. At first we lived in a small house, and things weren't too bad; there were just very strict rules in place, but then the family bought a bigger house in the country to accommodate more future foster kids (as you may know, foster parents are compensated financially for taking in kids!), and within a very short period of time, about 1-2 months after moving, there were more foster kids moving in, and let me tell you, things changed pretty dramatically! There are a few things that happened there that really stand out in my mind---at the ripe old age of 10, I found out what having a real job meant. For my birthday I got a bucksaw and was pretty happy until I realized it meant that I had to cut firewood every day after school for hours at a time, and if I didn't, I was punished. I was punched, kicked, slapped, thrown into walls, and had my head bashed repeatedly on the wall, by both foster parents. I also remember a violent incident in the kitchen one night (because I held my fork in the wrong hand) that traumatized me so bad; I still can't eat corn to this day! Needless to say, I didn't I didn't like the way I was treated at this home, so I complained to CAS, but the caseworker's response was disbelief; she thought I just wanted to go to a different house like I had done in the past. When one of the foster kids got his nose broken, the foster dad got scared of all the complaints by kids to the CAS, and in order to avoid investigation he phoned CAS and said they couldn't keep foster kids anymore, and to help speed up the process of getting rid of the kids, the foster parents referred a friend of theirs who was looking to adopt a little boy, to the CAS. It was this place that I was shipped off to next. I don't know what kind of screening process the CAS had, but all I remember was that I went to live with a single man in his forties, in a RV camper, in somebody else's front yard, on the outskirts of H. I remember the first day he picked me up and brought me to the "house," and I thought that while it was a little weird, it was sort of adventurous, like a camping trip. I guess the bottom line in my head was that ANYTHING was going to be better than the last place!

In the beginning of my stay with this guy, life was great. The people's property that he had his camper parked on had a few three-wheel ATV's that I was allowed to go on all the time. I also remember having a bear cub to wrestle with, and I looked forward to that every day. One day I remember the dad moving the camper to another yard, which just happened to be at the house where my brother was staying in foster care. Within the first week of moving there I remember waking up from my sleep in the middle of the night with an erection, and the dad naked beside me, and I was still in a sleepy haze and wondering what was going on, and why he was giving me oral sex, as I was only 10 years old and didn't have a clue about sex, or anything to do with sex. He explained to me that this was a normal part of growing up, and that I would be rewarded if it was kept it a secret for life. Although I didn't like what had happened, I trusted the "adult" in the situation, and found out what being "rewarded" meant--- the very next morning he took me down to the motorcycle dealership and bought me a brand new Yamaha dirt bike. The thoughts of the night before were quickly pushed to the back of my head. The bike was dangerous for because I had never driven one before and it was too big for me, but I LOVED it! Even though the nightly rituals continued and he made me "return the favor," I loved my bike and it was a great escape for me, as I was getting more and more confused. He also taught me how to weld and got me a three-wheeler, and basically anything a kid can dream of; however, things didn't appear to be quite right to people on the outside, like family and friends (but not CAS), and they started to ask him questions, to which he responded that he had seven children that weren't with him and he missed so much, and that was why he was so generous with me. Right after that we moved into a house in H. and the camper became a sort of vacation place for us and our friends. During one of these "vacations," he sexually molested one of my friends (who committed suicide at a young age a few years later). My friend wanted to "experiment" with me too, and I really came to hate all of this and finally decided that the "rewards" were not worth the act, and told the dad that this was going to stop and that I wanted to move away from him, or I would reveal my secret, so he took the appropriate steps to make sure CAS would put me in a good home, and I would keep his secret.

From here I moved to M. once again, in with another family. By this time I was beginning to learn that when things didn't work out, all you had to do was move away and start over again. My molester dad visited me there a lot for weeks to come, made friends with the family, and even brought me my three-wheeler to make sure I would keep quiet. I remember my last conversation with him, when he took me for a car ride---he told me that this would be our last time seeing each other, unless something was ever revealed about what had happened between us, and then he made it very clear that I would be hurt if it ever came out. I felt threatened, blackmailed, and scared, and in addition to all of the confusion I was already feeling, I now had to adapt to a new school and a new family with three kids. I didn't take to this home real well; my three-wheeler was my best friend. I didn't want to spend any time with the family; I just wanted to be alone and forget about everything that had happened to me with the last two families I had stayed with. Those experiences forced me to grow up way too fast and I trusted no one. At the age of 11, I started smoking cigarettes, stealing cigarettes, and developed a "bad attitude." My school grades went down and I never paid attention because I was too busy thinking up scenarios and solutions in my head, like "what if this happens next, or what will I do next, and where will I go next," etc. I had decided that no one was ever going to hurt me again, and no one would ever get close to me. Things weren't working at this house, so CAS moved me to a temporary home with a family in M., but I only stayed there for a short time, and then I moved to another temporary home in M., and a short time later, I was moved to yet another temporary home in M. I was moved into and out of six or more homes before I was placed at a foster home on a farm. While I was living there my brother, who had often visited me in foster homes and parties, committed suicide, and although he was one of my closest family members, once again I did not get to say goodbye to him. Despite this, I was generally happy at this home, and stayed there for four years, but things weren't going well at school, and I had started smoking marijuana and drinking heavily at age 12. I found that doing these things was a wonderful escape from reality. Then one day I started to lose my values and all hope to have a decent life and I attempted suicide with one loaded gun on each side of my head; fortunately for me, someone found me and stopped me, and after this the family talked with me and tried to help me. They put money into an account for the work I did on the farm, and when I had enough money saved I was able to buy a three-wheeler. They also bought me a skidoo to give me some freedom, and I felt like I could be happy again. For the first time, I was able to experience freedom without having to give anything in return. I was able to stay with them for four years because they were very patient and understanding. I didn't act the best way there, and I guess this was the reason I eventually left their house, but thanks to them I learned a lot about machinery and gained a lot of operating experience, which has helped me to this day.

At 16 years of age, I was placed into my last foster home, in H. I stayed there a few months, until one day I decided to get away from it all; I quit school and moved about an hour away from H. and enrolled in a program, a program that made it mandatory to go to school, and as long as you did you could stay in a sort of group home, which was kind of like a room and board situation. On a side note, all of the residents of the group home came from the same type of background as me, and since we all related to each other the drug use only escalated, and at this point I was doing a lot of cocaine. After a few months of being there I ended up in the streets of T., where I lived for a few months. I came back to H. and lived on the streets because no one wanted to help me, and I was rejected by society. Some of my immediate family wanted to help me, but they were sickened by my self-destructive attitude and my daily drug use. By this time I knew that there was only a short period of time left before I was going to get an undetermined amount of money as a settlement from the car accident, to be given to me when I turned 18 years old, so while I was waiting I decided to check out the rest of the country, and I hitchhiked my way across Canada.

The day that I turned 18 years old I was in T. to collect my money, and I spent the next few months living large and partying with my friends. I moved back to E. and provided a good time for a couple of friends and myself, and when the money was almost gone I moved back to H., where I had non-stop parties, drinking, and cocaine, until the money was totally gone. When that day came I got a reality check and knew I had to change my life, so in 1988 I checked myself into a group home for drug and alcohol re-hab. I wanted to go to O. because my brother lived there and I really wanted to be reunited with him and have his support, so I stayed there for about eight months and got clean, and got a job right after re-hab. I met a girl when I was 19 years old, and I really felt a need to have a child because I had missed out on so much love when I was a kid, and I just wanted to love a child and give that child the kind of life that I wanted for myself, so my girlfriend had a girl, to whom I devoted all of my time, energy, and love into, but within a year of her birth my girlfriend and I separated. We had a verbal agreement about child support and visitation, and up until she was 6 years old I paid for almost everything she needed and also took her home with me every weekend. My ex seemed fine with these arrangements, but one day I got a call from a man who said he was in contact with my ex, and he asked me to come to his office to discuss some issues, so without even knowing his name or who he was I went there and he said he was a mediator, to help my ex and me iron out our problems; I answered some questions on a piece of paper about child support, etc., and then signed it. He told me I'd never have to worry about arguing with her again. After everything I had been through in my life, all I wanted was to be able to live peacefully without arguments, so I signed it; however, two years later, after filing my income tax, the government withheld my income tax return and sent a letter stating that I was in arrears for child support since 1990 (close to $16,000), which I was very confused by, so I called the maintenance office and was told the paper I had signed was actually a legal document, that the guy I had seen was her lawyer. Further, there had been a verbal agreement about child support and my ex never once mentioned in the two years following the signing of the document that I owed her more money, or that she wanted more money for the previous two years! It seemed to me that I had "been had" by the system once again.

The government ran my life through CAS in my past and I didn't like the way that turned out, so naturally, I was angry that the government had once again stepped into my life to try to control it. I felt that I could take care of my situation on my own. I understand that child support is a law, and I wanted to take care of my daughter, which I was doing, but not having known what the legal document meant, by the time I found out, I was already very behind in payments; also, everything that I had paid for and payments that I did make, were not accounted for by the government. Since that day, I have tried countless times to get this situation settled by hiring lawyer after lawyer, but I ran out of money, and the situation only got worse; every one of my income tax returns was garnished, as well as my GST refunds. I've been charged $400 a month in child support payments for the last fourteen years, even though half the time I was without income, and on top of that I haven't even had a relationship with my daughter for the last seven years because of my bad relationship with her mother, but once again, I needed a lawyer to legalize the visitation rights, which had never been established. I used to take her with me on my truck trips across Canada every summer, to places like Canada's Wonderland, until the last time, when I was two days late dropping her off at her mother's because the truck broke down; even though my ex knew about the delay, she forbid me to take my daughter again. I know this broke my daughter's heart; she loved being with me and even did a project in school, saying that "the best time in her life was traveling with her daddy." I called her after that and sent her birthday and Christmas presents, and still attempted to see her, but the last time I called my daughter, her mother told me that I might be able to have lunch with her, but that was it, which would have been nice had they not been so far away. Anyway, my ex told me that my daughter didn't want to come with me anymore, and I know that was not a decision she would have made on her own, given our relationship, so once again I'd been had by the system---a father has no rights unless he has lots of money for courts.

I was living in S. at this time, where I met another girl, and things went well for awhile, and I thought when she got pregnant that I would have another chance to make the kind of family that I never had, but unfortunately things didn't work, and one day I found her in bed with another man, so we separated and my daughter is with her. This time I didn't make any formal or verbal agreements for child support or visitation rights, because I already knew where that would take me! So I did what

I had always been shown---when things don't work out, you pack up and move on to the next house, the next town.

In 2000, I had an opportunity to lease a semi-truck, and I believed that I would finally be able to make enough money to hire lawyers and finally get everything settled, but by that time I was so far behind that short of winning the lottery, there was no possible way of ever coming back. I had met another girl and we went trucking together, so I tried the trucking bit for a year before I started getting phone calls from the MO, who threatened to garnish my wages and take away my driver's license, which I needed to make a living, so I cancelled my truck contract and moved to E., where I tried a few different things. I started off with an idea that I came up while trucking and pursued a patent on it, and after spending thousands of dollars on it, I found out it wasn't going to work because of an error conducted by my lawyer, and then I tried to start my own landscaping company, but that didn't work either, because my bad credit wouldn't allow me to get the materials I needed. I then tried working as a welder, but didn't make enough money, so I tried my luck in another city; I got another truck, and the money looked promising, but the truck ended up costing me $19,000 in repairs, so then I was even more behind, so I tried landscaping again, with the help from a business man this time, so things went smoothly for a few months, but, alas, it was too good to be true. My second ex started calling me and wanted me to sign over my rights to my second daughter, so her new boyfriend could adopt her, and she also wanted child support, which I knew would cost me more money in lawyers, which I couldn't afford, so I packed up again, and moved to H. By this point, things were so bad financially for me and my new girlfriend that we were seriously considering bankruptcy, and H. seemed like an easier place for that to happen. I also wanted to come back to the place where everything in my childhood had happened to me, and try to get some questions answered in my mind.

There are a lot of things I don't remember from my childhood, such as dates, etc., that I wanted to sort out in my mind; for example, the order of houses I lived in, the length of time in them, or why I left a particular house (when you're a kid, sometimes it may seem like a year, but was in fact only a few months), so I decided to visit some of the "good" families that I stayed with, to hopefully get some questions answered. After visiting a few of them, I went to the CAS to request all my records, so I could get all the answers, and was told, "Of course, they're your records, and you have every right to them," so I received them in about a week, since they were in another town. When I went to collect them, I was told that the Director had gone through them and had made the decision that I could only see some of the records, such as "how I was taken care of, taken do the doctor and dentist, etc.," so I was discouraged and left it alone for a few weeks, and then decided some were better than none and went back to look at the ones I could, but was told I would need a court order to have them handed over to a lawyer on my behalf, so even though I didn't have the money, I sought out a lawyer and found the cheapest one would charge $2000 just to obtain my records; of course I couldn't afford that, so my records are still at the CAS today. I came across a web site called Canadian Afterfostercare, written by another former foster care kid, named John Dunn, and as I read his story, it was like reading about my own life---he's my age, was also abused, sent to many different homes, and separated from his brother, and he also mentioned many behavioral traits, lifestyles, and habits that are consistent with people who have gone through what we have, and he is also fighting the CAS to obtain his personal records as well. After reading his website several times over, I contacted him by email and by phone because we both believe in the same things and want the CAS system to change.

While I was researching my past, I stumbled onto another business idea, so my girlfriend and I started doing some research and engaged two business partners who were friends of mine from the past, and pursued it. At the financial point we were in, I felt that it was my last chance to set things right, so my partners and I sought out investors and started the background research to start a recycling company, to not only benefit me, but also to create employment and change the economy in northern O., and after nine months of preparation, the plan was done, and I was ready to find funding. This achievement didn't come without a price, though. We consulted a bankruptcy firm to determine our options and was told that if I did declare bankruptcy, I would forfeit my rights to pursue my case against the CAS FOREVER, and I might also lose my rights to any money that would come in the future, to me from my sister's settlement. There is absolutely no possible way that I will give up my rights to fight for the rights the government took away from me when I was 5 years old. At this point, however, I have put every dime I own and all the energy I possess into trying to make my business succeed, so much so that I can't pay my rent, put food on the table, have a telephone, or pay my car insurance, and

I also can't go to work for a company because the government will either garnish my wages or take away my driver's license. The only option I have would be to try to borrow $25,000 from someone to make a proposal to my creditor, which is one step above bankruptcy, and if I could do this I could keep all of my rights, but who is going to lend me $25,000 with all of the problems I already have??!! I have been fighting this for 27 years, and it will be another few years before anything is even settled, costing me an undetermined sum of money for a lawyer, which of course I don't have. Just when it seemed that the recycling business was going to take off, things went sour with my business partners; they weren't the most legitimate people, and one of them ran into money problems, and then decided the solution was for him to take the business for himself and the other partner. He was crazy, frantic, and desperate, and made it very clear he would stop at nothing to get us out of the business, so we decided our lives weren't worth risking over money, and even though it killed us to leave something behind that we had put so much time, energy, and money into, we had to leave town. We had about $15,000 worth of furniture that we sold for $2,000, so we could eat and have somewhere to live for the next two months.

At this point, I have lost all faith and hope for life itself. I feel like I am boxed in, with no way out, and I don't believe in miracles anymore, and top of that, my health has deteriorated so much over the last two and half years that I am scared for my life at this point. I am also up against a wall, because if I get any health care all my government problems will come up again, but on the other hand, I don't have enough money to pay cash for all the doctors' fees and tests. So I sit here, sick, losing weight, and wondering what my next step will be.

All I know for sure it that, thanks to the CAS, I have lived in twenty-one foster homes, numerous "temporary" foster homes, attended eight schools, lived in twenty-four cities in Canada in over eighty homes, and have had over fifty different jobs. When I think about it, there are so many things that could have gone differently; for example, if the CAS had placed me back with the nice family after things didn't work with my brother, I feel my life would have taken a completely different turn, as those kids became teachers, due to the support they received, and I believe I would have been given the support, guidance, and love that I needed to become whatever I wanted to be. I am still in contact with this family today, and they still give me all the support they can, so using my own judgment, I know my life could have been a lot different. They aren't the only ones who are supporting me in my pursuance of this case. Anyone who knows my story does not understand how I am still alive today, and how I am not in jail. Statistics show that the majority of people who have gone through what I went through lean towards certain behavioral traits, and a lot of them continue the cycle of abuse (physical, mental, emotional, sexual), others turn to crime, others turn to drugs and alcohol, and there are those that simply refuse to deal with scars they have, and they end their lives. Rather than end up being just another statistic, I have other goals I want to accomplish to help stop the thousands of cases that are similar, or worse than mine. By placing a lawsuit against the CAS, I want to raise public awareness on the flaws and wrongdoings made by the CAS, and try to stop it from happening to other helpless kids. I also want some sort of compensation for what I have gone through, and a chance to start over and make things right in my life. Instead of looking at things negatively, with self-pity, I choose to appreciate all of the experience I have gained in my life, to know that I could make a solid life and career for myself, if I was given the chance. Right now my fate is in God's hands, but I don't expect Him to come knocking at my door and take away all my problems.

It is now March of 2003. As we were leaving H., I gave a long time friend a call and told him what was going on and he invited me to stay with him for awhile, and he also got me a truck driving job. I was overwhelmed, so we packed up and went there, and within a month of getting back on my feet, Bang! There it was in my face! I saw the potential for a business that would give me one more chance at success. The first month of driving the truck all I could think about was what I could do to get us out of this situation, so I slowly started to investigate the business idea that I had and found out that it was potentially a multi-million dollar venture, and after the background research was done, all we needed to do was find ourselves a team of about five people to help us move forward with this new venture, and since my friend had been living in this area over seven years and we had been best friends for over 16 years, we trusted his advice and hired the people he had suggested, since we were fairly new to the city and didn't really know anyone else at the time. We gave my friend the title of Vice-President after building our team, and we started doing our preparation to go find investors, and after five months of research and having the business plan in place, the unexpected happened---my long-time friend got an urge to own the business for himself. After we had all of the work done to start the business, my friend found out that another employee was going to make more money than him for the first two months, so he decided that since all of the major work was done, he didn't need us anymore, and went behind our backs and basically brainwashed all of my staff (that were also his friends) and got them to hate me. He got them so well that one night he suddenly regrouped the team to come and beat me up in order to scare me away from our home, so they could take over the business that I had founded. I was so devastated.

For the second time in a row, a "friend" had stabbed me in the back. I can't believe how much money changes people. That night I had to call the cops to get my stuff out of his house and had to borrow money for a place to stay because my friend had drained us out. I called a friend in the city and we stayed there for a few months and tried to start the business anyway; however, the more time passed, the more we realized that it just wasn't going to happen, and we realized we needed help very fast, or we'd be living in a shelter, so we decided to move back and stay with my girlfriend's family.

After all this time of trying so hard to succeed, the unthinkable happened. I hit rock bottom. I lost all faith in life, people, and I just could not see the light anymore. To me, nothing mattered anymore, whether I was breathing or not. I decided to give up! UNTIL..........Thanks to my fiancée, whom I love so much, and who has been put through so much since she has been with me. I am still with her today because of her love, support, and wonderful stubbornness to not let me go! I also love her wonderful family for believing in me, and patiently giving me a chance to be able to leave all of my past behind (friends, family, and everyone I have ever known in my life). With the help of her family I was able to find myself with God again.

My new life with God by my side

It was in the New Year that I started praying every day and asking God to help me to get through the pain and suffering from my past, and to give me strength to carry on. I woke up one morning feeling completely different. I felt like all of my anger towards others that had been consuming me was gone. My thoughts were so clear, and I had the answers to so many of my questions. To me, it was a miracle. I finally realized that God wasn't going to knock at my door, but that instead I had to go knocking at His door!

This was just a start of what I was going to go through. A few weeks after I was getting closer to God, I could feel something was not right; I felt very suicidal. I felt like it was not possible to have a second chance, and I felt like it was not worth it to keep going, just to name a few.

Resume

In the past year I have tried to declare bankruptcy twice, with no success, and was given many reasons why we shouldn't or couldn't do it. My case is so complicated that even the bankruptcy trustee told me to hide from all my creditors until I figure out how to get myself out of this mess! That just blew me away! I have tried many different ways, with no success, to get myself out of this situation. I recently found a law firm that had interest into starting a class action lawsuit against the CAS, which was some of the best news I have received in years. It was a short-lived joy, however, because shortly afterward, the lawyer emailed me to give me some bad news. I don't have long to go before all of my problems catch up to me.

I have so much potential in life, but yet I have the potential of nothing with the situation I'm in. At the age of 34, I finally realize what went wrong in everything I've ever tried. Because of my past, I always ended up trusting the wrong people. I always taught myself not to trust the "good" people, because they will abuse you in any way they can. The other side? Well, I always had a friend to lie, cheat, steal, scam, and get high with. It seemed like these people always understood, and they were always there when I needed them. Now I know that I was living my life the wrong way, and choosing the wrong path. All of the businesses I have tried that would have been successful have failed because of lies, and scam artists that I thought I could trust. I wrote this story with the hopes that whoever reads it would take on a different outlook on life. Since I don't know what the future holds for me, I really hope that I can make a difference in some way.

Reality

I have dug myself a hole so deep that it is impossible to climb out of unless I would get some help.

Harley Joe Carnes

Luckier Than Most

I decided to share my story because I figured with all the horror stories out there about foster care, it might be encouraging to hear a happy (or at least happier) one. Although my family has had its share of tragedy, we've been luckier than most families in similar situations. Our family managed to remain intact throughout the whole foster care ordeal and still remains intact today, for which I am very grateful. Certainly things were bad for us to be put in foster care, but I realize it could have been so much worse, much more tragic.

Tragedy struck my family when I was very young. I am the sixth born (1960) of ten children (seven girls and three boys), and in 1964 when I was only 4 years old, my oldest brother, who was 15-16 years old at the time, was murdered in Joliet, Illinois, stoned to death with flag stones while he was out having fun with some friends, and his body was found by some railroad tracks. He just left one day and never came home. This was tragedy number one and unfortunately tragedy number two was soon to follow. In 1965, just a year later, my mom died of stomach cancer, which through our family into further turmoil and grief. Not only was my dad grieving the loss of his wife, but he was also overwhelmed by all of the responsibility of caring for nine children, some of whom were still very young and in need of much attention, which he simply couldn't adequately provide. Although there was a woman named Hatti who helped our family some, between working to make ends meet and care for his children, it just became too much for my dad, especially since he was a disabled veteran from WW11, and we were already poor and living in the projects. My maternal grandma lived down the street from us, but we didn't see much of her for some reason.

I remember when it all began to happen, our entry into foster care. We were all (dad and siblings) sitting around a big table at my aunt and uncle's in Joliet one day and my dad talked to them about us, and said he couldn't keep all of us, but as it turned out it didn't work out for him as planned, as he really didn't have the means to keep any of us, so the decision was made to get help from the state.

Two of my younger sisters and one brother went to a nice foster home on a farm in Nauvoo and were eventually adopted. Another younger sister was adopted into a real nice family in Joliet. Since my dad was a DAV I was able to go to ISSCS (Illinois Soldiers and Sailors Children School), along with my four older sisters, who watched over me a lot there. I was only 5 years old when I went to ISSCS and I was very shy at first, but I had real nice cottage parents who made me feel welcome there. Really, the worst memory I have of my time there is wetting the bed and feeling humiliated by having to hang my sheets out to dry on the clothesline where everyone could see them. I was probably wetting the bed because I was insecure, and having to be humiliated like that sure didn't make me feel any more secure, but all in all ISSCS was not a bad place; it's just that I would have preferred to be with my whole family. I ran away from there several times, mostly because I just wanted to have fun and not have to do any chores. My older sister also ran away, but she wasn't able to return to the home; she was put in a girl's detention home for one year, which was a very strict, lock down place, the kind of place that you'd get shot at if attempting to escape.

One thing I didn't like about at the children's home, of course, was being away from my other siblings in care, but both of the adoptive parents made sure we all kept in touch with each other and they treated us all like family. My dad only visited me about every two years while I was there and my maternal grandma only visited occasionally, so having a connection with the adoptive families compensated for my dad and grandma's lack. The adoptive parents in Nauvoo were so nice and caring; in fact, they still took in more foster kids, even though they had their own children and my siblings to care for.

Between the ages of 9-14 the ISSCS staff was trying to find foster homes for the children there because the home was being closed (it closed in 1979), so when I was 14 years old I went to live with an aunt and uncle for two years, which was all right, except for their daughter accusing me of trying to rape her, and my alcoholic uncle trying to hit me. His son stopped him from actually hitting me, but I didn't want to stay there after this happened, so I went to live with another aunt and uncle between the ages of 16-18, until I graduated from high school, and then joined the Navy, being a responsible young man.

I was married in 1980, but my wife didn't want to go overseas with me when I was stationed there, so when I got back to the States our marriage was annulled. In 1984 I was out of the Navy and met my second wife in 1986, who I have three girls with. She recently died of an accidental prescription drug overdose and I miss her, but life goes on. My girls are still young adults and I have them to think about and I hope to remarry again someday.

All in all, I feel that foster care was good for our family, mostly because we kept in touch with each other, and for the most part our family has kept intact. I'm the mediator in the family, the one who goes in between to keep the family together, and we still manage to have a family reunion every year, so our family is ok. Of course it isn't perfect, but what family is? I have one sister who is a backstabber and some sisters don't get along with each other, and there are some other family members who don't get along, but I'm the neutral one and get along with everybody, and my older sisters who took care of me when I was younger, now look up to me. Our family was like the black sheep to my mom's side of the family, but my dad's side treated us good, probably because my dad came from the country where people are more down to earth and family oriented. I am close to one brother, and we keep in touch, even though we don't see each other a lot. My dad died of natural causes (probably a heart attack) when he was only 56 years old.

At one point when I was younger, I didn't understand the whole family situation and why we had to go into foster care, but now as an adult, I understand, and my attitude is "forgive and forget." Some of my older sisters didn't understand and held a grudge, but I didn't. We don't talk about the past much; at least I've never really brought it up. I have one sister who says she doesn't remember a lot, that she didn't like it a lot and wanted to drown it out because she doesn't want to remember, but I realize we are all different in how we react to things and she may have been more impacted and traumatized by the past than I was. Mostly though, we lead normal lives and there aren't any alcohol or drug addicts in our family, and nothing real sordid.

Yes, my family was lucky, and we have kept pretty intact, but I also realize not all families in this situation have been able to do that. It would be nice if more foster parents let siblings know each other, as I feel a lot of kids don't, and it is important that they do. The state is the main problem with this, and I think the laws regarding this should change, that children should have the right to see their siblings, and they should also be able to know their personal information. I also think that the state is way too lenient in selecting foster homes. The homes need to be investigated better by doing background checks. Foster kids are already vulnerable; these children shouldn't have to be subjected to further abuse and/or neglect. People need to become more aware and help more, especially wealthy people. Foster kids deserve love like everybody else.

Heather Milne

Longing For Lost Family Memories
Because Family Means Everything to Me

I am sharing my story because I have so many missing parts of my childhood and feel that by sharing what I do remember, it will somehow help me to connect to the lost memories. I also desire creating more dialogue within my family about our past, in order to bring about more closure, and bring us even closer together. My family is very unique; we are very open and receptive to one another, so I feel that by me opening up and sharing, it could encourage other family members to also do so. This is my hope, as family means everything to me.

I've never really thought of my family as being dysfunctional, as it was all I ever had and I just accepted them the way they were, but I suppose that by society's standards, my family could be classified as dysfunctional. My dad had problems, and my mom was the good co-dependent, trying to keep her family together, which consisted of five children (I'm the fourth born). There was another child, my mom's second born, but she died in a car accident at 14 months of age; my mom had removed her from her car seat, and due to the car's break problem, the baby girl was killed when she hit the dashboard. I think my dad's behavior increased after that and I know my mom suffered from guilt, as she confessed it on her death bed.

My dad worked for a brewery and helped the business by drinking up his paycheck, money that should have gone toward providing for his family. When I was 13 years old my parents divorced for five years, but then remarried again and stayed together thereafter; they even burned their divorce papers at the marriage ceremony. My mom was heavy built and my dad was small, so he knew better than to mess with her, but the beatings were inflicted on me and my siblings instead. My dad would line all of us up and belt us if nobody admitted to something we were accused of. Even though things weren't perfect at home and my dad could be pretty abusive at times, I never really had a lot of anger toward my parents. My dad was sober for the last twenty years of his life and did his best to apologize and make amends. My dad was an abused foster child himself, and no doubt passed on what he got, to us. My parents are both gone now, and nothing I went through in my childhood compares to how much I miss them now.

I don't know who turned our family in to social services. Our family was too close for it to have been an extended family member, such as an aunt or uncle, and I don't think it was a neighbor, but somebody must have thought our family was dysfunctional and in need of help, and turned us in. I tend to think it could have been my own mother, as I believe she was overwhelmed by the responsibility of caring for five children and an alcoholic husband. We moved around a lot as a family, but I don't remember all of the places we lived.

I do know that our whole family was placed in an independent (not through CAS) group home when I was about 9 years old. We were there about two years, along with some cousins and their parents. I believe I was in there two or three time, the first time with my whole family, but later just by myself. This group home was intended to help rehabilitate my dad and help restore stability to our family, but apparently it didn't, or only worked temporarily, as shortly after that, I was placed in a girl's home, where I stayed about 6-8 months. I think CAS put me there because I had emotional problems; I don't really know for sure, but I know that my dad refused to sign any papers for continued care and I was removed from there and returned home. I was 12 years old when I left there. I remember, because I was supposed to go home for my 12th birthday, but wasn't allowed to. I was alone there, and I missed my family.

I was also put in a receiving home at some point; I believe it was in between the two group homes sometime, when I was about 10 years old, but my memories are sketchy, so I can't be certain. I remember things that happened when I was with my parents, but I don't remember much about being in foster care, except that I know this temporary receiving foster home was bad; it was hell. My sister was there with me, and I remember seeing her being punished by having to stand on one leg, and I got very upset by it. I ran away after this, and hid in ditches to get home, but my granddad, who was there when I got home, called CAS, even though I begged him not to, and I had to go back to the foster home. I was very angry at my granddad about this.

I wish I could remember more, but like I said, the memories are vague. Grades 2, 3, and 4 are gone or very broken up, and I don't know for sure how long I stayed with my parents. I do have a memory of sexual abuse by a friend of my parents when I was 10 years old, and I remember being told that I was just trying to get attention. As far as I know, it only happened one time. To my knowledge, I was in two group homes and one foster home, but who know if there was more. I may have been put in another CAS group home, but I'm not sure. I have a lot of mixed up memories. Maybe I don't have all the memories because I don't have the emotions that are attached to the memories. One thing I do distinctively remember though, was that I wanted to be around my parents when I was a child and was removed from them. I don't believe there is one child in foster care that is really happy there, even if they appear to be. Children will still have an undying love for their parents, no matter how much you give food, clothing, and shelter to them, if they feel loved by their parents, which I did. I think my parents put me in the homes, but I'm not angry at them about it because I don't know why I was put there. They were CAS homes, so it was through the system, and although I don't hate CAS, I have apprehension toward them, especially since I've had to deal with them in my adulthood.

Throughout my adulthood, I can't be without my family and have great anxiety, always having to know what's going on with everybody. I worry about them a lot because I care so much. Even in my childhood, we strived to stay together, and as adults, we still strive to remain a family, no matter what. Foster care has a tendency to repeat itself, and unfortunately, it has in my family. My older sister is homeless in a sense (she's staying in a house where she hasn't paid rent), has seven children who aren't in her care (the three youngest ones are in foster care); she is very exhausted and depressed and just wants others to rescue her. I try to encourage her the best I can. My oldest sister is taking care of ten children, four of whom are our brother's kids who were born with defects. There have been problems in our family, but we don't want our grandkids going to CAS, so we do our best to take care of them to prevent that from happening.

I had to go through a lot to get custody of my granddaughter, but she was worth it. I call her "Beautiful Spirit" because she is so precious. I had to go through a kinship program with CAS to get custody, because the mother of my granddaughter is drug addicted and irresponsible. I don't hold a grudge against her and try to support her, as she has her own CAS history of abuse and has had a tough time. I also had to make a choice between my boyfriend at the time and my granddaughter, as he gave me an ultimatum; the choice wasn't too hard to make, considering he was very dysfunctional. This was my third bad relationship, and even though it wasn't easy letting go of it, and I was even engaged to him, my primary concern was my granddaughter. CAS termed me a transient because I've moved around so much, and they didn't see me as a stable prospect as a caregiver for my granddaughter, so I really had to prove myself, but I did not want her getting stuck in CAS.

It has been through letting go of abusive men and getting custody of my granddaughter that led me to a women's service program for battered women, and it's where I'm learning how to feel emotions, and even cry. There was so much commotion and turmoil in our family that I just learned how to hide my feelings, but I'm emotional now and have done a lot of emotional growth. Sometimes I have anxiety and feel like I want to scream, but at least I'm feeling. I'm in the process of trying to recover my childhood files, at least from the children's home, and hope to make some connections between my emotions and memories.

Foster kids go through so much, but we all need to have faith, and believe that there are people out there to help us, because there truly are. I am finding this out myself. As for the lost memories, I'm working on them…

Janette McCrary

The Wolf Outside My Window

I started working on my autobiography when I was 12 years old. I'm 28 now, and although I plan to finish my autobiography, I'm not sure if/when I will be able to, so it only made sense to take advantage of the opportunity to share my story in this book, as I want my story to be heard. Because I was in so many placements, in so many towns, my story is probably one of the more severe cases. It needs to be heard so that people realize how bad it is for foster kids and so other foster kids who have gone through what I did will realize they aren't alone. Sharing my story along with others allows me to be a part of a collective voice for foster kids, and although I can't change anything about my past, perhaps I can help make a difference for future foster children.

I'm not even sure exactly how many foster homes I was in, but I know I was in between 20-30 from the ages of 6 ½ to the time I aged out of the foster care system at age 18. As I got older I wanted to be adopted, so I would have a "real family," but the option only presented itself once, and the family chose not to adopt me.

Altogether I was in thirty-four placements and twenty-nine different places (I was in two shelters more than once). My entry into foster care began at age 6 1/2, but before I elaborate on that I will share my earlier life and what brought me into foster care to begin with, which was poverty and sexual abuse.

According to what I have been told, as I only have a vague memory of the incident, I was either sexually abused by a cousin or a distant relative (it was documented in my state file as my cousin), and I told a male friend about it, who told his mother, who called the cops. The police asked me if I wanted the perpetrator to go to jail, or if I wanted to go into foster care, and I chose foster care, because I loved my cousin. The fact that my parents weren't capable of caring for me also contributed to this decision. My mom had problems and my dad was mildly mentally retarded.

This is a picture of me at age 2,
when I was still with my biological parents.

Until the age of 8 or 9 I had monthly visits with my biological parents, and then for some reason the visits stopped. After I was removed from them they unofficially adopted at least two children, which my mom confirmed after I saw it noted in my file. I had a good relationship with my dad and a so-so one with my mom. The last time I saw my mom as a child was at the age of 11, when I went to my dad's funeral. I hadn't seen my dad for 1-2 years before he died. There are two stories about his death---the one told to me by the DHS is that he died of diabetic shock, and the other story, told to me by my mom, is that he committed suicide because he couldn't get me back. I'm not sure which story to believe.

There are also other stories flying around about my family, which I choose to take with a grain of salt, since my mother doesn't always tell the truth. My mom and my half sister were adopted by the same woman, who was not a blood relative, but a relative by marriage, and this woman also adopted several other children, one of whom my mother believes is her supposedly "still born child." My mom's imagination runs wild a lot, so who knows what the truth is. I didn't see my mom again until I was 20 years old, but have since tried having a relationship with her, which isn't easy. It was ok meeting her, but there was no "I love you," and no apologies, and no real warmth. Sometimes she's talkative, sometimes she's a loner, and sometimes she's mean and snippy. I've learned to just accept her for who she is and not expect much, so I don't get disappointed. She is on disability and remarried, living near my half-sister.

And now I will tell my story, which has both good and bad moments.

My **FIRST** placement, at age 6 and ½ was at a shelter. I'm not sure how long I was there, but I know it was only a temporary placement until a permanent home could be found, so I couldn't have been there long. The only reason I know I was there is because as a teenager, when I went back there again, I saw a picture of myself there as a young girl, holding a McDonalds happy meal box. I don't remember the actual experience of being in the shelter; all I have is a vague memory of going to McDonalds on the way to the shelter.

I'm not exactly sure when I went there, what city it was in, or the foster parents names, but I do know my **SECOND** placement was a foster home and that the reason I was removed in December 1989 was because I broke the biological child's toy.

My **THIRD** placement was with Mr. and Mrs. Harper, I believe, but I'm not sure. I was only there about two months because it was found out that I was being bothered by the foster dad. How this was discovered, I'm not sure, but I think it might have been through some play therapy that was being done with me for previous abuse. I don't remember if I was happy to leave this home or not, but I'm assuming that since I was sexually abused, I was.

This is a picture of me at about age 7.

My **FOURTH** placement was with Nelson and Ivy Pendergrass, where I stayed about eight months. I remember that I moved with them from their first house into a big mansion on a hill. These foster parents weren't perfect, but all in all they were pretty nice. The only reason I was removed from this home was because they were opening up a group home for teenagers and I was too young to stay, and although I didn't stay in personal touch with them, I did occasionally listen to Nelson's Christian radio show.

My **FIFTH** placement was with David and Debbie Henry, where I stayed for almost a year. They wanted to adopt me, but David had enrolled in seminary in another state, and DHS wouldn't allow them to take me out of state. Apparently it wasn't the end of their connection to me though, as I received a group letter from all four of their children, whom I'd never even met, calling me their sister, so I guess I meant more to them than I realized. This was confirmed a couple of years ago, when I found out that Debbie and David had been showing the kids photos of me and talking about me, as if I were another one of their children, who just never visited. It made me feel very special.

This is a picture of me at about age 8.

My **SIXTH** placement stands out in my mind because it the only time I was given a choice about a placement and it was the longest placement I had. I got to meet the foster mom and her daughter at the DHS office before I went there. Unfortunately I wasn't given a choice about staying there after I was attacked by the foster grandfather, who had Alzheimer's. Of course I didn't really want to stay after that, but I didn't relish the idea of moving again either, plus I really loved being there on the farm around all her farm animals and dogs. Even though the placement ended I've still had an ongoing relationship with them and their whole family, even going back for occasional visits.

This is a picture of me at age 10, with my biological mother, at my dad's funeral.

So, here I go AGAIN, back to the shelter, my **SEVENTH** placement, this time for about two months, from March-May of 1994.

The shelter was only temporary and then I went to Larry and Gwen McBride's, my **EIGHTH** placement, which was a foster home, where I stayed for two months. They were pretty nice people, with their own children. All I really remember about this place is doing arts and crafts and going next door to the foster grandparent's house to play video games and do puzzles. One outstanding memory I have though, is going on a family vacation with them, a first ever for me. I never knew why I was removed from this home, but I am still in contact with many members of the family today on Facebook.

My **NINTH** placement was with a single woman who had a career as a therapist. I was there about five months and then things went haywire. During this time I was in day treatment, which is a cross between a school and mental institution, and I was frequently being restrained for any little thing I did wrong. There was an incident when the foster mom came up behind me to hug me, and I thought I was being restrained and freaked out, kicking and screaming, etc. What bothered me the most was a necklace she had given me being broke during the struggle. All I remember after that was her daughter wanting me to leave. I was sad to leave this home because I really liked the foster mom and her daughter. Before the incident I started to get an eating disorder, barely eating for a few days, which the mom recognized and helped me with, so I really appreciated her.

My **TENTH** placement was a foster home, but I don't remember where or who with, only that I was there for about six months, and then had to leave because the foster mom resigned.

My **ELEVENTH** placement was in a foster home with D. and M., but I was only there about a month. I don't remember the whole story of why they asked me to leave or what happened, but I do recall that when I first got there, I told the social worker that I didn't have a good feeling about this home. I didn't get along with their daughter, either. The only good memory I have of that time is going to the mall and buying HUGE jaw breakers.

My **TWELFTH** placement was a good home, where I stayed for three months, until she decided to let me go because of the stress of being a single mom and having her work hours increased.

My **THIRTEENTH** placement was an ok home and I babysat for their two young boys while I was there and went to ballgames, but for some unknown reason I left there after only about three weeks. Maybe it was a temporary placement; I don't know. I tried to find them on Facebook, but there was no response.

My **FOURTEENTH** placement was with JM, who was a very nice lady and also a school counselor. I don't remember a lot about my five months there and I don't know why I left.

I don't remember anything, not names, location of my **FIFTEENTH** placement, not even how long I was there, but it wasn't any longer than a month.

I really liked my **SIXTEENTH** placement on a farm in S. They had three adopted kids, 2-3 foster kids, and three adult birth children, but I didn't get along with their adopted daughter and had to leave after seven months. The adopted daughter and I are now in touch, and we get mad and make up just like "real" sisters.

My **SEVENTEENTH** placement was just a stone's throw away from the previous home, but it was short-lived, only about a month. I don't remember a lot about this home, but three things stand out in my memory. One memory is of them having giant pigs. Another one is of me and the foster sister fighting a lot; in fact, we fought so much that one night the foster mom came in the room, sure we were killing each other, and I was dead asleep! Apparently I was fighting her in my dream, and was actually yelling at her in my sleep too! The third memory is a very unpleasant one, of having lice, and after no results with the over the counter mix, having the foster parents pour gasoline over my head in the bathtub, which burned my skin, mouth, and eyes. I don't know why I left, but I sure was glad to after that incident!

My **EIGHTEENTH** placement was only temporary, but could have been permanent, had I not done something stupid and had to leave. I was 14 years old by this time and beginning to be interested in boys. The foster mom went out on a date with her lawn guy one night and they decided to have his 17 year old son stay at the house and keep an eye on me during their date. I had a crush on him and he started trying to convince me to have sex with him. I didn't want to have sex with anyone yet, so I kept trying to say no, but he wouldn't give up and I finally gave in. It wasn't even good sex; it was BORING. I'm not sure why I left this home, but I think it had something to do with her not "keeping an eye on me," and me having sex.

Placement number **NINETEEN** was very short-lived, only about a week. I got in trouble because I was in the garden and had to pee so bad that I didn't wash my hands before coming. When they called DHS to try and get me out of their home, the foster mom said I was crazy. I called a friend who was in foster care and his foster dad offered to take me temporarily.

I don't even remember the foster dad's name, but I was only there overnight or at the most two days. Because there was a teenage boy in the house, I wasn't able to stay per DHS rules, so that was the end of placement **TWENTY.**

Placement number **TWENTY-ONE** was with a family, where I stayed for a week or so before being removed after I got bothered by their two sons. After being bothered for two days, I asked my foster mom if I could go to work with her. She worked at a private treatment and foster care center, which was also where my social worker worked. I wanted to go there to tell my social worker about the incident because she wouldn't call me back when I tried calling her; however, my social worker wouldn't talk to me, and sent the foster mom down to find out what I wanted. I told her I didn't want to tell her, that I only wanted to tell my social worker, but no one would let me talk with my worker. I knew the foster mother wouldn't believe what her sons did, but I finally told her, just so I could get her to tell my worker. The social worker sent me back to the house, where I was locked in a screened in concrete porch area for about two hours to wait for my social worker to pick me up. While I was waiting, the foster mother and her sons called me names and I felt threatened, but at least they stayed on the other side of the door. I was so happy to leave this place!

Placement number **TWENTY-TWO** was another temporary one, at another shelter, which only lasted about a month. I don't remember a lot of it.

My next placement, **TWENTY-THREE**, was another shelter of some sort, and I'm not sure how long I was there, but I know I was in six homes during November, so it couldn't have been for long, only a few days or maybe a few weeks at the most.

Well, the shelter, here I come AGAIN, my **TWENTY-FOURTH** placement, which was of course temporary, lasting only a few days, if that.

I guess I was pretty messed up psychologically at this point, so they decided to put me in a diagnostic center, placement number **TWENTY-FIVE**, where they did psychological tests and education aptitude tests on me.

From this place I went to my **TWENTY-SIXTH** placement, at another shelter, another temporary place, where I was probably only at for a couple of days. I had a very bad experience there, when a guy who should've been in jail, but wasn't, started bothering me. I told a worker that he was harassing me, but they didn't do anything. One day he threw a pencil at me and the sharp end hit me, and then he came toward me and I didn't know what he was going to do, so I stabbed him with a pencil enough to put a little bit of pencil lead in his arm, which landed me in the psych center. I think the guy needed psychological help more than me, but they said they couldn't find a place for him, so they moved me.

I don't remember anything of my **TWENTY-SEVENTH** placement, a psychiatric center, but I do know I had a lot of psychological problems at this point. I felt like I was being punished for what happened to me. Two years after the incident another foster kid, who had this social worker, told me that the social worker told her about my incident and that I was a problem child and fabricated it.

My **TWENTY-EIGHTH** placement was at a group home, where I managed to stay for about 2 ½ years, until I ran away at the age of 16. It was an ok place, but some of the girls needed to be in the nut house or jail, and some of the housemothers were all right and some weren't; some felt like my mom and some I absolutely hated. One way the place was good for me was by making me more outgoing and assertive. I always joke that I was "ghettofied" there. When I first went there I was very gullible, shy, and nerdy, and got picked on a lot and even beat up, so I learned real quick that you had to fight back. While I was there I found out that my past incident hadn't even been handled properly. My new social worker tried to open the investigation again, but it was too late. Some of the things at the group home were really bad, and some of it was really good, but one thing is for sure, it wasn't boring! I got grounded a lot there and I finally ran away because I thought I was "in love," at which time the police took me back to the home, where the social worker came to pick me up to take me my next placement, which was, guess what?

That's right, the shelter AGAIN, my **TWENTY-NINTH** placement, where I stayed for only about two days, before I was placed with a previous placement again.

I was placed with DR again, my **TIIIRTIETH** placement, where I stayed for about five months, until I got in trouble for violating rules when I was grounded and had to leave. The foster mom said I could go next door, so I figured I could just go anywhere (testing her rules, I suppose), so I went out with a friend, and my sister said she'd tell unless I took her and a friend with me, and we went to the bank and my foster grandmother was there, and we tried to beat her home, but failed. When we got home, my foster mom was calling over and over, waiting for us to answer. She told me she was disappointed in me and for me to pack my bags, that my social worker would pick me up, which she did, to take me to, guess where again?

This is a picture of me at age 15,
with my fiancé who broke my heart, at the Military Ball.

I was placed with DR again, my **THIRTIETH** placement, where I stayed for about five months, until I got in trouble for violating rules when I was grounded and had to leave. The foster mom said I could go next door, so I figured I could just go anywhere (testing her rules, I suppose), so I went out with a friend, and my sister said she'd tell unless I took her and a friend with me, and we went to the bank and my foster grandmother was there, and we tried to beat her home, but failed. When we got home, my foster mom was calling over and over, waiting for us to answer. She told me she was disappointed in me and for me to pack my bags. She told me my social worker would pick me up, which she did, to take me to, guess where again?

That's right; I went back to the shelter AGAIN, my **THIRTY-FIRST** placement, but this time for three months, until a very traumatic experience ended my time there. I got in trouble for taking too long of a shower one day. I was very mad about this and demanded to talk with the shelter director, which I was allowed to do, but he didn't do anything to the worker, except send her to the young children's area. About a year ago I found out this worker, who was still at the shelter, got in trouble.

I was 17 by this time, so I was put in Independent Living, my **THIRTY-SECOND** placement, in a house with one other foster girl, where I stayed for about two months. I was engaged to marry the guy I ran away with in while at the Group Home, and when he dumped me for another girl I was really hurt and angry, so I slept with three different guys. One of the rules of the Independent Living Center was that I wasn't supposed to have sex, so I got kicked out, just before graduation.

My **THIRTY-THIRD** placement was at another shelter, where I stayed for only about two weeks I guess.

I would also like to add that somewhere during placements number 26-34 I went to stay with my best friend and her family for a few days, followed by my mother's adoptive mother for about a week. I don't know exactly when, but I remember that it was one of the summer holidays for veterans, like Memorial Day or Independence Day, or something. One thing that always stuck out in my mind and I thought was astounding was the fact that it wasn't a proper home, but the social worker just ignored the facts.

By this time I was about to "age out," so I was sent to my last placement, number **THIRTY-FOUR**, with a couple, where I stayed about three months, until I turned 18 years old. They were very strict, and very religious. I remember the birthday party they gave me before I left. They filled a trash can and a laundry basket with various household goods and taped about $30 worth of dollar bills around them.

This is a picture of me at age 19 at my high school graduation, along with my first husband, my foster sister (DR's daughter), my foster Grandmother (DR's mom), my foster sister (DR's daughter), and my best friend and godmother to my son. Diana probably took the picture.

One thing that has troubled me about this last home was a foster boy who lived there. About a month after I left I responded to a card the foster parents sent me and found out this boy, who was ten years younger than me, got sent back to his very abusive father, which was why he was in foster care to begin with, and I have often wondered what happened to him, and have even tried finding him on Facebook, but to no avail. He was the only person in foster care I really wondered about and worried about being dead. I sure hope he isn't.

Aging Out

I don't remember my first day out on my own, exactly…But I remember the first few years very well. I had been saving up my money since I was about 15 years old, to get an apartment, but when I went to stay with my biological family temporarily, my birth cousin, who was in middle school, told me she didn't have clothes for school, which was about to start back up, so I took her to the mall and bought her about $200 worth of clothes. When I got out on my own, I was given some gold-plated money from Belize, left to me by my father, as well as about $600 in Survivor's benefits.

I sold the gold-plated money (at a loss, I later found out) to a dealer for only about $50.

When I moved into my apartment, I was fine for awhile…But I guess about 3-6 months after I moved in, I lost my job, and then I was evicted because I couldn't pay the rent. I was still attending high school, and I had to temporarily drop out while I found another place to live and a job. I moved in with a friend's family, and the mother taught home-school. I went to her school every day, but since I wasn't enrolled, when I went back to school they refused to let me back. I had to wait until the next year, when I was able to re-enroll. During my time in high school, I moved around a lot, because I kept getting evicted. At one point, I even ended up in the local homeless shelter, but it freaked me out so badly by dinnertime the first day, that I paid a friend $50 every two weeks to sleep on his couch. Shortly before I expected to graduate, the Indian Services counselor at my school helped me get set up with food stamps, Section 8, and some money for my cap and gown.

I got married two days before my high school graduation (at age 19). Only a few people came up to my graduation; even though I invited several of my former foster parents, DR and her family, the worker that helped me with some independent living things, and a friend, were the only ones who came.

I left for the military a month later. While in the military, I discovered that I didn't have enough credits for graduation. I was also injured in BASIC training, so I was sent back home two months after I started my military career. We used the money I earned to put a down payment on a house, thinking it was the best decision. I decided to go ahead and finish up my high school credits, which I did online, mostly from the library. I was unable to work because of my injuries, so my husband and I ended up getting evicted from the house, and had to move in with my sister. Shortly after that, we found out I was pregnant. We used our tax refund to put a deposit on a trailer, which was to house us, my mother-in-law, my sister-in-law, and our baby when it came. I started working at a daycare center and he was working minimal hours at a restaurant…And his mother was taking all of our money. We had to get food from food pantries to eat, since his mother would accuse us of stealing if we ate her food. We weren't able to get food stamps because we lived with her, but I did get WIC. We found out that she wasn't going to give us his sister's room when she went away to college, as she had promised (leaving us with a bedroom the size of a large closet, with a VERY small window and no heat or AC, for a couple and a baby and all of our various things!), so we decided to move out. When she found out, she said, "If you want to leave, do it before I get home then!" even though our apartment wouldn't be ready until the next day, and we wouldn't have a car the next day, and I was eight months pregnant in the middle of summer and we were there alone…So I had to help move our furniture and stuff out of there. We then had to sit out in the heat until someone could pick us up. We spent that night in Wal-Mart, fell asleep in one of the chairs, and woke up to security asking us to wake up before customers started arriving. The next day was my 21st birthday. I was officially too old to get ANY help from DHS or any service for foster kids. My last service was my car and the furniture for the new apartment, which I got for free. We moved into our apartment.

Thank you for reading my story.

Jasmine Utley

Not Just Another Boring Biography

Hi everyone. My name is Jasmine Utsey, and here is my story. I promise you that you won't fall asleep reading it, as this is not just another boring biography, but then us foster kids don't have your average, run-of –the-mill "boring" life, do we?...not unless you want to call being moved around all over creation, being physically, sexually, and emotionally abused, and generally battered, and even suicidal, "average." After reading my story, you may not even think it's your average foster care story, if there is such a thing. We all have our own unique tale to tell, and here is mine.

I'm an 18 year old African-American, who was born into a very dysfunctional family. My dad, or at least the man I called dad, was a Vietnam Veteran. In reality, I'm not sure who my real dad is. There are five of us siblings (I'm the middle child), and only my half brother, who I've never met, knows who his real father is. The rest of us will probably always be kept wondering who our real dads are, as my mom was the neighborhood drunken whore, who had so many men, it would be impossible to find out. I basically thought I didn't have a dad, and then when I did acknowledge one, my grandma told me that he didn't want to have anything to do with me. I was 16 years old when I was finally in touch with my dad. Most 16 year old kids these days want cars for their birthday, but I was exhilarated just to get a birthday card expressing that he loved me.

I don't have any memories of my early childhood, or early pictures to even help me out, to refresh my memory. I remember being happy at 4 years old, when I was home with my grandpa, who I called "dad," and I also remember my 5th birthday party, which was a happy event, complete with cake and everything, but other than that, I draw a blank. I wish I had more happy memories. I wish I had a time machine where I could go back and get what I didn't get, and I wish I had a delete button on the side of my head where I could delete the memories I didn't want, but I don't. Unfortunately the bad memories are still with me; I've just learned to live with them, and try to make new, happier memories.

As for the bad memories...well, when I was 7 years old, I was living with my grandparents, which is considered "kinship care." Some people might think that kinship care is better than regular non-relative foster care, but believe me, that isn't true, at least it wasn't in my case. Although my grandpa was real nice and I was very close to him, my grandma wasn't. One Thanksgiving something bad happened there. The only thing I was grateful that Thanksgiving was that I wasn't killed! I ate ok, if you want to call eating beans all the time eating ok. My grandparents got money from the state, but my grandma sure didn't buy me any decent clothes with any of it. She dressed me in old, lady-like, hand me downs. I wanted to look adorable, but I couldn't; instead, I looked like an old rag doll, and I was teased about it at school. Are you bored yet?

When I was 7 years old, I tried to set the house on fire. I struck a match and put it in a garbage can, and then I put it in the bedroom, not realizing that my grandpa was in there, which avoided the whole ordeal. God must have been watching over me. Maybe my mind wasn't right from all the Prozac I was on for depression, or maybe I was just messed up from all of the mistreatment I got; most likely it was a combination of both. I wasn't happy with my grandma or aunt. When I was 12 years old my grandpa died and I tried overdosing on painkillers, which was my second suicide attempt. My grandma and aunt moved us to another house about ten minutes away after my grandpa died. I was always moving around in my childhood, not so much with different people, but to different houses; it was basically the same dysfunctional caregivers, who created another dysfunctional home, and it just seemed to get worse over time.

With my grandpa gone I was now stuck with my grandma and my aunt. I think the only way I could escape the pain was by drinking, which I did heavily between the ages of 13-17.

I wasn't comfortable with my aunt but I never said anything about it. I was also concerned for my aunt's child. It was at this point that my brother and I were both put into Emergency Protective Custody. My baby brother had been acting out criminally, so they placed him in a children's home, and my other younger brother was placed somewhere else. I was put in a group home because there wasn't enough room for another girl at MH. I didn't like this place at all. The staff girls weren't nice and the girls living there were terrible. It was like a giant clique there, and I didn't fit in. There were fist fights there. There was another home next door, where I wish I could've gone, as I think I would've been treated better there, but when you're in this type of situation you have no choice; you just go wherever they put you. I was only at this group home for three months, because according to the judge there wasn't any proof about my aunt mistreating me, even though the forensic woman who evaluated me said that I was telling the truth. Not only did they let my aunt go free, her lawyer had me looking like the bad one, the whore, because of a past incident when my mom had sent me on a bus to get the mail and I had stopped by a friend's house, and was accused of having sex with her boy. I cried in the courtroom, and if I was in the same room with her today I would tell her off! The day I got out of the group home my caseworker came and picked me up and took me to my great aunt's funeral, an aunt who was very nice to me.

And guess where I went---back to the same dysfunctional home that I'd been taken out of, with my grandma and aunt. I got tired it, so I went to live with my older sister, and my mom was living in the same neighborhood, and she showed up there a few times, but I really didn't want to see her. It's the honest to God truth. She would try hugging me, but I didn't want to hug her, and I don't feel sorry for her. I love her, because it's hard not to love the woman who gave birth to you, but she didn't care about me, so why should I care about her? I wish there was a rehabilitation place where my mom could be forever, because that is what she really needs. I gave up on her a long time ago, when she said she was going to get me, when I was a young girl, and living with my grandparents, but didn't. She never ever showed up. She never visited. Never. I realize that my mom was probably passing on to me what she got from her mom, my grandma, but it still doesn't make it right. When the chips fall, it doesn't work that way. My dad has apologized for not being there, and my mom has had so many "Hollywood" (fake) tears, but I know she doesn't really have any remorse and she doesn't care about me. She had the choice to change, but she didn't. My baby brother still thinks she's going to change, but I tell him that he's dreaming. I guess he's still waiting on her, but I'm not. I'm done with her. I don't want anything to do with her.

I worry about my brother, because he is still filled with rage. He was very self-destructive. I never liked physical pain, so I did it the easier, softer way, with pills. I'm so glad I'm not suicidal anymore. I feel sad for my brother, because he was so artistically gifted. I miss him and I feel responsible for him; in fact, I feel like everybody is my responsibility. I worry about him and who he's going to run to for help, now that we're not together, but I'm going to keep running far, far away, if I have to take care of other family members. As far back as I can remember I always had to be an adult, taking care of other siblings because we were left unsupervised so much of the time. I can remember waking up, especially on Saturday mornings, and finding the house empty, nobody home. I've decided that I don't want any children because of my childhood. I also don't like moving around, because I did so much of it in the past. I'm stable right now, until I move again, to go to college.

I think the only way I can make it out of this whole mess is to complete my education and stay away from bad peers, who are using drugs and alcohol, and girls who are getting pregnant. There were so many pregnant girls at one school I attended that I called it "pregnant high school." The boys and girls are troublesome, and it's these dysfunctional behaviors that cause dysfunctional homes. My family is still broken up and dysfunctional, but I want to take my negative experience and turn it into a positive. I use school now as a positive outlet and am looking forward to college, and a decent career, probably as a nurse. In the past I was defenseless and I felt stuck; there was nowhere I could have gone. I felt like nobody loved me. I felt like everyone deserted me. I get along all right with my siblings and I have an older cousin who is a father figure for me, but that's all. My parents abandoned me. In the past I felt worthless, and I thought I might as well "off" myself and be off the face of the earth, but in reality, I think my experience only made me a stronger and better person. I have a fear of abandonment; I don't like getting too close to people because I'm afraid they'll leave me, but I believe God has always been there for me and loves me unconditionally. I don't believe in hell, fire, and brimstone, as I've already been there. If I could, I'd have fourteen cats, because they never let you down like people. I've always felt old for my age. I'm only 18 years old now, but I feel like I'm at least 30, with an achy body. Sometimes I feel jealous of people and think, "Why can't I have a better life?" It all seems so unfair. It's survival of the fittest though, and foster kids are survivors. Foster kids aren't really all messed up; we're just different because of the way we were raised, but I think being raised that way broadened my view; I'm not just looking close up; I'm looking all around and my view is magnified on everything. I like myself today and I am glad now that I didn't "off" myself from the planet. In the past, when I was sent to a psychiatrist, they thought I'd kill myself, but they don't understand how resilient we are. What doesn't kill you makes you stronger. Foster kids are amazing. We are awesome; people just don't realize it yet. Maybe other people don't know how to be there for us, but foster kids need to stick together, because if we can't be there for each other, then we're really screwed.

Well, you're still awake, aren't you? I told you it wasn't just another boring biography.

Jason Murphy

A Voice for Hope

My name is Jason Murphy. I have always made jokes that I was born in a ditch, but as far as I saw my life unfolding, I might as well have been. Life was not easy from day one. My parents were already on a destructive path in their own world and I would become the obstacle in their partying ways. I became a permanent ward, but the dysfunction didn't stop there. That's where this story begins.

This is a story of a boy who has survived and overcome obstacles in life that would have taken most people to insanity. My life has been insanity. From birth to age 17 there have been over forty different foster homes. Some were good, some were bad, and some should have never been allowed to take in foster children.

I often wonder how I made it to where I am. I read the paper or hear on the news about someone accused of a horrible crime and most of the time they blame it on their past. I am in total disagreement with that. I am the maker of myself. I have made a lot of mistakes in my life and they were all decisions that I made.

I hope to change someone's outlook on their life. The possibilities are endless. Anybody can be or do anything they want, if they set their mind on it. It's all a choice. I wish I was encouraged more to finish school and get the proper education that I could use today. I know it all came down to money and the decision of a social worker. The bare minimums were provided, and that's it. I feel for the kids out there that think this is as good as it will ever get. That is so not true. It will get better. I am proof of that. I shouldn't be here by all accounts. My life has been spared so many times. I was the only one that put myself in these places and am very thankful that I made it out to give my children the life they have today.

Don't give up. Be strong. Stand up for yourself. I think I over killed that one. I spent so many years of everyone telling me what to do, where to go, what to say, that I stand firm on NOT being walked on or taken advantage of. I am not shy to speak my peace and sometime I do hurt feelings in the process. I am working on this.

I have faith today that all will be OK, as long as I take care of myself and keep my side of the street clean, which means treating people as I would like to be treated. I know what compassion for another man is and understand it. If I make mistakes today and acknowledge a mistake, they are mostly amended shortly. These are tools that I have been taught and use them whenever the situation arises.

I was told we are all good and caring people, but I can't understand the truth to that. Why are there just horrible, nasty people in the world? I know that I was not a very nice person. I was bred to be a survivor of my environment. I also know today that was just wrong. Everyone has a story. Everyone has parents, siblings, friends, and loved ones. There are so many children in foster care, as a result of the society we live in today. I feel that the compassion for another human being is lost. Why can't people just slow down and see and listen to their innermost feelings? To put your hand out and offer help is rare, unless it's an obvious dire circumstance.

My purpose for writing this story is to bring you into the minds of the children that are placed in foster care. I hope it brings inspiration to this struggling system. My hope is that lessons can be learned from the mistakes that have been made. But to continue a cycle of dismal failure is not the outcome I would like to see. Please listen to what the kids are saying. They are not as naive as you may think. They may be small and meek, but they do have a voice. Please hear it. These are the people that will be running things in the future. There are so many people that think they know better and their way is the only way. Usually the social workers that are put in charge of us are like this. It's not. The kids have a voice and should have a choice in the decisions made in their lives. I know for myself, as I cringed when my social worker would tell me what was best for me. These kids were placed in care for a reason. Those reasons might require the child to have aftercare once they are settled in. I didn't get any of the aftercare. I was expected to adapt, and feel lucky I had a home to go to. I didn't come from a normal existence, so why was I expected to act like a normal child? The social worker would drop me off at another home and would not to be seen again for some time. That was it. They wondered why it didn't work.

My inspiration for writing this story came in the paper one day. The little boy's name was Matthew Vaudreuil. It was 1992 and this little boy died at the hands of his own mother. The Ministry had given this little boy back to this unfit mother, over and over, and finally she took Matthew's life. It upset me very much. I couldn't stop thinking about this incident with this little boy and so many others that are damaged in the hands of their caregivers, this being their own parents or in homes that the ministry has deemed fit for taking care of children. I have been in multiple homes that were unfit to bring up children and the people in charge should have known this, but it was ignored or swept under the rug until it was too late and there were casualties. It was always the children that paid the price for this irresponsibility and not doing of the right thing.

My life today is beyond fabulous. It is quiet and uneventful, but it contains everything I could ever want or need. I could never have imagined at 12 years old that this is where I could be. At age 12 I couldn't see past the day or week. Everyone has a bad period in life and they think it will never end. It will pass, and life will go on, if you don't give up. I still have a lot of demons in my closet. They will take time to heal, but for the most part, I have become the person that society says we should be.

I would like to give the new social workers that are almost out of school and ready to step into this world an understanding that their work will affect many lives. They need to be able to make the right call on the kid where that decision is so critical. I could have used more people that were involved with me to really care. I felt as if I was just paperwork for these people. I felt the workers involved left their emotions and feelings outside the door when they started their day. I understand why, as the emotions would drain the strongest person; that's probably why they shut them off. But it doesn't help when that's what these kids need. They need someone to be emotional for them and with them. You are removing these kids from years of neglect, abuse, and whatever else, and now basically you're their new parent. Big task. Most aren't up for it.

I'm hoping my experience, strength, and hope may inspire workers in the system and foster children that think there is no hope, to see there is hope.

Jeannie Lynch

Legally Kidnapped

I am sharing my story because I believe that we, the foster children, have a God-given responsibility to help other foster kids. I believe God will not burden or hold accountable a bent rod, which means that people who are broken or challenged, the Lord gives a special grace to. I believe foster kids have a special grace from God. I believe there is a special portion for foster kids. I believe we are a special selected group of people set apart by God to give the secret of abandonment, in order to make sense of it to give back to others. My husband has told me that I am the conscience of society, that my observation of human beings is that they are selfish and don't want to spend their "quality" time listening to other people's tragedies. Nobody wants to hear it, so when the opportunity came for me to be heard by somebody who did want to hear it I couldn't resist it. After all, don't we all want to feel valued? For years I thought I was the only foster care survivor. I NEVER talked about it. I felt like I was on the precipice of insanity. I began therapy in my 40's and I talked about it there, but never to my friends and family. But ever since I contacted the Foster Care Alumni of America about two years ago, I haven't been able to shut up, nor do I care to, as it is very liberating. I feel like I'm a 60 year old woman trying to work out and overcome a trauma from when I was 7 years old, feeling like a young girl again, but I find it very healing, as there is healing in revealing.

As for my story, it is quite colorful. My dad was the product of a rape by a physician and was raised by his grandparents, then went to work to support his grandma. He was about 35 years old when he married my mom, both believing she was pregnant. I actually came along five years later. My dad was in and out of work (during 1940's) as a machinist and he also dug clams sometimes for a living. Our house (in the 1950's) was actually a garage, two 8' x 8' rooms on a piece of land given to him by his grandma that was part of her lot. I remember the house well. One room had a bed, a bureau, and a small television, and the other room was the kitchen, with a table, two chairs, a kerosene stove, and a sink.

My mom was mentally ill (bi-polar) and was quite bizarre. I called her the "head in the bed" because she spent so much time in bed when she was depressed. She hated living out there in the garage because it was so remote, and during the winter she would get my dad to rent apartments, but due to her bizarre behavior we got evicted a lot. My dad was real sweet and even though my mom was mentally ill, he was totally devoted to her and stayed married to her until she died suddenly in a hospital at age 66. He was a saint, very stoic, with a stiff upper lip, in control of his emotions. My mom was just the opposite, very emotional and sexual, especially when she was manic. She was very sexually inappropriate when she was manic and I remember one time when I was playing Spin the Bottle as a preteen and she gave me and my girlfriends condoms for party prizes, which mortified me, as I was hypersensitive, worrying about the state and the school watching us and taking us away from my home again. And as for me being taken away from my home...

The first time I was taken away from my home I wasn't actually taken from my home by social services. I was put in a home by my dad when I was only 2 years old. It wasn't a state run home; it was run by a woman who took children in for money, but it FELT like a foster home to me. I don't remember how long I was there, probably anywhere from 6-months to a year, but I do remember being very apprehensive when my dad carried me in the house. I remember 3-4 teenagers sitting on a couch and the mom yelling at me for being hungry. She was very cruel and I remember hiding under a table to get an away from her.

I was 7 years old when the state got involved and I was put in an actual foster care home. Things weren't going well at home and I wasn't being properly supervised. I remember a hobo by the name of Bill the Indian, who smelled like tobacco, coming by one day to keep me company while my dad was at work and my mom was in bed. He brought me a copper teakettle he got from the dump. He also gave me lice, and my dad then put an end to that relationship! My dad was fearful of him and maybe jealous of my relationship with him. I felt like I was raised in isolation in the woods by bears, and then thrust into society. One time when I was 4 I walked four miles to a lady's house who was a friend of my parents to get a tuna fish sandwich, so that I could learn how to open my own can of tuna at home. My dad let me help him make homemade cigarettes. Being alone, (mother was sleeping), I made my own cigarettes out of pencil shavings. Having seen the Loretta Young Show, I also poured a "pretty" glass of vinegar to go along with the cigarette. One rather bizarre memory I have is of a neighbor friend down the road from us going down to a farm to get a donkey and then putting the donkey's head in my mom's bedroom doorway. Another memory I have, unfortunately, is of being violated by a 17-year old boy who had asked me to come see his kittens. My only natural preservation at the time was to detach from the whole situation by looking at a broken kite I had. The incident was reported to the police, but nothing was done.

I remember the day I was taken away from my home and put in foster care. It was a cold, frigid day in January. I remember it was unusual that my mom was out of bed and my sister stayed home from school. I also remember I had some new clothes for the first time and I twirled around because I felt so good in them. They all went into a large room, but my dad came out without them, and he picked me up. He carried me to a strange woman's car, and then there was REALLY trouble, with ME! I was so absolutely petrified I almost peeled my nails off of his neck, clinging to him with sheer desperation. After a long road the social worker told me to look for number "14" on a house and I remember thinking in my head, "NO WAY!" because I thought I'd go back home if I didn't cooperate. Once there, the first three months I wasn't allowed to see my parents, then I had supervised visits for 3-4 months, then unsupervised visits every other week for 4-5 hours.

I HATED foster care! I felt like a throwaway child and I was never comfortable living with strangers who weren't really equipped to deal with me. A soul can't thrive without love, and in a lot of cases foster parents can't/don't love us. I was depressed while in foster care and survived by feeling like I wasn't even there, disassociating myself. I disassociated myself so much one time at the age of 9 that when I broke my neck by falling on the ice while ice-skating alone, I thought the ice cracked! The physical pain wasn't any worse than the emotional pain though, so it kind of balanced me out because I had physical pain to focus on instead of emotional pain. I was dying inside and fantasized about a fairyland, storybook place to replace the terrible reality, not so much of the foster parents, as they were nice enough (even though I'm pretty sure the foster mom fostered for money), but of the reality of being yanked away from my family. I remember there were several foster children who came and went during the almost six years I spent there and I remember when I was about 9 years old I took care of a baby, from the day she came to the home at 5 days old until she was 18 months old. One day I came home and the baby was gone, just like that. There never was any discussion.

And at age 12, just like that, a social worker came and told me I could home now with my parents! But unfortunately I came back to the same reason I was taken away. I went to live in an apartment with my mom and dad, but by August that same year my mom was manic again and acting crazy, and got us evicted again because she got a friend to take an ax to our attic door.

And so just like that I was whisked away again to another foster home, but I was so traumatized that I blocked this day out of my memory. I think the foster parents were ok, but I just shut down. I don't remember crying. I was dead inside. I think I was there about five months, but I have very little memory of being there.

The best way for me to describe foster care would be to say I felt like I was being flushed down a very smooth toilet, with nothing to hold onto, just going down into the abyss. I called my story "Legally Kidnapped" because that's how it felt. The foster care system is legally righteous and I felt like it was me against the government. I even hate the word "system" because there isn't a system. It is chaos, and it isn't just sometimes chaotic; it is always chaotic. I found that if I shared my heart with people they say, "At least you were with parents," but the reality is that I was either with a mentally ill mom or in foster care. I think I did better than some other foster kids because I always felt that my parents loved me, but it was still rough and has had left lasting scars. I'm so sensitive and afraid of rejection that a look from a person in the grocery story can blindside me. Even though I grew up in a middle class neighborhood, I was the poorest kid in the neighborhood. It was bad enough being a foster kid, but now I was a poor foster kid, and the parents of other kids didn't want their kids to make contact with me and didn't want me in their home, not exactly something that builds self-esteem.

How have I survived my foster care trauma? Well, I have been a workaholic, a shopaholic, a cleanaholic---anything you can add "aholic" to I can do. Anything to zone out. I have also been overly responsible. But then came God…and I believe He hasn't wasted one experience in my life. He has taken every thread and woven it into a rich fabric and then allowed me to put that fabric into my life quilt (Romans 8:28). I take every thought captive and if there's evil, I give it to God, and when temptation comes knocking on my door, I say, "Holy Spirit, come and get the door." I believe my 60's will be the crowning glory of my life.

Jeff Campus

It's Getting Better All the Time

Although I want to share my story, it's a daunting task to write down memories from so long ago, especially since I like to classify my stay at ISSCS (Illinois Soldiers and Sailors Children School) [which hereinafter will be referred to as "the home"] as a love/hate relationship. Looking back, I know it kept me from going down the wrong path and I will elaborate on that, in addition to a few other things.

Before my time at the home my life was somewhat normal. We always had good clothes, plenty to eat, went on vacations, and did what I consider the normal things a family does. My father was a career military man and I grew up not knowing much about him, and at times being afraid of him. My brother and sister never got punished like I did, nor did I ever know of any type of abuse to them or to mom. I only saw one fight between my mom and dad and that was when we were living in Germany. Both of my parents smoked, but I never saw them drink, and none of us kids ever smoked. Later on I learned that my dad had done something, which prompted our leaving Germany without him and returning to the states.

I wound up at the home because my parents divorced a few years earlier and I had become a borderline juvenile delinquent. I was living with my mom, along with my younger brother and older sister. I was the troublemaker, getting into a few minor scrapes with the law. I was caught throwing rocks at cars from the top of a building across the street from our apartment complex and I started skipping school. I also knocked off a coke machine and riding horse, without getting caught. Looking back, it would most likely have led to more brazen and bolder crimes. I was 12 years old when the court made me a ward of the state and I was off. I really hated being at the home.

At the home, I was immediately separated from my siblings and thrust into an environment I detested. I had been used to being pretty much on my own before, and the home was a very structured living arrangement, which I didn't like. I felt like I didn't belong there and that the other kids simply weren't my equal. I had been in a few fights before the home and although I didn't seek out any fights, they came my way. When you're 12 or 13 and try to demonstrate some independence, somebody is always waiting to make you capitulate to their way of thinking. The details are unnecessary, but you either have to pound the crap out of a bully or they'll keep hounding you. After one such incident, which was supervised by the cottage pop, I went through the rest of my five year stay there pretty much without incident. This is but one of those events that have helped shape my outlook, that being if more parents took disciplinary action against their children, our news today wouldn't be filled with school violence. I also strongly believe that liberal attitudes have contributed to the demise of the family structure, but hey, that's just me. I don't want to get off on this tangent, but knowing this about me helps define my position. Something else I have reflected upon since those days of adolescent fighting is that what I thought was natural progression towards maturity, that being once you got a little older, people were able to civilly work out their differences without resorting to physical violence. The reality was that not everybody moved along at the same pace and some never moved along at all.

Although my mom came to visit me regularly during my stay at the home and I had plenty of extended visits at her place during vacations and holiday seasons, I felt a little abandoned by my mom and blamed her for my situation, which resulted in our relationship suffering somewhat. It took a long time, but I eventually came to the conclusion that she did what she could at the time and that the best thing I could do with that information was to use it to better myself. We have a good rapport now and try to talk once a week. We sometimes go more than a year without seeing each other, but only because we're 1100 miles apart. My siblings are even further away. My sister and I were never really close, but we get along ok and still communicate. My brother and I were close, but that became strained by money problems. That old axiom about not loaning money to friends or family or you won't have any, is all too true. Our friendship has improved tremendously over the past year though, and has all indications of getting back to the level it once was.

I have also maintained a life-long friendship with one of the kids I met out there at the home and this beginning has helped us to provide each other with insight and support throughout our lives. There have been many twists and turns since then, and I am looking forward to a few more.

My stay at the home impacted me on so many levels that it's hard to say what worked in my favor. One thing I can be sure of is my intention to marry the right woman and to raise a family was very strong. I didn't want to wind up in divorce court and split up yet another family, repeating the mistakes my parents and so many others did with such regularity. I made the commitment to not put my children in the same type of situation I had been in, but that was compounded by my somewhat shitty attitude, which made finding a mate a tad more difficult. As of this writing, my wife and I are coming up our 24th wedding anniversary and my son graduated from college 12/09 with an Engineering degree, with the distinction of Magna Cum Laude honors. My daughter just started her senior year and I hope she is as fortunate as my son, who has a fantastic job already.

Another survival technique I think I acquired from living amongst so many other kids was the ability to judge a person's character pretty quickly. I can't be absolutely certain that is where this came from, but I don't have anything else to compare it to. Maybe this is something innate to me or it's a learned behavior; I don't know, but it has helped me to avoid what I perceived to be bad situations and some bad people.

Words of Wisdom? The usual ones, like, "Don't do anything you'll regret" and "Be yourself" will help if there's a decision to be made. I am fond of biblical verses and have found great satisfaction belonging to a church I enjoy. Another pearl of wisdom I can pass on is that not all churches are created equally, so you'll have to do your homework and pick out one that fits. Before I close, I want to include one last saying that I really like, which I try to practice. It is by Rob Bell and goes, "When we're still hanging on to how things were, our arms aren't free to embrace today."

Make your life count.
Jeff Campus
September 2, 2010

Jeremy Brown

Nothing Lasts Forever

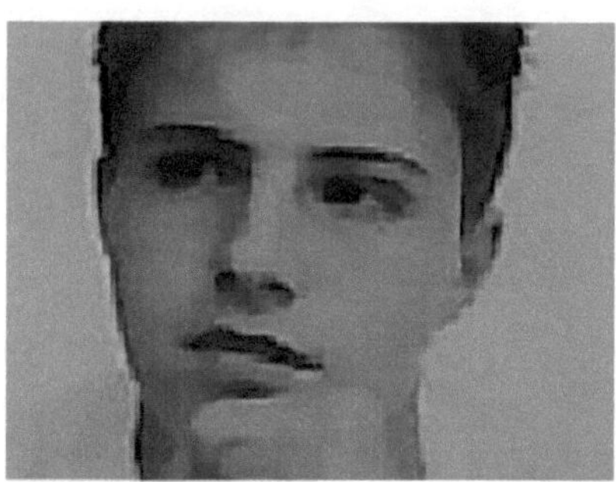

I want to share my story because I think people need to know all the bad things that go on within the foster care system, but they not only need to know what happens; they need to know our feelings about it. I am thankful to have an opportunity to share this with other foster kids.

Sadly, the foster care system isn't 100% safe and has the reputation of not doing much in terms of mainstreaming children, especially difficult children, like myself; it's just that an abundance of problems stem from its role as emergency or temporary shelter. Given even the best of motives, child care workers, who each have 60 or 70 cases at one time find it impossible to cope with the flood of children washed up into the system and to monitor foster parents closely. Because the families they are dealing with are often in crisis, children have to be whisked out of one environment and into foster care, and the children slide backward in priority as the heavy caseload spawns another crisis, and yet another placement. Child and Family Services found ten placements for me.

I can only tell you how I felt. I was so angry and so bitter over what had happened to me that when I was placed with my first foster parents, I resented every nice thing they did for me. I wanted to stay bitter and angry forever. I mean, you don't just say that you love someone and just walk out like that! I waited by the window of my first foster home for weeks, waiting for my birth mom to come back and get me, but she never did. I have tried to find her, as I would like to have the chance to tell her everything I want to say, but she is nowhere to be found.

But I always say that, sometimes the richness of life lies in memories we have forgotten. If you never remember things in your past, who is to say you won't make the same mistakes? People today look to the future as if it holds the keys to everything, but I've been looking at people and how they've changed with the times. Lately, all I've been seeing are people throwing love away and losing their minds; or maybe it's me that's gone crazy, because I can't understand why all these people keep hurting each other, when good love is so hard to come by. So what's the glory in leaving? Doesn't anybody ever stay together anymore? And if love never lasts forever, tell me, what's forever for? It's not just love between boyfriends/girlfriends, husband/wife, or any other combination, that is going to waste. What about children and their parents? I see kids all the time, running away because they "think" they hate their parents or their parents hate them. If you had no choice but to be taken away from your parents or the other way around, you'd understand why I have such a problem with runaways. Don't get me wrong---some kids have to run away just to be safe, but if you run away just because you fought with your mom, then you're the one missing out. Love isn't free, but between parents and their children, well, that's as close to free as it's going to get, so take it while you can.

Ten years ago, when I was only 7 years old, my mom gave me up to Social Services, not because she couldn't care for me, but because she wouldn't. Her love stopped short of what I needed, what any kid needs, and the truth is, I never forgave her.

When I say the richness of life lies in memories we have forgotten, it's not always the best memories that make life rich. I think that by learning to trust again by looking at why your trust for people went away, is what makes life worth something. By learning to love again, learning the meaning of your life, or learning that setbacks happen for a reason, makes "Forever" sound like my kind of heaven…

It was hot, the sun was shining the quiet breeze was warm and dry. The sand was flying everywhere as I kicked it. Sand filled my shoes as I crossed the playground to the swings. The swings. My sanctuary. The place I went to when my mom and Mike, my step-dad, were fighting. It was so quiet here. I loved the way the wind blew against me as I went higher and higher, reaching for the sky. Mike and my mom were fighting again, so I left and went to the park. But this time something was different. It was two weeks after my real dad had died and I couldn't take the fighting anymore. I just wanted to forget. I just wanted to be alone and in the place I loved before I had to go back. I had just started swinging when mom pulled up and yelled at me to get in the car. By the time I got there, her face was streaked with tears that were pouring down like rain. I had never seen my mom cry before, not even when she fought with Mike. "Mommy, what's wrong?" You're a problem child! Always getting into fights; we can't take it anymore! I've had enough, Jeremy! That was all that was said, and I didn't understand. The car started moving, but we weren't headed for home.......I stared out the window, trying to hold back tears that were making my eyes burn, but I couldn't. Streams of tears rolled down my face as I watched the trees fly by and something I couldn't see. The rest of my life was passing me by and I didn't even know it. Mom pulled into an old, rough parking lot that needed to be repaired and told me to get out and go inside. With tears still pouring down my face, I put my head down, whispered, "I love you, mommy," and went inside, into the Social Services building. I was so confused, so hurt, and my first foster home was hard. I got in even more trouble than usual and I was passed from foster home to foster home, changing last names every time I was in a new home. Wishing I was back on the swings...

I was 14 years old and in another foster home with another family. A lot of the homes I had been in had other kids---group homes was what they were called---but Jason and Sara were the first kids who looked up to me; however, they didn't look up to me because I set good examples...

The foster mom was the one who worked to provide for the family and I admired her for it. She would work all day, every day, at three different jobs, while the foster dad sat at home. One day things got out of hand.

That wasn't the first time he had come after me, but it wasn't the last time, either. I also learned that fighting back just made everything worse.

I remember the fear in the kid's eyes every time I took them next door. Sara would cry and cling to my shirt as her brave brother would grab her hand and tell her everything was going to be okay. Jason was my little hero, my soldier. I love those kids.

But the last time was too late...

The foster dad was in one of his moods. Both kids booked it to the neighbors. That night was spent in the hospital. He just wouldn't stop. My entire back was raw from his belt; I had cuts all over my chest and arms, and at one point he twisted my arm until it snapped in three places. I don't even know when I passed out, but I spent the entire night in the hospital...right next to Sara and Jason. Sara had a broken arm and Jason had a concussion.

The next day Social Services took them away to a better place. I wasn't so lucky. I was happy for them; they needed to be in a better place, but those kids broke my heart that day. They had just found out that they were leaving. Both of them ran up to me, wrapped their arms around me, and said, "I don't want to leave without you!" I'm not afraid to admit that I cried my eyes out for the first time in 8 years, and melted like the kids did, clinging to my soggy t-shirt. As they walked down the hall, holding the social worker's hand, I remembered every time they smiled, cried, and every time they made me play with them. I even remember when they each lost their first tooth, lying in bed hoping the tooth fairy had already come...

I was living on the street again. I had run away for one reason and one reason only---the foster dad. I got in trouble for coming home late from skateboarding. That night was the only time the foster mom said anything in my defense. She came to the doorway, a drink in her hand, and said, "Honey, you're hurting him."

I ran away that night---packed my backpack and jumped out my window. I was sitting in the park now, when I realized something…More haunting than the darkness that surrounded me was the realization that I was alone, totally alone with myself. And it scared me. The next day I went to school early so I could talk to one of my teachers. We sat in his classroom talking, and this is how it began: "What were your real parents like?" I replied, "I don't have a dad. Well, he didn't live with me. I had a step-dad, though. I remember in first grade, I went out for soccer. I had to beg Mom and my step dad to come watch me. It was like they were ashamed of me. They finally came, after I got mad enough. And then we lost. You'd have thought I was the only one on the team, the way he acted." We talked about other things, and then the school bell rang.

I was sitting in first period, when a boy tapped me on the shoulder and whispered, "Get in a fight with your Daddy last night, Jere?" I jumped up, knocked my desk over, picked him up by his shirt and threw him against the wall. He got up and we started fighting. Fists were flying, and every punch James landed had no effect on me. The teacher called the principal, who came with the security guard on duty. The security guard pulled me away, dragging me all the way to the office. The teacher I had talked to that morning was there and followed us into the office. The officer stated, "Learn your place, or you'll have a rough time here!" Mr. S. asked me, "What were you thinking, Jeremy? Did our talk mean nothing?" I replied, "I wasn't thinking. I just…I need out." Mr. S. said, "A lot of people have already paid dearly for your anger and lies. You have bigger problems than getting out of this place. And why don't you tell the principal why you have those marks. Tell him what you told me." Looking away, I yelled, "Nothing happened!" They both stepped outside the door, but I could still hear them. Mr. S, said, "Him and his foster dad got into it last night. We talked about it this morning before the first school bell…" Tears came to my eyes. I thought I could trust Mr. S.! "I don't know how life gets so mixed up. Some kids become our most successful citizens, while others crowd our prisons. What's the difference? Jeremy has will and courage, but also a lot of anger. So what do we do with him? Seriously, I don't know how to heal emotional and physical damage. Scars run deep…," the teacher said softly. They both walked back in. I stood up, but Mr. S. pushed me back down, putting his hand on my chest where one of the welts was. I winced. I yelled, "I'm leaving, just let me leave!" Mr. S. said, "Jeremy, we're giving you another chance. So…" "I don't want another chance!" I screamed, and then ran out. Mr. Scott ran after me, yelling, "Go ahead and try it. Try manipulating a storm or lying to your hunger! Try cheating the cold! Let us help you. You don't have to live on the streets, JEREMY!"

So, here I am now, up in a tree in the park. Total darkness surrounds me as I try to find a comfortable position to sleep in. I can't because of the welts across my chest, back, and arms. Another sleepless night I guess…

In the morning I was found, and placed in a new home, an actual home, with people who loved me. I was in a good family. A family that loved me for real. A family that took care of me, and helped me with anything I needed. They had one biological child, Isaiah, and four other foster kids. I loved those kids so much. Every moment I spent with them is one that I will remember forever. They made me laugh, they made me cry, and sometimes they made me angry, but only for a second. I would never hurt those kids. I would protect them. I cared about them, and I still do, but I'm going to be leaving them soon, and not just because I'm aging out of the foster care system.

Lately, I've been thinking about when I turn 18 years old. Eighteen is when I age out of the system. It's when I'll have to make it on my own again. It makes me nervous and scared, not because I will probably be living on the streets, but because I won't get to see those little kids here anymore…

I heard my case worker and my foster parents talking last night. My caseworker said that this would be the last opportunity to adopt me before I age out. They both looked at each other and the foster dad said, "We're not planning on adopting him. We never were. He's great with the kids, but his criminal history is what's holding us back. He's a strong kid; he can make it on his own. He's too dependent on us and the foster care system; it's about time he learns how to be a man." There was a pause and the foster dad said, "We loved Jeremy when he first got here, but I'm afraid our love ran short when he started stealing from us. At first, money went missing, then my jewelry, then the gun we kept in the house for safety. I'm afraid he's gone too far…"

I never stole from them! I didn't even know they had a gun in the house. They haven't asked me about any of this; I don't know what to do. I'll admit I stole from a store before, but that was when I needed food to survive. I even ended up paying the store back when I got the money. I explained to the manager why I stole food and she cried.

I just want to go back and never hear that conversation. I want to go back to never meeting them, so my heart and head weren't filled with pain. Physical pain hurts me less than emotional pain, because honestly, I'm used to physical pain...

I'm going to miss those kids so much, and I just can't think of another place without them. I just can't. Those kids look up to me and I want to make them proud, but how am I supposed to do that when I can't see them anymore? How can I protect them? How can I teach them to play soccer, or help them with their homework? I am like their real brother, but in a couple of months I won't be there for them.

The foster care system is what it is. It's a way for kids to be safe, but in some cases, kids are put into a home that is no different from the one they were taken out of. So I guess what I'm trying to say, is that the caseworkers are doing all they can, so don't blame them. It's just that some little things need to be changed.

Each day I regret getting in so much trouble as a kid. I regret not planning sooner for my future. I regret acting out to the point where my mom gave me away. I like to think that everything I went through wasn't my fault, but the truth is, I still do. All these things are what make aging out so hard. However, there is a message in all this. It is, that no matter how hard life is, no matter how much you think you hate someone, the truth is, you can change your life, and you can love the person you thought you hated. You can be free in your heart and in your mind, if you just do something about it. SO STAND UP! You have to stand up and be strong; otherwise you will fall down in the rubble of your past and get lost.

Playing sports is a healthy outlet for me, a way to cope
with all of my anger and frustration.

Snowboarding

All around me the mountains shimmer in the fading colors of sunlight. It was the place I longed to find. The place I could be free. It was time for me to face my fears. It was time for me to face the beautiful mountain laid out before me. I am not alone. With me I carry a small black patch that reads: In Memory of Steven E. Brown. Inside that patch and inside my heart rests the resilient soul of my father. In this moment we're connected. If I fall, we fall together. That patch gives me courage, especially when I hear his voice again, telling me to believe in myself so I can shine like the sun, overcoming any enemy.

At the top of the mountain I see millions of lights off in the distance as the bright sun gives way to a silvery moon. I'm at the edge. The edge looking down with my snowboard strapped to my feet, ready to drop into a white wonderland of fresh sparkling snow. I drop. Relaxing immediately as I remember that my dad is here. I look to my right and there he is! A transparent shadow, blue against the snow. We're racing. I'm racing the dead, the lifeless, the one I love so much. My entire body is electric, tingling with an intensity so great I feel untouchable. Carving down the mountain never felt so good! Breathing the cool, crisp air, catching a glimpse of my father's spirit, it's all a wonderful reverie that I hate to leave…

As I make my way down the mountain for the last time, I look back and already the almost tangible shadow of my father is fading away like the mist across the moon. Carving my path down I still feel his presence, but not the same connection as before.

Looking back at it all, the mountains, the way the moon falls across the magnificent peaks that seem to break through the sky; looking back I realize something...

Snowboarding is more than just a sport to me. It's an adventure. Through snowboarding I have learned to trust myself and challenge myself to do something great. I have seen true beauty in the form of the perfect winter night. With snowboarding I have become stronger physically and emotionally. I have become a leader and a role model by teaching kids how to snowboard. I have learned to believe in things no one else thought possible. I have learned to be somebody people depend on because of the discipline snowboarding offers. Most importantly, I have learned humility...

I tap the small black patch in my pocket, turn and walk away from it all, realizing that my next encounter with natural beauty, outstanding peace, and the courage I need to fly is just days away, waiting for me to return to freedom.

Anonymous

I Am Not Alone

I want to share my story in the hope that other former foster children might identify and see that we're all not so different after all. We are all related.

When I was a little girl before the age of 6, I had what seemed the "normal family life and home." I had a mom and dad, school, friends, neighbors, aunts, uncles, etc., but one day this all came to a screeching halt when I was pulled out of class by a neighbor who took me to her house, placed me on her bed, and told me my dad had died. I don't really remember what I felt. I just cried and cried. Shortly after my dad died my alcoholic mom had a nervous breakdown and was committed to a hospital and I was left with the next door neighbors.

Sometime later some friends of my deceased father picked me up and got guardianship of me. This household had a mom, a dad, five children, and all the family in the world, and we went to church on Sundays, etc. On the outside it looked like the perfect, typical family life. Geez....how lucky I was...

Well, not long after being placed there the verbal abuse started; I was belittled all the time. I was also sexually abused. I was a brave child and told teachers and family members, etc., but I was told that I was making it up to get attention. After years of this abuse I finally ran away in the middle of the night and told the police what they were doing to me, and Thank God, I never had to see them again.

I was placed in the foster care system and was taken from home to home, until finally a girl's home was found for me. I had a 'house mom' and a 'house dad,' along with seven other girls. At least now I had some stability, consistency, and normalcy. I became somewhat of a normal teenager and graduated from high school. I had weekly required counseling and group meetings at this home, which I believe helped me to grow up and understand at the least that "nothing was my fault."

I moved out of the girl's home at age 17 to live with my high school sweetheart and we were together for the next ten years. He was wonderful until we got married, then the abuse, etc. started. He owned me and dictated my life. He made me feel like no one would ever love me but him and that no one would ever treat me better, so I believed it and stayed. I finally got up the courage to save money, and with God's help and a friend's help, I was able to leave him and start my life on my own again.

I've always had a hard time 'being alone.' Not having a man meant that I was truly alone, since I don't have any family whatsoever. So shortly after leaving my first relationship I had another boyfriend, but there was no true love there; he was just someone to have, and it didn't last long before I was on my own again.

Then a year later I thought I found the man of my dreams again.... "Yeah, right!" I moved out west to live with him and once again I was lied to, misled, and cheated on.

After divorcing my last husband and being on my own again I turned my life over to God and let Him have control. I had spent so many years trying to find somewhere to belong and someone to turn to, and all along I did not realize that there was only one being I needed to turn to, and that was "God." What an enlightening, wonderful wake-up call! My life has changed so much and now God has blessed me with everything I could ever want and need. I have a wonderful man now, who has deep spiritual roots, and we pray, study, and work hard together to have the best life possible, with God in the center of our life and our relationship.

I discovered FACT when I was looking for resources and tools to help me deal with my underlying feelings and loneliness. I hope that by other former foster children reading my story, they won't feel so alone, and know that there are others who experience the same feelings and pain, etc. that we've all been through and feel.

I believe that God is in control, not us. We have to have faith and rest in His wondrous, unconditional love, knowing that He will provide, and He will never give us more than we can handle.

Thank you all and God Bless!

Kelli Schoen

A Survivor

I hope that by sharing my story other foster children will be encouraged and inspired to realize that in spite of their upbringing they can be strong and survive, that they can live a successful life, as I have been able to do. If you can survive foster care, you can survive anything. I was in the process of writing my own book about my survival of foster care and other traumas, but had to put it on hold due to health issues, so it only made sense to take advantage of this opportunity to share, and although it isn't the easiest thing in the world for me to do because I learned early on to be "guarded" and afraid of rejection, I am willing to share my past if it can help others to have a future.

I can't tell you anything about my original home because my entry into foster care happened at birth. My mother voluntarily gave me up for adoption---why I do not know. I have an older sister, who my mom raised, but for some reason unknown to me, she chose not to raise me. It was discovered at birth that I had a hole in my heart, which made me unadoptable, so I was made a permanent ward and started my foster care journey through twelve homes. I have no memory of the first four foster homes I was in, but I remember the fifth one. My earliest and rather vague memories of this home are of sitting in my bedroom playing with toys, and feeling fearful when I heard my foster mother come up the stairs. I suppose by then I was emotionally triggered just by her presence. She was also emotionally abusive toward me, telling I was ugly and that nobody wanted me, not even my own mother. I had a bed-wetting problem. Her favorite name for me was "piss pot." When I got my foster care file later on, it stated in the home study on this family that "This would be a loving family that wouldn't put any demands on any foster children." If they only knew the truth about the demands being put on me there, that home study would have been trashed and I would have never gone there.

One of the demands being put on me was for sex by my foster father from the age of 8-13, which frightened and confused me. He was very forceful in his sexual approach, and although he never blatantly threatened me, he strongly insinuated it. He'd be cleaning his gun and saying to me, "I'd hate for you to say things you shouldn't tell, because I wouldn't be able to protect you. Remember, you can't tell." This happened a lot. I don't know if it was with the same gun or not, but I would come to find out later after I left the home, that he committed suicide by shooting himself. My foster mother sent me a Christmas card, inviting me for a visit, so I responded to her invitation and spent a weekend there, but was uncomfortable because I wet the bed while I was there and was afraid of punishment, so I left before she found out. She told me her husband died from a heart attack, but I knew she was lying because I lived in a small town where everyone knew everyone's business.

I got pregnant at the age of 13 and didn't know it, but my foster mother kept track of my menstrual cycle and did know it, and demanded that I abort the pregnancy. Not only did she demand an abortion, but she performed it herself by using a coat hanger. When I came home one day she was waiting for me at the front door, with a very pissed off look on her face, and grabbed me by my hair at the back of my neck and dragged me down the hall to the bathroom, where she performed the "abortion." Of course I tried to resist her, but to no avail. When she first came into the bathroom with a coat hanger, I thought it was to beat me with, but she started screaming, "I'm not going to have a slut in my house and having the neighbors talking about you being pregnant," and then she held me down while she used the coat hanger to abort the baby. She said she was "doing me a favor," that she had to make my period start so I wouldn't have a baby. I was so naïve and uneducated about sex at that age that I wasn't aware of what was happening, that I was pregnant and aborting the baby; all I knew was that the foster mom took me somewhere because I was bleeding so bad and I remember crying myself to sleep. I'm not sure whether or not she knew I was pregnant by her husband, but I think she did, or at least suspected it. My foster father never did know about the pregnancy. I missed some school because of this, and then was eventually I was ok and was allowed to go back, but I can remember dreading having to go back home after school. The foster mom never beat me again after this incident and the foster dad seemed to leave me alone for awhile after this, but in time he started sexually abusing me again and the foster mom resumed the emotional abuse. I remember one afternoon when she asked me to go to the potato bin in the garage, and because she didn't like the potatoes I brought in, she started telling me how stupid I was and that I would never make it in this world, and then she grabbed me by the arm and dragged me out to the garage and forced me into the potato bin and shut the lid, leaving me there until it was dark, with crickets crawling all over me, crying myself to sleep. To this day I have a fear of closed in spaces.

I was afraid to mention this to anyone at first, for fear of what else she would do to me, but I finally got up my courage and two months later I told the school counselor about the sexual abuse. Up to this point I had only told the school counselor that the foster mom talked mean to me, but I was so nervous and scared one day after having been sexually abused the night before, that I finally broke down and told her about the sexual abuse. I begged her not to tell the foster parents that I told, and she explained that she would have to tell my social worker, but that I would be protected. I was so frightened. She contacted DSS (Department of Social Services), but the social worker told the school counselor that I was lying. I can still remember her saying she didn't believe me, questioning why I waited until now to tell her, and me telling her that I had just learned the week before in my health class where babies came from, and that I was scared I would have a baby by the foster father, but she still didn't believe me. I was so scared and humiliated by the time she got done questioning me that I didn't tell her about the bathroom incident. Even though the social worker took me to the doctor to see if "I was telling the truth or not," and the doctor confirmed that I was, she still didn't want to believe me and took me back to that awful foster home. I was scared enough from having to go back there, but when she told me she had talked with the foster mom, I really freaked out and started crying, begging her not to take me back there. She said, "If there is any sign that your foster father knows, I will take you out of this home tonight," hugging me and acting all sweet with me, assuring me I would be fine. When we got back to the home I could hear the adults talking from my bedroom, and when I heard the foster dad coming toward my bedroom I grabbed the medicine bottle the doctor gave me and headed up the hall, making the excuse that I had to check with him about how to take the medicine, and as I passed him in the hallway he grabbed my arm and said, "If you are going to continue spreading lies about me, you will get out of my house," and when I wiggled free he said, "I will see you dead." I went outside where my social worker and foster mom were talking and said to them, "He knows, he knows," but I was reassured by both of them that I would be safe, that the foster mom would stay by my side and protect me, and that she would call me later to check up on me.

The foster mom took me to her son's store and explained the whole situation and my sister-in-law actually believed me, saying that "It will be hard for people to believe because dad is the kind of man who will give the shirt off his back if needed," but also saying that she knew "This was the kind of man who would do such a thing." I was then taken to my sister's house, and when I told her "yes," in response to her question of whether or not it was true I was sexually abused my her dad, she said, "You know, if this goes to court I will have to stand behind my father," and then got up and left the room. This was the hardest thing about exposing the truth, as I felt very close to her and even felt like I was a replacement for her twin who had died. I babysat for her five children and one night while I was there I had to wear one of my sister's nightgowns, and while she was still gone her husband came home and started touching me and kissing me, and the next thing I knew he convinced me to lay in bed with him and keep him company until my sister came home, but when he started trying to make me play with his penis I jumped up and went in the girls bedroom, but he ended up coming in there and laying on top of my back (I was sleeping on my stomach), and I just pretended to be asleep, which was easy to do, since I learned how to zone out with the foster father. I never did tell my sister about that night. I remember the phone ringing later that night and my foster mom answering it and saying, "She is just fine; she is sound asleep now."

Explaining the rest of this will be tricky because what I remember as far as time span and the true time span is different. My memory is of the social worker removing me from the foster home the very next morning, yet the records show that it was a month before she removed me from the home. The only thing I can figure is that the last month was so horrible for me there that I just blocked it out. What I do remember is going to my bedroom and packing up my belongings, making sure I didn't forget Lucky, my stuffed leprechaun that my sister gave me that I always slept with, and I remember getting into the back seat of the car and turning around to watch my foster mom looking at us as the car was pulling away, and me tearing up. My social worker said, "I can turn around and you can stay if you want," and I turned around and said, "No, mam." She then started driving toward the other side of town and began telling me about the family she was taking me to, but to be honest I was only half-way listening; my head was filled with things that my foster mom had said over the years---things like, "You are nothing," and "no family will ever want you." Throughout this whole awful ordeal the one person I am grateful for, the one person who stood up to the social worker on my behalf, was my school counselor. She became somewhat of a mentor for me and she is still in my life today. I have told her she saved my life.

Between the ages of 15-21 I lived in seven different foster homes, but I don't remember much about them, except that they were ok homes and the foster parents were decent, caring people. I'm still real close to three siblings in one foster family today, and I also have a foster father I am real close to.

As for my biological parents, they never visited me while I was in foster care, but when I was about 16 years old I met my real mother, in a roundabout way. I was in a new school and when the teacher took name roll one day, a boy showed up with the same last name as mine, and I found out he was my cousin. I asked him if he knew my mom's last name and he said, "Yes," that she was his aunt. He didn't believe me until I showed him my birth certificate, and his family denied this, but he eventually got tired of being in the middle and gave me her home phone number and I called her. Her husband knew something wasn't right because I asked for her by her maiden name, not her married name, and when I went to school the next day the school counselor told me not to contact her anymore. My foster father told me she was my mother, but that she didn't want to talk at this time, but apparently she changed her mind, as about two weeks later she called my house and told my foster father that she wanted to see me, so the social worker and he set up a meeting for us.

It was a really weird experience meeting my mom for the first time. I remember walking down the street toward a restaurant and seeing this woman who looked so much like me that it was like looking at me when I was older. She just walked up to me and said, "Oh, you must be Kelli. I'm sure you have some questions to ask me." As a matter of fact, yes, I did have some questions to ask her, but she wasn't very willing to answer them. The main question I wanted to ask her was, "Is the man you're married to my father?" She said, "No, and I don't want to talk about him." The only thing she would say about him was that she had thought she'd have a better life without him, but she didn't; she ended up with same kind of life anyway. I don't remember what else we talked about, but she took me to my grandmother's house. An older woman came walking outside and asked my mom who I was, and my mom told her to go inside, and then when we were all inside the house my mom told her who I was and she said, "I always wondered what happened to her." Although I had a good, loving relationship with my grandma, and we talked on the phone a lot, I couldn't get any more information out of her than I did my mother. I think I was the best kept secret in the family, but I don't know why; maybe I was the result of a rape or something, I don't know. I have learned not to ask questions. Why ask questions if you can't get any answers? I thought I deserved to at least know my history, if for anything, medical reasons, but I wasn't willing to risk what little relationship I had with her, so I quit asking questions. Although we are not real close, and she's rather distant with me, we do talk occasionally. I have somewhat of a relationship with her and I'm fine with that. I've learned to accept my mom on her terms. I've also learned to accept my foster care experience on its terms. People in general have always been apologetic, offering sympathy about my circumstances, but I tell them, "It's ok, although I wouldn't want to live it again; it made me who I am today." I'm very strong-willed, which is something I learned from being in foster care. I had a social worker who discouraged me from going to college (because of financial funding), but I stood up to her and was determined to get my education, which I succeeded in doing. Foster care taught me to stand up and take care of myself. I have been treated for Post Traumatic Stress Disorder and Depression, and having been a mental health counselor for 15 years, was able to treat others with mental health issues, but due to a physical disability (I suffered a stroke while being operated on for a brain aneurism), I am now unemployed and not liking it, but am accepting where I'm at in my life because I have to. What else can I do? When you've gone through foster care, you just have to learn to accept life for what it is and survive.

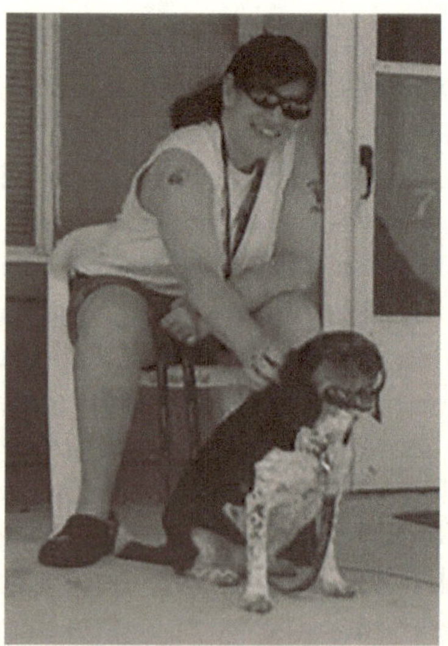

K.R.

Experience, Strength, and Hope

When I started to write this my heart was pounding and I was starting to feel sick to my stomach. The tears started to flow with the idea of "having to go back there." However, I decided I could not give up on writing it. If my story could make a difference in someone else's life, then I am willing to tell it. I kept going over in my mind, what should I say and what should I not? Do I want to tell all or just some of the details? I then decided that I am going to write about what has made the most significant impact on my life and what has been on my mind and heart the most.

I was born two months after the blizzard of 1978. I usually tell people, jokingly, that this happened in preparation for me to come. I am the youngest of three girls. When my mom gave birth to me she got sick with pneumonia, so my dad and aunt took care of me for a few weeks. Then when I was four months old my mom had her first nervous breakdown and my sisters and I were taken care of by my dad, aunt, and family friend. My mom was in the hospital for four months.

She was diagnosed with Bipolar Disorder and severe P.T.S.D. (Post Traumatic Stress Disorder). When she was stable, she sang us songs and played games with us, took care of us when we were sick, and cooked for us. It was like being raised by a single mother since my dad eventually became sicker than she was. She was suicidal at times and angry at parents and other family members because of the neglect and abuse that she had as a child, especially by her mom who was an alcoholic. Her parents divorced when I was 2 years old. My grandmother died from lung cancer when I was seven. I only remember seeing her once, on Christmas when she gave me a mechanical Beagle puppy. It now makes sense to me that as an adult I have a dream to have a real puppy someday when I own a house with a yard. My grandfather died when I was fifteen. It was awful when he passed away because I was very close to him. He was three quarters Italian and one quarter German. He would sing to us in his car when he would drive us to the shops in New Hampshire. He called me Bella (beautiful in Italian). I still miss him to this day.

When I was three years old my parents went away for the weekend and left us girls to stay with my grandfather's girlfriend, who was also an alcoholic (my parents did not know this about her at the time). She got very drunk, locked me away in a room with her, and beat me up really badly. My sisters were in the other rooms and could not help me. They heard me screaming in the other room. They were only 6 and 8 years old at the time. I found out that I was in the hospital for a week with really bad bruises. My mother said she didn't recognize me. It wasn't until I was fourteen that my sisters told me about this incident. I was shocked when I heard this from them because I have no recollection of this happening. They cried as they told me this, sorry that they couldn't help me. My grandfather didn't believe my mom, and from that point on their relationship was strained.

My dad ended up in the hospital not long after that incident. He suffers from Schizoaffective Disorder and P.T.S.D. He grew up in Cuba and left when he was nineteen to escape from Fidel Castro during the Cuban Missile Crisis. I met his parents twice, since most of his family stayed in Cuba. He received shock treatments during one of the several times that he ended up in the hospital. I don't ever remember him being a "normal" father. He is always in his own little world and it always feels like I am talking to a wall. He answers when you talk to him, but that's it. It feels cold and unloving; however, I know that he does love me because he sometimes tells me so, but I can't go to him for advice, comfort, guidance, or protection.

When I was 41/2 my mom had another nervous breakdown. I remember her lying on the kitchen floor on her stomach, banging her head and her fists on the floor saying, "I just want to die." I don't know who called 911, but the police came and took her. We rode in an ambulance to the hospital, and then the Department of Social Service's put us into our first foster home. I was terrified, but I never told anyone. I think this was the beginning of me becoming numb emotionally and repressing my feelings. I don't remember much about that foster home, except for when I got chicken pox. I was scratching so much, crying and making a lot of noise so my foster mother made me sit by myself in the dark on the top of the stairs. Thank God we did not stay at that foster home too long!

After that we went back home to our parents for about a year. Then I ended up in another foster home by myself for six months. I was about 6 at the time. I actually liked this one. It was a young married couple who owned a house in the next town over. They had a German shepherd that was much taller than me when he stood up, but he was so gentle. I loved going to the parks with him and my foster father. It was nice having two parents, and even grandparents, that were stable. My foster father owned an ice cream truck where he also sold pizza and subs. I loved it. He used to read to me at night and tuck me in at bed time. I never had that from my own dad, so when I had to leave there I was really sad; however, I acted as if I didn't mind coming home because I didn't want my parents, especially my mom, to feel worse than they already felt for not being there for me. Soon after that I ran away from home with a bag packed with rice and clothes to my aunt's house down the street. I said to my mom, "You're crazy, so I am going to auntie's house," and then I left. My mom followed me to her sister's house where they fought. In her mind my aunt was trying to take me away from her. When this happened her oldest son had to break it up. He has been my favorite cousin ever since!

Until the age of 13 we went back and forth from my parents to foster homes. We were sometimes placed together in the same home, but not always. I was in three other homes that I can remember. I lived in one of them for a year. While I was there I contracted lice and scabies. Once when I was sick with a stomach bug, I was forced to eat my dinner, otherwise I was going to be sent to my room. It was awful! In another foster home, I remember there being a strict policy of how much toilet paper, one or three squares, you could use, depending on what you needed to do. It was the strangest thing ever for me, because even while in the projects with my biological parents we never did that. My mom somehow always had enough to provide for us girls and even helped others who were less fortunate.

We did not have extended family that would or could take us in. We only saw them on some occasions, except for my uncle (my mother's older brother). We couldn't live with him because he was working full-time; however, he did take us out every Saturday for bowling, or a movie, or the park, and he always took us out to eat. I remember thinking he was crazy because he always told us jokes and I was not used to that. I was more used to the depression, dysfunction, and fighting in the house with us girls, mom, and dad. I argued a lot with my mom and oldest sister. My sister and I fought because my mom would not set limits with me. I believe she was too sick to. My sister thought it would be better if I stayed home and not spend time with my friends. I didn't want to be home because I didn't want to see my parents sick. I just wanted to be a kid and have fun.

My sister tried to be my mom, but I didn't like it because I felt she was too controlling. It got so bad that we started fighting physically, so when my sister turned 18 my mom made her leave, and she went into a group home.

I felt like my mom was a broken record, repeating over and over what she had gone through as a child. She sometimes took her anger out on us with regards to this. She would talk to us kids as if we were her therapist, but we always felt bad because we couldn't help her. She wasn't getting the help she needed and was carrying the burden of raising children on her own. Because of my dad's illness and shock treatments he became extremely introverted. My mom could not accept that about him. I stood up for him on numerous occasions when she kept nagging him to talk to her. I would say "Leave him alone!" I was very angry at her because of this and because of her being sick. She would try to explain her illness to me, but I just got madder.

She would say that I was so stubborn, that I never wanted to lose an argument, and that I should be a lawyer because of it. Then I felt even worse when she would say that I was the "strong one," that I could somehow handle things better than everyone else in the family. I felt that maybe she was right, but more than anything I felt that I couldn't help but be strong because of the weaknesses I saw in the family. It's like I carried the family "problems" on the weight of my shoulders, but wouldn't allow myself to feel the hurt and pain that went along with it. I was afraid that I would just fall apart and end up in the hospital like both of them. During these times I don't remember ever crying. I suppressed my feelings because my mother's were so extreme at times, and I didn't want to be like that. My older sister tried to keep the peace and was more passive like my dad. She got along with all of us and tried to mediate between us since we were arguing most of the time. My mom tried to get us all help with individual and family counseling, but it wasn't enough to fix our problems. She really fought hard to keep us kids at home as much as she could.

In the midst of all of this I was teased by kids at school and in the projects about my looks and my mom being "crazy." They thought I had a big nose so they called me Pinocchio and Gonzo. The saying of "sticks and may break my bones, but words can never hurt me" is a lie! Whoever came up with that nonsense, anyway? These kids even started physical fights with me for no reason. I further withdrew into my shell and wanted to be invisible. I felt unpopular, unloved, and didn't fit in, except among kids whose families were somewhat similar to mine. I found myself spending time with kids whose parents had a substance abuse problem and/or emotional problems. Somehow we never got around to talking about how awful it was; at least I don't remember ever talking to anyone about it, including any teachers. It was like they didn't even care. They were oblivious to the fact that I was thinking "If I got hit by a car and died tomorrow, would anyone miss me?" I felt so alone and abandoned. And I couldn't voice this to my parents because I didn't want to make things worse for them. I was even afraid to because I thought it would make them sicker. I didn't want to over burden them with my problems, needs, and fears.

While all of this was going on, I didn't have a healthy outlet. I found my escape in several things, including video games, movies, music, sports and finally, romance novels. These are the only things that got me through those awful times. I listened to songs by Mariah Carey including *Can't take that away…*"They can say anything they want to say, try to bring me down, but I won't face the ground," and her song *Hero,* "It's a long road when you face the world alone. No one reaches out a hand for you to hold. You can find love if you search within yourself and the emptiness you felt will disappear." The romance novels taught me to fantasize about the perfect romance of a woman being swept off her feet with the notion of "happily ever after." The more I read those books the more I got lost in them, and the more I read them the more those other things that used to help me get through weren't as mesmerizing. Reading these somehow started to fill that void that I had in myself of needing to feel loved, accepted unconditionally, nurtured, and happy.

This then lead me down a destructive path of "looking for love in all of the wrong places." I met a boy who knew my sister's boyfriend. Our relationship started quickly and we were together for about a year. We didn't get along very well at all. We were very young and immature. He was disrespectful to me and also called me Pinocchio. He spent more time with my older sister, to whom I felt inferior, because she was my mom's favorite. She said that she wasn't difficult like I was and that she was pretty and I was only attractive. My mom told me once that if a guy met me, and then my sister, the guy would want her and not me. She even said maybe if I got a nose job I would look better, that I was too pale and that I should wear some makeup, especially blush.

I finally couldn't take what I was going through with my boyfriend anymore, so I broke up with him. A few months after that I realized something was wrong when I still had not gotten my period. When I realized this it was the first time I had cried in a very long time. I was pregnant at the age of 14, right out of 8th grade. I never told anyone except her father and a close friend of ours. We didn't tell our parents because we were afraid to. I also avoided the doctor. You are probably wondering how this could have happened. No one else knew? I was in denial. I felt like if I never said anything to anyone then it wasn't really happening. Then I could just wish it away just like I had done with my parent's mental illnesses, however unsuccessfully. I wore my older sister's clothes, which were baggy on me. I slept upstairs in the living room on the loveseat because I felt too ashamed and guilty to sleep downstairs with my mom and older sister. I lied to people, including my best friend, when they asked me if I was pregnant. I said that I had never had sex and that I was just depressed from the break up, that I was eating more and gaining more because of it. Finally, my mom decided to make a doctor's appointment for me, but I never showed up because I knew what they would find out. I told my mom that I forgot about the appointment.

My mom didn't find out until I was in labor about two months after this. We didn't know if I was in labor or having a miscarriage. My mom asked me if I preferred a boy or a girl. I told her, "If I have it then I want a girl." I didn't want people to know because I was embarrassed, so I made sure we went to the hospital in a cab instead of an ambulance. When we got there the person at the desk asked me, "Who is your doctor?" "I don't have one," I replied. "When was your last period?" "I don't know." They then whisked me away in a wheelchair to the maternity ward. After they did an ultrasound they found out that the baby was breach (feet first instead of head first), and that I would need a C-section. The nurse who did the ultrasound said she knew the sex of the baby, but she was not going to tell me because she wanted it to be a surprise. She also said that since I was not eating healthily and hadn't gone to the doctor, that I had toxemia (bacterial toxins in the blood) and my blood pressure was so high, that I could have had a stroke if I hadn't made it to the hospital in time.

Several minutes later my bed was wheeled away into the delivery room, where my mom met me. She wore blue hospital scrubs from head to toe. She was there with me the whole time while they delivered my daughter in to my arms. She was a healthy full-term baby weighing 6 lbs. 11 and ½ oz. Since then we have called her our miracle baby. I had never even baby-sat a child, so I was totally clueless as to what to do with her. The only experience I had with kids was the summer before this, when I worked at a camp with pre-school kids. I didn't even know how to change a diaper, so my mom showed me. With the help of my mom and sisters I was able to slowly learn how to take care of her. Her father also moved in with us for a short time. We felt we should stay together for our daughter's sake, but we still continued to argue, so we broke up again.

I was a freshman in high school when I had my daughter. I like to say that I was 15 when I had her, but she will tell you I was 14, ten months and fifteen days. I was out of school for two weeks, and then I was able to go back, because my mom took care of my daughter for a few months before she ended up in the hospital again. Thankfully my older sister was eighteen at the time, so I did not have to go into another foster home. My mom was only at the hospital a few months, and while I went to school my daughter stayed with my best friend's mother who owned a family daycare. From my sophomore to senior years I ended up bringing her to the day care that they had at school. I wasn't the only teen mother there, so I am grateful that my school provided the daycare and a program for teen parents. I brought her to school on the bus with me, where I would get looks and snide remarks like, "You are just a baby having a baby," and "Are you married?" With a curt reply I replied, "Yes, I know," and "No way would I ever be married to him!"

My life was not the life of a 15 year old. I went to classes on the days I decided I didn't want to skip them, and then I went to work at the teen health center at the high school. I picked my daughter up from her aunt's (on her father's side) and then I went home. When that job ended I then worked at a jewelry store near where I lived. I don't think I ever did much homework, but somehow I was still able to graduate. It was very difficult for me, but with the help of my mom, sisters, and my sister's boyfriend's family, I was able to get through it. I don't remember anything I learned, but I do remember graduating, and that my daughter was 3 and ½ years old at the time. More recently, I have come to realize just how common this part of my story is among foster children. On October 21, 2010 I went to a book signing for "Hope's Boy" by Andrew Bridge, who is also a former foster child. He mentioned that statistically, girls who end up in foster homes are more than twice as likely to become teen mothers. When I heard him say this I started crying. I am one of these statistics!

At the end of my senior year I met the love of my life through a family friend. On a deep level I still felt alone until I met him. He was my best friend and became my boyfriend, and eventually my fiancé. He loved my daughter and me very much. He understood me and communicated with me like no other. He accepted me for who I was, and when I told him about what my mother had said about my nose, he kissed it and said, "I love your nose." I didn't know until a couple of months after we met that he was an alcoholic and a drug addict. I had never touched a drink or drug because of my mother constantly warning us that we would end up an alcoholic like her mother. I am so glad she decided to break that pattern! I didn't understand what was going on with him. He told me I should start going to Alanon meetings, which is a 12-Step recovery group for family and friends of alcoholics. At the time I was living at a shelter for women and their children because my mom and I were not getting along again.

A year later on May 2, 1998, five days after my birthday, he died from a heroin overdose. I was devastated. I was in so much pain from his death that I wanted to die. I remember that week after his death. I went to his wake and funeral. I had a court date for visitation for my daughter's father, where I couldn't even function at the courthouse. I was so distraught with grief that I threw up near the bathroom. I had to leave. I couldn't function at my job or through the classes I was taking in college. I didn't even tell my supervisor what had happened because I was ashamed. Because of this, I got fired and failed several classes, and withdrew from the rest. Since we were living in the shelter I was told that if I didn't get another job, we were going to be kicked out within a week. By the Grace of God I was able to work as a cashier at the same job that I had before I went to college.

People from the Alanon meetings kept bringing me to meetings, which helped me get through all of this. I got to be around people who understand the affects of alcoholism and drug addiction. All I did was cry in those meetings for years because of it. They accept the fact that because of my past I still don't feel comfortable or safe around people who drink even moderately, or take drugs. They help me understand my mother and have compassion for her. Before I started to go to those meetings I thought she was making up the abuse that happened from her alcoholic mother, but hearing the stories in those meetings I then knew it was true. They also taught me to "Let Go and Let God" and to "Turn my will and my life over to the CARE of God." I never felt that anyone or anything cared about me, so this has been such a foreign concept for me. I learned that "feelings aren't facts" and about *"God* as we understood Him." I have embraced my own faith, which is Christianity. My faith story is another story altogether!

At the age of 6 my daughter started to act out and I received calls from her school almost every day because of it. Her behavior was so bad that they decided to put her in Special Ed. She got moved to a different school with a smaller class size. They gave her an I.E.P. (Individual Education Plan), which included a team of teachers and a counselor with whom we met individually and as a family on a weekly basis. I think all kids should have this! I remember I started crying during one of the team meetings with the teachers and counselor. I was too upset to say anything, so the counselor explained to the teachers that the reason I was crying was because my mother couldn't be there for me the way I was there for my daughter when I was her age. During these times we got a lot of support from my sisters, my mom, my uncle (later his wife), and friends from my meetings and church. I also joined Codependents Anonymous (CODA), another 12 Step group, where I am finally learning how to set healthy boundaries. Why don't they teach this in schools? God just kept bringing people and situations into our lives to help "carry" us through it, just like the Footprints prayer.

My daughter's father was mostly in her life until she was 10. He then moved out of state with his wife and their children. They have only seen her a few times since they moved. Thankfully, since then my landlord and his wife have been a huge support to us. He and my uncle have been like father figures to my daughter, which has really helped me because it is really tough being a single mother. Speaking about single mothers! What also helped us during these years was watching a TV show called Gilmore Girls. It was about a single mother who had her daughter at age 16, and at the start of the show her daughter was 16 and in high school. We could relate to it in a lot of ways. We have since bought all of the seven seasons because the series ended a few years ago. One of my close friends recently said to me "Kristina, it doesn't take a village to raise a child! It takes the Body of Christ to raise a child." He is so right!

Even though I have made a lot of progress in other areas of my life, neither Alanon nor CODA have helped me work through my foster care experiences. Only maybe one or two times did I mention it in those meetings, but no one "got it." They couldn't relate to what I had gone through during that time. Actually, until sometime late in 2009, I hadn't really talked about it at all. It all happened when my mom went into the hospital because she got really physically sick, which exacerbated into her having a mental breakdown. As you know, this was nothing new for my sisters and me, because it had been going on for much of our childhood. The big difference was that we were now adults, and we actually began talking about what happened when we were younger. You are probably thinking, "What do you mean you never talked about it?" Yes, we never talked about it when we were younger, even amongst ourselves. I think it is because we were so confused and scared about what was going on. I think it was also our defense mechanism to help us get through it. It was like we had to deny that it was actually happening to get through it.

We talked about how difficult it was for both of our parents to have mental illnesses and for them to keep having breakdowns. We talked about how afraid we were and how awful it was for us to keep going in and out of foster homes. We talked about how alone we felt and the fact that we didn't know anyone else who had the experience of being in foster homes, aside from the three of us. We cried and hugged each other. We then ended up becoming my mom's "social worker" to finally get her the help that she really needed. We made calls to different nursing homes and rest homes because the hospital social worker wanted to send her home. She was too isolated at home, since we no longer live there and my dad has been in his own nursing home for several years. We knew that she didn't belong back there. I remember I got angry with the social worker and said to her, "If this was your mother, would you send her home?" She got upset with that question and replied, "She is not my mother." Fortunately, I was able to convince the social worker to transfer our mother into a nursing home. My stubbornness sure came in handy that time!

A few months later my older sister started to talk about how she had been thinking about starting a non-profit organization for kids who had been through what we had been through. She even mentioned this to a friend of mine from church. But how could one person like her start something so important, she asked? My friend reassured her that God can help by bringing more people around to help. I started to talk about how I wanted to be a temporary foster parent and advocate for children and parents to become more stable so the kids wouldn't end up in foster homes. I wanted to do something that I wish had been done for us. I said jokingly to my friends and family "Of course, my future husband would have to agree to something like this, especially being a foster parent."

After we had these conversations we did not think about it again until about a month later, when something so amazing happened. It was the weekend of May 14th-16th, 2010. I was on a 20's & 30's church group retreat up in New Hampshire. Before dinner on Saturday the 15th, I was reading this book called *Will I Ever Be Good Enough*. The section I read that day, on page 44, said:

"In many parenting-time proceedings, the discussion focuses not on what is in the best interest of the child as the law dictates, but on what is the best for the parent. It is a sad commentary on our culture that many parenting-time evaluators and judges listen more intently to what the parents wants than what is truly best for the children. There is even talk about which evaluator is 'for the father' and 'which is for the mother.' What about being a child advocate?"

I thought, "Oh My God, this is *exactly* what I had been talking about only a few weeks before." So I underlined it in my book and put stars next to it. It was just so amazing to me that I decided that this would be a *perfect* place for me to stop. I left the cabin and went to the dining hall for dinner.

I grabbed my food, and then sat next to one of my friends. Only a few minutes later, another woman wandered over to my table. Although I had seen her in passing at my church group, I had just met her the night before at the prayer meeting. I never had a conversation with her. I asked her how she was doing, and she said that she was tired from a very busy work week. I then asked her what she did for work. That's when she said she had founded the Massachusetts Chapter of a non-profit organization called the Foster Care Alumni of America (F.C.A.A.) for former foster children to be advocates for foster kids. I then asked her to repeat herself because I was shocked by what she said. When I heard her the second time I started crying. I could not speak for several seconds, but when I finally spoke up I told her that I was in foster homes. This is when she started crying because she was also shocked. Before she came to dinner she prayed to God, asking Him, "Where Are You God? Should I continue to do this work? I have been doing this for almost two years, unpaid, without funding. It is just getting too hard!!! Please God; I need a sign if I should continue to do this." It took us at least an hour to absorb what had happened. We cried and we laughed during that time because we were just *so* overwhelmed and in awe with how amazing God's perfect timing was. Even consider the fact that the invitation to their yearly Alumni BBQ that she sent out months before said to R.S.V.P. by May 15th, the same day we made this connection. Also, May is Foster Care and Mental Illness Awareness month!

Since then, other amazing things have been happening. I became the Treasurer for the MA Chapter of F.C.A.A. I was referred to Carol Lucas, who compiled this book, and another woman who is starting a FACT (Fostered Adult Children Together) support group right in MA. I never thought something so awful could be used for something good. I just kept thinking over and over, "You will no longer regret the past nor wish to shut the door on it," which is part of the Promises of working the 12 Steps in Alanon.

Where are we now? I am so happy that I am going to be a part of this FACT group! I have P.T.S.D. because of the trauma I have endured. I am 33 years old and still have night terrors. I have to sleep with the light on and listen to the Veggie Tales song *God is bigger than the boogie man*. I am terrified of being abandoned and am always expecting that to happen. When someone leaves my life or dies I can't handle it. When it does, I fall apart emotionally. I suffer from low self-esteem and trust issues. I still sometimes feel those familiar feelings of being invisible and not cared about. I tend to be very serious and don't know how to have fun because I am still waiting "for the other shoe to drop," for something bad to happen during the good times because it is what I am used to. My relationships, especially with men, have been rocky at best. I still have that ache of wanting a "family unit" of my own, one with a mother and a father. I feel I have not been able to give that to my daughter, or even the wounded child still within me. I'm afraid to go on psychiatric drugs because of the side effects; I feel it is a temporary band aid. So not only do I go to my meetings, I go to church (including Celebrate Recovery), acupuncture, energy work-integrated awareness, and I see a Christian therapist that works with E.M.D.R.(Eye Movement Desensitization Reprocessing-treatment for P.T.S.D).

I came to realize that I internalized my mom's negative beliefs about herself passed onto her by her mother. Her mother would also compare her sister to her the way she did with us. What has been helping me change those "negative tapes" and heal from the past is to read the book *Captivating: Unveiling the Mystery of a Woman's Soul* and listening over and over to songs by Johnny Diaz called *More beautiful You:* "Well, little girl 14, I wish that you could see that beauty is within your heart and you were made with such care; your skin, your body, and your hair are perfect just the way they are," and Kirk Franklin's "*Imagine me* loving what I see when the mirror looks at me."

Most importantly, I have been praying and meditating on the following Bible verses:

"But the LORD said to Samuel, "Do not consider his appearance or his height, for I have rejected him. The LORD does not look at the things people look at. People look at the outward appearance, but the LORD looks at the heart." 1 Samuel 16:7

"No one will be able to stand against you all the days of your life. As I was with Moses, so I will be with you; I will never leave you nor forsake you." Joshua 1:5

"He will wipe every tear from their eyes. There will be no more death or mourning or crying or pain, for the old order of things has passed away." Revelation 21:4

"Though my father and mother forsake me, the LORD will receive me." Psalm 27:10

"A father to the fatherless, a defender of widows, is God in his holy dwelling. God sets the lonely in families, he leads out the prisoners with singing; but the rebellious live in a sun-scorched land." Psalm 68:5-6

"For your Maker is your husband—the LORD Almighty is his name—the Holy One of Israel is your Redeemer; he is called the God of all the earth. The LORD will call you back as if you were a wife deserted and distressed in spirit—a wife who married young, only to be rejected," says your God." Isaiah 54:5-6

"And we know that in all things God works for the good of those who love him, who have been called according to his purpose." Romans 8:28.

Just like The Fray's song "Lost and insecure you found me, lying on the floor," I am no longer lost but now I am found. I had no identity, but learning about my "Identity in Christ." I have embraced my love of dolphins and am going back to school to become a Financial Planner to teach people money management and to invest in Socially Responsible funds.

My dad calls me every Saturday to spend time with him. I make time to see him every few weeks, just us. We watch movies together, sing songs in my car, and I even open up to him and share some things that are on my heart. I make him laugh a lot. After reading *The Unavailable Father* this past year, which even has a Chapter on the Schizophrenic father, I have had some insight into our relationship. It has helped me understand him and myself more. I feel this has helped a lot. My mom is doing better because she has better social workers working for her and now she is in assisted living. We have made amends and are getting along better. She can't believe she ever said those awful things to me and now says that I am beautiful, that I deserve the best, and that I am a "Diamond in a rough." She has apologized to all of us and feels badly that things weren't better for us when we were younger. I keep reminding her that she "did as best as she could with what she had." My daughter is now 18 years old. People always think that we are sisters. Because of all the help we received, things got much better. She got out of Special Ed in only a few years' time and has been on Honor Roll since then. She is now a senior in high school and will be going to college in September. This past year we have had several family gatherings that have been enjoyable and fun. Even better is that there have been no arguments. I never imagined that what they say in Alanon "The family situation is bound to improve" would ever come true. It is also true that "God is doing for us what we could not do for ourselves." I definitely "Came to believe that a Power greater than ourselves could restore us to Sanity." Thank you God, for everything! As they say in meetings, thank you for letting me share!

Written by Kristina R.
Kristina R.
Recovering Codependent
Recovering Fostered Adult Child
Grateful believer in Jesus Christ

Footnote:
McBride, Karyl. *Will I Ever Be Good Enough? Healing the Daughters of Narcissistic Mothers.*
Rosenthal, Sarah S. *The Unavailable Father: Seven Ways Women Can Understand, Heal, and Cope with a Broken Father-Daughter Relationship.*

Lisamarie Kerr

A Far From Normal Life
Growing Up Too Quick

As I write my short story I am fairly fresh out of foster care in Ireland, being only 19 years old. I want to share my story because I think others need to realize how abnormal our lives are as foster kids. I'm sure other foster kids who read this will relate to just how abnormal our lives are and how it affects us.

I was in foster care from the age of 3 ½, or so I have been told. My life was far from normal, as I had to grow up quicker than some people. I had to take care of my younger brother (he is 13 years old now) who has health issues from the time he was born until I finally got to move out of the foster home at age 18.

I met my biological dad for the first time about two weeks after I left my foster home, but it wasn't a good experience. I was living with my fiancé and working in a training center and one day after work my dad followed us up to our apartment. He stayed for hours and did some things he shouldn't have, and when my foster dad came to visit to see how we were doing, my real dad ran out of our apartment fast!

When I started suffering from panic attacks I was admitted to a hospital, but my foster sister came to the hospital and told the doctors and nurses that there was nothing wrong with me, that I was just faking it, which was the biggest pile of crap! I wasn't faking my panic attacks! I did everything for my foster family when I lived with them and this was what I got in return! I only saw my real mom once a week for an hour visit, which was supervised by social workers, and I only saw my older brother once a month.

Aging out and trying to move on with my life has not been easy. I would probably write more, but my life has been so hectic for the last few months that I just can't.

Loraine Mink

Fortunate, Considering My Circumstances

I was born in 1925 in Aurora, Illinois. I had one brother a year older than me. My mom died from tuberculosis when I was 5 years old. I have no idea why my dad didn't take care of me and my brother, and if for some reason he was unable to care for us, I still don't understand the circumstances and why my other relatives didn't take us, especially since there were so many of them. I resented this.

I was put in a children's home in Aurora sometime shortly before or after my mom died, but I don't know exactly when. My brother joined me there at the children's home after he got out of the sanitarium for tuberculosis. I just remember being real happy to see him. We were there about two years. I don't remember much about the place, but I don't think it was a bad place. I also don't remember if any relatives came to visit me while I was there.

We were taken out of the children's home in 1932 or 1933 because my dad couldn't pay for our care there, and put in ISSCS (Illinois Soldiers and Sailors Children School). We were able to go there because my dad had been in WW1. I don't have any complaints about the home, at least not as far as the basics go. They were good to me there, providing the essentials. I was well-fed. The school was good; I think I got a good education there. I had a lot of kids to play with. It was as good a place as any for children who needed a home. My only complaint was the lack of nurturing there; I don't remember any emotional warmth and hugging. The kids there used to call me "little miss touch me not" because I would tighten up inside if anybody got too close to me. I don't really know why I was so afraid of being touched, but I had a fear of closeness. I don't remember anybody ever hurting me, but I just wasn't comfortable with physical closeness for some reason. Maybe I was afraid of getting close and people leaving me, abandoning me, like when my mom died and I was pushed around in homes. The highlight of the year at ISSCS was Legion's Day, when we were treated very special, getting to ride on a big truck, going on picnics, getting candy, playing games, and getting gifts. It was a real treat.

In 1939, after my 8th grade graduation, I was taken out of ISSCS and put in a home with my aunt and uncle, but I wasn't happy there because me and my aunt didn't like each other and we didn't get along, so I only stayed for about one week. A social worker just came there one day and told me to "pack my things," which wasn't much, because "things weren't going well there," and I was put in another foster home in Elgin, Illinois, with Mr. and Mrs. Chelsey Fritz, for about two years. They were real good to me, but the woman's mother had to move in with them when her husband died and there was no room for me, so I was taken out of that home and put in a temporary home with the foster mother's niece and her husband for about three months. They were also very nice to me. From here I went to live at the Nelson's home and stayed there one year, using their daughter's bedroom while she was away at college. The Nelson's were also very kind to me and their three daughters even thought of me as their little sister. When their daughter came home from college though, there was no room for me and I had to be put into another foster home, this time with Mr. and Mrs. Lester Walters, which was just as nice as the other homes; in fact, Mr. Walters gave me away when I got married.

I was fortunate, considering my circumstances. I had such nice homes and the people were so good to me, treating me like I was part of their family. Most people don't realize what foster kids are going through these days. I know a lot of kids, especially these days, aren't as fortunate as I was. Perhaps part of the reason all my foster parents were so charitable toward me was because they were all involved with their churches. I was lucky, but the majority of the kids nowadays aren't, and I just wish they could have a better experience like I had. One thing I believe though, is that having a tough childhood like that makes you tougher and more resilient. Growing up without your own parents, you feel like you have to take care of yourself. You have to be strong.

Lu

A Tragedy

I was born in 1941, along with my twin sister. I was the last of seven children. My mother was only 13 years old when she married my dad, who was twenty years her senior. My dad died 13 days after my birth. When I was about 2 years old my mom remarried and I acquired two half siblings. My step-dad was very abusive, both sexually and physically; he was a real SOB. I don't know exactly when it started, but I think around 5 years old, I remember waking up and him bothering me, sexually molesting me. I told my older sister about it and when we switched the sides of the bed to sleep on, he molested her also, so she told our mom and her mom. Thereafter he threatened me, so for a long time I slept under my bed. He also beat us a lot. One day I watched him make a switch out of braided twigs and he told me it was for me, that he was going to beat me with it. One day I came home and saw him beating my twin sister and when I confronted him about it, he began beating me with the switch. I then grabbed the switch from him and started beating him with it. I wanted to kill him!

I never did understand why I was being abused. It was very confusing for me. My mom also beat me a lot; in fact, every chance she got, she hurt me, not only physically, but also emotionally. She told me that I was made for sex. My twin sister was favored over me. She was a parasite and I never felt safe around her. I still don't feel safe around her. The family laughed at me like it was a game. They were a bunch of sadists, doing whatever they could to antagonize me.

The one bright spot in my childhood was my grandmother. I bonded with her. The first five years of my life was spent being shuffled back and forth between my mom's and my grandma's place, which was just across the street. She died when I was 10 years old and I felt like a part of me died with her. If I could have gotten in the grave with her, I would have. I had a meltdown; I didn't want to come out. I wouldn't even take a bath then. I was in a state of shock for years.

My life was one tragedy after another. When I was 10 years old I had a foster home set up for me, but they took my older sister and left me. I was always getting left behind. I was 11 years old when I started living with an aunt and my twin sister lived with another aunt right next door. My aunt sat me down one day and told me she didn't really want me there, that the only reason she took me in was because the other aunt wanted my twin sister and nobody wanted me, so she took me. A few weeks later my aunt informed me that my twin sister would be adopted, but not me, and then she gave me a piece of jewelry to make me feel better. I still loved that woman, even though she didn't want me. I felt like I was the scapegoat in the family. Somewhere along the line I felt like I lost my childhood. I saw everyone else have one, having a good time being a kid, but what happened to me? Where was my childhood? I don't think I ever had one.

When I was 12 years old I was put in a foster home (the Center) for 24 hours. The social worker took me there, even though she told me she wasn't supposed to. Before going there, my sister and brother were dropped off at a foster home. They were crying and clinging to me. I had a big frog in my throat like I wanted to cry, but I didn't cry. I asked the social worker to tell me a funny story just to put my mind somewhere else, so she did. In my childhood pictures I'm never laughing. There was no laughter in me.

In 1954 I went into a children's home in Illinois. The cottage parent told me I wasn't supposed to stay long, so I kept thinking somebody was going to come and get me. I liked the home and was very grateful to be there. I was fed, clothed, and educated. One day I was sulking about and I told one of the workers there that I felt bad because I didn't have anything on my bed like the other girls, such as a doll or a stuffed toy, so she took me over to a building and unlocked this huge room that was filled with toys and let me pick out something for myself. I can remember standing in the middle of that room and just being awestruck by all those toys and stuffed animals. I was my own worst enemy there for the first two years. I was a sleep walker because of the emotional stress and I had nightmares. I also had trouble in the classroom because I kept thinking about being home and where I would hide. One bad experience I had there was when I got hit in the face with a paddle by one of the girls in my cottage and I had to go to the hospital. The cottage parent told her to hit me and I never understood why.

I left the home when I was 18 years old and I lived with the same aunt I lived with before. We got along ok, but then I started running around, met my husband, and got married. He was a nice man and we had four children. I suffered another terrible tragedy when my husband shot himself because he was sick and didn't want to suffer anymore. I felt suicidal afterward and I seen a psychiatrist, who told me that as a child I lived in a "nest of sadists."

My experience has affected me a lot, especially in my relationships with people. I don't trust easily and I don't like being hugged; I feel stiff and ready to slap. I am emotionally distant. I feel like I am on the sidewalk watching people go by. I have always had depression and suicidal thoughts; it's a way of life for me. I felt like I was a worm in the dirt; the dirt was cleaner than me. I will probably always be angry about my childhood. The hurt doesn't go away.

It doesn't do any good to tell others going through this experience that they will be all right because they won't believe you, but if I could paint a picture, I would paint a blue sky and say good-bye to my past and hello to my future. I was a worm at first, and then I was left hanging in the air. I am still hanging in the air, but my feet aren't up there yet and the air is never new and fresh. I'll never climb the rest of the ladder up to the air because I don't think I will ever be over it. As for my family, I don't talk with them much because they still try to play mind games with me, but I do miss my one deceased sister who was at ISSCS with me. My life was a tragedy, but I think my childhood experience made me a stronger person in raising my children, and whereas I used to have trouble being alone, today I can be alone. In the past I couldn't laugh, but I am laughing today. Humor helps me to cope, but as long as I'm alive I'll probably always be climbing that ladder to the sky.

Margaret Raycroft

Bitter or Better

I am sharing my story to offer hope to other foster kids. I hope my story helps other foster kids out there to realize that "You can go on, in spite of your past, and that God loves you and will never abandon you, even when it seems that way."

I wasn't born into good circumstances when I entered the world in 1931. My dad was a WW1 veteran who had been badly gassed and was living with "battle scars." My mom and dad were both alcoholics; my dad no doubt drank to relieve his Post Traumatic Stress Disorder from having been in the war, and my mom probably drank to relieve the stress from having to take care of ten children and put up with an alcoholic husband who beat her. Maybe she thought, "If I can't beat him, then I'll join him," I don't know, but I do know that our home life was badly affected by their drinking. Even though my dad had a job as a finished carpenter, there was never enough food, because booze and cigarettes were more important to him than feeding his own children. I think my mom became overwhelmed by the responsibility and got discouraged, and just gave up.

I was the oldest girl in the family (I had five older brothers), so I took on as a mother, where my mother left off---in other words, I became the mother and caretaker for my siblings because my mother was too drunk and preoccupied flirting with men at taverns to take care of us. From the time I was only about 7-8 years old, it seemed my life was consumed with taking care of another baby. I was a child taking on adult responsibilities. One of my earliest memories is seeing my dad beat my mom because he was angry about her going to the tavern; she was a very pretty woman, who had no trouble attracting men, and he was fully aware of her infidelities. My father would have me go fetch my drunk mom from the tavern, and I remember one time when we got in the taxi to come home, the taxi driver headed toward the country instead of our house, and I got so scared of him hurting me and my mom that I started beating on him, telling him to take us home, which he did, thank goodness. I was responsible for bringing my mom home, so I was also afraid of what my dad might say or do to me if she didn't get home. I was always the caretaker. In my foster care file it said that, "She has a sad expression, which brightens with an occasional smile. Evidently, she had a life of worry and responsibility. The father of ten sent her to nearby taverns to hunt for her mom, to see if she was with men. She has had responsibility beyond her years and even now, at 10 years old, worries about her brothers, praying for them constantly. Her bitten nails show the nervous strain."

Not long after the taxi incident, a police car with two policemen and one policewoman came to our house and picked up me, my three younger siblings, and two older brothers. The police officer asked me where the rest of the kids were, because my older brothers weren't around when they first arrived, and me being the faithful caretaker, I went to fetch my brothers who were at a neighbor's house. So there we were, hauled off in a police car. As if it wasn't bad enough that I am being hauled off, I'm being hauled off in a police car, without a clue as to why or what is happening. I was too petrified and too preoccupied with taking care of my three siblings to even cry. I was 9 years old when this happened and never even knew who turned our family into Child and Family Services until years later. At first I thought it might have been our neighbor or the school that turned us in, but I eventually found out it was my aunt Margaret who did it. I hold no grudge against her and believe she did the right thing. There would have been a great tragedy had we not been taken away, as things were getting really bad at our home. My aunt probably saved our lives. We had two house fires; one was caused by me when I hung some washed diapers too close to the stove. We were going so hungry that I used to steal food from the grocery store and the store owner let me do it because he was aware of our circumstances.

So off to foster care we went, just like that. I realize that we needed to be "rescued," but I can't say it's a beautiful life being in foster care, because you keep moving; you pack up your "Jew bag" and you're off again, always wondering, "What did I do? Was I bad?" I recall that the first night we were removed from our home, we were temporarily put in a nursing home, where we all huddled around a crib where my younger brother and sister were. The two younger ones were in the hospital. After this temporary placement we were all placed in separate foster homes; none of us were together in the same homes. I went to a Catholic Children's Home, but for how long, I don't know, but I do know I didn't like it because the nuns strapped me for resisting doing the performance of Catholic rituals.

One of the hardest parts of being in foster care was missing my siblings. I had been like their mother, and although I never felt guilty about our separation, because I understood they weren't my responsibility and it wasn't my fault that this was happening, I still missed them and worried about their welfare. It was especially hard to know that my siblings weren't being treated as good as me. It sure didn't make me feel good when I found out from my social worker that my younger sister was in a foster home where she was tied to a tree outside for the whole day. I was in foster care about two years before I finally seen my siblings, and only got to see them because they demanded it. I remember that my two older brothers came to visit me and took me to an ice cream soda shop, and they visited me regularly after that.

I believe my baby brother committed suicide later in life because he was so badly affected by his childhood and foster care. He kept calling me in the middle of the night, telling me how much he hated life, and I could sense that he was "finished." He was a loner who didn't trust people, and he just gave up. The pain was too unbearable for him. My baby brother, who I'd cared for like my own child, was gone. How can this possibly make you feel good? The only thing that made me feel better was having my husband say to me, "I think your brother is gone. We'll have to leave it to God." I like to think my brother is safe in God's hands now.

I wish I could say that my parents were as eager to see me as my siblings were, but unfortunately, that wasn't the case. In the beginning my mom really never visited at all, because she just couldn't get it together enough to do it. I don't know if her maternal rights were terminated or not. I don't think she even cared one way or the other and she never apologized for the mess we were in. When I was about 11 years old she apparently tried to visit me, as according to my file, "Her mom allegedly took her to a nearby street where her boyfriend was parked, and told her of her intentions to divorce her father and marry this man. She was so upset and sobbed so much that she induced a 105 temperature, which according to the doctor, was brought on by her nervousness." I was aloof with my mom. By this time I was in a stable home and wasn't remotely interested in returning to my drunken mom and a dysfunctional home. When I was 16 years old my father was permitted to visit me. He had gotten sober by this time and we ended up developing a good relationship; he even went to church with me. He did at least apologize and tried his best to make amends with me. My parents never did divorce, even though they no longer lived together. My aunt Margaret never forgot me; she visited me and even brought gifts.

My saving grace was being put in a good Christian foster home when I was 11 years old. I believe I would have become bitter toward society if I hadn't been put in that home, but being there ended up making me a better person; I was able to accept my station in life and move forward. The foster parents were very nice. They didn't have their own children and really loved us as their own, and told us so. The foster mom had a heart condition and the doctor had recommended a "state kid" for her, to help her out, so I ran a lot of errands and did a lot of chores, but I was always treated nicely and never just felt "used." They took me in first, and then the state convinced her to take my three younger siblings also. My two older brothers were in a nice Christian home by this time. I was here at this home from the age of 11-19, and then the foster mom died in her sleep one day when I was 19, and I thought my life had ended. I loved that foster mom so much that I tried to chase a girl down on roller skates because she had made fun of my foster mom's straw hat! I missed her terribly.

Back then girls stayed in the system until age 21, so I still had some "time" left, and I was worried about not graduating, and about my future, and what would become of me. I ended up staying with another set of real nice foster parents (the foster mom was my Sunday school teacher), as Mr. Brown wasn't capable of caring for me after his wife's death. I stayed at this home until I married my high school sweetheart at age 21, a very nice Christian man, who I'm still with today and have a family with. At first his parents were a bit hesitant about their son marrying a "state kid," but we were intent on marrying, and they accepted me. I was afraid; I had trouble believing that my husband would ever love me, due to my low self-esteem from being a "state kid," but he wouldn't leave me alone. I think part of my low self-esteem had to do with the fact that I had learning problems in school, as I was so emotionally distraught in the beginning that it affected my education, and I was labeled as "mentally deficient" and of "dull intelligence," but I wasn't stupid; I was just upset. I gradually improved in school, though, as I became more settled and secure; I even won a spelling bee! I wasn't dumb after all, but still, my self-esteem was lagging behind some, and I was insecure at first with my husband. When you're a foster kid you live with a fear of rejection and abandonment that isn't easy to overcome, but I realized that my husband loved me for who I was and didn't see a "state kid"; he just seen "me."

I'm not ashamed of my background, because there's nothing to be ashamed of; I didn't do anything wrong. God has worked miracles in my life, and one of them is being able to use my past experience to help others. My husband is a pastor, and as a pastor's wife, I have consoled many people, and I feel that my foster care experience has enabled me to do a better job of this; I'm a more empathetic person. I can't think of anybody who goes through as much as foster kids do. If you've gone through what we've gone through, you should be able to be empathetic toward anybody in any situation, so I feel that because of my past, I have a stronger capacity for love and compassion.

Martin Kenneth Hollingsworth

A Happy Ending

I was born the youngest of four children. I have two brothers and one sister. My earliest memories are of watching my alcoholic father beat my mother, and when my brother and I tried intervening we also got beaten. My mother ended up leaving my father, taking me and my siblings with her to live with our grandparents (my dad's parents) temporarily. We were all living in the attic of their house, but along with other family members living in the home, it became overcrowded and eventually we were all turned into the Child and Family Services; by whom, I don't know, perhaps by my grandparents, but I don't know for sure, just like I don't know for sure about a lot of things about my past. There are still a lot of memory gaps and unfulfilled questions about my family history and childhood, that will no doubt always go unanswered, but from what I was able to gather my mom ended up having a nervous breakdown and my dad ended up in a military prison.

A 40 & 8 Society "train" from Voiture 529 in Peoria, Ill. in the Legion Day Parade, June 13, 1954. (Courtesy of ISSCSHPS Archives)

When I was 4 years old I was put into ISSCS (Illinois Soldiers and Sailors Children School), which ended up being a blessing from God as far as I am concerned. It's no telling where I would have ended up at, in the streets or whatever, had I not gone there. Other than a couple of inappropriate things happening there, I have fond memories of the place. The home not only gave me an opportunity to be in a safe environment, but there were also a lot of other children there and we all pulled together. The other boys were like my brothers and I thought of the cottage parents and the boys there as my family; we were like one big, happy family. When I got older I became like a big brother to the younger kids coming into ISSCS, encouraging them and lifting their spirits. One of the greatest times at the home was Legion's Day. It was the most exciting and fun day for me and the other children, with games, picnics, gifts, and 150 parents, so you never felt alone. I remember one Legion Day when I was sitting all alone and I felt a warm hand on my shoulder; when I looked up I saw a woman with an angelic face looking at me, and she asked me to go with her. This woman was a Christian woman and she ended up inviting 6-8 of us boys over to her house on Saturdays to let us watch television programs about Jesus and read to us about Him.

While I was at the home I was sent out to a few foster homes, but the first three didn't work out—two families were too old and one family just wanted to use me as a farm hand. I got lucky on the fourth try though, and at the age of 11 I ended up living with some real nice foster parents, the Hollingsworth's. My foster dad played sports with me and my older brother, who also went there with me, and my foster mom had the biggest heart you can imagine, and they were both real active in their church. They were unable to have their own children and wanted to adopt us, along with two foster girls they had, but my biological mother wasn't capable of signing off for me, and I don't know about my dad.

I never saw my real dad again, and my mom only came to see us once while we were at the Hollingsworth's, not expressing much though, just telling us, "Farewell; it looks like you're in good hands." When I was 18 years old I became of age to sign myself off, so I decided to be legally adopted by the Hollingsworth's. My brother didn't want to be adopted, but for me, it just seemed like the natural thing to do. When I was at ISSCS I felt sad at Christmastime because I wished I had a real family to celebrate Christmas with and I didn't, but with the Hollingsworth's I felt like my wish came true. I lost touch with my blood siblings, except for Chuck. I hadn't seen Richard since 1953 at ISSCS and I lost track of my sister in the late 1960's, but I heard that she didn't do too well, that she was in two real bad foster homes, and sexually abused in one of them, before finally running away. I don't know her whereabouts today. My experience was a good one, with a happy ending, but I know that many children today aren't as lucky and are just being thrown around from foster home to foster home, many of them never finding a good home, where they might possibly be adopted. Just as I tried being an inspiration to the newcomers at ISSCS, I want to give hope to the foster children today and let them know, "There's hope. Just keep the faith, have a positive attitude, and know that you have choices in life. Don't let your past beat you down. Rise up against it, no matter what."

Nikki Daniels

A Walk Down Memory Lane

"I Remember…."

I am happy to share my story because I want the world to know what happened to me while I was in foster care, and that the foster care system is bad all over the world. I am from Australia. I have so many words in my head about this subject that I was hoping to write a book one day, but it puts me in a big void and messes with my head to think too much about my past. Mostly I am angry now that I'm an adult and look back and realize how I was treated worse than a dog, and that there is nothing I can do about it, as the law won't help me unless I have $$$. Altogether I was in three foster homes and seven group homes/orphanages, was sexually abused by two people (that I remember), raped by one person on two different occasions, and emotionally and physically abused in five unsuccessful placements. Although I am happy to share my story, it is not a happy story, only one that should be told, for my own sake as well as others.

According to my file I was cared for by my natural mother during the short time I was with her, but at about 5 months of age she gave me up for adoption because she couldn't afford me and there was no single mother's pension to help her. I was admitted to the Care and Protection of Department of Children's Services and placed in a temporary home for two days, then placed in a foster care home to be adopted; unfortunately, the adoption never happened at the Sander home as planned. I remember some things from this home, many of them not good. I remember getting a yellow bowl with a suction cup on the bottom of it to stick to the table, which filled with hot water, and a spoon fork to match. I remember crawling down the table and grabbing the father's beard. I remember the mother standing in the backyard with her arm outstretched, holding a pair of my soiled underpants with feces on them, and I remember knowing that I had to eat my own shit, and I remember chewing on it and swallowing it. It wasn't the first time this happened, either. I wasn't allowed to use the inside toilet of their house; I used the thunder box (outside sawdust toilet), and if I didn't make it to the toilet in time and made a mess of myself, I had to eat my own shit, and I also had my wet underpants rubbed in my face. This home was on a farm and I remember there were pigs and sunflowers. I remember sitting on their stairs, watching the school bus come and take the children up that long red road, and I remember longing to go on that bus with the other kids. I also remember being burnt with a cigarette on my left abdomen, which I still have the scar from, done to me by the children in the chook pen, as a threat to not tell on them for smoking. I remember not being allowed to have dinner if I didn't get the dog inside its house. I remember one time when it was getting dark and I still couldn't get the dog to go in the dog house, and having somebody come down and approach me, coaxing me out of my hiding spot (why was I hiding??), asking me what I was doing, and for me to take him up to the house. So I did, and then when we got up to the top of the stairs on the porch and knocked on the door, the mother opened the door and asked me who was with me, to which I replied, "I don't know," and then he took off his wig and everyone was laughing. I remember I was then locked in a cupboard. I also remember I was not allowed to have a pillow for my bed. The only happy memory I really have of this place is having some men carry me around, and I remember one man in particular was a neighbor, who I felt very safe with.

Although I don't remember any sexual behavior at this house, I have a BIG FEELING that there might have been, which would fit in with all the other things happening there. The BIG THREAT—the police would get me if I told anybody how naughty I was. I figure now, in my adulthood, by reading all the documents from my file, that it was about how naughty THEY were. My file even stated that "It was not known at that time, but has since been revealed, that these people told others she was being taken away by a policeman for being a naughty girl," and that "She was afraid of the police and talked constantly about death." Why would a little girl talk about death??

This first foster family was given several options to adopt me, but prolonged the adoption until in the end when the social workers gave them an ultimatum, which the parents responded to by saying, "Francine is a naughty child, causing embarrassment to their family, that I was promiscuous to male callers on the farm and often talked about sex." Why would a 5 year old child talk about sex?? My file states, "The adoption was supposed to be finalized, but their resistance took the form of assertions to the effect that Francine had become a behavior problem. They stated that she was defiant, disobedient, deceitful, causing great worry and embarrassment, and was more difficult to manage than their own children." I think they may have been using me for something. I remember being horrified of the police. Why?? Whenever I tried to tell an adult or authority figure that somebody was hurting me, I was told I was a liar and just making it up, or that I was just "too active" for a 5 year old. Bloody hell! What 5 year old has those kinds of thoughts?!...none that I know of!

These people were only in it for the money, which they knew would stop once I was adopted, so they declined and the adoption was deferred. My file said, "The adopting parents asked that proceedings be delayed, as another child had been born and they found the State allowance very helpful. From that point all attempts to finalize this adoption met with resistance." Potential foster or adoptive parents should be required to attend intensive training courses before attempting to foster or parent a child. They need to prove themselves. Fostering should not just be about money, as this leads to children being abused.

Talk about abuse! I remember a time when I was put on a horse and I was bucked off, and fell right under the horse. I remember looking up and seeing the horse's foot coming down to my stomach, and I remember thinking it was going to stand on my stomach, but instead it brought down its leg and just chipped the top of my stomach and put its foot more forward so it didn't stand on me, like horses do to logs in their path. I also remember that when the horse's foot was coming down, I was able to see up to the veranda from the bed of grass I was lying in, and watch the parents and whoever else was up there, laughing. I could have been killed, and they thought it was funny!

I remember the foster mom beating me around my head when I was about 2 ½ years old, and somebody made a complaint to the Child Welfare Department about "possible signs of abuse," and yet I was still left there until my 5th birthday. When I was taken away from the Sanders my file states that "Francine was withdrawn and shed no tears when Mrs. S. left! No warmth from Mrs. Sander to Francine (and visa versa). Francine hadn't been told this placement was permanent, and believes she is only in B. for the holidays!!" A quote from Child Care Officer's Report stated "The child informed her that the mother (Mrs. Sander) said she hated her and did not enjoy her involvement with the family. Beatings were also mentioned. This was confirmed by Francine." I never even knew the Sanders weren't my natural parents, my file stating that "She had also apparently never been told that this was not her natural family and had been given to understand that she would be returned home to the family within the week." Hell, I didn't even know my NAME! All through my state files, I am referred to as Francine/Nicole---take your pick I suppose. Seriously, my real name is Nicole, but my name had been changed to Francine, and I wasn't even informed of my real name (Nicole) until I was 12 years old, so I started to doubt anything they ever told me about myself. I remember they were making me a "life diary," so I could place parts of my life together, perhaps as some kind of therapy. I remember one time the nun leaving the room, and I was frantically trying to take note of any information in the files that she had left there, and I managed to get an address, but later checked it to no avail, because of the lack of support.

The next home I went to was like an intermittent church based home, which I only stayed at for a short time, a very short and unhappy stay. I thought I was going there because I was naughty and the police were going to get me. I remember there was a house mother, along with her own kids and the other foster kids. I was now living in the city with normal toilets and no outside toilets, but since I wasn't allowed to use the inside toilet at the last house, I was shitting under the table downstairs and hiding around under the house to go to the toilet. My behavior was referred to as "problematic and abnormal," with me "threatening the house mother with soiling my pants and refusing to use the toilet." They said I was regressing, because I was crawling around on all fours. I was hiding because I was afraid I would have to eat my shit like I did at the Sanders. My file even states that "The foster parents suggested that difficult behavior could be expected from Nicole, though they are confident that she will be unaffected by the separation." Hmmm….it also says that "In view of the apparent ease with which the foster parents had arrived at their decision to send Francine/Nicole back, it now seems very likely that she may have suffered some degree of emotional neglect as a member of this family." Maybe this emotional neglect was why, according to my file, my "Behavior towards strangers was also abnormal, affectionate to the extent of having a claustrophobic effect on my recipient."

I was only in the next foster home for six weeks, but I remember it. I had issues with the boys there, which the adults around me were starting to get embarrassed by. My file states that "There was the question of some activities with one of the boys," and that "This type of behavior at 5 years old, seems premature." Seems…?

Due to my "abnormal" behavior it was recommended that I be removed from this home and placed in a children's psychiatric home/hospital) for "assessment and/or treatment," so I was admitted there. I was only there for six weeks, where I underwent psychotherapy and was drugged on Neulactyl, but the drug had no effect on me, other than probably making me a vegetable for six weeks. The final doctor report said, "Not responding to treatment."

They were hoping I would be able to return to the children's home "less disturbed," but apparently there was a change of plans, as in the next spring I was instead placed with another foster family. I was subjected to more abuse in this home. In between visits to this family, first for weekends and then finally to live, I was given back to the psychiatric hospital at the end of a weekend, and according to a doctor report I have from my file, I denied any physical issues I had, but I wonder why they thought I did to begin with.

All these weird questions come to me now that I'm an adult and I realize I have been wronged, and that it wasn't my secret; it was the dirty mongrel's secret, them trying to hide their misdoings. I stayed with these foster parents for a few months, but it seemed longer to me. I was now 6 years old and when I started to speak about it to his wife, she made me wear nappies (diapers) to bed, and she would check my nappy in the morning to see if the pins had been changed. In the end of my stay there she made me wear a nappy to school and I would cop a beating when I got home from school if it had been pinned different to when I left home in the morning. I remember that before I was taken out of his home and placed back in foster care, the foster father, knowing I was leaving, asked me, "Is there anything you want me to do before you go away?" Do what?

In reference to the foster parents care of me, my file states that "Possibly a normal child would react in the same way as other children, but Francine's background cannot be considered normal in any regard, and she may interpret the foster parents' management as further rejection." I agree, and it also isn't normal for 6 year old girls to be sexually abused!!

The foster mom couldn't cope with me and my "limitations," and so I left their home and went to Tuffnell, another group home. I remember one day they sat me down and said the foster father was going to work far away, and that I had to be put back into foster care again... The same man who took me from the first house came to take me from this house and put me into this orphanage. I lived there until I was 10 years old, and then moved into a family group home in the suburbs for awhile.

I was later fostered by an older couple for ten months, but it wasn't a good place, either. The lady had some serious issues, always nagging and threatening me all the time, telling me, "If you don't be good, you can go back to the orphanage," which I considered would be better, at least I wouldn't be nagged, and I would have other kids to play with. I felt lonesome there. The mother was dealing with her son's suicide, and when I came along I was like a replacement for him, so she resented me. I held a grudge against this lady for most of my life, until I recently saw her---she was an old lady, all wrinkly and twisted, using a walking stick. I heard her say words to her own granddaughter to make her feel self- conscious, and it was at this point that I realized I am not going to be angry at her any longer, because she is going to die as an old, angry soul. That is punishment enough.

Eventually I was put back into care and went back to another children's home. I didn't trust the house father there. I had been put back into this home when I was 11 years old and now I was 13 (he wasn't my house s father until I was 13). I ran away from here when I was 14 years old and lived on the streets in, and learned the way of the streets, surviving by stealing canned goods and sanitary items. I was introduced to drugs, and overdosed on heroin at age 16, but never touched drugs again after that incident. The house father never approached me for sex while I was in the orphanage, but he paid me for sex later on when he found me on the coast, and he offered me a job if I went back to live in his home town. Eventually I went back to get this job as a nursing assistant, but the real reason he wanted me there was to have me close by so he could get certain favors by giving me money. I was 17 years old at this time, and learning how to prostitute.

I remember another time while I was in care, having weekend parents, and the grandpa acting strange. I remember being out in the horse stables (he had race horses), and having him pick me up and pin me against the wooden stable wall, with his face, spiky beard hairs, and big lips coming down my way for a kiss….and then the door opened and all this light came in, like in the movie Close Encounters….and I seen the silhouette of his wife standing there. He just put me down and she told me to go up to the house, so I ran all the way up to the house, and I never went back there again. Thank God his wife caught him, but still, these men and women get away with it. They need to be caught and held accountable!!

I was 24 years old before I realized what happened, and I was 33 before I realized I could speak out and make a complaint to the police about the things that happened. When I was a child and spoke up about it, I was drugged, or told I was lying, or had to go see a shrink chew on his tongue while he interviewed me. I think the shrink needed a shrink! An investigation took place with the one foster mom, but of course she denied the abuse and the case was closed. Later I received a state apology and a federal apology, as if an apology will resolve it. It's a dirty world we live in.

I also wanted resolution with my real mom, so I met her in 2009, when I was 41 years old. It was an odd event, really weird, not what I dreamed of. I had this image in my mind of how meeting my mom was going to be like, like being lost at sea from the voyage….I wondered who she was, what she looked like, how does she smell, sound? I had built up this image of what it would be like from reading stories and seeing movies, but it wasn't anything like that; in fact, it was weird, because I just treated her as if I had left the house in the morning and just walked in and said, "Hi," sat down, and had a chat, with tea and dinner. I was sitting in front of a complete stranger, who I have no feeling for, but should. She is so much like me, rather detached and unemotional, avoiding eye contact. I didn't really talk too much about 'how or why' about the past; it seemed as if she didn't want to give me much of the details. I already had my own ideas as to her lifestyle at the time of my birth anyway, and I don't have any bad feelings for her, but she is my mother. I remember driving away after three days of visiting and thinking, "Was this it? I waited all my life for that?" And there it was, and now I have to drive away from it, and that's it. I really knew it then, and I knew it before I arrived for the visit. I would like for her to visit me and my four kids, after all she is their grandmother, but I'm not going to worry much about it. Whatever happens, happens.

So much happened to me while I was in "care," as it does to so many other foster kids, and my words of advice to others would be to let your voice be your greatest weapon. Saying "no" to the abusers is saying "yes" to you. If you're being abused REMEMBER, it is not YOUR secret; it is THEIRS, so don't be afraid to come out and speak up about the truth, and if somebody doesn't listen, keep speaking---tell the world---somebody will hear you. Foster kids need to be brave and make the abusers accountable for their abusive actions. By doing this, you could be saving a life, including your own. Educate yourself about the world and things you don't learn in school, in order to find yourself. Be creative. Find your talent and use it. It's important to stay in school and become independent. Don't have babies when you are real young, but if you do, keep them close to you and aware of their doings. Don't let them fall into the Child Welfare System. Families should work together and stay together. The most important thing I did for my children was to protect them from what I never was protected from, and they didn't get molested or abused. My children all have different fathers, and I never married any of them, mostly because I worried about them being sexually abused, as it was always the fathers in my childhood who molested me.

My foster care experience has deeply affected me as an adult, but I am surviving to the best of my ability. I am so glad I am who I am now, and I don't want to be any other person, but I'm messed up inside myself. I think if this happened to the normal person, they would be insane by now. I don't trust people, men or women. I don't build close relationships with women, and it seems I resent them, due to my original abandonment by my mother, and then the abuse I suffered by my first foster mother. It was always the woman who was in charge, the one who was hired by the state to care for me, and a lot these women are horrified when they were notified that their husbands did this evil deed, this sexual molestation to a child, to such a degree that they took their anger out on the child, almost like an act of jealousy, but it is never the child's fault, even if the child consents, or even asks for it. I don't feel comfortable around a lot of people and tend to feel inferior around them. I suffer from depression and anxiety, and although I have traveled to other countries (India, Indonesia, and Malaysia) and felt safe there, I also suffer from agoraphobia. I make up excuses in my head to not go places, and it takes me forever to leave home when I do. I started to do an art course in order to get some structure in my life, but the thought of putting myself somewhere outside of my home where I would have to socialize with normal people was too much for me. I like my privacy and isolate myself from the rest of society by living on a big piece of land that gives me space from my neighbors. I have grown up to be "angry at the world person," living my life like a crab, sticking my head out of my shell every now and then to see what's going on in the outside world. I like the Internet because it brought the world into my home, giving me the resources to communicate with others while I confine myself to my home. I am hyper vigilant to signs of disapproval and do not have relationships with men or women. I am heterosexual, but am actually asexual by choice because I feel like nobody can take anything from me if I don't give them sex. I am not on medication because I fear being a zombie and falling into the big pharmacy system. I have headaches so severe that I'm bedridden for two days at a time, rendering me useless to take care of my kids. I've been to counselors and therapy, but it didn't really do any good; the only good that can come out of it is if people read and hear what I have to say with horror, finding it impossible to imagine that abuse happens within the Child Welfare System and within families, but I know it does. I am disappointed in the CWS, as it did not protect me and over 500,000 other Australian foster kids who were abused in "care," which is recorded federally, many who have died and weren't able to speak out about their abuse, and many, many more who would like to come out. It seems most of the women I know were sexually abused; in fact, I only know one who wasn't. I think it would be good for the sake of statistics to take an anonymous vote to see how many people were molested as a child, and I'm sure it would open up a big can of worms.

What is particularly difficult is having the realization of the impact that my "black" childhood has had on my children. My one son in particular suffers from my past and is embarrassed by it, taking it personally, seeing it as a representation of himself and his parentage. There is a loss of family, as there is no other family, no aunts or uncles, grandparents, cousins, etc., which makes Christmas and other holidays crappy for them, and makes me feel bad for them. It is a letdown for them, and I feel bad for them, but I can't change the fact. I have remained single and I will remain single to the day I die; that's just the way life goes for me. And I am happy in my own company---it's about the only company I trust.

I could go on and on, but one thing leads to another, and there are so many loose threads, all connecting at some point, but there really is no closure because it hasn't been addressed properly. All these people who abused me should be held accountable. I was speaking out as a child, but nobody heard me, and even as an adult, the authority figures still don't want to hear me. I guess they can't be bothered; it's just old news to them. So strange, this world we live in, that this can happen, to be detected and then pushed under the carpet. Is a child's life so unimportant for this to happen? I hope in the future foster kids will be important, so they don't have to remember all the shit I've remembered. And "I REMEMBER."

Pamela Jane

My Journey Home

My name is Pamela Jane and I was born in South Africa. When I was born, my mother was training to be a nurse at the hospital and my father was working as a coal miner at the mines, where we lived in a caravan. One day, there was an explosion and the mines collapsed, forcing us to relocate. Dad got a new job at a hospital as a maintenance man. While my parents were away at work, I would spend the days with my paternal grandparents at their home.

My baby picture

It was in the early 1980's that my grandparents, an aunt, and my great grandmother were travelling for a summer holiday when they were involved in a fatal car accident that cost them all their lives. My uncle was following behind on his motorbike and witnessed everything. My grandmother was the only one who didn't die at the scene. She went into a coma and was taken to the hospital where Dad was working. He never left her side until she passed away, which inevitably cost him his job.

We moved out of the caravan park and into my grandparent's house, which was left to Dad, Uncle P., and Uncle M. The extent of their grief led them down a very dark road. Whereas they may have only dabbled in partying before, the sudden loss of four of their family members gave way for them to become consumed by it, seduced into doing whatever it took to block out the pain, until there came a point where the money was spent and reports of child neglect reached the social services. A social worker came by the house to follow up the complaint, but Mom assured her that we were coping.

One day a telephone call was made to inform the Child Welfare Services that a 3 year old girl had been abandoned by her parents. That little girl was me. We were homeless and were sleeping rough on the roof tops of shopping centres because we had no-where else to go. Out of desperation, my parents had schemed and decided cheque book fraud was their only means of getting money, and so they left me with a stranger in a coffee shop, asking her to mind me for a couple of hours while they went about their illegal activities. When they returned for me, I was no longer there. I was placed with a foster family for the next three years while my parents tried to rehabilitate themselves.

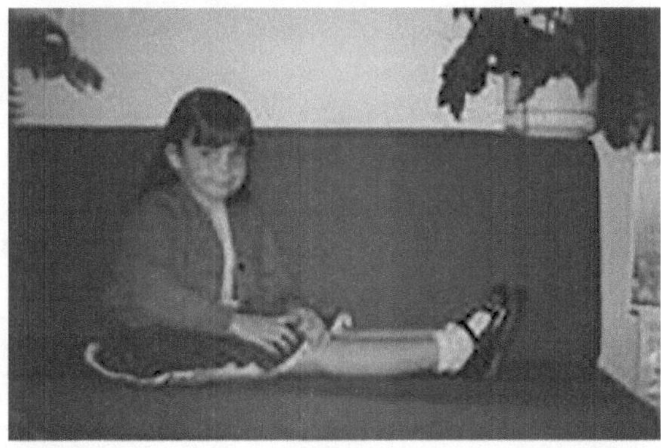

Age 3/4

One day, when I was six years old, I was helping my foster parents build the largest puzzle I had ever seen. The pieces were all green and blue and tiny and they all looked the same. I was trying to find all the edges so we could build the boarder, when the phone rang. She left the table to answer the phone. Her back was to me awhile as she spoke, and then she handed the phone to me. I was told that I had a new baby brother and that I would be going home. It was good news because everyone seemed excited for me, but as far as I was aware I was home with a family I loved and who loved me. I had an older foster brother who playfully teased me, and another one my age, who was my best friend; we did everything together. We'd all go to church on Sundays and come home and have family meals around the table. I started my first day of school while living with this family and I cried my heart out for my foster mom when I got lost in the school corridors.

My 1ˢᵗ school picture, Age 5

Nevertheless, the day came that I had to leave to be reunited with Mom, Dad, and my brother. My social worker collected me and we drove to where the Social Services had arranged a flat for us all to live in. I don't remember how I felt, and to be honest, much of the move itself is a suppressed memory, but it was here in this flat that my life changed for the worse.

I became better acquainted with my real family and came to know and love my Mom's sister and her husband. Aunty J. had an ex-husband, Uncle M., who was the father of my cousin, M. Jr., with whom I spent many a day playing with. Dad's brothers, Uncle M., and Uncle P. were also involved in our lives, but Uncle M. more so. He and Dad were as thick as thieves.

As much as my parents tried to hide it from me, I was exposed to their partying ways. Things got out of hand one day. The sound of my mother's screams still haunts me to the core of my bones.

One day Dad came home and he was covered in blood. Mom was in a panic, demanding to know what had happened. I was of course worried too, because his shirt was drenched from the blood running down his face from a wound in his head. Dad and Uncle M. had apparently decided to hitch a ride on the back of a Coca-Cola lorry without asking the driver's permission, and of course the drivers thought that they were stealing. When the drivers stopped the lorry to confront them, they decided to run, and then thought it best to split up. Unfortunately for Dad, the drivers decided to pursue him, and when they caught him they smacked him over the head with a glass coke bottle.

Dad was hopeless at holding down a job. At one point he did have one, and I remember that Mom and Dad had enough money to buy him a bicycle so he could travel to and from work, but one day the bicycle was gone and Dad said it got stolen, but Mom could have bet her life that he had sold it.

One day, because I had lied to the neighbor for Dad, he decided he would lie to the school for me to have the day off school to visit Mom in hospital, who was having her tubes tied so she couldn't have any more children. We walked to the school and told them I had tonsillitis and that I needed to go to the hospital, and then we walked all the way to the hospital to see Mom. It was the longest walk ever. Mom and Dad didn't have a car, so they used to hitch hike a lot, and it helped to have me a long with them, as it made the drivers feel sorry for us and stop. I remember many a time getting into a strangers car and them telling me that I had the most beautiful eyes they had ever seen.

Age 7

Mom eventually decided to run. She took my brother and me and sought refuge with the Salvation Army. We were given a room and food, and felt safe. Mom lay on a single bed, with my baby brother next to her, and I settled down for the night on a mattress on the floor. Suddenly and without warning, Dad had somehow managed to get into the refuge and barged the door open. He began yelling at Mom, and then grabbed the bottom of the bed and just tilted it up against the wall. I just heard a couple of thumps, Mom screamed, my brother cried, and I shouted at Dad and told him that I hated him, and that he had to leave.

We eventually went back to the flat for a while. I don't remember much about the last day I spent with my parents. I was 7 years old, my brother was 1, and I remember that we had visitors around and a fight broke out. I remember a pan of rice falling to the floor and rice grains were scattered everywhere. My brother and I cowered in the kitchen behind the cooker. The police were called and came charging in. The next thing I knew I was being sent off with my uncle and my cousin. My uncle took us to the Drive-in to watch a film. We ended up watching Dirty Dancing, which I remember finding extremely difficult to watch, as it was very raunchy for my little mind. On the way home my uncle stopped the van on a very dark motor way and told me that the car had broken down, and that if we didn't get it started soon, we were going to be killed by bad people in the night. I was petrified. I cried and screamed with fear, and he just laughed and said he was joking as he started the car back up and started to drive again.

Because of the troubles at home I had to stay the night at my uncles's house, which ended up being a bad experience.

The following morning, I was told that I would not be going home. Instead, I was going to be placed in a foster home. I had to spend all morning with my uncle, who taunted me as we played a game of monopoly, by not letting me move my own pieces, and claiming he was doing this because I wouldn't let him do what he wanted the night before. Eventually the time came to leave, and my social worker collected me.

When we arrived at what was to be my new foster family's house, Mom and my brother were there, too. Our new foster mom was taking my brother out of my mother's arms, and he began crying for Mom, not letting go, and Mom was begging for a few more minutes to say goodbye, and calm him down. It was a horrible moment, and both my brother and I were shunted into this new house of strangers.

Although my foster parents may have been strangers to me, personally they were no strangers to my family's plight. Being of the Baptist Christian faith and regular church goers, they knew my late grandparents, because they attended the same parish services. This is why they agreed to take Charlie and me in at such short notice. They had three children of their own, two daughters and a son. I shared a bedroom with their youngest daughter, and she and I played, and went to school together at Dinwiddie Primary School. Every Sunday I attended Sunday school while my foster parents attended the service. Mom and Dad would visit occasionally to take my brother and me out for the day, but sometimes they had to be turned away because they came to visit us drunk.

My brother and I.

On one visit, Dad took me to the grave yard to visit the graves of my grandparents and aunty. On the way he taught me a song called 'Under the Board Walk,' and he sang it all the way there, and I believed he was singing it about us.

'Under the board walk, down by the sea
On a blanket with my baby, that's where I'll be
Under the board walk, out of the sun
Under the board walk, we'll be having fun
Under the board walk, board walk'

When we arrived, the graves were nothing but mounds of soil. He shed a few tears and confessed that there were no headstones, due to them not having enough money.

One weekend, the Church invited people to come forward and give their lives to the Lord. People would stand up and tell their stories. I asked for Mom and Dad to come. I believed with all my heart that they needed saving. For the first time in my life, I remember crying tears of joy when both Mom and Dad did exactly that. I felt hope in my heart that they would be safe, and maybe try to change, and turn their lives around.

One day, I was playing in the living room with my brother and I was doing rolly polies on the living room floor. My brother would smack my bum as I went over, and I became emotionally distressed. This led my foster parents to think I had emotional problems. A visit to a doctor confirmed their suspicions.

As my placement with these foster parents was only temporary, a day came when a place in a children's home became available, and I had to leave. It seemed like hours before we arrived at the place, which was to be my new home. Great high corrugated steel fencing surrounded it, and as we drove through the gates, I noticed a sign, 'St Mary's Children's Home.' We were greeted by an old familiar face, Mrs. S. She had been a part of my life for as long as I could remember. Something told me that whatever it was happening that day, it was not going to be good for me. As far as I could see it seemed like a really nice place. There were about six cottages and I observed all their names. We stopped when we reached St. Anne's, and I followed everyone inside, and was introduced to my new house parents. I greeted them, and at the same time peeped around the corner. There were other boys and girls, sitting in the lounge. They looked happy and like they were having fun. Mrs. S. told me that I was going to live in this cottage and make a lot of friends. My foster parents couldn't keep both my brother and me, and since my brother was young, he stood a better chance of adapting to the family, and so we were separated. A lump formed in my throat when I realized I was going to be away from my brother, as it was hard enough already having said goodbye to Mom and Dad, but now I had to say goodbye again, and as I watched their car drive out of view, a tear slowly rolled down my cheek, but I wiped it away, because I promised myself I was going to be brave. Back in the cottage, I was taken to the dormitory that I was going to be sharing with four other girls. It was made up of five beds, all in a row, all in pink bedding, with little side tables beside each one. The carpet was a softer shade, but along with the curtains was also pink. I decided that day that I hated pink. I put my suitcase on the bed, which was the closest to the bedroom door. I was allocated a cupboard, and then shipped out for a grand tour. The cottage consisted of 4 bedrooms, 2 bathrooms, a big lounge and dining area, a kitchen, and lastly, the house parents' private courters. I was warned that we did not go in there unless it was an absolute emergency. There was also a very big garden with loads of flowers, and a tiny wooden shed at the bottom. Further I explored with a new found friend, past all the cottages, and round the back of the grounds. There was a main kitchen where African dinner ladies cooked meals for the whole children's home. One of my duties was to collect the food for my cottage and carry it back. A bit further on we came to a chapel, which was where we had our Sunday evening services. My mind was so overwhelmed with information---duties, in-weekends, out-weekends, and hundreds of new faces.

My best friend from the Children's Home and I on a day out

I again started a new school, and the walk would take me past the hospital where Mom was living and working. Every afternoon after school, for a while, I would stop outside the Nursing Home and wave to Mom. One day she came out and gave me a picture, which I took back to the children's home and put in my dormitory. I was told that I wasn't allowed to speak to Mom, and so the after-school visits were forced to stop.

For the first few out-weekends, which was every second weekend, I went to stay with my ex foster parents, and it was lovely to see my brother, but then they too stopped. The next out-weekend came, and I had the surprise of spending the weekend with my first foster parents. The next few out-weekends, I had to stay at the home, until one day I was called to the office for a meeting. This was when I met a couple. They wanted to foster a child, and I met their requirements. I spent a few months visiting their home on out-weekends. They lived on a five-acre plot of land in. They had 36 cats, 5 dogs, 3 horses, a pig, a ram, geese, bonze chickens, and turkeys. They had done a room especially for me, painted in a soft peach, with pretty white and pink floral bedding. On my first visit, I dropped the milk on the floor and cried uncontrollably for making the mistake. I was so scared they wouldn't want me after that. A day came in 1989 where Mrs. S. approached me and asked me if I wanted to live with them. I told her that I was afraid of what would happen if I didn't like it there anymore, and she told me that I could always come back to the home, and so it was that I packed up all my things again, said goodbye to all my friends, and my house parents, and moved to the countryside.

Cuddling the Kittens

Riding Sally

At first, life was ok, but then it seemed that I was always getting into trouble with the foster mom. She was always angry with me for something I had done or hadn't done. She was a very religious woman and believed in discipline. I had an endless list of duties to perform--- feeding the animals, grooming the animals, cleaning out water troughs, hanging up, bringing in, and ironing the laundry, vacuuming the house, litter picking on the whole of our land, and sometimes even manual labor, like lugging bricks from one place to the next, and digging soil. School life became unbearable, because she would dress me up in dresses below my knees, and make me wear boy's shoes to school. I was brainwashed with religious mumbo jumbo, so that all I spoke about was Jesus, and the other children thought I was a freak. On days we were able to wear civvies to school, I would have to wear church dresses, while the other kids wore jeans and trendy tops. I wasn't allowed to listen to music, or watch television, and so I became an outcast, and spent most of my lunch breaks hiding in the girl's lavatories. The boys teased me, saying that nobody loved me, and the girls just didn't really want to be my friend.

Age 11/12

If I didn't brush my teeth – SMACK! If I forgot to clean the horses water troughs out – SMACK! If I took a piece of bread without asking, I would be grabbed by the tops of my arms, nails dug in so deep it would pierce the skin, and I would be shook so hard that my head would just wobble back and forth. I would then be dragged to the phone to call the minister, and was told to confess my sin. I was frightened of being in the car with her and always tried to sit in the back behind the front passenger's seat when she was driving, because it was the one place she couldn't reach me. If she was upset with me and I was sat behind the driver's seat, she would grab my legs by the calves and pinch her nails into my skin.

One day I wrote Mom a letter saying how unhappy I was, and exposing my foster mom's abuse. Unfortunately for me, the foster mom was an all-seeing-eye and found my letter. When I got into her car I saw my letter on the dashboard, and then I saw the back of her hand come flying towards my face. I felt blood pour out of my nose, and pain spread into my eyes. She didn't even give me a tissue, let alone offer me any comfort. She had broken my nose.

One day she came to collect me early from school during a sports period, and because I had left my trainers at home, I played barefoot. To teach me a lesson not to forget my shoes, I was dragged by my ear through a thorny field filled with broken glass and debris, all the way to the shopping center car park where she had parked.

I ran her a bath one evening, and when she got in she screamed, and came running out with scolded feet because I had accidently made it too hot. She yelled at me, and then went and started shouting at her husband that he never supported her with me. He shouted back at her that he didn't know what she expected him to do. I went into the bathroom to start running cold water, when the foster dad came into the bathroom, and hit me around the head. The force of his hit sent my head spinning, and my face hit the washing machine with such force that it broke one of my front teeth. He told me I was lucky that was all that got broken.

The most frightening experience I had ever encountered up until this point came a few months later. They had fostered another little girl, who was 6 years old. With the foster mom being on nightshifts at the hospital, and the dad leaving for work at 6:00 am in the morning, the little girl and I were at home alone until we left for school on the school bus, which we caught just up the road. It was a Thursday morning and I heard our five dogs barking, but they sounded distressed, and so I opened the kitchen door, and saw a black man standing at the end of our driveway. He looked distressed, too, with all these dogs at his heels, so I went outside and got them under control, and asked the man what he wanted. He said that he was looking for work and wanted to speak to the 'boss.' I told him he would have to come back later, because the boss had left for work at 6:00 am. He then asked to speak to the 'missus,' and I told him she also wasn't here, and wouldn't be back until 9:00 am. He thanked me and left, and I never thought any more of it. A week passed. It was Red Nose day, and she and I were getting ready for our school photos to be taken that day, and we were in good spirits. I heard the familiar sound of the dogs barking again, and they sounded very agitated, and so without thinking, I opened the kitchen door again to see what the commotion was, when I saw four black men striding with purpose towards our house, kicking and swearing at the dogs. Something inside me told me to shut the door quickly, and lock it, but I couldn't lock it. I fumbled for a while, but the lock was stuck, and so I left the door unlocked and ran to the lounge, to the telephone, and dialed the neighbors who lived on the plot of land adjacent, at least five minutes away. I had just enough time to tell him what I saw, and to come help. I had just hung up the receiver, when I was on my way to find K., and I saw one of them coming towards me. He was shouting at me, demanding I tell him where the money was. I was petrified as he waved his knife around. We'd been broken into not even a month before, and I told him as much. I said they took everything; we have nothing. I could hear the others smashing around in the rest of the house and then I heard K. scream. At this point the phone rang, and the man with the knife grabbed me, and said if I answered it he would kill me, holding his knife to my neck. The next thing one of them came into the lounge dragging K., and shoved her in my direction, telling me to make her shut up. It was a nightmare. I heard gun shots in the distance, and the four men just scattered, leaving out the backdoors. I don't remember much else. My foster parents got home, and the police came, and I told them everything I knew. One of the men was shot by the neighbor and was wounded, and arrested, but the other three escaped. It was discovered that our property was being watched, and that the man I had spoken to the week before was one of the armed burglars. All said and done, I still had to go to school that day, albeit a bit late, whether I was suffering from shock or not. A few days later, a reporter came to write a story about the incident, and K. and I had to pose for a picture in front of the house. We also had a panic button installed, in case anything like this ever happened again, to alert the neighbors and deter the burglars, but we continued to be left alone in the house. After the event, I was a nervous wreck. Whenever we were alone, I would spend most of my free time lying on the kitchen floor, looking out of the cat flap at the front gate. The only time I felt safe enough to not do that was when it was raining. I figured no one would want to rob a house in the rain. But whenever the dogs barked, I would get hysterical.

One night not so long after, I was in bed in my room, and it was raining, and the dogs were barking that same aggressive bark, and I just screamed. The foster dad came into my room, and I was too afraid to be on my own. K., lucky for her, was fast asleep in her room, and I begged my foster dad if I could sleep in his room. "I'll sleep on the floor," I said to him, "you won't even know I'm here," and so I took my pillow and duvet, and made an attempt to sleep. Half an hour later, he got up. I could see him walking out of his room, naked by the moonlight that was shining through a gap in the curtain. He went to the bathroom, got something, and then came back and picked me up off the floor, and lay me in his bed. I pretended to be asleep, as to not confront his nakedness. He covered me and then got back into bed on his side. I was lying on my side, my back was towards him, but he came up close behind me. The next thing I felt was him pulling up my nightdress, and taking my panties off. I continued to pretend to be asleep, because I didn't know what else to do at this point. I was so scared. He then applied an ointment of sorts to his fingers and rubbed it onto my private parts, but still I was frozen in shock, and it wasn't until I felt him close, the stiffness of his penis trying to penetrate me, that something inside me said, "get up, get up, get up." And so I did. I stood right up, and I turned on the light, and I looked at him and said to him, "What are you doing?" and then I walked out of the room to the bathroom, locked the door, cleaned myself, and went back to my room. I felt so alone and vulnerable, and that I couldn't trust anyone ever again.

Kim and I grooming our horse in the front of the house

The next day was unbearable, really. I dreaded seeing my foster dad, but when I did, he just carried on like nothing had happened, and so I didn't say anything. Weeks went by, and life changed a little after that. K.

left us. My foster parents hired a gardener, and a maid, and built them a little hut to live in on their land. Soon a little black girl came to live with them; she was their granddaughter. The house maid, was ill; she had cancer and wasn't with us for very long, but I grew close to her, and I was very sad when she died. Her funeral was the first one I ever attended. R. had to come and stay in the house, and share a bedroom with me.

I started running away from home when I got into trouble. One day I took the dogs out for a walk, and decided to hide under a bush not far from our land. I could see the house, but I made the dogs go home without me. I sat for hours in the rain, until I saw my foster dad's car pull up. It was safer at home when he was there. The foster mom wasn't as abusive to me in front of him. Still, it was enough to get me into even more trouble.

A few weeks later after our Sunday Church service, my foster mom and I went shopping. I was happy when I went to church, as it was the only time I ever felt like I was 'good.' When we got home she got mad at me, because of some bacon that was missing from her bags. She blamed me for the mishap. She said that if it weren't for me dancing around, she wouldn't have misplaced it. She told me to get out of the house, because the sight of me made her mad, so I went outside. My foster dad was doing the horses hooves. I asked him if I could help, and he said that I could by holding the horses' reins while he went to fetch something. While he was away, the horse reared up, and being only 12, I wasn't strong enough to hold him, and so he got away. My foster dad came back, furious because the horse didn't want to be caught, and told me I was useless, and to go back inside. My foster mom shouted out the window, "I don't want her inside," and so feeling completely unwanted, and useless, I ran to the bottom of our land, cut through a corn field, and went to a friend's house, and told my friends mother what had happened. Of course, a few hours later, my foster mom called, and told me that if I didn't come home now, I shouldn't bother coming back at all, so I decided to go home, as I didn't have much choice really, but I was so scared of the trouble I was going to get into, that I snuck into the house, and hid under my desk in my bedroom for hours and hours. I could hear my foster mom ranting about me. There was no way I was leaving that spot! She sounded like she was going to kill me. Eventually she found me, and I held my breath tight when I saw her feet enter my room; then she saw me, and dragged me out, and gave me the beating of my life! I was so bruised it hurt to move for days.

The final straw was when the other foster girl wet the bed. I was on my way to school, when my foster mom demanded that I wash her bedding. I refused. It wasn't my pee on the sheets, and I didn't see why I was responsible for it. She smacked me, and left the room, and I climbed out of the window to escape in her brief absence, but she caught me, and dragged me back through the window, and then hit me across my face. When she left again, I ran out of the house. I had had enough. I ran all the way to the neighbors in tears, and asked them if I could please use their phone to call the social services. The neighbor kindly drove me to the city, to their offices, and there I was seen by a social worker, and told her everything that had been happening. Later that afternoon I was taken to a children's home, where I spent the night, not knowing what was going to happen to me. I didn't speak to anyone, and I didn't eat; I just cried, and cried, and cried, and cried myself to sleep.

The next day I was collected by one of my friend's mom, who didn't want to see me in another home. I spent a few weeks with her, until a meeting took place with my foster parents and the social workers, to discuss my future. The foster mom made a promise to never raise another hand to me, and told me she had bought me a puppy, so I agreed to return.

Sandy and me

Things went ok for a while. I named my puppy Sandy. On one shopping trip, the foster mom asked me if her husband had ever touched me, and I lied, and said "no." I didn't want any more trouble. But trouble came not long after my 13th birthday. After a nasty confrontation with the foster mom, she called a friend, and told her to take me, before she killed me, and so I left them with the clothes on my back, and my pillow.

The friend who collected me was a vet. She had recently married a man, and lived with him and her two daughters from her first marriage. I knew the girls from school. I stayed with them for a while, and then my foster mom called to say she wanted me to come home, and I refused to go, and so it came to be that this couple asked me if I would like to be fostered by them, and I agreed. They were a nice family, and for the first time in a long time, I could be a young teenage girl. I listened to music, went to a school disco, had my first date with a boy, had my hair cut nicely, messed around with makeup, and I felt happy mostly. I started high school, and things changed. I made new friends, friends from other schools that didn't know me from primary school. With my new look, I had boys chasing after me, and good girl friends so that life seemed to be pretty normal.

My first makeover

But with everything that had happened in my young life already, by the time I reached the age of 15, I wasn't normal at all. I had issues---very big issues. I was a little rebellious at times, but I guess that is normal for any teenager, but it didn't serve me well. I had met a boy who lived quite far away. He was my first true love. I had racked up a massive phone bill talking to him, and so was banned from seeing him. The woman accused me of having sex with him, and told me I would probably be pregnant by age 16. I hadn't had conceptual sex with anyone, because I was so afraid of it, due to my sexual abuse in the past. Also at school, my friends were into this 'happy clappy Christian Church,' and in a ceremony at school one lunch break, I acquired the gift of speaking in tongues, or so I thought I did. When I told my foster mother this, she told me that there was no such thing as heaven and hell, and that basically everything I had believed for most of my life was a lie, so I was banned from seeing my friends also, not to mention that my entire spiritual belief system was left in tatters.

The family took me on holidays, and it came to light that I was struggling to accept my new family. All I wanted was my mother, my father, and my brother, and upon our return, I had an argument with my foster mom about everything from my parents, to God, to my friends, and boyfriends. I just couldn't take it anymore. I wanted to die. Life was just a struggle, and happiness seemed to constantly be taken away from me, and so that night I overdosed on a cocktail of medications, gulping handfuls of pills, and writing my emotions down in my diary.

I was taken to the hospital and had my stomach pumped, and spent a couple days there before returning home, but the reception upon my return home was a very frosty one. My foster sisters didn't want to talk to me; they were angry for what I had done, and so I went to my bedroom and stayed there for three days. Even my meals were brought there, and on the third day, the foster mom just shot into my room, screaming at me, and slapped me across my face saying, "How could you do this to our family, I want you out!" She told me to pack up my stuff, and the next day drove me to a new place. I had no idea where I was going, and I wasn't able to say goodbye to any of my friends.

NH was a place of safety, a halfway house, a home for juvenile delinquents awaiting placements in Industrial schools. I was sent there until a place became available in a children's home. But to me, it was jail! Upon arrival, my bags were checked, and razors and aerosols were confiscated. My personal belongings were displayed for everyone to see, and I felt so degraded, as the girls were going through my clothes. I had to sleep in a dormitory with about twelve girls, wake up to ringing bells, have dormitory inspections, allocated bathroom time, eat with everyone in a massive dining hall, with iron gates being opened and shut after every section. They boys and girls were separated apart from school time, which was also a section in the institution. I was locked up, trapped, and very depressed.

It took a week before I was seen by a social worker. I went to her office, and in front of her she had a file. It was the fattest file on her desk, and it was mine. I can tell you that at that moment, I realized that was all my life amounted to was just another file on someone's desk. I was also sent to see the psychologist and started a course of anti-depressants, and counseling. If there was one thing I looked forward to, it was my meeting with my psychologist. She was so lovely and understanding. I didn't have to pretend with her. She even allowed me to use her phone to call my boyfriend, so that he knew where I was, and was able to come to visit, because apart from Bridget and Mark, no-one I cared about knew where I was.

I turned 16 while I was there, and soon after received a postcard from Mom, saying that she was leaving South Africa, and returning to her parents in the UK, because things weren't working out for her. Dad came to visit me there once, as well. I started smoking, and self-harming, which were difficult things to do, considering cigarettes and razors were banned, but these objects had a way of getting through, as they do in any correctional facility. While I was there, one girl committed suicide whilst in an observation room, by hanging herself with her bed sheets, and another girl was gang raped by a group of girls in the school toilets with a roll-on bottle. There were frequent spats of violence amongst the inmates and all in all it was three months of hell!

Finally, a place became available for me in a home for troubled teens. After a year of being there, my boyfriend's parents grew to love me, and agreed to foster me, and give me a home. I was age 17, and again had a new family. They looked after me well, and I grew to love them dearly, but I was troubled, and when my relationship with Nate failed, home life started to take a strain, and I became bitterly unhappy, and so at the age of 18 I left home to make my own way in the world. The night before I left, J. said to me, "please don't leave; stay," and I said him, "J., I am damned if I do, and I am damned if I don't."

I remember one day I sat and did a timeline of my life, and discovered I never spent more than four years in any one place. I held on to every memory for dear life, because surely if I didn't, who would? Who would remember what I was like as a child? There have been times that it has just been too much, and I haven't been able to cope with all the memories, and feelings of worthlessness that my childhood experiences have left me with. It is sad to admit, that on more than several occasions as a young adult, I made attempts to take my life, because I felt so insignificant, and I had no self-worth. The scars that remain on my arms from my years of self-harm bare testament to the emotional pain that I was in. When you grow up with no stability, with no sense of belonging, with the constant feeling of being 'unwanted,' and never knowing real love, is it any wonder? So as illogical as this may sound, I have written this story of my childhood to release the memories, so that I don't *have* to remember them anymore.

I also wanted to share my story in the hope that it may inspire anyone who has ever felt the way I have growing up. I want to say to you---never give up, because you don't have to let your past define you. Find strength from the fact that you *have* survived whatever it is that life has thrown at you, and love yourself. Love yourself with abundance, because you *are* worthy of love. Learn to understand the weaknesses of those who failed you, and know that you are not to blame for the choices they made, and lastly, forgive, because forgiveness is the only way for you to let go of all the negative emotions you harbor inside you against those who have wronged you. I hope and pray that every child in foster care---past, present, and future, finds the peace and love that they deserve. Thank you FACT!

A New Beginning

In 1999, I came to England, and reunited with my mother as a young woman. I can't begin to even express how much I love her. I found my maternal grandparents, my two aunties, an uncle, my two cousins, and finally, in 2001 I found my brother in Scotland. It's not been an easy journey finding my place in this life, and I have had so many emotions to deal with, and still do, but I have found my family now, and I can finally say, "I'm home!" I am still searching for my father in the hope we can make peace with the past and build a relationship.

Today I am 31 years old and I have a 4 year old son, who I treasure with all my heart. Sometimes I swear he is the most loved child in the world, because not a day goes by that I don't tell him how loved he is by me, and the joy he brings to my life. Every day he heals me a little more. My experiences as a foster child have taught me many things, but understanding, forgiveness, and love above all.

My Beautiful Son and Me

The Guardian Angel

I had a dream one night
About a man I went to see
He was surrounded by a holy light
He was only real to me
I found him on a mountain
My face stained with tears
He said to me, 'Come my child, tell me all your fears.'
I told him of my anger,
Of all my hurt and pain.
He said he'd purify my mind
With the gentle falling rain.
He told me of my life ahead
Of why I was placed on earth
'This is only the beginning, my child,
This is your birth.'
I tried to touch the light
So it could take me away
'It's not your time to die,' he said,
'Not tomorrow and not today!
You are not alone, my child,
I am watching over you
You have not yet reached your destiny
And it is something you must do!
I will walk beside you
And hold your precious hand
Give you all the guidance
Until you understand
There is magic in your future
Happiness and love
Then I'll be watching over you
From the heavens up above.

Paul Kannenberg

It Could Have Been Worse

I want to share my story because it was my experience. Some of it was good, and some of it was bad. It hope the good will make other foster children hopeful, and the bad will make other foster children be able to count their blessings, and give others a look into reality about what foster children go through.

I came from a very large family (I'm the youngest of fourteen children). We lived in Illinois. My dad became ill and my mom was overwhelmed, and unable to care for us, so we were put in foster care. I went to ISSCS (Illinois Soldiers and Sailors Children School) in 1948, where I stayed for four years, until I was placed in my first foster home, which was a very good home on a farm. Unfortunately, the father died after I was there a little over a year, and back then single parent foster homes weren't allowed, so I was removed and sent back to ISSCS. I wasn't happy about leaving this foster home, but what could I do? I was only a child; I didn't count.

I stayed in ISSCS a couple of years before I was put in my second foster home. This was a single parent foster home (by now the laws had changed). I wasn't happy there at all. I felt unwanted there, and that the only reason I was there was for her convenience, for the money. I was about 14-15 by now and felt I had more control than I did when I was younger, so I ran away and went back to ISSCS, where I was accepted again. I spent another 2-3 years there, before I left for the last time.

I went back to my home town and stayed with my mom for awhile, about six months, then took on various jobs, and got an apartment with my brother, but due to problems stemming from my brother's retardation, this arrangement didn't work out for long. When I was 17 I moved out to Colorado and joined the Army shortly after, when I was 18. I spent six years in the Army, in communications, and was married while I was in there (I was 21), and we had three children together. I felt like I was happily married, but after twenty years of married life we drifted apart, and went our separate ways.

I remarried about five years after my divorce and we had one child together. We are still happily married today.

What are my thoughts on foster care? I don't think any kid wants to be taken away from their home with their parents, but who's going to listen to children? There wasn't anybody there to listen to me when I was taken away. I was just a child. Everyone else seemed to know what was best for me. They had all the answers, and they never asked me what I wanted. I think foster children are herded around like cattle; at least they often feel that way. Sometimes I felt that way. When I got older I was able to accept my experience better, but as a child I felt rather helpless. And as for the foster care system and foster homes, I think the social workers need to screen people better, and listen to the children more, taking into consideration what they want, and how they feel. My experience could have been a lot worse, as you will see when I share a story about another foster child. His story is much more tragic than mine.

There was a foster boy who lived down the road from me when I was in my first foster home. We took the bus to school together. He would get on the bus wearing mix-matched clothes, and wires for shoelaces. He was very skinny because he was underfed; he didn't eat with the rest of the family, and only got scraps of food, whatever was left over, and if there wasn't any, he went hungry. He slept on mattress springs with only a blanket on top, and he was beaten on a regular basis, whipped severely. He was just used as a farm hand. Some people in the area knew about the situation, and yet nobody turned the foster parents in. There had been other foster kids there before him that people also knew were being abused and neglected, and everyone turned a blind eye.

One day this foster boy apparently just couldn't take it anymore, and when he was alone with the foster father at home, he killed him, blew him away with a shot gun, and when the foster mom came home, he blew her away, also. He was only 12-13 years old when he murdered them. I was of course shocked by it, but it wasn't hard for me to see why he did it. He was sentenced to sixty-five years of prison, but he didn't serve all of them. I happened to run into to him one day years ago, and we resumed our friendship. The past was never brought up by either one of us. He got married, and has since passed away. This was a worst case scenario, and I am grateful this wasn't my experience, but it just goes to show you how bad it can get for foster kids.

Ray Reese

Hell

I would share
A long story about
my foster care
experience, but it was
HELL,
and I don't want to
talk about it. It is
too painful to relive.
It affected me for life.
I am 77 years old,
and a loner. I love
and trust animals,
but not people.
A lot of foster kids
have been to **HELL,**
and don't know it,
but I do…
and it was **HELL.**

Richard Powell

Finally Over the Anger

I was born in a small town in Illinois in 1940. My earliest memories are of our family, which included my parents, along with me and my older brother, Ed, living in a one-room shack with a dirt floor and an outhouse. My dad, who was called "fish," because he drank so much, was known as the town drunk. He spent a lot of time in the bar, and in jail, and my brother and I spent a lot of time fetching him from the bar for our mom, so she could get his paycheck to feed us.

I'm not sure exactly when, but my parents eventually were separated, or divorced, and since my mom was unable to provide for me and my brother, we were placed in ISSCS (Illinois Soldiers and Sailors Children School) in Normal, Illinois. We were able to go there because my dad had been in the Navy in WW11. I never seen my parents much after that; my dad only came to visit me once at ISSCS, and my mom only visited me a few times while I was in foster care. The story was that my dad was killed in Chicago, and I'm not sure how he died, but I was led to believe he was murdered, and found in a motel room.

Although Ed and I were put in the same children's home, I had a different experience and recollection of that time, probably largely due to the fact of me being younger. I was only 6 years old when I entered ISSCS and I was confused, probably not understanding what was going on; therefore, I became a very troublesome child who was belligerent, rude, and boisterous, and very difficult to handle. I was a very troubled and angry boy.

I only stayed at ISSCS for about 1-2 years, and then I was put into a detention home in Galesburg, Illinois. I don't have a lot of memories of this place, other than being watched over very carefully. This was only a temporary placement until a foster home was found for me, so I wasn't there long, less than a year. I went from the detention home to a foster home in Rantoul, Illinois. I was 8-9 years old at the time, and was also at this place less than a year. The foster father, Earl Scarberry, was a Christian minister, who was a very nice man, but I was still very rebellious, acting up and mouthing off, so they couldn't handle me, and I was removed from the home. I went from this home to Cunningham Children Home in Urbana, Illinois for a few years. It was a good place, and I don't have any bad memories from here. I was older by this time, so I was allowed some freedom, which I liked. When I was about 15 years old I was put into a very nice, private foster home that was intended to be an "aging out the system" home. Child and Family Services watched over me very closely there, and when I was age 17, they made arrangements for me to go into the Navy. I got married when I was 18 years old, and remained married to my wife until she died in 2008.

I was very angry growing up in the foster care system, and it took me a long, long time to get over my anger, until my late teens or early twenties, but eventually I did get past my anger, and got on with my life. I was fortunate to have a very nice social worker, who was like a mentor for me, a big ego booster, who gave me some confidence. We kept in touch with each other for about 50 years, until he died in 2008. If it wasn't for the love and support I got from him, I probably wouldn't have done so well in my life. I was a Navy airplane pilot, a deputy sheriff, a city police officer, and a manager of an engineering department in a hospital. I have three children, two boys from my first wife, and one boy with my present wife, who I have tried my very best to be a good father, and provider for, giving them what I wished I'd had as a child.

Today I feel like I was lucky to have my foster care experience; at least some good came out of it. The only remorse I have is that growing up, I wasn't with my family, but I am still grateful to have been in those foster homes. I never really resented my mother for being unable to care for us; I understand that she had a tough life and did the best she could do. I loved her as much as any boy can love his mother, and was happy for her when she remarried, this time to a very nice man, who was a good provider to her and my five half brothers. It wasn't easy for me growing up in the foster care system, but I am comfortable with myself today and don't have any ghosts or gremlins to dwell on.

Roberta Manning

A Lost Childhood

It isn't easy for me to share this story, but I think it is worth telling, especially if it can help somebody else in the process. I had a very chaotic childhood, to say the least. That is putting it mildly, considering what I went through, and how it affected me.

I was born in 1954 into a very large African-American family in Illinois. I am the seventh one out of nine children, six boys and three girls. My dad had health problems. My mom abandoned the family. She just took off one day, leaving our disabled father to care for us, which he was unable to do. My dad asked my oldest brother, the oldest of us kids, to take care of us, but he said he couldn't, that he had to graduate, and that he wanted to go into the Navy. I was angry that my brother didn't at least try to take care of us. I think he purposely wanted to get away from home, because he had already shouldered a lot of the responsibility for our mom, and he was tired of it. I had an aunt on my dad's side that helped out some, at least at first when my mom left, but she had a family of her own to care for, and didn't want the responsibility of taking care of us also. She was the one who turned our family into Child and Family Services.

I was 5 years old when I went into foster care. My younger brother and I went into a foster home together with an older African-American couple, but we only stayed there about one year, because the foster father had a mental breakdown and CFS decided it was best that we be removed. This wasn't too bad of a home, except for a few abusive incidents, once when I got hit with an extension cord for making a mess in the bathroom when I had diarrhea, and another time when I had to stand in a corner on a hot day for calling her grand kid a fool. They were a very large, religious family. During this time my mom had called and asked my dad about our whereabouts, and he said he didn't know, but through a lawyer, an aunt found us. CFS ended up telling my parents where we were at, but that they would need a judge, as my mom had been declared an unfit mother.

After I left this home I went into another foster home, which was hell. It was also with an African-American couple. The dad was a lawyer, and very nice, but she was nasty, very mean. At first she was somewhat nice, but she ended up being very abusive. She was a stay at home housewife with two kids of her own, a teenage daughter and a younger son, who never had to work, but I was treated like a slave. When I was about 6 or 7 years old she made me get on a step ladder and iron clothes, and I would have to get on my hands and knees, until my knees were raw, to scrub black marks off of the kitchen floor, and if the floor wasn't clean enough for her, I got beat on my back side with an extension cord. She tried keeping the abuse hidden from her husband, because he was a nice man and didn't like it. I would hear her telling her own kids that we were dirty. She told us, "you're not my kids; you guys are raggedy, and come from a dirty family. I don't have to treat you good. You're just dirty, poor foster kids." Maybe she thought of us like slaves because we were darker than her kids; I don't know. We were also denied food that her kids ate, and we weren't allowed to sit on the living room furniture. Once when I tried sitting next to the foster father on the living room couch, she got real angry, and wouldn't let me. She told him he should only be close to his own kids. We didn't have any good clothes, and when she got us some clothes at church, I asked her why we didn't have new clothes, and she slapped me when I got home. I asked her husband why we didn't get new clothes, and when he asked his wife why we didn't have new clothes, when the state provided money for us, she told him she took the state money and spent it on their own kids. The father went out himself and bought us some new clothes, but she got real mad and told him to return the clothes, but he wouldn't. He told her he would turn her in himself if she didn't start treating us right, and she threatened to leave him if he did. The next day she threatened to throw the clothes in the garbage, so I hid them, and she chased me around so she could beat me. I was always getting beat with the extension cord, for any little mistake I made.

I told the caseworker about the abuse and she told the foster mother if she abused me again, she would be arrested. The foster mom tried getting the bruises off my body before the caseworker came to visit, and there was a surprise visit once, but the bruises were already gone. After this the beatings stopped, but the verbal abuse continued. She still called us "dirty little black kids" and slapped my face. The dad intervened, and told her to keep her mouth shut, and even tried taking us to work with him in order to protect us from her, but she made life hard on him. I was even afraid to go to school, because I didn't trust the mom with my younger brother. She came right out and told me she hated me, and I asked her why she was a foster mother, if she felt that way. I told my foster dad I wanted to go home, that I didn't want to stay there, and he tried talking to his wife, but nothing changed for the better, so the caseworker ended up telling my real dad that we were being abused in this foster home, and he got a lawyer, who was able to help get us out of there.

The case went to court, and the foster parents got their foster care license revoked, and the judge gave my mom a second chance. My older brother came to pick us up, and took us back home. It's a good thing we were taken out of that foster home, or I might have ended up dead. There was a family next door with a lot of kids, which she forbid us to play with, and years later, I found out she ran over one of the kids with her car, and broke his arm and leg, how, or why, I don't know. I was ten years old when I went back to live with my parents, but my mom took off again two years later, and left the family in a predicament again. Maybe part of the reason she left this time had to do with the fact that there were things happening with me and my sister and she felt guilty. Also, my dad knew some things that my mother was doing and she was afraid he would find out. My dad tried taking care of us, and we all tried helping out (there were four of us kids then), but things weren't working out. We were poor, and I used to use dish soap for laundry soap, which was leaving my clothes dingy, and the school principal noticed, and tried contacting my mom. He asked me if my mom left again, and I broke down and told him the truth, and he contacted Child and Family Services. I didn't want to go into foster care again because of the bad experiences I had, but they had no choice.

All four of us went to children's home, and I was there about three years, from the ages of 11-14. It was a good place---strict, but not abusive.

My mom visited me while I was there, but I refused to see her, and ran down to the cemetery close by to hide from her. I was very angry while I was at the home, and acted out a lot. I was very rebellious, and got detention. I got therapy while I was there, but I don't know how much it helped, because I still misbehaved.

The state ran out of money and wanted to move some of us, so we went into another children's home. Three of us went there, one by one. My brother went there first, but he didn't adapt well, so he was brought back to the previous home, and some foster parents who used to take him for weekends eventually took him into their home until he graduated. I went to this home about two months after my one brother, and my other brother went there about one year later. I spent three years there, from the ages of 14-17. I loved the home, and adapted well. I didn't get hit or yelled at, so I felt safe there, at least up until I had the unfortunate experience of being raped by a boy there. When I was 15 years old, I earned privileges to cook and bake, and when I was about 16, I got privileges to leave the grounds, met a boy, and got pregnant. The people there at the home were real angry at me, especially since I had done real well in school, and they considered me a good prospect for success. They said I was a bad influence on the other girls there, and decided to move me to an unwed mother's home.

When I was about two months pregnant, before I left the children's home, I got raped by a white boy on the grounds. It was a boy I was acquainted with, who had a crush on me, and one night when I was walking home to my cottage, he threatened me with a switchblade, and took me over to a cornfield, and raped me. He wanted to be my boyfriend, and when I told him I already had a boyfriend, and that I was pregnant with his child, he got crazy, and said he would cut the baby out of me, and I told him if he killed me, we wouldn't be able to be together, so he let me go, but told me if I ever told anybody, he would cut my throat. His mom had abandoned him at birth, and I guess he couldn't take the rejection. He was obsessed with me. I reported the rape, and the boy was removed from the children's home and put in psychiatric facility somewhere, but I still worry about him killing me.

I went to the unwed mother's home and had a baby boy, who I kept. I stayed with my brother for awhile after this. My dad was dying of liver cancer, and he wanted to see his grandchild before he died, so I stayed there two years before he died, and helped take care of him. My dad asked my brother to find our mom, and she came back to help care for him, also.

She wanted to leave after his death, but we talked her into staying, and then she died two years later.

While I was staying with my brother, I had the second unfortunate experience of being raped, this time by a friend of my brother's. My life didn't get any better after this point; in fact, it got worse. He ended up getting a rape conviction, and spent three years in prison, and when he got out he told me he had been drunk, and apologized to me. He also said he loved me, and wanted to marry me, that I needed a man to take care of me and my child. My dad had a neutral attitude toward the marriage proposal, my mom discouraged it, and my brothers encouraged it. I didn't see any reason to listen to mom---why would I listen to her, when she abandoned me, but I sure shouldn't have listened to my brothers. I know it sounds insane, but I married the guy.

The only reason I can come up as a rationale for marrying him, was that I had a fear of rejection. I was 18 years old at the time, and stayed married for 17 years, and had one daughter with him. I never trusted him with my daughter, because he raped me, and I was afraid he would hurt her. I tried leaving after three years of marriage, but stayed for the security, if you could call my life with him secure. He was an alcoholic, and very abusive, and you guessed it, hit me with an extension cord! He hit me with his fist, threw burnt food at me, kicked me, and tried choking me. He even put a gun to my head and stuck my head in a freezer, and I talked him out of killing me somehow, but he was crazy with rage, accusing me of cheating on him. There was a man I was friends with, and he found out about it and accused me of being unfaithful, but he was the one who was cheating, not me. He was even having an affair with my best friend, and her mother told me about it. I ended up leaving him after this. In retrospect, I think he wanted revenge for me putting him in prison. He died of liver cancer at the age of 43. I had a relationship with the man I had been friends with, and he had two kids, a boy and a girl, but this guy was a crack head, and was also abusive, so the relationship ended, but the chaos didn't. He came over to my house one time with his new girlfriend, wanting to stay there, and when I told him he couldn't, that they had to leave, he tried to murder me by stabbing me in the chest, but I was able to block him with my arm, and he only got my wrist, which I had to get nineteen stitches for. I was upset, because this guy wasn't prosecuted, and I found out later it was because he was a drug snitch for the prosecutor.

I still worry about him trying to kill me, and I believe this fear largely contributes to my depression and anxiety.

I forgave my mom for the abandonment, but it wasn't easy. I was very angry, and blamed her for the fact that I was put in foster homes, and abused. It hurt being in foster care, because I wanted to be with my whole family. Living like that makes it harder in life. I think I felt like I had to grow up quicker, in order to survive, otherwise I would just die. I asked myself, "Why does all this stuff have to happen to me? Is our family cursed?" It seems so unfair. I didn't have a real childhood to enjoy. I lost my childhood. I have depression, and anxiety, and have gotten therapy off and on throughout the years, but sometimes it's too painful to talk about. One of the biggest issues I have is with not trusting men. I know I have to keep going, though, and be strong, not just for me, but for my children and grandchildren. I am overprotective of my kids and grandkids, because of my past, and they didn't understand why, until they found out about my childhood. My oldest son told my grandchildren and younger daughter that I was broke down from the abuse, that I'm not real strong, but to be patient with me. What has been particularly painful is watching the past repeat itself. My daughter had problems with her children. I was a kinship provider for awhile, but she is doing better now, and has custody. We still fight sometimes, and she doesn't believe that her father raped me.

I feel bad for foster kids, and what they go through. For those of you going through this today, don't give up. There is hope, and when you have problems, talk to somebody you trust. I know it's hard to trust, but you need to try. Even though I didn't have good foster parents, I believe there are good ones. Sad to say, I don't regret being in foster care, because I think I was probably sexually safer there than I was in my own home. My mom and dad were southerners who trusted everybody, and left their doors open all the time, which left me vulnerable to sexual abuse. It was while I was living at home that I got raped by my first husband. It was also while I was home that I was raped (attempted) by a family acquaintance. After this incident, my parents were more careful about leaving their doors locked. My mom had been gone at the time of the attempted rape, and my dad talked her into coming home, and told her that she needed to be there for her baby girl, who was going through so much, so my mom returned for a short time, only a few days, and then left again. My greatest hope is to be the kind of mother my own mother wasn't, and to find a good man someday, somebody who will love and respect me.

Ron Huber

Never Complete Closure
Author of *A Ward of the State* and *Facing the World without Love*

I would like to dedicate my story to the millions of children who have grown up without knowing the warmth of a hug, or the true feeling of being loved. I know the feelings of loneliness and the yearning that you feel to love someone and be loved in return. I know your fear of rejection. At your lowest moments, it may be hard to believe that there is someone out there who loves you, but there is. You may not be able to see Him with your eyes or feel His arms around you, but if you look deep inside of yourself, you will find that God has always been there, and believe it or not, He has been protecting you. It took me nearly thirty years to learn this, and because of this, I have unintentionally hurt many people in my life, for which I ask forgiveness from. I pray that each of you who are going through this will learn to believe in yourself. It doesn't matter what anyone may ever say about you; know and believe that you are unique and a wonderfully made individual. While no person, especially a child, should have to endure the pain and sadness that you may feel, know that inside you there is strength stronger than anything you may face. With God's help, you will only grow stronger. Learn to let go of the past, and take hold of your Heavenly Father's hand. He will never abandon you. You can be anything you want to be, as long as you believe in yourself. God believes in you, and I believe in you, and I salute you, the unwanted child.

My story has already been written in my two books, *A Ward of the State* and *Facing the World Without Love.* For those of you who are unfamiliar with them, here is my story. If it can help even one person, it is well worth telling again. It is a story that must be told and retold in the interests of future generations of orphaned and abandoned children, whose lives could be wasted without early proper care.

One unpleasant memory I have is being embarrassed in the classroom, and being branded as stupid by my peers for not knowing my own mother's name, which burned a permanent scar on my heart, but what they didn't realize was that my ignorance of who my mother was didn't come from having a faulty memory or from being some mentally retarded misfit. I didn't know my mother's name because I never got the chance to ask. Her name was Helen Somerville, but to me and my three brothers, Vic, Ralph Jr., and Simon, she was a ghost. The local bar saw more of her than we did. My grandfather was our primary caretaker, but unfortunately, he was an alcoholic also and only looked in on us sporadically. If he was sober, he'd bring us food, and if he felt real kind he would clean our bodies of the terrible stench from having sat in our own excrement for days, though I imagine it was more for his own personal comfort than sympathy for us. A meal usually consisted of peanut butter and jelly sandwiches. The rats in the building lived better than us. My dad worked on a boat and was often gone for weeks at a time, sending his paycheck. Maybe he didn't care that his money was spent on booze, but I'm more inclined to believe he forgot his kids even existed, as he barely noticed us when he was home. I remember Vic and me amusing ourselves on the cold and dirty kitchen linoleum floor. It was a dismal existence, to say the least.

Then life changed for us one November day in 1948, when a big black sedan with two women came to our house. I remember them looking at us, then at my mom, who led them into the kitchen, where they spoke in hushed tones. A chill ran through me that had nothing to do with the cold, and when they came out to the front room I was so nervous that I wet my pants, which didn't go unnoticed. Ralph Jr. was grabbed out of the crib by one woman, while the other women took care of Vic and me. Simon had not yet been born. When Vic got upset, she told him she'd smack the daylights out of him if he didn't shut up. My eyes welled up with tears as I hung my head and walked slowly to the car, looking back toward the front door, feeling chilled by the coldness of my mom's indifference, and having a feeling of hopelessness and abandon sweep through me as the door closed us inside.

It was a silent ride to the Covenant Children's Home, except for our grumbling stomachs. We were very warmly welcomed by the Reverend, who carried me inside because I was so frail and malnourished that I passed out while walking from the car to the stairs. We were immediately fed a hot meal of turkey and mashed potatoes, which we shoveled in our mouths with our hands, and then we took a bath, and put pajamas on, and were neatly tucked into bed, where I lay wondering about Ralph Jr., if he was being treated as well as us. If this was a dream, I didn't want to wake up.

I was diagnosed with Rickets from malnutrition, but got stronger after eating regularly. I was initially very withdrawn, but gradually, the constant love and encouragement forged a crack in my shell and I was running around on the playground with the other children and flourished in school. I loved to sing; it made me forget where I was. Christmastime was a new and warm experience, with tree decorating, cookies and cider, caroling, and gifts, but as other children left for holiday home visits, I was left wondering why my mommy and daddy didn't want us, their absence creating an empty feeling inside my little heart, the feeling slowly subsiding when I realized I wasn't alone, that there were others in the same boat as me. I remember hearing the sniffles of children who couldn't understand why they had to come back to the Home, while my sniffles came from wondering why I had never left.

In January, our parents came to visit Vic and me, and brought us gifts, but it was an awkward visit, with my mom uncharacteristically affectionate, my dad expressionless, looking at me like a stranger, and me unsure if I wanted them to go away for good, or if I should go home with them, wondering if it would be different than before, as I wanted to feel like a family and have them tuck me into bed at night, but it didn't matter what my young mind was contemplating, because they weren't there to get us anyway. I felt crushed as I watched them leave, and wondered what was so bad about me that they didn't want me. I was initially despondent after their visit, but slowly returned to my usual self, my confidence gradually improving.

Then in the spring, the Reverend awoke us, packed our bags, and informed us that we were going on a "vacation." We left with a social worker, who took us to a foster home. I thought to myself, "Why are we here? Did we do something wrong? How long will we be here before they send us away again?" My mind raced and I felt troubled by questions that I had no answers to, such as why we had to leave the Covenant Children's Home, if we would ever go back, or if we'd see our friends again. The first few weeks in this foster home I slept in my bedroom closet, where I felt safe. The foster dad was pretty nice, but the mom was mean and strict, and withheld food from us as punishment. Once Vic got in real trouble when he did something wrong. We slept together that night because we were both so traumatized.

The mom seemed a little nicer after this incident and we even got a new tricycle, but the hopeful feeling was short-lived. When I tore the screen door netting trying to get the bike outside one day, the foster parents decided we were too much trouble to deal with, and I was awakened the next morning by a vigorous shake from the social worker, who had our bags packed. We were leaving, and although I had mixed feelings, part of me feeling happy and part of me feeling sad, assuming I would be returned to the Covenant Children's Home and wondering how long it would be before we'd get another family, these feelings didn't compare to the shock I felt when I woke up to see my parent's faces. I didn't know whether to be happy or sad, nor did my parents seem to be.

We were returned home---to a cold house, blankets for beds, meager meals, and a new baby, Simon, along with Ralph Jr., who had also been returned. Vic and I were left alone to care for Ralph Jr. when my dad worked and our mom left with baby Simon. We were receiving spankings regularly ever since we got in trouble for making a fire because we were cold, and we were getting thinner by the day. I went to bed with hunger pangs, wishing I could be anywhere but here.

My wish came true shortly after Christmas, when my dad took off for good, leaving my mom alone to care for four young children, which she was unwilling and incapable of doing. She blamed us for our dad's departure. I figured I must be a bad kid for my dad to leave like that. About a week later we were taken away from her, again, and placed in another foster home on a farm. These people didn't want boys, and had told the Child Welfare Services so, but since our mom had made it clear she wouldn't take us back, and we needed a home, they consented to at least give us a try, but I sure didn't feel very welcomed, not from day one. She inspected us like we were puppies and her gruff manner made me have bad thoughts about this new home, but I had no choice in the matter, and so for the third time in less than three years, Vic and I stood at the end of the gravel road, waving goodbye to Mrs. Booth, our social worker, in her black sedan.

For the third time, we had no idea of what we were in for, but for the millionth time, I was scared. Things got off to an awkward start, with the foster dad accusing me of being a dummy because I was too shy to talk at first. Did they ever consider how I might be afraid, considering the circumstances? I felt the foster mom only tolerated me, while the dad found us amusing. Apparently, what they wanted was farm hands, as we did farm chores from dawn to twilight, like hired hands. We got beatings a lot, for reasons I didn't understand. I think hardly two days went by without us getting beat. After a little over a year of being there, we got a visit from a social worker, who disregarded our complaints about abuse, and instead believed the Borg's "nice act," telling us how lucky we were to have them. I sure didn't feel lucky to have them. School wasn't much of a reprieve from the mom's abuse, as I was always teased about something---my clothes, my smell, my speech---you name it. I began to wish I was invisible.

One day I just took off from school and wandered through town, hoping somebody would have compassion on me and take me home with them, but of course it didn't happen. Despite my desire to stay with my brother, my unhappiness at this foster home caused me to hit the road several more times over the next two years, usually after a disheartening visit by one of the social workers, when our complaints were ignored, and were reminded of how fortunate we were to have a home. After each visit, things got worse for about a week, the beatings becoming more frequently, and I would continually run away, only to return to face the music of my punishment. It was a vicious cycle, but I was desperate, so I kept trying to escape. Apparently I was stuck with these foster parents, at least for awhile yet.

Things changed drastically when the foster dad lost one leg due to a tractor accident. Vic and I all but gave up school, since we had to do all the farm chores now. He turned into a different man and one night things got out of hand. The very next morning, a social worker came to take us away. The foster mom tried talking the social worker into letting us stay, expressing a concern about who would do the farm chores with us gone, but the social worker told her that it was her problem, and then told Vic and me that she had just the right place for us. It wasn't until the blue Chrysler began to roll down the driveway that I really believed we were leaving this awful foster home. After eight long years of wishing, hoping, and praying, it had finally come true. It looked like my prayers had finally been answered. I turned in my seat and watched from the rear window as the farm, the animals, and the foster mom's permanent scowl faded into a cloud of dust.

Vic and I were taken to ISSCS (Illinois Soldiers and Sailors Children's School), a large area of land with several cottages, a school, gymnasium, recreation room, and indoor pool. Vic and I were put in separate cottages, due to our age difference, yet another decision I had no control over. Vic was my best friend, and for the first few days I was very lonely, and even though I saw him during meals and at the recreation room, he seemed to have made a lot of new friends, and although he didn't ignore me, I didn't feel as close to him as I once had. I began making friends with most of the thirteen cottage boys and I wasn't treated like an outcast, as I feared I would be, but my stuttering wasn't completely gone, only in hiding, and so I worried about being teased for it. I didn't like school because the teachers wanted me to participate, while I preferred obscurity. One teacher always questioned my being withdrawn, which I responded to with a blank stare, not knowing how to explain to her that I'd spent most of my life being invisible and didn't trust the spotlight. It seems to me that she should understand why I was withdrawn, but she didn't.

Overall, life for Vic and me had been much better since we'd arrived at ISSCS. The adult workers there were nice, and even though we had chores ad homework to do every day, we weren't treated like workhorses and we were allowed to have fun. ISSCS turned out to be the best place for us so far. While I was there, I became acquainted with a family outside the grounds, the Huber's, who made me feel very welcomed. Though my life experiences were limited, the Huber's weren't like any family I had ever imagined. The parents were patient, understanding, and interested in their children, and extended this to me. All the kids treated me like I belonged in their family, a feeling I had never had before. Their acceptance was the most precious thing I had ever received.

After high school graduation I was expected to leave ISSCS, but leaving ISSCS was not easy for me. I worried about where I would go and what would become of me. I was afraid of becoming homeless. Things were looking extremely bleak, but when the Army recruiter came to ISSCS, my decision was easily made. The Huber's gave me a farewell party, which I was completely overwhelmed and overjoyed by, yet at the same time, I felt saddened and tremendously hurt by the realization of what I was deprived of as a child.

In my third year overseas, Barbara and Lonnie came to visit me and informed me that the whole Huber family had decided they wanted to legally adopt me. To say I was happy would be an understatement. Years of feeling unwanted, unloved, and worthless fell off my heart like dead weight. When we called the family to tell them my agreement to the adoption, their rejoicing over the phone was like music to my ears. I didn't know why they had chosen me, but I was so glad they did! When I went back to the States on leave, before going to Vietnam, I was given a warm homecoming and only had to sign a few legal adoption documents, which was simple and quick, and the feeling of being part of a family swelled my heart with pride and a deep sense of love and gratitude that was wonderful. I was 21 years old at the time, but my prayers had finally been answered.

The journey of my life was far from over after the adoption, though. I saw combat in Vietnam, and I got married and had two girls, but unfortunately, my lack of experience and my inept social and relationship skills made me a poor husband, and the marriage failed. I flourished, however, in my occupation as a broadcaster. Amazingly, the stutter that had plagued me for so much of my life had done a permanent disappearing act, which I credit to the growing confidence I got from the love and support of my new family, the Huber's. I retired from the Army and continued in my broadcasting career, working for the Voice of America. I met and married my beautiful wife, and have a son who I hold very dear. Their love and patience continue to strengthen me.

Although I have a good life today and am blessed in ways I never thought I would be, for me, complete closure will never come. The scars will be hidden, but they will never go away. My prayers go out to those who are going through the system, which the federal Health and Human Services Agency describes as handling more than 200,000 children a year, as well as those who are now out of the system and have to live with those scars. God bless you all.

S.S.

Through a Child's Eyes

They say that the eyes are the windows to the soul,
With no words spoke her eyes had said, "That life had took its toll."

Behind her personality she tried to hide,
Not realizing that imitation was suicide.

Pretending as if everything was in its place,
But I could see the pain in her face.

I never knew the true meaning of unfair,
Until I asked her how did she end up in special care.

And her soul she had begun to pour,
But my heart could not take it anymore.

Just visualizing her life experiences through her eyes,
And through her testimony hearing her cries.

From being nurtured and cared,
And now she is scared.

She once was happy with her mother,
Until her uncle had the misconception that she was his lover.

It started out with just a touch,
Until he started to feel that wasn't much.

He wanted more but she wasn't willing to give but he was willing to take,
And so her he decided to rape.

He raped her and threatened to kill her if she would tell,
And eventually she noticed that she didn't feel well.

Her uncle poisoned her just to conceal,
He didn't want to get caught so her he was willing to kill.

Eventually her mother had walked in when she found him having sex with
her other kids too,
This was something that no one should have to go through.

But her pain didn't stop there,
Although it was already too much for a child to bear.

Just when she thought her nightmares were ending,
More problems were beginning.

Because her mother wouldn't have sex with the landlord he put them out,
Which was sad because rent wasn't what it was all about.

Living in the street,
Just trying to find food to eat.

Just trying to find a way to survive,
They were living, but didn't feel alive.

Seeking help from a shelter,
But they didn't take time to help her.

Back on the streets again,
Giving her most prized possession to men.

Just trying to make it through,
What else was she to do?

She's been in seventy foster homes within a year,
And now at 15 she's ended up here.

And now she's putting on a façade,
So her life won't seem so odd.

She is concealing her pain,
And at times she doesn't feel that she is sane.

All her sorrows has taken its toll,
Of thoughts what tomorrow holds.

At night she cries herself to sleep,
Because that is the only time that she feels she can weep.

She dreams of her death,
Because she feels as if she has nothing left.

But the streets changing is symbolic because it's God's way
of showing you that things won't be the same.

And your death just meant that that's where you will end up if
if you keep feeling shamed.

And it's not ok to be uncertain about your aspirations and your dreams,
Because Faith without works won't get you anything.

And there is no need to fear,
God didn't bring you this far in order to leave you here!

And stop thinking that you have to give your most prized possession,
And you are not gay so stop thinking that girls are your obsession.

And I understand that you had a hard time trusting another,
Don't let your past stop you finding a lover.

Looking for love in all the wrong places,
Seeking help from all the wrong faces.

They found an abandoned house but to them it was their home,
A family united together and not alone.

Her mother eventually found a boyfriend to help them out,
Staying together was what it was all about.

Even though he sold her drugs,
He showed them love and gave them hugs.

It was the first father figure that the children had,
Seeing him being murdered made them sad.

They shot him six times in the chest,
Taking the only father they had left.

And although one suspect is in jail,
Eight victim's lives were nothing but hell.

So when the police came to investigate the crime,
They realized this family had been living in an abandoned house the
whole time.

So protective services came in and separated them all,
This was just the beginning of Troy'neisha's fall.

Without her family what was she to do?
Without them she felt she couldn't make it through.

Just thirteen,
And already she's experienced these things.

A lover as in Christ,
Because He loved you enough to save your life.

And all would be in vain if you just gave us here,
Vista is your journey but your destination is not here.

God is trying to mold you into the person He wants you to be,
But you must open your eyes and see.....................

That through Christ Jesus you T. can be all that you want to be!!!!!!!!!!!

Anonymous

THEE Restorer

I want to share my story so I can hopefully give hope to the hopeless, the foster children. I don't want to elaborate about all my foster homes and everything I went through, because I don't want to rehash everything, nor do I want to talk much about all my personal life since then, because it is personal to me, but I would like to share about HOW I am overcoming my past, which is by the grace of God.

I went into foster care at the age of 5, along with my three younger siblings (two sisters and one brother), because our mother was mentally ill. I'm not sure what mental illness she was diagnosed with; I just know she was mentally ill, to the point that she was unable to properly care for us. I had a very unstable childhood, bouncing around between my mentally ill mom and 21-22 foster homes. My mother's maternal rights were eventually terminated, but for a long time Social Services kept putting me back with her, only to have her fail their expectations again, and so I would be moved again, into another new foster home.

Being bounced around like I was made me feel very abandoned, and I always felt like I was a puzzle piece that didn't fit in the puzzle anywhere. I had a lot of anger, resentment, and shame about being in foster care, and I grabbed onto everything I could to try to overcome my past, which often wasn't good for me. Even when nothing made sense, and it seemed like everything was disastrous in my childhood, I tried everything I could with what I knew. I tried so hard to fit into the puzzle, but it seemed to no avail, was another fail.

I had the idea that I could somehow heal my own childhood by building my own family as an adult, but that was easier said than done, an illusion that would be shattered, to no avail, another fail. I had two children, a boy and a girl, with my first husband, then divorced, and remarried, only to divorce him also---not exactly the idea of my dream. My relationships with my children are being restored today; in fact, my son is actually living right across the hall from me, with his girlfriend and daughter, in my apartment complex, but you know how it is when there is an upheaval in the family….people tend to take sides, which I guess wasn't mine, so for 10 years I was estranged from my son, nor did I see my daughter much, which was hard for me. She is married with two children today, but lives 100 miles away from me, so we still don't see each other often. I am in contact with my mom today, and I have an ok relationship with her, but she has never even apologized about the past, let alone really be a mom, but it is what it is, and I realize today that she is mentally ill, and can't help her shortcomings.

When I was about 38 years old I began searching for God, or maybe I should say He had been searching for me, and found me, as I wasn't really looking for Him, but somehow I found Him. My life was a mess, and I figured He could help clean it up, as I wasn't doing a very good job of it myself. It's been a journey of hope from the beginning, as scripture says, "Hope does not disappoint." I can say I've reached a place of strength, renewal, and great peace in my soul, which I completely lacked before. And although I began seeking the LORD years ago, surrendering came later, because of my unbelief. But He's shown me His patience, and a love I never could imagine. He is intimate, and completely faithful, which I'm so grateful for, since I'm a real work in progress. I will close with a biblical verse…one that I hope brings hope to every heart:

Jeremiah29:11

"For I know the plans I have for you, says the Lord, plans for good and not for evil, plans to give you a hope and future. He is awesome and Mighty to save."

Sebastian De Carss

Pictures Could Tell My Story

I want to tell my story because I think people should know the horrors that some foster children have endured while being "cared" for in orphanages. I am a survivor of attempted murder at the age of 4, and I became a handicapped child who was retarded, autistic, and spastic, with a speech problem, for twenty years. I was a migrant slave during the 1960's because of this crime, and unfortunately, experienced many horrors myself, but fortunately lived to tell my story. I have many pictures I would like to share and documents of proof, but I am not allowed to share them, so I will only tell you what I can.

This page should be filled with pictures, but I couldn't share them. Read my story and then fill in the blank page with your imagination.

This is picture of me while I was in the orphanage.

This is a picture of me before I went into the orphanage.

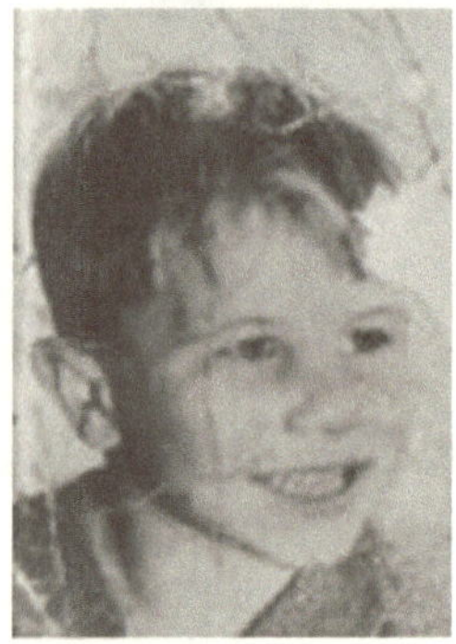

This is picture of me while I was in the orphanage.

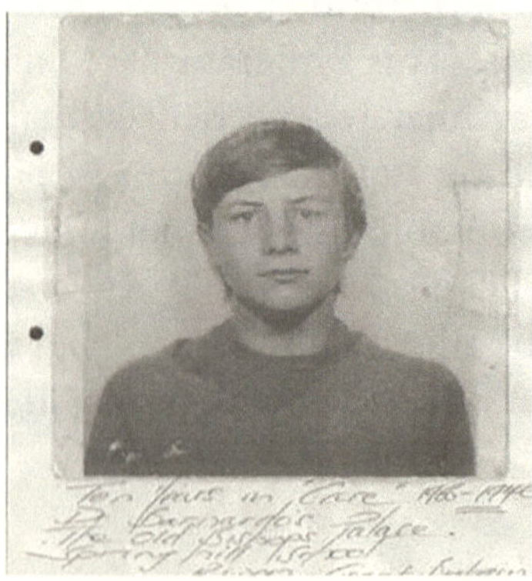

Although it is true that my pictures would tell a story, my words will elaborate on them. I wish I had imagined all of this, that it was just a nightmare I eventually woke up from, but unfortunately it was a horrible reality, one that not only lives on in my pictures, but also in my mind. I hope by sharing my story it will help other survivors of abuse to come forward and speak out. Abuse survivors, especially of the magnitude in my case, need to speak out, not only for themselves, but for the benefit of all abuse survivors. Maybe if we speak out enough, people will finally wake up and do something about the horrible realities facing so many innocent children.

Because of these crimes I became a child migrant slave for about ten years, from. I was shipped off to an orphanage, which was supposed to be a "care" home for disabled, unwanted child migrant slave children. I became a handicapped person for twenty years, a retarded, autistic, and spastic boy, with a speech problem, but I wasn't so handicapped that I couldn't take pictures with the camera that was given to me by the headmaster at the home. He probably thought this retarded, autistic, spastic bastard wouldn't know how to even use the camera, but I did, and I exposed things about disabled children not only to his own family, but to the whole world, and he is now behind bars for eleven years. He is done! He was convicted and now he is being investigated by the police concerning the many large "bonfires" that took place on the grounds.

When I came to France in the 1980's, I was very lucky to be adopted into a wealthy French family, and had many great years with them. I went on to study law, and brought a civil court case against the people at the orphanage, which I won with legal aid. I now have another legal case concerning the bonfires that took place on the grounds, which the police are investigating, and I hope to win. I want to see justice done.

I had many pictures I wanted to share with this story, but was unable to for legal reasons. But believe me, my pictures DO tell my story.

Terri Rimmer

And then…

I want to share my story to help bring about more awareness to the foster care issue, and to give other foster kids hope. Foster kids go through so much, and sometimes there seems like there is little hope, so if I can offer even a glimmer, then sharing my story was worth it.

My original home was dysfunctional, very chaotic. I had a stormy relationship with my abusive mom, and an inappropriate one with my dad, which led me to foster care as a teenager. I am close to my sister, who rescued me from my dad twice. In June of 1980 I went into a children's home, where I stayed for a month, and then was sent to the state hospital for two months, and then back to the children's home for awhile, and then into another hospital where I stayed for a month, and then I went back to my dad's. I was bounced around a lot. And then….

Having spent the summer being subjected to more of my dad's behavior, and having kept my sister updated the whole time to the progression of his behavior, that things had escalated to the point where I feared for my life, and was terrified that he was going to cross the line with me, she and I went to a church agency hoping to get some help. It was called AGAPE, a foster care placement agency where Church of Christ members take in abused and/or neglected children temporarily, sometimes leading to a permanent placement later. Although my sister and I had attended this particular church a few years earlier, we were not currently members, but had no other resources at our disposal; this seemed to be our only hope at the time. It's all rather fuzzy as to how I managed to break free from my dad that day, but I'm glad I did. I feel like foster care saved me. I'm sure I felt traumatized that day. The only thing I know is that my sister rescued me, and took me to the church, and then…

A counselor there drove me a temporary foster home close by. The foster parents in this home were very nice, churchgoing people, with two young children of their own. The mom was a homemaker, and the dad was gentle, loving provider who reminded me of Mr. Cunningham on the television show "Happy Days." It was peaceful there from the beginning, the most calm I'd ever felt in a home. There were no fights, no throwing of dishes, no craziness, and no parties. I was given a few chores, though not many, and basically all I had to do was go to school, do my homework, and be the 15-year old I was. Although my time there was brief, only three weeks, I have fond memories of my stay. The mom cooked every night; the family ate together, doted on the kids, watched television, and did the typical domestic things a "normal" family would do. I remember going to a beach on Labor Day and calmly sitting on a beach towel, watching the foster parents tend to their children, and then later having a picnic, with no drama or trauma, just being a "normal" family. During this time I was touch with my sister through letters, visits, and phone calls, and we were both grateful I was in a good home, even though we knew it was only temporary. I was hoping the permanent home I was about to go in would be as good as this temporary one. As part of wanting to please this couple, I got baptized in their church. Except for maybe being angry at God about my childhood (though I didn't know this at the time), I had no religious learnings or beliefs, but I saw how important being baptized was to them, so I volunteered one Sunday night, much to their extreme excitement. They got on the phone immediately afterwards and told my soon to be permanent foster parents, who were also church members, and they were all so excited for me, so proud. I couldn't let them down. I didn't have any behavioral problems while living here, because I felt accepted, loved, and I also didn't want to jeopardize my permanent placement. I was a very "good girl." I didn't know at the time that I was angry about the past or present circumstances, because I wanted so much to have a permanent, good, safe home. So I just stuffed my feelings, and put all my energy into pleasing everyone. It touched me that the foster mom trusted me with her kids, and she made special meals for us, asked me about school, and hugged me goodnight. I felt safe with her husband, which was very important to me after the sexual abuse I went through. I remember lying in bed fantasizing about being a majorette on a squad and being admired, something I'd dreamed of since I was 10 years old, but was too shy and awkward to do.

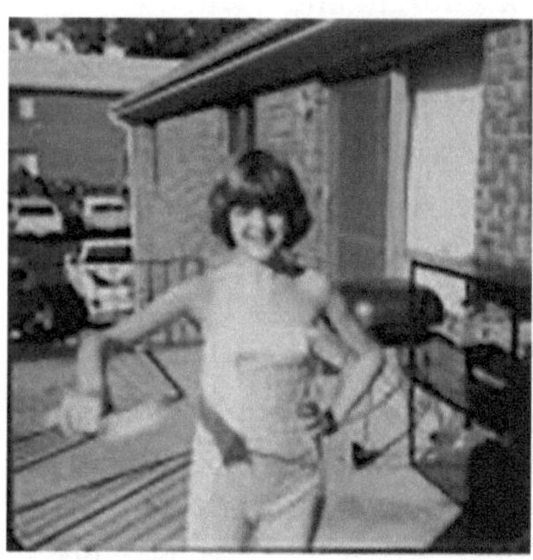

It was all I could do just to survive and get through a day. It took all my emotional energy to tend to what I had to do every day. When I hear stories about foster kids being abused in their new foster homes, I am always so grateful that it didn't happen to me, and very sad for them because they were being re-abused. Being abused in your original home is bad enough, but to be subjected to further abuse by foster parents who are supposed to be rescuing you from your abusive home, only perpetuates the situation, and breeds more distrust. I said a sad goodbye to the Letchworths, but was hoping and expecting with all of my heart that my permanent foster home would be just as nice, if not better. And then…

What was supposed to be a permanent home for me ended up being a three month stay, because I sabotaged it out of guilt and blame, believing I didn't deserve any happiness, so I went back to my mom's until January of 1982, and then I was placed in a girls juvenile group home, and stayed there until I was 17 years old, and then…

I went to live with my dad for three weeks, who was behaving strange again, and I called on my sister to rescue me again from his sick clutches. I remember sitting in the DEFACS (Department of Family and Children

Services), awaiting our turn to speak with a social worker, and then having her introduce me to my third set of foster parents, and before I knew it, we were off, me saying goodbye to my sister promising to visit, call, and write, which I knew she would, and me getting into a car with my familiar blue, battered suitcase.

I don't remember if the foster mom and I had much of a conversation on the way to her house, but I know I was shy and intimidated by her stealth, and the prospect of where we were going. I ended up at her country home, which accommodated numerous foster children throughout the years (the Stricklands had won numerous awards from DEFACS for their years of service), and tried settling in, but as I was sitting in my new bedroom, the foster mom put down my bags and sat on the bed across from mine, eyeing me reassuredly in what I foolishly thought was a maternal way, and then said, "So, you're here because of your father?" I said "Yes," looking at the floor, ashamed. When she heaved a heavy sigh, I thought she was going to sympathize, but instead she asked me if I was responsible for it. "Well, some girls do, you know; I just wondered." I sat there, silently disbelieving what I was hearing, while she stared at me for a minute, and then she told me to get settled in while she finished making dinner. I didn't feel very settled in at this point. I slowly unpacked, shell shocked at what just took place and also at my new surroundings. I was pretty adaptable, having moved around so much by now, but there was still a period of getting adjusted. Despite the shaky beginning, it ended up being a good home for me. The foster mom bought me clothes with the allowance provided to her as a foster mom, took me to the doctor, gave me chores to do, took me on errands with her, and generally listened. She even bought me a fire engine red electric typewriter after letting me use her blue manual one, when she discovered I loved to write. I wrote a lot of great things on that typewriter. I would perch precariously on a high stool, bent over, banging away at the keys, as it hummed along to the tune of my imagination. I'm sure this was a healthy emotional outlet for me. She even wanted me to write a novel about her experiences as a foster mom, but we never got around to it.

One day I went to court, but nobody told me what to expect, only that my dad was going to answer to charges, and I wouldn't have to see him. I was shocked when the social worker told me, "Your parents signed away their rights. You're a ward of the state now," so matter-of-factly. I had no idea that's what this court date was all about, and as we waited to pay the parking lot attendant, I saw my dad in his car ahead of us, giving me a nasty look as I met his gaze. I was numb by the time the social worker dropped me off, and she told my foster mom to keep an eye on me. I started my fourth high school in four years not long after that.

One day I received a package from my dad, which not only surprised me, since I had turned him in for sexual abuse, but devastated me. Inside the box were black and dead roses, shredded baby pictures of my sister and me, ripped up stories and poems I'd written, and a big note addressed to me from my dad that read: "Thank you for ridding me of you at last." That spun me into a depression that I must not have ever recovered from. I had no idea my dad could be so cruel. My foster mom told me I needed to forget my dad, but that it's easier said than done. He was my dad. And then…

After being at this foster home for about a month, the foster mom informed me of a couple who lived down the street that wanted to adopt a child because they couldn't have children of their own, and even though they wanted a baby, they took a liking to me and decided to foster me, so I was off again. It initially seemed like a good place for me, but the honeymoon period at the home was brief. Unfortunately, following the same pattern I pursued with the other foster home, in the name of fear of being loved, I sabotaged that placement, and was returned to the previous foster parents within two months, where I remained until I graduated from high school.

I went back with the foster parents and I slid into a depression that nearly killed me. I was getting ready to leave foster care in five months, and had been accepted by two colleges, but I was terrified of leaving a system that had taken care of me since I was 14 years old, so the following month I took a bunch of pills from my mom's medicine cabinet, in hopes of checking out. I was struggling in school, didn't have much contact with my mom, none with my dad of course, and I was paralyzed with self-hate. I had made a few friends at school, but for the most part no one even knew I existed. I wanted so much to be popular, or at least well-liked, but it seemed everything I tried for was out of reach. It ended up being vitamins I had taken, not pills, but I still had to go in the hospital a week, for attempted suicide, and had to convince the doctor I no longer hated myself. My sister called me the first day I was there, upset and crying, not only about me, but also about the fact that my mom who only lived 20 minutes from the hospital was too busy partying with friends to come see me. She was infuriated by it, disbelieving my mom's behavior, and of course I was hurt by it. I graduated from high school and then…

I spent the summer of my 18th year emancipated from foster care, and living with my mom for the summer, before preparing to leave for collage. I spent a lot of time with my sister, and dated some, but was very afraid of having sex because of what my dad did to me, and my mom and step-dad still thought of me as a child, and were very strict with me. My whole identity all my life had been victim, abused child, and the past four years, ward of the state, and now I was about to embark on a new role as a college student, majoring in English, and was excited and thrilled to get out of the house, but scared to death of living in a dorm on my own. I remember standing in the dorm room alone, looking at all my stuff, and wondering what my life would be like now. It was strange to be in a new town, alone, knowing no one was with me and my belongings, and no social worker to tell me it was time to go again. I wondered how I would fit in with these normal kids from good homes, how to act, dress, speak, and laugh. Who would I become now? As I looked over my class, my heart skipped a beat. I saw my journalism class listed and knew I was there to pursue a dream, no matter what. And so, with enthusiasm and energy, all contained inside, I began to imagine what it would be like to be a real writer, something I knew I wanted to be at the age of 8. I was here for that dream, that hope, and in my mind, nothing or no one could stop me from believing in myself in that area, the only place I felt I belonged.

Life After Foster Care

Anger. Hurt. Frustration. Loneliness. Abandonment. Confusion. Emptiness. If you spent any time in our nation's foster care system, more than likely you know those feelings intimately. You understand what it is like to be taken from the only home you ever knew, and left to fend for yourself in the foster care system. You know too well the baggage that comes with being labeled as a "foster child."

Perhaps you eagerly awaited the day that you "aged out" of foster care. Or, maybe, you were scared, and worried about your future. Regardless, life after foster care offers hope. It's a new beginning. Here are some tips for life after foster care. These are geared more towards foster children who recently aged out of the system, but are written for all former foster children.

Ten Tips for Former Foster Children

Tip # 1: **Think Positively About Your Future No matter what happened before, and during your years** in foster care, now is a fresh start. Don't let anybody tell you differently. Be optimistic about your future. Try your best not to dwell on what has happened in the past, but rather, what can happen today and tomorrow. Have a good attitude and positive frame of mind. Try not to let anything in your past control how you feel about yourself, and your future. You are not "broken." You are not "abnormal." You are not "damaged." In order to succeed you must be strong, hopeful, and confident. Avoid letting feelings of anger and resentment take over your life. You deserve the best. Think positively!

Tip # 2: **Find Support** Okay, the thought of getting together with other former "foster kids" might not sound too appealing at this time. After all, you probably had to deal with a roommate who stole your stuff, or a foster brother who treated you like dirt, but the thing is, other former foster children know what it's like. They know the feeling of seeing other happy families laughing together, and you wishing you had that. They know the frustration of not having a parent to turn to for advice, on everything form doing laundry to buying a house. They've been in your shoes, for the most part, and they "get" it. You might meet older adults who can offer you free advice, or people your age who are going through similar situations. I highly encourage you to at least try to find the support, encouragement, and friendship of other former foster children. Ideally it's great to have a real-life support group, such as FACT, but online support groups can be beneficial as well. For resources and links, read "Online Resources and Web Sites for Former Foster Children."

Tip # 3: **Get Counseling** I highly recommend finding a reputable therapist who can help you cope with life's issues. He/she can assist you in everything from dealing with past trauma, to your current relationships today. Unfortunately, counseling can be very expensive. If you can't afford it, and you don't have insurance that covers is, call 211 for referrals. Ask the worker for free or low cost counseling recommendations. Most universities have a program where master's level students provide free or low cost counseling. (In some cases, they might actually be better than therapists who have worked for years and years). Also, most communities have programs where you can get free counseling through a center. Some agencies that serve victims of domestic violence will offer free counseling to anyone who has been abused at one point in their life. Look for one in the phone book, and call and ask. Some churches provide free counseling as well. If you had a counselor while in foster care, get in touch with him/ her for referrals. If you lived at a group home for abused and neglected children, in some cases the counselor on staff will counsel you at no cost, even though you no longer live there. Just call and ask. Getting counseling is a sign of strength. It is not absolutely essential, but it can really make a difference.

Tip # 4: **Join a Church** I advocate finding a loving church family to belong to, if you don't already have one. Church is not just a place to grow spiritually and learn about God, it's a place that offers you support through challenging times in life. If you go to a church and don't feel welcome, please don't give up. Keep trying until you've found a good match.

Tip # 5: **Keep in Contact With Siblings, Think Wisely Regarding Family Contact** If you have any younger brothers or sisters that were in foster care as well, by all means, keep in contact with them. Do your best to be a positive role model and example to them, as all siblings should. If you lost contact with your biological family, I am not completely against getting in touch with your parents, but I think this decision should be made after a lot of careful thinking. I encourage you to discuss this with a counselor. In some cases, you might just want to have letter/phone call relationship for now. Or, you might want to see them, but if the situation is not appropriate, do not stay in active contact with them. If you have no desire to find them, this is definitely, absolutely okay, and the best decision for you. If your mother or father contacts you, and you don't want to contact him/her now, do not feel guilty about saying no. Please seek advice and counsel regarding this issue.

Tip # 6: **Enjoy Life Without Children for Awhile** This tip is geared more towards foster children that have recently aged out. If you are reading this, and already have a child or two, this does not apply to you. (Yes, you can be a wonderful, nurturing parent regardless of your age, background, and past situation). The fact that you're reading these shows that you are very proactive and wise. However, if you don't have children yet, please, I urge you to wait awhile for children. I personally feel that it is ideal to be married at least two years before becoming pregnant. This is not to say that single moms can't be good parents, but is so much easier (and better for the child) to have a partner. You've had a rough childhood, and you deserve to enjoy life without the responsibility of another human being that needs your devotion about 100% of the time. That doesn't mean that you won't be a great parent one day (I'm sure you will), but that it is an excellent idea to wait a few years.

Tip # 7: **Volunteer** If you want to, I highly encourage volunteering. It can be very therapeutic to help someone else in need, and there are numerous social service agencies that would be thrilled to have your help.

Tip # 8: **Stay Away from Drugs** Please, do not experiment with drugs. Nothing good can come from it. I urge you to never, ever, try any illegal drug, not even once. If you find yourself in bad company, it's time to make new friends. If you need to, move to a new area. I know it sounds extreme, but drug abuse will only lead to future problems. Do you really want your future children to live the same childhood you did? As you might know, drug abuse is one of the main reasons why children are removed from their homes. I know it sounds trite, but just say "no." Stay away from individuals who use drugs.

Tip # 9: **Speak Out** Were you abused while in foster care? Did you keep it a secret? If so, please, I urge you to report this horrible crime. Whether you were abused physically, sexually, or verbally, it must be reported. If you were sexually abused, call a rape crisis center in your area for help on reporting it. I would simply call the child abuse hot line for reporting physical or emotional abuse while in foster care. This needs to be done to prevent it from happening to another child. If you were in a group home, and feel that some of the things that happened to you in foster care were not appropriate, by all means report it. I recommend contacting the board of director's president, perhaps writing a letter, and asking to meet with him/her to discuss your situation. You might share ideas on how the home can be improved, etc. Do it for the sake of future residents. Your voice does matter.

Tip # 10: **Ask for Help** Do not hesitate to seek assistance if you need it. By that, I mean if you find yourself in a crisis, and needing help with food, utilities, medicine, etc., don't be afraid to ask for help. Call 211 for help.

That being said, however, I highly encourage you to have a budget, and practice money management skills. I recommend reading books by Dave Ramsey. If possible, take his course-"Financial Peace University" if it is offered in your area. Join an online money management forum for advice. Avoid the temptation to get into credit card debt.

These are just a few tips for life after foster care, along with others, such as having a mentor, somebody who will encourage and inspire you, writing about your experiences, or/and going to college, or pursuing something in your life that you're passionate about, and no matter what, don't give up! Take it easy, relax, and hang in there! Enjoy your life!

How Being a Former Foster Child Can Affect an Adult

Having been in four foster homes as a teenager, I can tell you the many ways it affected me as an adult.

For one thing, entering my first foster home at age 15 after being in some other places, I learned not to trust, feel, cry, or express my emotions, except anger. I also felt guilty for any happiness that would come to me, and that is still true today. I blamed myself for everything, and sabotaged things for awhile in my life. This is common.

I learned not to count on anyone, or anything, except for my older sister, who was in a separate foster home for awhile. The upside was that I got good at packing fast, since I would often be moved to another home without much notice. I learned resourcefulness, too. I got into survivor mode, but it later did not serve me well, because any kind of common sense went out the window in favor of fear. I learned that I had to work extra hard for anything, and that there were two types of people in my life---the balcony people who lifted me up, and the basement people who tried to bring me down.

I got the lesson of compassion, and empathy, and feel sure that had I not gone through these trials and tribulations, I wouldn't have those qualities. That part I am grateful for. I became especially sympathetic to the underdog, stray cats and dogs, and abused and neglected kids.

I learned to be a people pleaser. For instance, I got baptized once just to please my temporary and future foster parents. I got the art of being a chameleon down. That's a hard habit to break, still. Sometimes I would joke with people that "I'll be whatever you want me to be."

I learned that I couldn't be a parent, no matter how good my intentions were for my child. I have no coping skills.

I associate certain smells, sights, and sounds with being a foster child. Songs can also trigger emotions in me.

I learned to be a comedian for one of my foster moms, who only wanted me that way. Later, when I went through a depression, she just wanted me to joke around all the time. I learned that some people want you for their own unmet needs.

I became a child advocate. If I hadn't been in foster care, I probably wouldn't have pursued this. Because of my detail-oriented personality and passion for the cause, I wound up testifying in one of my cases, which resulted in the biological mom losing custody of all four of her kids, due to long-term abuse and neglect.

It learned to be obsessive, another trademark sometimes of being a former foster child. Sometimes it a good thing, but other times not.

Placing My Baby Daughter Up For Adoption

Now, I would like to elaborate on the sixth issue of being a former foster child, that of "being unable to be a good parent, no matter how good my intentions were for my child."

At age 34, after 14 years of thinking I couldn't get pregnant, and feeling safe to be off the pill, I was shocked to find out I was with child, and immediately knew I would have to place the baby up for adoption, due to financial, emotional, and physical reasons. It took about three years to make peace with my decision, which I did through therapy, and lots of prayers, and the decision didn't seem like a choice, but something that just happened over time through writing, talking to other birth moms, bonding with the adoptive mom, and spiritual guidance. Many people judge me for my decision, but I can assure you that it was not an easy one, and was made out of love and concern for my daughter, not selfishness, and I was deeply affected by it. I felt like someone died, like my heart and guts were ripped out, the most excruciating emotional pain you can imagine. I was so traumatized by it that I couldn't eat or sleep for two weeks, and had to be medicated, and was in a trance most of the time, barely able to function. I knew I was doing the right thing, but it was still very painful, and since I suffered from depression, it took me a lot longer than other birth moms to get past the pain. The love the decision sprang from came from a deep knowing in my soul, from the bottom of my heart, to every inch of my being, that it might be ok to drag myself through hell financially, emotionally, and physically, but I couldn't do it to a child, and that I would regret it if I did. I would not have been a whole mom in any sense of the word. Being Bi-Polar, I'm not mentally stable enough to parent a child, and having no coping skills, I was afraid of abusing her. I also had no support system in place to help me raise a child. Though I wish I could've raised my birth daughter, I don't regret my decision, because I know she is happy and well cared for, and we have a semi-open adoption arrangement that allows me to see her 2-3 times a year, and I have also written her letters through the years, which the adoptive mom will give her when she's old enough to understand them, and deal with them, along with a scrapbook I made for her. She has also seen her "baby tapes," the DVD of her Placement Day (the day she was placed with her adoptive parents in a ceremonial setting), and her time in the hospital when she was born, and loves them.

I have tried to use my experience to help raise awareness about adoption, a I think there is still a lot of ignorance surrounding the issue, with many people in society thinking birth moms don't love their child, and just give the baby up for adoption without a thought, which couldn't be further from the truth. The truth is, my hope was that my child would have a better life than I had, a life I knew I was incapable of giving her. I gave her up to give her a good life. Giving my daughter up for adoption was an act of love.

Testimony Iyore

Abandonded
Author of the book *Abandoned*

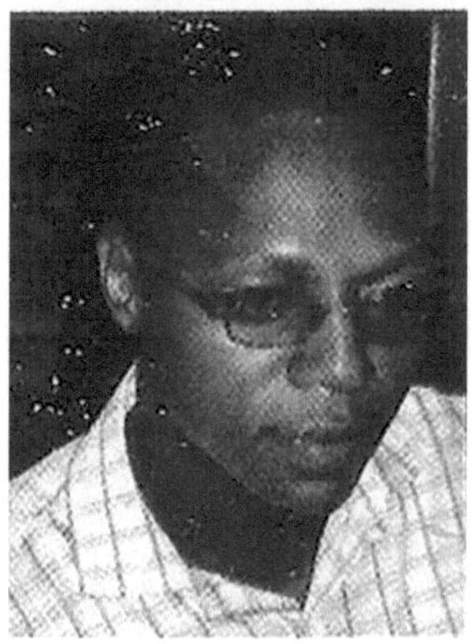

I chose to share my story for the same reason I wrote my book ***Abandoned***---to warn and guide teenagers, and the general society about the evils of unplanned relationships and abandoned children, but more importantly, that an abandoned child can fully live a positive life and succeed, through good morals and hard work. More than anything, I want to give HOPE to all abandoned children.

I speak of the evils of unplanned pregnancies because in Nigeria, Africa, where I am from, I am one among many of other abandoned children who are the product of this. My father deceitfully impregnated two women at the same time, and chose to abandon me and my mother, in favor of marriage to the other woman. Luckily, my mother's parents promised NOT to abandon us, and when my mother left her village to get a better job to help support me, I was left in the care of my grandmother.

I grew up extremely different from my peers. When I was first enrolled in primary school at age 5, I wasn't doing well, but with my grandmother's encouragement, I soon took over the first position in my class work, and also in other areas of life. Even at such a young age, I was already filled with wisdom, and brighter than all my school mates, but unfortunately my excellent pattern of living began to attract jealousy, envy, and hatred within my peer group, and even among older boys. I was embarrassed on a daily basis because of my background, my peers calling me a bastard, knowing my father never cared about me, and even questioning whether my father was a human, or a ghost. My grandmother led me to believe that my father was off traveling and would return, but he didn't, and when my mother came home to visit, I called her "sister," as the only person I knew as my mother was my grandmother.

Even before age 10 I was doing some menial jobs, just to make sure I was able to meet up with my other friends. One of my jobs was fetching firewood to sell, and one day when my grandmother came to help me haul the wood to the roadside where buyers could easily reach it, she lost her step and fell, the wood falling on her leg. Surprisingly, it became serious and she ended up in the hospital, where she died four days later. I was very upset over the loss of my loving and caring grandmother, and cried myself hoarse. It was at this time that I discovered the woman who just passed on wasn't my mother, but my grandmother, that the person I knew and addressed as my sister, was my real mother, and it was also during this time that I realized my father didn't travel, but that he abandoned me when I was barely one week old. I became devastated by all this news.

Meanwhile, my mother had remarried and had other children, which gave me no other choice than to remain in the village, with nobody there to take care of me. I was left feeling like a sheep without a shepherd, suffering humiliations, and emotional depression. Thank God for my mother's younger brother, who tried to come to my rescue, especially with my education, but despite my uncle's efforts, I was no longer happy over the way things were going, especially with the knowledge and information at my disposal. I saw myself as an empty vessel on a flowing river that lacked direction, protection, and a future. I saw life in its real and raw state, desperate to swallow the unwary, me. The situation was burdensome, uncertain, and gloomy, and I began to struggle for survival, trying to make sure I got for myself what other children at age 10 had access to.

There was rumor going around that one of my father's cousins lived in Nineb, but I was never interested in meeting with anybody relating to my father. I grew up with the belief and desire to become a man of myself, choosing to have a wife and children, like my relatives and friends, and it was this desire and belief that made me principled, disciplined, and independent from childhood on. Though my background was always a burden, I was always exceptional, and was always honored and valued among my peers, and I continued this way, always feeling rejected and dejected, but never ceasing to encourage myself. I often peeped into the future, and each time, I saw a great, distinguished, and independent personality. I had a dream about myself.

When I was 14 years old, my aunt in Sogal sent for me to come live with her, and considering all the hard experiences I had passed through, I accepted this offer without delay, seeing it as the greatest opportunity to ever come my way. The first week was like heaven on earth for me, with everybody pampering me like a prince, but the tune of their music changed from the third week on, when I began to experience the true side of life. "Come, let me take care of you" became "Come and be my slave!" They started reminding me that I was homeless, helpless, and hopeless, loading me with work, and mistreating me, and accusing me whenever anything went wrong in the house. Their new song for me was "Pack your things and leave my house!" And they said it repeatedly, whenever there was a misunderstanding. The condition of the home became unbearable, and I lost concentration at school, and in everything I was doing. I started to lose my dream. Desperation crawled into me, to the extent of me considering suicide as a solution to my numerous problems.

Luckily, I had a best friend I could confide in, telling him all the hard times I was passing through, and how confused I was, but he encouraged me to go back to my parents, not realizing I didn't really have any. I remember telling him, "I don't even know what the face of my father looks like; I was told he abandoned me when I was just one week old," and when he asked about my mother, I explained to him about her being married with children, and how uncomfortable I felt whenever I was at her house, feeling rejected and dejected. I told him that I had never slept under the same roof with my mother, except perhaps when I was still a baby, and she had never invited me to spend a weekend with her, not even to talk of a whole holiday, and I wasn't even used to my brothers and sisters. I told him that the whole thing turned me down, to the extent that sometimes I felt like I was not even worth living on this planet earth. My friend was a great encouragement to me during this time, telling me how strong I was, and that I was going to make it in life, and that he would be there for me at all times, but I just couldn't shake my depression, and life became unbearable. I told my friend, "I just don't know how to start. It's like I should look for poison, drink it, and forget about this whole stress," and he said, "Don't disappoint yourself. Papa God has ways of doing things, if you are able to withstand all these battles now, and tomorrow you'll become great, and all these people, including your so-called father, will be the first to start running around you, and praising you here and there. But if you kill yourself now, nobody will care." He encouraged me to leave my aunt's place, telling me, "I still give you my words…you are going to be very great, if you don't let all these problems overcome you." His words of encouragement reawakened my dream. I felt like a drunk trying to wake up from a deep slumber, but I had a plan---to go back to the village school to complete my secondary school education, looking into any work I could do to save up enough money to enable me to further my education to the university level. I vowed from that point on that I never wanted to live under anybody again in my life. My friend was a real God send at this time, not only encouraging me, but also helping me to save money on a daily basis until I had a reasonable amount saved to leave, and helping me to finally escape. I felt happy to be leaving for freedom, but sad about leaving my friend behind.

I left on my four hour long ride back to Nine, believing God had a reason for what I was passing through, and that I was now a man, capable of fitting into the village society, and joining the other boys in whatever they did for a living, all the while living in my deceased grandmother's room, while I completed secondary school. When I went to see my mother, it felt strange because I had grown up thinking she was my sister, and when she questioned me about being there, and not at my aunt's, I told her I ran away, that "It was better to die while standing, than to live in chains." I believe my mother began to see me more as her son at this time, because when I told her, "If God has created me to come and suffer humiliations, and depression on earth, if that will glorify Him, then who am I to question God?" she replied, "Come on, don't talk like that. God didn't create you to come and suffer! I knew from the beginning that you were created for a purpose," and then tears began to flow between us, but still, she clearly made it understood that I couldn't stay with her, but it didn't matter, because as I bluntly told her, "I don't think I would even want to stay with anybody again in my life. I've had enough of people." When my aunt came to fetch me to go back to her place, I told her I left her home to get away from depression and oppression, and that she should "Go back to her family, and let me who does not have a family, he who does not have a home, and hope, stay on his own, so that peace can reign," and I made it real clear that I didn't want to live under anybody else's roof again, that I would survive on my own, and let God run my life for me.

Things were still tough in the village, and I felt sad, but I remained ambitious and determined, and reasoned within myself, "My God! What kind of life is this? I know you live, and that you will never let me be put to shame, though I am in a poor and local background; whatever any of my mates from good backgrounds, those who are taken of by their parents can do, I can equally do it." This belief made me a distinguished fellow among my mates, and I stayed in the village, where I finally rounded off my secondary school education.

After I completed school I was in a quandary about where to go from here, and decided to move into the city with a friend until I could get my own apartment. My friend seemed concerned about my welfare, but I reassured him I could survive. I was a construction laborer for awhile, until I got involved in an oil business, which enabled me to secure an apartment, and I thought to myself, "I can tell the world, I did it myself!"

About eight months later on a visit to my mother's I had a most unusual experience on my bus, which I guess was fate. I ran into a cousin of my father's, who quickly recognized me, and persisted in telling me how "It is not that we don't want you; it's just that other events have taken away our attention from your matter. We discuss you always. Your uncle is so concerned about you, to the extent that the whole family has come to the conclusion that we are coming for you this year. I thank God I found you today, because that has been one of the problems facing us." He wanted to come visit me, but I told him I had no home, and continued on my journey to my mother's, where as usual, we exchanged 'pleasantries without pecks.' I guess the main reason I visited her was because she was the only person I had at that time. When she noticed me looking unhappy, I told her about the bus incident, to which she responded to by encouraging me to not be so biased toward my father, seeing it as an answer to prayer, as in this part of the world, for one not to know one's father and his people, especially a male child, is unthinkable. A mother is easily acknowledged, but a child without a father is a bastard, a stigma every responsible family would want to run away from.

One day, while I was walking along the street, I ran into three men, one of which was my father, who addressed me as his "son," and then proceeded to embrace me, with tears in his eyes. I must admit, we were both in tears, and I was thoroughly shaken to hear someone call me "son." I guess the saying "Blood is thicker than water" is true, and even though I was a bit leery of him visiting me, I was finally persuaded to let him and my uncles come to my home, where it was like a ceremony on that day. He encouraged me to visit at Christmastime, and told me to thank my mother and her family for all they had done. The role of the father in this part is to sow a seed, and he may decide to disappear, only to reappear when the seed he planted some years back is ready for harvest, maybe not being interested in the pains and agony of childbirth. My mother was very happy to hear about me meeting my father, as she didn't want me, or her, living with the stigma of me being a bastard. She encouraged me to visit him at Christmas, and I was unsure, thinking of it as another challenge, but I figured it could be a double blessing, meaning, all my plans with their support would be achieved faster. At least that is what I hoped.

It was very exciting at first, being at my father's, with everybody rejoicing over my arrival. It felt like the happiest day of my life; I felt so joyful! I imagined the whole scenario to be a dream. But my joy soon turned to sorrow, when my father, and his wife and children arrived, as other than my father's first daughter, I was given the cold shoulder, and I was left feeling cold, depressed, disorganized, and confused. Abandoned again. I felt like I jumped from the frying pan into the fire, and I questioned God. How could He allow this? After all, I never expected anybody from anywhere to come and tell me about my father! I thought to myself, "Have I not been a father to myself from the beginning?" I knew I wasn't really wanted there, so I decided immediately to leave Ugune, but it was the saddest day of my life. I was leaving a dream.

As I pondered over this experience, I received a message from one of my uncles, asking me to come to Truocrah-trop, which I honored. My uncle reassured me that even if my father didn't care about me, other members of my family did, telling me, "We love you, my dear." I had plans for traveling abroad, but my uncle encouraged me to continue my education before going abroad. He promised to take care of all my responsibilities. I knew I was at the crossroads, and I wasn't sure which way to turn. People had promised me heaven on earth before, and at the end, I was disappointed, so I was confused again, but decided to inform my mother, then close up my business, quit the house I rented, and go live with my uncle, which ended up going well very well for awhile, until some money came up missing, for which I was accused of stealing. Calling me all sorts of names, I felt like they were just waiting for a day like that to remind me of who I was. I was discouraged and fed up again. This was the road I thought I had abandoned when I left my aunt's, and now here I was again, feeling trapped, unwanted, and regretting that I had succumbed to the lure of my uncle's proposal. Even though after about a week it was discovered who stole the money, and everybody tried being friendly again, I felt wounded, helpless, and hapless.

A year and a few months later, I got admission into a higher institution, a university, but due to a lack if finances it became a struggle, and out of desperation I went to my father for help, but the enthusiasm that followed our reunion had unbelievably died, and he advised me to go back to my uncle's, as he didn't have any money to spare. And I thought, "A dream…?" This was why I never wanted to further my education until I was capable of handling things myself, and here I was in a mess again. Abandoned again. I thought, "God! Did you create me to come and pass through all these pains and agony all my life? Why is it I have never been happy for one whole month since I grew up? Damn! I think I should put an end to this life. Imagine I don't even have a place to call home; I turn stranger wherever I go." I called my uncle, who suggested I go to my mother for help, and I wondered how I became a victim again, and whether I could survive this, but I had nowhere else to turn, so I went to my mother. I told her I felt nobody wanted me to live, and it would have been better if she had aborted me, to which she hysterically replied how much she also suffered because of my birth, and when I told her I never really cared about meeting my father, she told me she thought it was a good thing I did, because now I could talk about having parents, but I told her, "I was better off not knowing him, because now I still can't boldly say I have a father in public. At least when they call for those who don't have a father, I can easily identify myself as one, but now, where do I belong? I have a father, but I can't go to his house happily. I am a stranger even in my father's house!" I told my mother I needed school money, and she told me not to worry, that God had plans for me, and I agreed with her. My mother was able to gather up enough money for me to go back to school. I told her I was grateful, that I wondered how life would be without her and her family, and she said, "That is why people say when one way closes, another one will open, but at times we concentrate on the closed door for so long, that we do not see another open door beckoning." I made it through that semester, and then went back to my uncle's for help, who refused me, so I started thinking I should look around for whatever people do for money, even if it was armed robbery. For three days I didn't go to school, and became so confused, and depressed I couldn't do anything, and even to have a bath was almost a forgotten issue. People around me started noticing something was psychologically wrong with me, and after a few days of no solution, I went back to my mother, who was once again able to raise some money for that semester, only to be forced into asking for her help again after me being refused by my uncle, but this time she encouraged me to find work, so I tried a motorcycle business, which went well for a few months, until the motorcycles began breaking down. I was once again under stress, feeling and looking like a mentally deranged person, but still, I wouldn't ask for any further assistance from my mother.

Things got so bad at this point that I stopped going to school, church, and was indoors for four days, and on the fourth night I was awake all night, in sorrow, with tears pouring out from my eyes, and as they poured out I became hostile, going to some friends who belonged to a secret cult to get a gun, so I could kill everybody, but I finally came to my senses and decided it was a drastic decision, and that I needed to live and walk according to my belief from childhood, so that people could see through me that with God, one without parents can make it, but life without parents assistance really is not easy! I was once again confused, trying to figure out where to go, and what to do. That whole night I paced up and down in my room, thinking of what a solution would be, and at a point when all hope was almost lost, I came up with the idea of leaving the coast of Nigeria entirely, so I sold all my belongings for money, and left to see my mother, to tell her of my new development. I called her "mummy" for the first time that day, and told her, "In case you no longer hear from me, or see me any moment from today, do not be worried. If God says I will live, then I will live. I must confess, mother, I am tired of the kind of life I have been living. Let me go into the world to see if I can find happiness, and whatever happens to me, I will accept it to the Glory of God." For the first time, my mother and I embraced that day.

I left Nineb for Sogal in a state of devastation, inquiring where I could get transportation to the nearest neighboring country, and I paid for a vehicle going to Accra. The trip was very hard, and whenever I set my eyes on my bag during the journey, and remembered that I didn't know where I was going, and that I had nobody to meet, tears flowed freely, and I continued crying until I got to Accra; then when I realized I had enough money to travel even further, I decided to go to the next neighboring country, Cote D'Ivoire. I met a French man on the bus, who put me up for the night after arriving at Cote D'Ivoire, but again, I was vulnerable and taken advantage of. The man explained that there were three types of businesses men did there---GUY-MAN, which is known in Nigeria as 4.1.9, when you search the Internet for people to send you money under the pretense of having a business, which of course is a fraud, the second one was drug-peddling, and the third one was buying and selling, popularly known as ocarina business. My friend encouraged me to join the GUY-MAN business, and I chose to, but after some time, when the money didn't come from my relatives as I told him it would, my "friend" threw me out, even though I had given him enough money up front for about four months rent, and I hadn't even been there one month.

I figured I had to face whatever came my way, so I packed my belongings, and went to a church I worshiped at, explaining my situation to the founder of the church, where I stayed about four months. One day I met up with a man who tried to get me involved in hustling money from prostitutes, but I told him, "It's a pity if you don't know what you're causing to yourself; hear me, it is a curse to be attached to a prostitute. Ah! God forbid I begin to feed from the money a woman gets through prostitution. If there is not other means to survive, my dear, death is preferred." So I went back to the church, and doing the GUY-MAN business instead, but people said it was through the same means by having prostitutes that money was raised to browse the Internet, so there seemed to be no way out. I eventually turned a mendicant in the church, which I managed to feed myself with, and sometimes go to the Internet to browse. In my second year of doing this, an American lady responded to my format, and I began to receive money from her, but my conscience began to trouble me, and I gave up this dubious way of living, and even told the lady it was a scam. I then began selling fairly used clothing, and got myself an apartment. Then civil war broke out about three months later, and in the process of rioting people started breaking into shops, and unfortunately, I was the victim of those whose goods were made away with by hoodlums.

This incident brought me back to nothing, and things became very difficult again, and all the people who used to assist me stopped, because

I refused to continue with the GUY-MAN business scam. After a church service one day, a man approached me about drug-peddling, and I figured it was better than being a fraud star, so I decided to give it a go. In less than three months, my friend sponsored me to Pakistan, where I went to peddle cocaine down to Abidjan, and I had a successful trip, but on arrival there, I was set up and detained by the Cote D'Ivoire drug law enforcement agency, awaiting trial. I was given the option of paying some money instead of doing jail time, and since my "friend" ran away in the process, my only hope for money was my mother, so I contacted her, and she ran "helter skelter" in search for money to get me released. After 17 days in jail I returned home to find my room turned upside down, but I was so tired that I couldn't even tidy up my room, and in my frustrated state I thought, "Where can I go now? I can't live with my mother, and I'm not safe in my father's house. Will I again be able to face all the frustrations that almost turned me mad, and sent me into self-exile?" I thought of myself as a dropout, because I didn't graduate from college, but still, I believed I would be fine by God's grace, so I thought I would go back home and begin to walk in the channel that God had shown me, even if it took me sleeping at the bus stop!

On my arrival home I went to my mother's, where the whole family rejoiced over my return, welcoming me, and thanking God. My mother told me, "Oh my God, my heart is full of joy seeing you again!" And I told her how happy I was to see them all again, and that I thought it was the end of the road for me, that there would be no way out, that I went through hell. I also told my mother that asking someone to contact me on my behalf was just a test of faith, that I succumbed to the pressure mounted on me by one of the inmates in the cell. When my mother told me it was true that my stepfather gave out a huge amount of money for my sake, after being quiet for minutes, I went straight to my stepfather, and knelt down before him, and said, "Thank you, dad," to which he replied, "Oh! My dear, get up; we should glorifying God for the marvelous work He has done. Or, do you think it was because of the money that you are out? Don't you know there are people serving jail term today that had more than the amount of money you paid, and yet their money could not get them out? I thank God for you, my dear, but the only advice I have for you, is that you don't need to be involved in dubious acts before you can make it; just begin to do whatever you know you can do best, and see if you will not make it."

I was very touched by his words, and for a whole week I wasn't myself, thinking of what to do, but I still couldn't come up with a decision, and I had no rest of mind, for not having a place to call home to live comfortably in, so I began wandering about the states of Nigeria, moving from one cousin's house to the other, not wanting to turn a burden to anybody. Life continued this way for me, until I was able to discover, and was convinced, of what I was meant to do in life. Today, as God would have it, I have been able to put myself together and make use of the resources, which God deposited in me, and I am now living happily.

I discovered and believed a philosophy out of experience, that all issues of life lie in the mind. I was abandoned for success; I never knew it until I was drenched by the dews of life.

I am a strong advocate for abandoned children in Africa, and do everything I can to raise awareness to the issue of child abandonment.

This is picture of me and a baby that was
dumped in a pit toilet.

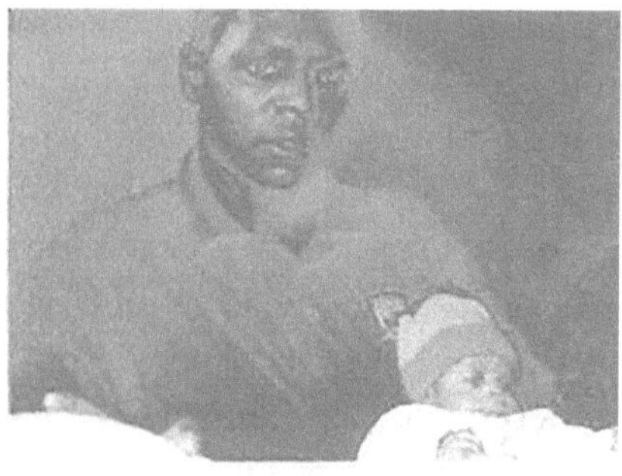

Theresa N.G.

(Written by Theresa N.G.)
Finding a Family to Call My Own

Dedicated to:

My mom, Jennifer, who gave birth to me. I know you are smiling down from heaven. For every child that has been impacted by the foster tare system. Cheers to all alums! We made it!

A Daughter's Journey

I was born premature at 2 lbs. and 10 oz. My birth mother passed away from lymphoma when I was 5 months old. At age 3, my father married my step-mother, who was mentally and physically abusive. My father carried on a cycle of "neglect" from his family history. I grew up hearing phrases like "Don't air your dirty laundry outside the family" and "Depression isn't any good."

I grew up in the United States under traditional Chinese culture. I am a proud second-generation Asian American. The oldest of three siblings, I have a half brother and half sister. Being of Chinese culture was the "excuse" that kept me from getting the help I needed. I was not even allowed to grieve the loss of my mother. In my experience, mental illness is not recognized in Chinese culture, and there is great shame associated with it. As an adult, I can see mental illness within my family tree, but it has never been dealt with. There is an inability to get help because of this perspective. In traditional Chinese culture people function as a whole family unit, versus where the focus is on the individual in the western culture. To admit that there is something "wrong" with a member of the family in Chinese culture is to bring down the whole family unit.

My father grew up in a poor family, with five or six siblings. His father, my grandfather, was a fisherman, and my grandmother was a seamstress. My father was the youngest, and was almost sold as a child because the family was poor. Fortunately, my father was raised by his grandmother.

My step-mother grew up the oldest of eight siblings. I don't recall much, given the trauma I endured. But she always referred to the differences in eastern and western child upbringing, that here in the United States, parents don't know how to discipline their children, that love means to cut you down to size, and that Americans use sweet talk, which is nonexistent in Asian culture, because 'fun' isn't in their vocabulary, that children are supposed to obey their parents and be perfect. A "Tiger mother's" best approach is no fun, all work, and no emotions.

Growing up "normal" for me would mean being scared to death to breathe or move, in fear of upsetting my step-mother, and trying my best. But my best was never reachable or attainable. At a very young age, I knew something was different. I was the unwanted child. References were made that I was to blame for my mother's death, or that I was a bad reminder to my father. Sometimes this made me wish I was never born, yet looking back I had a strong will in what I believed. I was born "American" after all. I didn't see a picture of my mother until I was 17, and then only because a therapist told my dad to give me one. Even then, he just gave me a rolled up class photo. From the moment I woke, the house was filled with screaming. No one in our family talked in a normal tone. I learned never to talk back or ask questions. I became an expert in "learn it yourself, teach yourself." Just because I wasn't blood related to my step-mother, I was always pinned to be the bad child. In reality, I did nothing wrong, or never knew what I did wrong, but everything just seemed to set my step-mother off. Being top notch in class grades was never good enough; I was always compared to cousins, brothers, etc. I grew up with the sense that nobody wanted me or loved me, that I would be better off dead, or that I ruined the family, that if I didn't exist, my family would be happy. Nobody talked about my mother's death, except to say that she was sick with cancer, and she had AIDS. Lord knows if that was a false fact. I thought, or assumed, that my mother died giving birth to me, or that my mom tricked my dad into having a baby, knowing that she was sick.

I recall one childhood experience with my step-mom. My dad just continued to read what he was reading, and I swear a bomb could have gone off and he wouldn't flinch. It was then that I really knew in my heart that there was no shred of hope that my dad would save me, or protect me, or put my step-mother in her place. I quickly took the blame for things that were not my fault, like when my dad broke the vacuum, or when my brother flushed my barrettes down the toilet. I figured I'd take the hits, because no one should ever have to feel this pain. My father and I swapped roles as father and child, where I would listen to his depression, and how he was neglected as a child. I grew up having to hear the phrase, "You're a worthless piece of shit, not even a piece of shit that can be used to grow a flower." Everyday, I felt that I was a speck of dust, getting smaller and smaller. School was my saving grace. I just wanted the teachers to take me home with them. It's not that I didn't LOVE my family; till this day, deep in my heart, I will always love my dad, my brother, and my sister. I never understood why my step-mom hated me so much. Nothing I did made her happy. Nobody loved me.

I don't like talking about these experiences, which don't even scratch the surface, or do it justice. I want you to focus on the positive that can come out of such a horrible situation. There is hope and life after. It isn't the end of the world; you can live the life you've always dreamed of.

To cope with all the pain growing up, I became depressed, and had nobody I could trust to talk to. In second grade, I skipped lunch, and figured since I couldn't control anything around me, and my step-mother refused to give me food, it would hurt less if I inflicted my own pain. Later in my teen years, cutting myself became a coping skill, to feel and breathe, since the trauma silenced me. I continued to be the outward perfect student, and teacher's pet. I excelled in all my academics to try to win my parents' love, to convince them that I was a worthy daughter, a smart one that they should be proud of. But even getting highest honors and teacher's outstanding remarks didn't melt my step-mother's heart to see that I was trying to make her proud. I just wanted her to love me and care for me. I simply couldn't understand why, just because I wasn't her blood, she would treat me second rate to her own kids. I honestly believed I could mold myself into the perfect daughter if I cleaned, did chores, and had no outside friends, since they were "the enemy" and couldn't be trusted. I once tried to make her a Mother's Day gift from a craft from school, but she never used it, or even thanked me for it. It was a pretty apron with sunflowers on it. I silently prayed all these years to my dead mother, to come and save me.

Nobody talked about feelings growing up, and it wasn't OK to talk back. Now, looking back, I was a quiet person, didn't do drugs, and got good grades. But what I didn't have back then was my voice, to ask for all the things I needed, and the courage to speak. My childhood, along with all of its horrors, had silenced me. In fourth grade, I finally got the courage to report it while, my best friend at the time held my hand. There was no life boat. In 9th grade I broke down and became depressed, and no longer saw the light in life. Finally, at age 15, I was placed in foster care. I was placed in four homes, had three different social workers, and was in three different high schools.

I lived with a traveling "trash bag," i.e. my suit case, which held a few things that I owned---my hope, my pride, the only thing left of me. My first home was a kinship placement with a step aunt. Then I was moved. In the second home, I was placed with a history teacher I briefly knew back at the Academy. Even in a home with a dog and a pool, I wasn't wanted. It was short lived, and they didn't want to be foster parents anymore. That was for only about a month.

Then I was in a new home again, new school system, with new friends, and new rules. Do I belong here? The social worker lied and told me that I was going to be with a couple, and I was going to be their only child.

The third home I was placed in was a "full house," I like to call it, with about 4-5 girls in one room. The guys had to share a room as well. I was moved again, to a new home, same school, and new rules. In this home, I met one 3 year old foster sister that would imprint my life, and speak volumes, and I had no idea how much of an impact she would have on me later on in life. I dream of a system that would care for and love her, and support her. I hope to create a bridge that all the little foster sisters and brothers can walk across into the transition of adulthood that would be less painful than what I experienced. Every night before I went to bed, she would say "Nobody loves me." I would let her get off her bed, which was the couch, and crawling from my bottom bunk, I held her in my arms and said, "I love you, and someday somebody will love us." She echoed words I couldn't speak. She was so brave to have a voice.

The fourth home was with a single mom and her son. I finally had my own room. Someone hung up my clothes and unpacked my bag. Looking back, I wish I could see and feel that she really cared for me, but it was hard, since she was a new foster parent. By this time I was so used to the thought that on one would want me, and the fear that I had to move again. All I knew was that I had to stay focused on getting a job, saving money, and getting my own place, wherever that was.

I met RD when his son, who was a friend and classmate, used to pick me up from the bus stop, since he had a learner's permit. As I sat quietly in the back seat during the eight or so minutes, we began talking. It was an interesting connection. Little did I know he was an ex foster kid as well. RD was probably the first relationship that someone invested in me, whose love was unconditional. I was so used to nobody wanting me, or people transitioning out, the illusion of my childhood that carried into my teen years. He taught me that I was lovable, and showed me what unconditional love truly was. I thank God that our paths crossed every day. He is truly an "angel" or messenger from heaven. I didn't know the weight of all my parents' wrong, or sin, I was carrying at the time. I grew up in an atheist household, and my biological dad always said religion was a cult. RD brought me on a church retreat to Calumet, in New Hampshire. It was where I met GOD, and learned about Jesus' Love. I just sat and cried my way all through the service. I never before experienced a room where there was so much love. The pastor had communion, and little did I know that day when I said "Yes," and didn't quite understand it fully, that my heart was forever changed. Before worship started, RD slipped me a little note that said, "You are not responsible for hurricanes, earthquakes, tsunamis, and tornadoes." I cried, because I finally understood that I was not responsible for my mother's death, that I didn't cause her illness. I felt a flood of peace, and tears, and just sheer love.

Upon returning home to my foster home, I was just a ball of light. I wanted to share Jesus' Love with everyone, only to quickly find that all the adults (foster parents and social worker) around me wouldn't allow it, and more over, they tried to make my relationship with RD out to be something it wasn't. I don't think anyone cared to get to know him, nor the profound impact he had in my life.

That year RD took me Christmas shopping, because I was determined to use all of my hard earned money on gifts for my foster family, especially my foster sisters and brothers. I wanted everyone to feel special, and so did I. I am not quite sure how we got on the topic of conversation, but while shopping for gifts, I mentioned how hard it was for me to make friends at my new school, my new social worker, and how it seemed like everyone in my life was only there for a brief moment. The universe seemed to take them away. He responded, "I will be your friend for 200 years." It was the first time I knew for sure that someone would never leave me. My life until then had been like a revolving door of adults coming and going. No one stopped for a while to sit and talk to me, or walk with me. It was like I had to be an instant adult, and try to mold myself into the perfect daughter, "to stay in a foster home." By that point, the changing rules, changing food, and changing school, were getting to be a lengthy list to maintain in my head.

I believe that every child deserves, and can grow and be nourished by a lifelong friendship, but many kids in foster care don't get the opportunity to do so. That is why mentors are so important. They should also be assigned to youth over age 14, not just to youth from ages 7-14.

By age 16, and in my second foster home, the current social worker I had kept pushing me to go to Job Corps. At age 18, I aged out of the system, and dropped out of high school to support myself. I didn't know of any resource that could help me. At the time I just wanted out of the system, feeling that I couldn't go back home, and couldn't live here. I wondered if I would ever belong to a family that would love me. I refused to go to Job Corps, because I wanted a high school diploma, and not a GED. I wanted the normal experience, something all my friends around me got. I highly don't recommend going this route. I support Job Corps very much, but the stigma of Job Corps was a "place for second chances" for those that ended up in jail, or in gangs. What about my First Chance? An option given to foster youth at age 16, it was a place for second chances. I kept thinking that I didn't do drugs, didn't go to jail, and I made honor roll every year. But I "needed" to be smart, and learn to fend for myself. I could feel that my step-mother always won in the back of my head, where she was convinced that I deserved a lower education, that I would drop out and become pregnant at age 16. The truth is that I was smart, a teacher's pet, and a huge geek at heart. Words can me made to build someone, or tear them down. One guidance counselor spoke up, and stood up for me. She called me into her office and told me that she didn't believe in the system, sending foster kids to Job Corps, that it wasn't the place for me. She told me that I was smart young woman, and that I should graduate from high school, and go to college. I was shocked and numb, because she knew that I wanted the normal high school experience. "But how?" I thought to myself. I needed a place to live, and I needed work to pay bills. I deserved my first chance, not a hand me down second chance, which was Job Corps. I didn't ask for this.

"Job Corps is the nation's largest career technical training and educational program for young people at least 16 years of age that qualify as low income. A voluntary program administered by the U.S. Department of Labor, Job Corps provides eligible young men and women with an opportunity to gain the experience they need to begin a career or advance to higher education."

My journal entry on my 18th birthday read, "Happy Birthday me, I'm turning 18. Honestly I am freaking---scared..." I was scared to death of trying to find where I was going to sleep and eat. I had so many doors close, and so many people turned their backs on me. My best friend and mentor, RD, believed in me, but didn't see how it was possible. I was next to homeless, and wanted desperately to get a high school diploma. Something needed to be done. He finally brought me to his church pastor. Saving grace. Thank God! I was linked up to a family that provided me room and board in exchange for helping with the kids, meals, etc., and a chance at getting my high school diploma! I repeated my junior year. During my senior year I had my own place, and at one point I juggled three jobs and full time high school. In 2004 I finally graduated with a high school diploma!!!

Job Corps. Website: http://www.jobcorps.gov/home.aspx

When I graduated from high school, I was the keynote speaker at the Department of Education Conference in Massachusetts. My messeage was entitled *Overcoming Homelessness in High School*. I presented it in from of 400 teachers and social workers.

Searching for LOVE, and Trying to Move Forward Only to Slide Back

I've prayed, and wondered about if I would meet anyone like me who understood what it was like to have lost a family, and not belong to a new one. Even after beating odds, I was still left navigating my own transition into adulthood. After leaving "the parents," i.e. the system, no one was there to help guide my steps. Trying to get a new start, I thought moving out of state would get me a clean slate. I was looking for love in all the wrong places. I moved there for a guy who ended up dumping me for another woman.

So I began a new relationship, a new job, and everything seemed to be on track. By age 23 I was engaged, and thought I finally had the chance to have the family I always wanted, but never could have. Little did I know at this time that I would follow in my biological father's foot steps, choosing someone who wasn't nice. After another argument, another fight, something clicked. It was like a voice telling me I better leave. At the time, I was eight weeks pregnant, and I realized in that instant that not only was I responsible for my life; I was also responsible for the one growing inside me, so my ex won the fight, and I had an abortion. The price I paid was a high cost that I wish for nobody. I will never forget the car ride home that day, crying on the Garden State Parkway, crying out to this God to "Come save me, just save me. I'm no longer mad at you for taking away my mother." I began to question what I wanted to leave behind, or the gift I will give to impact the world.

Thank God my story didn't end there. I am grateful for the support I received, and the love and care. I really hit rock bottom, but there is only one way up. Although my experience was scary, and I don't wish to relive this on paper, I do want you to know that you can find a LOVE that is healthy, giving, and real. It was a rough season, and I went back, and back again, until I realized I had in my hands the right to choose a happy life, that I was no longer hopeless, or a child that was 3 years old. It took a lot of work in therapy, and a dedication to "Get better, not bitter."

Breathing Again, Hope in Living Water

The next three years were filled with soul searching. My car would end up in a church parking lot. I would sit in the back pew, listen to the message the pastor would preach, and wonder why I never had a perfect life. Could this God love me? Is this stuff for real?

So I began a raw, but true dialogue with God, talking to this invisible God. Then a friend from work invited me to go to church with her. At the time I was contemplating this big dream of mine to help foster youth, so she asked me to come to a liquid church with her. "Liquid church, what kind of church was that?" From the moment I walked in, I had that same feeling that I had at Calumet, the feeling of being loved. The pastor spoke about how God is always with us. For some reason it finally hit me that I was no longer alone, that even in the darkest places, God would be there. I was no longer alone. The founder of *Charity Water* spoke of his faith story, and about the need for clean water in developing nations. There was a picture of a little girl drinking dirty water, and it suddenly hit me, "What are you doing here, T? I thought "If God can transform his life, he can transform mine, too, and there can be good." I felt like God whispered that it was time. You can make your dream a reality, so not another child of mine will be hurting.

The Leap of Faith

Dear God, how am I going to find former foster kids? Looking for former foster kids is like finding a needle in a hay stack. At the time, I was googling "foster care" and looking for a group therapy for someone like me. It began with a curiosity. I stumbled upon a website called *Foster Care Alumni of America,* a network of people that grew up in foster care. Foster Care Alumni of America FCAA's mission is to connect the alumni community, and transform policy and practice, ensuring opportunity for people in, and from, foster care. They didn't have a MA Chapter so I decided, oh what the heck, I'll start one!

Finding that Needle

One alumni I met forever changed my life, and made me not only believe, but know, that anything is possible. I met him accidentally after a church service. At the time, I was creating the alumni postcards, and I had a sticker on my laptop that said, "Hello, I am a foster kid." He sat on the pew behind me, and asked me about it. After I explained the project, and that I was former foster kid, I watched his eyes fill with tears of joy. He said he was a former foster kid as well, and we talked for hours. He called me his sister, and gave me a big hug. I knew right then that I found the very family I'd been searching for all these years. His name was Coach Ray, an Olympic coach, who was a former foster kid. If he can make it, so can I! One of my greatest joys is meeting other alumni. It is truly a gift we give each other, answering the question, "Is there anyone out there like me?" Anyone who understands knows what it is like to be a foster kid, losing parents, and having the messy transition of the foster care system take the place of your parents.

FCAA website: www.fostercarealumni.org

PEDS21, I Finally Have a Voice

In 2008 I was asked to speak on a panel in front of 2,000 doctors, and over the course of the week, it would reach about 50,000 doctors nationwide. We educated them about how to provide better health care to foster kids. Here is part of my speech at the PEDS 21 conference in Washington D.C.:

"PEDS21 Speech: Solutions for Better Health Care for Foster Kids"

"While my experience is unique to me, it also is typical of most foster kids, in that I entered the foster care system in need of mental health due to past neglect and abuse. And, like too many other kids, my experiences in and with the system then served to increase my need for this help, rather than being a place where I received it. Given my experiences in the foster care system, here are three solutions for providing better care:

1. Make sure foster kids have a consistent team of mental and health professionals.
2. Avoiding the band-aid approach---neither pills nor band-aids can change the facts of our lives so far.
3. Group therapy to help foster kids understand that their struggles are a normal reaction to an abnormal situation and let them know others in the same situation.

Having a Consistent Therapist in Care

Foster kids need consistent presences in their lives, people they can rely on to know who they are, and remember their story. A therapist can be one of these people, and frequently will be the only such person in a foster child's life. The child is often neglected, and not listened to, both by the foster families, and the parade of social workers they encounter. The last thing a child needs is a new therapist each time he or she moves. The model should be stability, and no more transitions. Every time a child moves, he or she should not have to also face a new therapist, with another request of, "Tell me your story…." This leads to the partly serious, partly embittered response of, "Why don't you just read my file?" In my case, I had four foster homes, three different social workers, and three high schools. A consistent therapist through all that would have made a world of difference.

Avoiding the "Band-Aid" Approach Re: Automatic Prescriptions

Prescribing medication for foster kids is an example of a band-aid solution. It is a joke in the foster care alumni community that every foster kid is on Zoloft. When you consider all that we lose when we go into foster care, you have to recognize that it makes sense to be sad, or angry, or confuse, or numb, or all of these things. It can really feel like the world is falling apart when you suddenly find yourself alone, and without a family. At that moment in life, the approach a health care provider takes is crucial, and all too often, it is easier to prescribe medication, and miss listening to the already neglected child.

I was very fortunate that my first therapist said I did not need medication. He said I just needed a friend. That was huge, and his observation gets to the root of the change that's needed. Foster kids need a health care provider who will meet them where they are at, not simply a change in medication to find the 'right cocktail.'

Medication can be extremely helpful in many cases, but first children need someone they can relate to, someone who can see and hear them. In my case, I couldn't verbalize my childhood horrors easily, so it would have been good to have a consistent therapist who I could eventually trust, so that I would no longer be silent.

Foster kids need support, understanding, and relationships, not pills. And even when they DO need pills, they still need those other things, too.

Benefits to Creating Group Therapy Customized to Foster Kids---Something Which Currently Does Not Exist

Group therapy does not yet exist for foster youth. The closest thing that exists to group therapy is the Foster Care Alumni of America. This is not truly a therapy outlet; it is just a way to socially connect and share stories with one another. Group therapy would provide many benefits to foster kids. First and foremost, it would help them understand that they are not alone. Being a foster child is unusual, in that there is no mechanism by which kids in the same situation can meet, and indeed are almost kept apart. Following out of this, group therapy would allow kids to discuss shared experiences. It would have helped me a great deal to have been able to discuss the organic side effects of being a foster kid with others who have shared the same governmental parents. I would like to encourage doctors to work with alumni to create a group therapy model customized to foster kids.

Conclusion of Speech

"My wish is for all foster kids, in and out of care, is to have a fighting chance to live happy and healthy lives. I hope that when foster kids come into YOUR office, you can see them, and hear them, and reassure them. Thank you for being here, and for caring about all of us in and from foster care."

First Chance, Dreams Come True!

Six years later I finally got my "First Chance." I never imagined that I could have this, but God heard, and did answer my prayers. I got a "First Chance" scholarship in 2010 for a full ride to the University of Phoenix, a chance to further my education.

I've come a long way since I aged out of foster care. I'm still navigating adulthood, and don't have all the answers. I'm finally at a place where I am not ashamed for being a product of the system who was not adopted, that I am a proud alumni, or "graduate" of foster care. I am brave, young, and beautiful. I've embraced and accepted my background and history. I can now say I am blessed with an "organic hybrid family" made up of friends, alumni, church brothers and sisters, and yes, even relatives. My wish for you is to find your own voice, love, health, wealth, and your own definition of what family means to you.

The END
Think Lemonade. *"You have the power to create your own ending. Life isn't perfect, but keep on making lemonade out of lemons and you will surely find the sweeter side of life."*

Thomas Bryson

Doing OK

My name is Thomas Bryson. I was born in 1946. I had two sisters and four brothers. Due to family problems, which I never knew of, I was removed from my home and moved to foster home. The only thing I knew was that my parents weren't taking care of us. The way I see it now, none of my brothers and sisters was kept at home; all of us were sent to foster homes. This was done by the state of Illinois, probably social services, or some other department. I was separated from my brothers and sisters. We were all put in separate homes.

The first foster home was all right, what I can remember of it. I can only remember bits and pieces. I really didn't eat much while I was there, but for some reason I would get hungry at night and sneak in the kitchen to eat some delicious sweet potato pie, but I got caught, and punished. My punishment was a switch or a spanking on the rear. I had to go to the back yard and get a switch or stick from a tree, or one that had fallen down on the ground, and if I didn't get a big enough one, I had to go out and get a larger one. The male foster parent did the beating job, and boy did it hurt! I also got my arm caught in the wringer washing machine while helping the female foster parent do laundry, which scared me to death, but all went well in removing my arm and going to the hospital. This foster home had no indoor plumbing, as in the bathroom. We had to go outside to an outhouse to do our business, even in the winter time. I bet the state of Illinois didn't know about that!

After this foster home, I moved to another foster home, which I don't remember at all, not a single thing, not who the foster parents were, where the house address was, or nothing whatsoever. I believe I was there about 2-3 years. I lived there with two African-American brothers, who are still friends of mine to this day. We have kept in touch over the years. While I was at this foster home I endured drinking beer, underage. I was also sexually harmed while I was there. I was forced to rub the back and toes of my foster family's son, which I couldn't complain about, for fear of having harm forced on me while the family was out. Social services said I was just a trouble kid while I was there, so now I wonder why---because I was abused? The foster parents gave the state of Illinois ridiculous reports on my time being there. I believe social services thought the foster parents had no reason to lie, or to take my word for it. I don't know what case was that caused me to be removed, but I am glad that I was.

From this foster home, I went to ISSCS (Illinois Soldiers and Sailors Children's School), a home for soldier's and sailor's relatives. I think going there really set me up for a good life in the outside world. As of last year, the state of Illinois sent me 20-30 pages of my life I lived at foster homes, and out at the ISSCS home, which included details of the house parents, the viewpoint of each child under their care, so stuff was detailed, but it was mostly their viewpoint. I was too young to go to Boys Row, and had to go to the Village, where it was for young kids over 7 years of age, I believe. Being the only African-American in the Village, I was a loner. I assume some of the kids never met a black boy, or was near one, or so it seemed. I barely got by in my school studies, but did do all of my homework. I was considered a cottage pet, meaning I stayed out of trouble and did what I was told; therefore the cottage parents really liked me. I helped them set the table, wash dishes, and other chores that other boys didn't like to do. After being there about two years I got into a fight, which was a tie, because we both gave up. I acquired a train set while I was there, but I don't know what happened to it.

I eventually entered Boys Row, which was for the older boys, and stayed there for four years, and then I left ISSCS. At Boys Row I was once again called a cottage pet, for the foregoing reasons. I got initiated by being taken out to the corn fields and depanted, and undressed, until I was naked, me and the boys, which was between 7-10 boys in each cottage, on our birthday, so I got it four times, but it wasn't anything new; the cottage parents allowed it, and didn't cause a fuss. I focused my energy in baseball, football, basketball, and swimming, and did well in all of those events. In Boys Row, I had a white house parent who really wanted to adopt me, but the state said "no" to that.

All the boys enjoyed Legion's Day, when all the legions that dealt with ISSCS had a child they sponsored, and bought a gift for. Each year, about the same time, ISSCS would have about 10-15 buses of legionaries for the annual trip of excitement, games, sports, and picnics at each cottage. A legion family that sponsored me was trying for me to get permission to visit their home in Peru, Illinois, but it was denied, but later on, since they were relatives of the cottage parents, they let me stay for the weekend. I met their relatives and was very welcomed there by all.

I left ISSCS in 1964, and had a job already to start at after leaving the home. A lot of my friends at the home would run away and end up at my apartment, which was a no-no. A few times I was called back to the home, and told that if they found runaways there, that I would be arrested, so the police came to my apartment a few times to search it, but they never found anyone there.

At the present time I'm still employed, and have never been laid off. I am retired, but still work. I have run a big company department, and was also a night manager, and relief manager. I have opened and closed departments, and also closed down a company. I have a two and a half story house, three vehicles, and a pension, and a pretty good life, but I never married, or even had kids.

Tianna (Tia) Marie Hartford

Scared to Tell---Scarred for Life

I wish I could say I was sharing my story to impart great words of wisdom and inspirational thoughts, but I'm not. The main reason I am writing it is to warn others about how much evil is out there, not only in the foster care system, but the world at large. I'm not saying there aren't good foster homes because I know there are, but I also know there are some really bad ones. I can personally testify to that because I was in a really bad one myself.

My foster care journey began when I was only a baby, just 6 months old, and didn't end until I was adopted at the age of 11. Since I was just a baby when I was put into foster care, I have no recollection of my original home; I only know what my sister told me and what my state foster care file said about it. According to what I've been told, my mom and dad were married and got divorced right after I was born. My mom had a lot of problems. My father was Hispanic and also had a lot of problems. Apparently she would do anything to hold onto her husband. There were seven children (I'm the fifth born) and we almost all have different fathers, which isn't surprising, considering my mom's behavior. My mom got five of her children, but it was still very dysfunctional. The father wasn't nice and my siblings have the scars to prove it.

Some of you who read my story may think my experience in this one foster home sounds too incredible to believe, but I can assure you it is all true, and I also have the emotional scars to prove it. I have battled with Post Traumatic Stress Disorder, Agoraphobia, Social Anxiety Disorder, Anorexia, and along with being diagnosed with Bi-Polar Disorder, this has been no easy battle, believe me, but I try to keep a sense of humor about it all. I tell my friends, "I have my appointment today with the crazy doctor to get my happy pills."

My first foster home that I went into as a baby was short-lived because of jealousy issues with the children of the foster parents. I lived in my second foster home from the ages of 1-7, and was there way longer than I should have been. Talk about being taken out of the frying pan and put in the fire! This foster home was an experiment in terror beyond words. The foster mom was a very strict Baptist and had a very warped idea about her abuse, doing things in the name of "religion," telling me and my brother who was there with me (he's a year older than me) that we were evil, children of the devil, and that we had to apologize to God and her for being bad, that we were evil because of the "sins of our parents." My foster father was real nice, but unfortunately he was gone most of the time traveling for business and wasn't around to prevent the abuse, and of course when he was home, we were now her little "angels." We were also put on display at church, so the abuse was also well-hidden there. It's hard for me to believe today that somebody could be that mean to a child, inflicting such horrific abuse on me the way she did, but I think she convinced herself it was ok, that she wasn't evil, instead trying to convince me and my brother that we were the evil ones, which justified her actions in her mind.

This evil witch called a "foster mom," bestowed daily belt beatings on me, and if I cried, it continued, and if I cried while seeing my brother being beaten, I got beaten again. She hit me so hard in the face that I had my jaw broken twice, which I was never even treated for then. It wasn't until years later that a doctor brought it to my attention and treated me for it. Of course she couldn't get it taken care of; it would have exposed the truth---I mean really, how do you hide the truth about a broken jaw? When she wasn't beating me she was locking me up in a bedroom for days at a time, with only sunflower seeds and cookies to eat, and a coffee can to pee in, since there was no adjoining bathroom, and then when she'd come in and smell the stinky urine, she'd punish me for that. I was beaten and left up in the attic also, and when she would talk in a strange voice that sounded like a witch to me, it frightened me and I would be screaming and yelling that there was a witch up there with me, and she would yell up at me to be quiet, that there was no such thing as witches, and then she's punish me more for lying about saying there was a witch.

If you thought the bedroom and attic incidents were bad, wait until you hear what happened in the basement on a regular basis. I was chained, yes, "chained," tied up to a pole for two days at a time, while my brother could only stand up at the top of the stairs to see me. All of these things happened regularly, along with other abuses. Whenever she caught me eating strawberries out of the strawberry patch in the garden, I was forced to stand in the middle of it where there were a lot of snakes running around, while my brother stood on the edge of the garden and watched, and he was of course punished if he went back to the house. I chewed my fingernails (wonder why?!) and she would hold my fingers over fire to "cure" me from that. She would take me to a bridge and dangle me over the bridge, fully aware of my fear of heights. She even put me in a long freezer, and I would be terrified, knowing I was going to die. It was all a mental game with her, bringing me to the brink of death, telling me that I was going to die, so I would beg for my life. She would push me under the water in the bathtub until I almost drowned, and she also dunked my head under ice water. Are you ready for this one? When I didn't do the dishes or other house chores right, she'd put dish soap in a dog bowl and force me to get on the floor like a dog and drink it, and eat soft dog food, and then I would get beaten when I threw up, and forced to clean up the mess.

If all this abuse wasn't terrifying and degrading enough, while my brother was gone to school, she would lecture me about hating her, telling me to kill her with the gun she had, and then when I would refuse to kill her, she'd put the gun to my head and threaten to shoot me. Her abuse was never a spontaneous reaction to me having an accident or something like that; her abuse was premeditated. The woman was EVIL. The only fond memory I have at all of this home is having the foster mom's mother let me watch Romper Room on television and of her making me "cry baby cookies," (if I didn't cry, I got cookies). She was real nice, but she could only be so nice to me, as she would get abused also. The social worker made visits here at this foster home, but we were told by the foster mom to "only say nice things to her, how well taken care of we were and how important God was to us," and she would warn us that she'd be listening in on our conversation in the next room, so we wouldn't be able to tell her about the abuse.

I guess there was divine intervention or something one day, as there finally came an opportunity for us to spill the beans. One day when the social worker came to visit us she took me and my brother out for an ice cream and my brother told her about the abuse, and I showed her my bruises (I was always well clothed to hide them). We were taken out of that home, but we had to wait for two weeks while another home was being found for us, in which time the foster mom, who had been presented with abuse allegations and had therefore stopped all the physical abuse, played mental games with us, telling me that my brother would stay at the home by himself and be killed, so that I would never see him again, and she destroyed prized childhood possessions of mine, including my pet rabbit, which I had to watch her kill.

The next foster home I was put in would be the one I was eventually adopted into, but at this point they were not interested in adopting me, so the home failed for the time being. The mean, evil foster mom kept contacting us at this home. She convinced the elders at her church that we were being abused in this home and they all had a plot to kidnap us. When she would call us, I would cry, and she's say it was because I was being abused, but it wasn't; I was crying because I didn't want to hear from her. She eventually stopped calling us and we never did hear from her again. The Child and Family Services thought we should be adopted and since they couldn't find people to adopt both of us, my brother and I were put in separate homes.

This next home I went into was a decent home and the foster parents (he was a pastor) were going to adopt me, but his wife was jealous of me and her husband's attention toward me, so it didn't work out. They were trying to iron out their marital problems and I was left with some of their friends while they were gone. One day I spilled some talc powder and the wife had a fit, and it was then that he took me upstairs and explained to me that he couldn't keep me. He made it very clear that it wasn't that he didn't want me. He told me he wanted to keep me, that I was his little girl, but that he couldn't. I cried and I was still crying two days later. I was 9 years old at this time and having a nervous breakdown. Really, I was. I was put in the state mental hospital for about a week. The pastor ended up calling the previous (third) foster home I was in and explained to them how much I needed some kind of stability and security, and pleaded with the foster parents to consider taking me back, which they did.

I was 9 years old when I was put back with these foster parents and 11 when I was adopted. The day before the final adoption date, the foster father had a heart attack (which the foster mom blamed me for), but the doctor encouraged him to go through with the adoption anyway because it was what he really wanted to do. It was a decent home and life was good there with the foster father; he was awesome. I was his little girl and we were inseparable, but not only was the foster mom jealous of my close relationship with her husband, but she never got over the bridge of me not being her own biological daughter; she wasn't very nice to me and always treated me like a foster kid. She also didn't understand and accept my abuse issues with my past foster mother, and so wasn't sensitive to my emotional needs.

When I was 11 years old I started babysitting for some neighbors and the father in the family sexually abused me, raped me, for years. He threatened me by telling me I would be taken out of my home and put back into foster care if I told anyone, so I never told. He also told me I would get pregnant if I told anyone (I didn't understand these things at that age), and then when I did get old enough to understand pregnancy, he told me that people would say I was a slut. Another fear I had around the age of 15 was that if I told, my dad would kill him; I took it literally when my dad would say he'd kill anybody who touched me, not realizing that all fathers say things like that to protect their daughters. This man did everything to be in my life---he chaperoned at dances, he took me places, anything to be around me. It wasn't until I was 18 years old that I was able to move away from him, but he still followed me wherever I went. This man used every ploy possible to keep me under his thumb. When I was 25 years old I finally broke down and told my dad and mom the truth about everything, and my dad told me how sorry he was. My mother never did believe me. My father died about a month later from a heart attack and I felt like I was to blame for it. This man stalked me for years. He even showed up at my husband's work place and came to a bar we were at and told my husband what a great person I was. I reported him when he broke into my apartment and pressed charges against him while I was working with law enforcement, but he begged me not to pursue it any further, that he had already lost his marriage, and would lose his farm and children, so I dropped the charges, but he still continued bothering me. It wasn't until some serious threats were made that he finally left me alone. I was told I had a strong legal case against him, but my adoptive mom didn't believe I was telling the truth and discouraged me from pursuing it. I found out later that I wasn't the only one he sexually abused, and as an adult I have lived with guilt about this, feeling as though I could have prevented it from happening to others if I had said something earlier. I have always been overprotective of my daughter and never left her wide open to anything that could be sexually abusive.

As is normal for any child in my situation, I had a desire to meet my real parents later on in life, so when I was about 24 years old, I met my dad and had a relationship with him for about two years, then broke it off due to personal matters. I guess if one parent doesn't work, try the other, right? Or maybe I'm just a glutton for punishment, I don't know, but my relationship with my real mom didn't work either. She was a downright "psycho bitch" when I met her. My brother and I met her at a hotel where we planned on visiting for a few days, but our mom went ballistic on us when we started asking questions about our childhood, ranting and raving about how much she hated our dad with a passion and how everything was his and the state's fault. She was in complete denial about her part in it and would take no responsibility for her own actions. She would not answer any of our questions, so we left after two days. I just couldn't handle her psycho behavior. It got so bad there at the hotel that my brother and I barricaded ourselves in a separate room from her. Needless to say, this was no happy reunion like you might see on Oprah Winfrey. The only other contact I ever had with her was about a year later, when I was pregnant. My sister had kept in touch with her and had told her I was expecting, and my mom called me, saying that she wanted to be a part of me and her grandchildren's lives, but apparently she had a change of heart, as I never heard from her again. I think guilt got the best of her and she just couldn't face me.

As I already mentioned, I don't have any good advice for others, other than to be strong and reach out for help when you need it, like I have. Not having good foster mothers really affected my ability to feel adequate as a mother. I really didn't really want children because I was so afraid of the prospect, but when I got married, I agreed to have one with my husband (I ended up having one pregnancy, but it was twins, a girl and a boy). Adjusting to motherhood was very difficult for me; in fact, it was so hard that I ended up having a nervous breakdown when they were little.

I was suicidal and felt that I was "damaged goods," that I wouldn't be a good mother, and it required some therapy for me to overcome my fears, but I have managed to be a decent mother in spite of my past, which is a miracle. I wouldn't have had to go through so much if there was more accountability of parents and foster parents, but there isn't. We go over to other countries and rescue the kids there, when the devastation is right here in front of us, with the foster care system creating monsters. Foster kids are just thrown to the wolves, where only the strong survive, but even the strongest of us don't survive without being left with scars that last a lifetime.

Tobias Michael Rogan

A Story of Resilience

There are many different reasons why children end up in the foster care system, and although the circumstances surrounding my case are unusual, and maybe even unbelievable to some, I can testify to the reality of it.

This is my story, my life, my challenges, successes, and my tale of resilience.

Back in the early 1990's I was born into a very big, religious family. In this I would include that my biological parents were divorced before I was even born. Because I was born into this very religious family, they taught me from the get go their "ways" of life. Some of the basic aspects of living with my family were: I ate nothing but organic food, and I was to be homeschooled. To even go more complex, they had told me that I was not to like the same sex and to be gay was unacceptable. My family explained that I wasn't supposed to feel this way, whether if I was a male attracted to the male gender, or a female attracted to the female gender. It was unacceptable. Because I was homeschooled, I was not allowed to watch basic television, or leave the small town I lived in. I didn't know anything about being gay, or even the basic fact that I was gay. I didn't know anyone my age and I did not know all about the society outside of my little town. I was very excluded from the "real world."

Fast-forwarding to 11 years old, I ended up going to school for the very first time in my life. It was a big culture shock from living on a farm for the past eleven years. When being homeschooled, biological parents have to pay for books and supplies and because my family was having financial issues in finding ways to pay for everything, my family sent me and my other ten siblings off to our first year of being in school. So I entered 6th grade, in junior high school, my very first year in school. A lot of parents in today's society tend to deny that their child might come out as a LBGT (Lesbian Bisexual Gay Transgender). Some parents are supportive, but for the most part, a lot of families fear that this could be a "new" aspect of their family. Because of how I express myself, I naturally am stereotyped to be gay. I am neither masculine, nor clearly feminine in my appearance. The technical term for this is androgynous, having both masculine and feminine characteristics. Because I didn't know anything about being gay, I was confused on why a lot of people at school tended to say that I was. I quickly learned that naturally I was attracted to the same sex; I didn't know where this was coming from. My family taught me that this was wrong, so, of course, out of curiosity, I asked my new friends in school what was wrong with me. For the most part, everyone simply said, "You're gay, and we accept you." It was an incredible feeling being accepted by my teachers and friends at school, knowing what my family stated previously about being gay. I have always considered myself a very talkative and outgoing person, so I have trouble hiding anything from my family. This was a major change in my life and I needed to tell someone.

Three months later, I found myself driving home with my grandma. Sitting in the passenger seat, my grandmother asked the usual question: "How was school?" I really did not know what to say, so instead I said, "Grandma, I have something to tell you. I'm gay." For the next few minutes it was nothing but silence. I asked, "Did you hear me?" She then replied, "We are not going to talk about this." The drive home felt like an eternity. When I did get home, I asked her when we would talk about it. She then replied, "When we have an emergency meeting this weekend." My heart sunk to my chest, knowing that the only reason why we have emergency meetings is either a good thing or a bad thing. We only celebrated weddings and the birth of a new family member; so clearly, I knew that it was not going to be a positive meeting. The following weekend arrived, without surprise; most of my family was at this meeting. I am from a rather large family and like I explained previously, I have ten brothers and sisters, so you can imagine that the site of my family is very, very large. I was told to sit in the chair across from everyone in the room and after hours of being questioned, yelled at, and harassed by my family, they decided to put me through a reparative program, which is basically a program designed to turn anyone gay, to straight.

I was forced to attend a camp that was designed to turn me straight. I went to numerous counseling and therapy sessions, and I was forced against my free will to go to a psychiatrist hospital where I spent three months away from my family. Personally, if you force me to do something against my free will, it's just going to push me further away, so after seven months of being forced to do all of these reparative therapy sessions, psychiatric evaluations, and hospital stays, I was not only pushed further away from being close to my family, but I was still gay.

My grandmother called yet again for another family emergency meeting. She told me to have a suitcase packed. This time around, my entire family not only attended, but people from the community, the church, and friends of the family were all there. I was forced to sit through and listen to my brothers, sisters, aunts, uncles, nieces, nephews, friends of the family, and down to my own father, saying that they all hated me. I was condemned to Limbo (I was condemned to the children's hell) and that I was dismissed from the family---in other words, I was kicked out.

I was only 12 years old when my family kicked me out of the home. What did I do? Where did I go? For the next year of my life, I was homeless. I lived in abandoned buildings, I couch hopped, and I lived on the streets. I had to live an adult life as a child. My choice of living or dying quickly came into view---should I live or die? I chose to live.

A year later, what seemed like a miracle, a teacher found me under a bridge. I was very unhealthy, sick, and on the verge of a mental breakdown. After staying in another hospital for three months to regain my strength, I became healthy once again. During my stay in the hospital, that is when Protective Services came into my life and I entered the foster care system.

For the next three years of my life, I not only faced the challenges of dealing with emotions towards my biological family, but trying to fit in with society. I moved on numerous occasions and went to many schools. When I was 16 years old, I decided that I wanted a change. I was sick of the abuse, the problems, and the negativity that I was constantly faced with from being in the foster care system, so I moved into an apartment and worked many jobs for the next two years of my life. By the time I was 18 years old, I was still emotionally exhausted and drained. I graduated at the top of my class and I thought about college. I ended up moving out of my apartment and into a dorm room at what is now my new home---college. I now am a sophomore in college and I am working for an awesome organization called Foster Club, advocating for young people in foster care. It is an amazing organization that I get to be a part of. I love it.

I now have a family.

Did you hear that?

Family.

Toni Liebezeit

Insecure

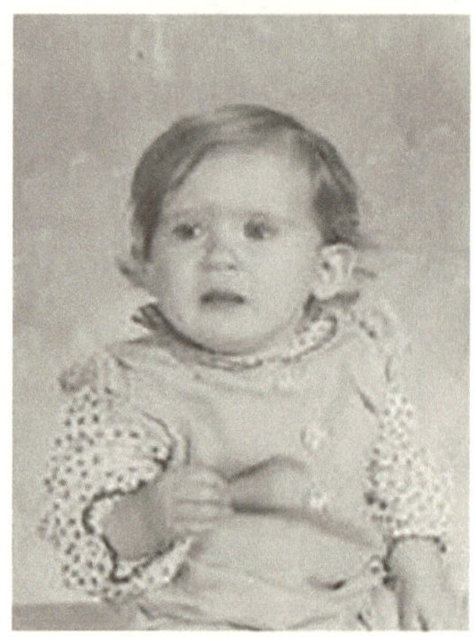

I am sharing my story because I believe it needs to be told and brought out in the open. We are still society's little secret, something to be shoved aside and ignored, and I think it's time for us to "come out" and share our stories; maybe people will begin to look at us like people instead of aliens. Really, have you ever noticed the response from people after telling them you were a foster kid? They just give you this blank look, like they don't know what to say….like "what's that?" People have no idea who foster kids really are and what we go through, how resilient we have to be in order to survive; we are like soldiers, in a fight for our lives. I also want to tell my story because I like to read anything concerning foster care, as long as it isn't clinical. I like real stories about real people, like these. When you read my story you'll get the real deal, not some "I Was a Foster Kid and Now I'm a Success" line of crap.

Now don't get me wrong; I'm not saying I haven't gotten better, but I don't believe I'll ever completely be over my childhood. I want to get over it, but it just isn't possible. You never get over it because you can't just erase history. Well, maybe some people do, but I haven't met them yet. Foster kids may have had various experiences, but at the end of it all we all end up with the same basket of shit---angry, hurt, insecure, mistrustful, that is unless you're delusional.

I'm very insecure. I feel as though I'm trying to navigate through life, but it's hard because of the way I was raised; I keep getting steered in the wrong direction. My childhood is always screwing with me and wreaking havoc in my adulthood. Sometimes I'm shocked at the way this stuff comes back to haunt me. I'm a 39 year old woman, and yet sometimes I can still feel like a lost 3 year old child yearning for her mommy. Given the right place and time, I can still be reduced to nothing, which I basically felt like growing up. I'm a Home Health Aide and I just recently started a new job, and have been feeling very insecure, worrying about making a good impression, doing everything right, pleasing the woman, hoping I don't look lost and stupid like I did when I was a kid. I tell myself, "I'm fine, I'm fine," but I'm not; I'm screwed up. If it wasn't for God in my life, I'd probably be in a mental hospital. When I was younger I felt like God abandoned me, but I now realize that He didn't. I was making a bed one time at a job and the woman scolded me for not doing it right, yelling "Didn't your mom teach you how to make a bed?" And I yelled "I didn't have a mom!" I didn't have a dad, either, or at least I didn't know who he was because my mom was date raped by a guy who was just a casual acquaintance, which resulted in me, an unwanted child.

When I was in my 30's years old I got my state file from my adoptive parents and found out that I was put in foster care immediately after I was born, that I never even went home with my birth mom. She was schizophrenic and freaking out when I was born, having delusions about having twins and thinking she lost the boy, so she had to be sedated and locked up in a mental hospital, and I was put in a foster care home. This scenario repeated itself many times throughout the first eight years of my life. My mom kept putting me in foster care when she put herself in a psych ward. It bothered me a lot when I read my file, as it really confirmed that my mom didn't bond with me. It was very weird to read it; it made me feel like a castaway, especially since I was an only child. Based on the knowledge that my mom probably wasn't nurtured herself as a child, I can forgive her today, but it still doesn't make me feel any better about the fact that I am motherless.

My uncle wanted to take me, but wasn't allowed to because he was an unmarried man, but I think the only reason he wanted to take me was simply because nobody else would, not because he had a strong love for me. I have an early memory of me crying in my crib, with a droopy diaper hanging off my butt, and my uncle picking me up. My uncle died right in the middle of the process of him trying to get custody of me, which really hurt me, as I felt like he was the only one in my family who cared at all about me and he was my only salvation. I can remember going in the bathroom after his death and running water so nobody could hear me crying. I had a whole system worked out for myself, so I didn't look like a cry baby. I wasn't allowed to cry, as nobody wanted a crying kid.

I don't remember feeling much of anything as a kid. You just learn to sit down and shut up and do what you have to do, with the attitude "I'll be good." I felt like I had to be good, even if I felt like I was screaming inside, and even though I had secret thoughts of a better life, I was smart enough to know that it was just "too bad," that there was no need in fighting it. I felt like I was just a nuisance, in the way, not wanted, and feeling like I should just be dead. Where in the heck does a 6 year old child come up with the concept that she wants to be dead, anyway? A regular child wouldn't do this, but there's a big difference between a regular child and a foster child. It's so miserable to be mistreated, neglected, and abused, that your mind just goes to dark places. I didn't have a mom sitting around playing patty cakes with me or giving me Barbie dolls; if I had the choice between a doll and some food, I'd take the food because I was so hungry. It isn't normal, the things foster kids go through.

There was so much chaos and complication in my childhood, I don't even remember how many foster homes I was in. I remember five of them between the ages of 4-15, and I think I was in one of them more than once, but who the hell knows? What I do remember is how I felt being in those foster homes---sad and full of despair, feeling totally alone and unloved. I had no energy or ambition to make trouble because I just wanted to be loved. The world seemed so big it felt like it was swallowing me up; I was so full of despair. I can remember being so upset, frustrated, overwhelmed, and pressured in my fourth grade math class because I couldn't do the long division, that I had a breakdown right in the classroom, crying at my desk and having an outburst, screaming out loud to the whole classroom, "I'm sad because I'm a foster kid!" Life was just too much for me. I couldn't learn because I couldn't concentrate due to being emotionally messed up, which made me feel inadequate and stupid, so I never liked school. It just seemed like another thing that I had to survive. As a result of my learning disability, I'm an uneducated adult, at least in the conventional sense. I'm lucky if I can balance a checkbook.

It isn't normal for children to be sexually abused, either, which happened to me some. My first memory of sexual abuse is being about 5 years old and being abused for a few months by a family acquaintance. At one time I lived with my mom, uncle, and aunt, and my one uncle who hung around degenerates; it was one of them who abused me. My mom was crazy and out partying or sleeping, so she wasn't paying any attention to my welfare, and if my uncle was in charge, it was all chaos and I wasn't safe. There was more abuse when I was about 7-8 years old, by another family friend who would come to our house and visit, and I was so hungry for attention that I welcomed him in the first time, not realizing what he was up to. It bothered me when he started touching me inappropriately, but when he started trying to have intercourse with, forcefully putting himself on top of me, I really got upset and told my mother "If you don't get that man out of our house, I'm going to tell the school and your welfare check will be taken away." I wanted sympathy from my mother, but she just couldn't give it to me. She couldn't even get her ass out of bed to go get me some apples when I asked for them, let alone give me any sympathy for anything. I was so mad, disappointed, and distrustful, and so annoyed and fed up with the whole situation that I lit a curtain on fire one day. I've had a life long history of sleep disturbance problems, waking up during the night scared, and I wonder if I may have repressed sexual abuse memories before these incidences, but I don't know. Shortly after the curtain fire incident my mom had a nervous breakdown and was put away in a mental hospital and I was put away in foster care.

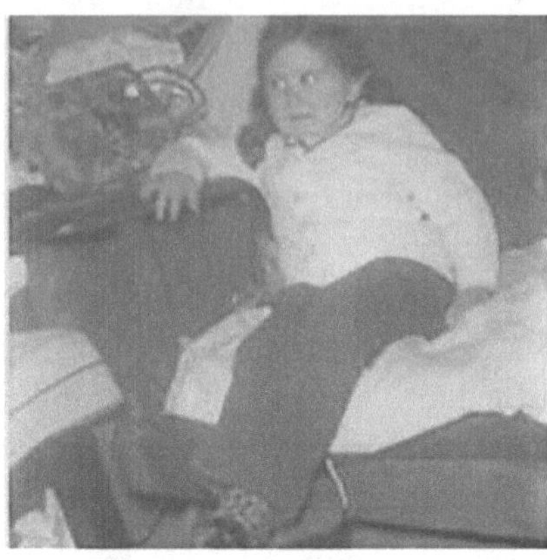

I felt like a wanderer in foster care. I just wandered around the foster care homes, feeling very lonely and lost in the unfamiliarity of everything, and feeling like I never "had a place at the table to call my own." Nothing belongs to you; nothing is "yours" when you're in foster care. When I left homes I didn't always get to keep things like clothes, toys, dolls, etc.; everything was just borrowed. I remember having a Raggedy Ann doll that my mom gave me when I went to a foster home, and when I left the home I wasn't allowed to take the doll with me, even though it belonged to me. The foster parents told me it wasn't mine, but I knew it was. But even if it hadn't been mine, why couldn't they just let me have the doll anyway? I was a foster kid, for crying out loud; I had no mother. The doll meant a lot to me; I even slept with it. They should have given me the doll! What nonsense! Years later, some people living in my mom's old house packed up some things of mine while moving out, and guess what was there?! A picture of me when I was about 2 years old, holding my Raggedy Ann doll!! What a blessing that was! I knew I had a Raggedy Ann doll!!

Finding pictures of your childhood can help fill in some memory gaps and remind you that you were a beautiful, innocent child at one time——unscarred and unblemished.

This is the picture of me holding my Raggedy Ann doll.

I treasure this picture!

It also isn't normal for a 6 year old child to be held at gunpoint, like I was. I had a gun put to my head by some man, who came looking for my uncle, and found me instead. It was like a hostage scene, with this crazy man saying, "You better say your prayers little girl, because your mom is a dumb bitch and wants to call the cops on me." Somehow I got away and ran to the closet, thinking I was safe by shaking and crying.

I don't remember being physically abused in foster care a lot, but the verbal and emotional abuse, and neglect more than made up for it. I always felt like I had to lower myself in order for people to accept me, and I tend to do this still today. There was also a lot of jealousy among the foster kids, so it was hard making any real friends. I can remember being in one foster home in a ghetto, with drug dealers, guns, and neighborhood whores. The foster parents were nice enough to me, but I just thought it was funny, strange, that I was thrown in there, in such an unsafe and unwholesome environment. I never thought much about it at the time, but as an adult I think it's absolutely ludicrous. I mean really, what was the Child Welfare Service thinking? I think the foster care homes are at a little better today and there are more resources available for the foster kids, especially with the internet. In the dark ages it was a foster mom's paradise; she could get away with about anything, but there's more accountability today, or at least I like to think there is. I learned at an early age not to tell anybody anything. I could have been a message in the bottle. I think authority figures, such as psychiatrists, teachers, and social workers, in their observation of foster care, look at us foster kids like we're lab rats, but we're not, and we're not bad kids; we're just sad and needy kids. I know I was.

Another issue for me being in foster care was not having enough food. Actually, this was an issue in my original home and didn't get any better with foster care. I can remember one time going in a convenience store with my uncle, and I was so hungry that I at a bite off of a meatball sub sandwich. I was embarrassed when I got caught, but I was so hungry I just couldn't help myself. When I was about 9-10 years old I had bulimia because I wanted to be thin. I got positive reinforcement; the kids thought I was strong and disciplined, but I was really pissed off and hungry. Right after this time period I was put in another foster home, where I starved.

I've had a by-pass operation because I became so obese, and I blame this not only on the fact that I went hungry with my mom, but also on foster care and the fact that I had such regimented meals, not being free to eat snacks and always having to ask for food. I was on a free lunch program at school, but I wouldn't use it because I was so ashamed and didn't want everyone to know how bad I had it. It was bad enough that I had no confidence and was made fun of at school for wearing crummy clothes; I didn't want more humiliation. When I was put in my adoptive home I was finally allowed to eat what I wanted, but I was so afraid and distrustful at first that I didn't want my foster parents to see me eat.

Not having a mother was the hardest and saddest part for me. My own mother never really wanted me and although I realize she didn't do it maliciously, she abandoned me, and the foster moms I had who were supposed to replace her were also inadequate. When I was finally adopted at the age of 15 I thought I would finally have a mother, but it turned out that she didn't want me any more than the others. At thought, "Now I'm being treated like shit and I'm stuck with her." My adoptive mom was angry that her husband had made an appointment at the Child Welfare office without her knowledge, knowing I was a girl and not a boy, like they had agreed on getting because they wanted a boy for their son. She denies that she was mean to me, and we act civil toward each other, like neighbors, but it could never be anything more than that. I always felt she had "evil resistance" toward me.

My saving grace is my adoptive father, who is awesome. I am real close to him, but I was deeply affected by my lack of mothering. Sometimes it felt like murder to even be walking planet earth. I felt so sad not having a mom to teach you things, like starting a menstrual cycle, or even do something as simple as putting on deodorant. I felt like a real horse's ass because I wasn't rinsing out my pantyhose and didn't understand why I smelled, but I never had a mother to teach me anything like that. I'm sure there are decent mothers out there, but I didn't have one. I have fantasies about what it would be like to have a mother, but I wouldn't know because I never had one. Around the age of 30-35 my motherless issue erupted, which I was unprepared for and made very uncomfortable by. I remember looking at myself in the mirror at the time of my surgery and thinking, "You do not have a mother." I felt so "out in left field." I realized that I had just plowed through my life, convincing myself it was all right not to have a mother, telling myself "I'm fine; I'm a big girl now," but deep down inside I felt so sad and tormented by it. I feel like I am damaged beyond repair because I never had a mother. At one of my lowest points, when I was at one of life's many turns, and realizing how screwed up I was, I wrote this poem:

Motherless

I was born on a gray winter day
I became motherless the same way
All alone, with feelings of dread
Delusions of grandeur going through my head
My life as I knew it was now dead
As my childhood slowly died
I longed for a place to run and hide
Gradually I discovered a way to feel numb
Anxiety soon succumbs as I swallow each and every crumb
Every meal I waited out in anticipation

Wishing my existence was only animation
Insecurity looming around each passing month
My face, belly, and feet stretched out like a balloon
Tears of failure and disgrace
Perpetually sting my fat face

I feel as though my mom died on me three times. The first time was when she was locked up and I was put in foster care, the second time was when I got adopted and had to say goodbye to her, and the third time was when she died for real, when I was 24 years old. I wish I'd had more time with her, taking her out and visiting her more when I was older and had gotten past the anger, but I was still annoyed with the whole situation and didn't. I can't be held responsible. Considering the circumstances, I did the best I could do, just like I suppose she did. It's just that I didn't have a mom. I feel like I am still waiting for my mother to come and get me, yet full well knowing she's not going to. Because I never had a mother, in the past I allowed girlfriends to run my life, but I'm getting better at keeping boundaries now. I'm more comfortable with men than women. I was socially stunted for years, suffering from social anxiety, but that's also better now.

I'll never be all right and I know that. I will never get over my childhood completely. I still get sad and overwhelmed and about 1-3 times a year I have crying episodes when I sit and cry for about an hour about being in foster homes. I feel debilitated and just cry and cry. Foster care was like a big prison yard and the first 30 years of my life I felt like a caged animal in a pen, very limited and cornered, and now I feel like I'm out of the pen and can go in the yard to stretch my legs and have fun, but I feel as though I'll always be in the yard, that nobody has come to unlock the gate so I can be completely free, and nobody ever will, because there is no key. I'll be buried in that yard because I was a foster kid.

I am very thankful for my husband. There have been times when he has come home to find me crying, and when he asks me why I am crying, I say "Because I was a foster kid."

Ty

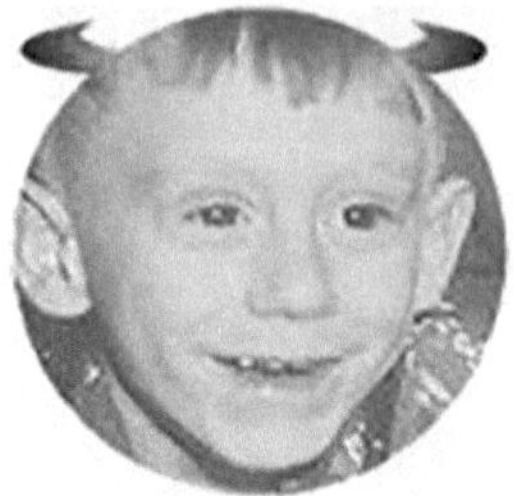

A Troubled Boy

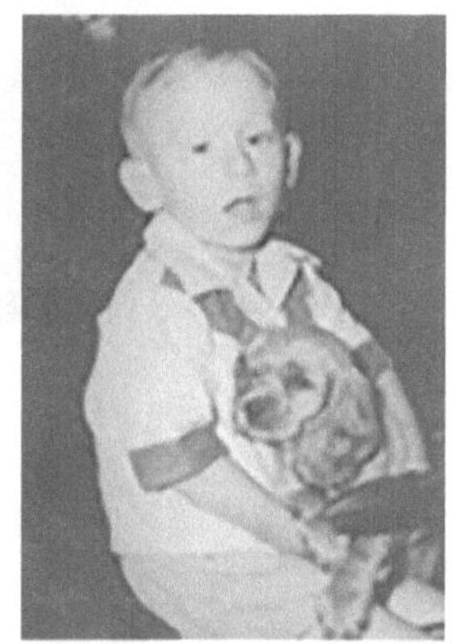

I have never really thought of myself as a foster child or made a big deal out of my bad childhood, but I have begun to realize, through writing my story, that I was probably more affected by my past than I care to believe. If after reading my story you think I'm crazy, you aren't alone; I've thought the same thing about myself, but now I realize there was a reason for my craziness, that my insanity stemmed from deeper, underlying reasons other than just some kind of personality defect. I wasn't crazy; I was just a troubled boy who acted out in belligerent ways. Here is my story. If it can help even one person from having to go through what I did, then it was worth telling.

I was the baby of three children; I have two older sisters. My mother took off when I was just six months old, never to return. The word for it is abandonment---not a very pretty word, is it? My sister went to live with an aunt and uncle and my dad kept me. His intentions were probably good, at least I like to think they were, but he was a raging alcoholic and he basically took up on me where he left off with my mother. The beatings he used to give her were now bestowed on me. My earliest memories are of being about 4-5 years old and singing in my swing; I would make up songs for my neighbor and sing all day long for her. I remember the beatings starting around the age of 6 or 7, but who knows what I might have blocked out that could have happened when I was younger. I became very withdrawn and not very sociable.

I had a babysitter from hell. She was my dad's best friend's wife, who had a daughter a little older than me. When I was at the babysitter's house I was forced to sit in a big, old rocking chair and if I got out of the chair other than to go to the bathroom, I got it with her hairbrush. If my dad was gone for ten hours, then it was ten hours in the chair. No kid can sit in a chair for 8-10 hours! If I got it from her, then when I got home I got it again. This went on every other day for about two years, due to my dad's work schedule. My behavior just got worse with each passing day.

As if the beatings weren't enough, sometime around the age of 7 or 8 an older teen boy who lived down the street started sexually molesting me. I am not sure how long that went on because my mind blocked it out for many years. I was 50 years old before I remembered any of that. God works in strange ways. If I had remembered the sexual abuse back when I was in my 20's or 30's, I would have wanted to go back to my hometown and kill the sob!

When I was 9 years old, I started setting fires---I tried three times to burn down my next door neighbor's house, I burned down a lumber company, and then I tried to burn down the church I attended. Years later I tried to think of why I did those things, as I had no idea, but then when I remembered the boy down the street molesting me, it all made since.

After the fire setting, when I was 9 years old, I was sent to a boy's school for three years. What made me really angry about this was to find out later that the state's attorney involved in my case, the one who was responsible for sending me there, had embezzled thousands of dollars and was sent to prison.

When I came out of there my dad had me put in a children's home. Things started turning around for me while I was there---I did well in school, was playing standup bass in an orchestra, played the guitar, and with the help of a really good teacher, was playing the piano and even writing my own piano music. Then my dad remarried and took me out of the children's home to live with him and his new bride, but things didn't go well. Within a month and a half they took all of my music lessons away from me, my school grades went from B's to straight F's, and it was at this point that I went completely crazy, berserk, and the new bride tried to have me committed. They tried putting me in a Catholic school, but that didn't even last one week. The nun cracked me with a ruler and I decked her.

After that, well, reform school, here I come, prison bound, but not quite yet; it still took a couple more things for that to happen. They put me in a foster home, but I ran away and was gone 3-4 months before they caught me, in Nevada, brought me back, and then they put me in a brand new detention center, where I was the first and maybe only person to escape from there. I set off the electric locks at 2:00 A.M. and was gone before they knew what was happening. It took those about six months to catch me and when they did it was bad, as I had been pegged for two stolen cars, an armed robbery, and something else that I can't remember. I had to go in a lineup for the robbery, which I did not commit, and the stolen cars couldn't be proven, but I got sent away to prison for escaping from the detention center. I came out on parole six months later, but I jumped parole on the second day out, and when I got caught this time I had stolen a car and taken it across a state line.

I went to federal court and got sentenced to two years federal time, which was much better than doing state time. I made some great friends there, got out around March of 1964, and I had some real good plans and intentions, but I met a girl, and when my friend, who got out of prison two weeks later and came to Illinois with automatic weapons to rob a bank and blow my parole officer away, who was a real jerk, I told him to come back in a couple of weeks, after I had enough of this young lass I was so into. Thankfully, he never did come back, and I am so glad!! It had been my plan and there wouldn't have been any witnesses. It is hard for me to look back and think that I even toyed with the idea of killing people.

Well, I ended up marrying that girl, we had three children, and then I became a junkie and had to put an end to that marriage, as I didn't want my kids growing up and seeing that shit, plus Marquetta and I fought from the time we got up until bedtime. We got divorced and I dealt drugs and did leather work for two years.

I made friends with a guy who became my roommate, got involved with his sister who had come to live with us, and was happy for a long while, but old ways were coming back and creeping in; the devil had me once again and I knew not why. I had a wonderful wife, but it just wasn't enough and I didn't know why, but sex with only one woman just wasn't satisfying for me; I had to have group sex. Well, that took care of marriage number two.

Now it's time for some real craziness---I got an older woman who agreed to an open relationship and brought home young women home to me for a couple of years, and the sex and good times were great, but then I eventually got tired of it and that "old thing."

After this relationship ended, I met a blonde lady about ten years younger than me, and this was LOVE, I just know it is, but she was a binge drinker, going from 6-8 months of sobriety to drinking 5-6 quarts in a day or two. I tried living with it for a few years, but then she wrecked my pride and joy, a 1970 Pontiac, and our marriage was never the same after that. She got a boyfriend on the side and I was about to bury him in the desert, but God got a hold of me, and for the second time, I walked away from taking another person's life. I have done all kinds of wrong in my life, but I have never taken life from anyone, and I thank God for that, for keeping me at least that sane.

Perhaps you're wondering whatever happened to my parents and my relationship with them. Well, my dad supposedly committed suicide, but it questionable, since my dad was an avid hunter, who knew how to shoot a gun, and shot with his right hand, not his left, where the fatal gunshot wound was found, on his left temple.

As for my long departed mother who abandoned me as an infant---well, when I was 21 years old I decided to look her up, partly out of curiosity and a need to know the truth about why she left, but mostly because I had a desire to know her, to see if there was a possibility of having a real mother-son relationship. She came out east for a two week visit, and then came out again two years later for about a week, but meeting her was a disappointment, not what my hopes were. She was a drunk. I'm not sure if she had always been a drunk; maybe she just started drinking out of guilt after she left or maybe she's always been a drinker and it just escalated with time. When I asked her why she took off on us, she said she wanted to get away from the beatings. I could understand that! She came to visit again 3-4 years later, this time uninvited, just out of the blue, with only the clothes on her back. She only weighed about 80 lbs. and was severely alcoholic. I kicked her out because she got hostile with a friend I was renting a room from and I was afraid she would burn the house down, since she smoked and drank like a fiend and would pass out drunk with lit cigarettes hanging out of her mouth. She was only there for three days this time, and this was the last time she ever visited. The only reason she came to visit the last time was probably due to her alcoholism and homelessness, as she had an apartment, but alcohol wasn't allowed there, so she moved out to the street where she was free to drink, then I guess she decided to call on me. Maybe the Salvation Army gave her a bus ticket to her destination; I don't know. I do know that I don't ever want to see her again if she's alive, which is doubtful. It's not that I'm hateful toward her; it's just of no real value to me. She's my biological mother, but she never raised me.

I guess the closest person to a mother I had was my grandmother on my dad's side, who was real nice to me--- too nice. She meant well and probably compensated for my dad's behavior toward me, but she spoiled me rotten, and gave me a lot of material things, which in retrospect, I believe contributed to my sense of entitlement and helped set me up for a life of crime. She would tell me stories about Al Capone and how she visited his bars in Chicago---not a very good bedtime story for a kid, especially one like me with emotional and behavioral problems. As for my sisters, I have good relationships with them and they are doing ok, but they didn't come out of their childhoods unscathed, either. All three of us are wacky in one way or another, but I am the wackiest.

I have forgiven all that have wronged me and hope for the same in return. If I could undo most of the wrong doing to others that I have done, I would do it in a heartbeat. I am getting old now and wish to leave this world doing no more harm to anyone. I never got any help or therapy for the things that happened to me in my childhood, and at my age now, I can't see bringing it all up. My demons are all asleep and I think it is best that I keep them that way. I could wake them up, but I don't want to. It's a frightening thought what my demons could do if I did wake them up. I basically stayed away from my family for twenty years because it seemed wherever I went, trouble was sure to follow, but I have good relationships with my family members now, and have tried my best to make amends to people I have harmed, especially my children and ex-wives. Looking back, it's unbelievable how much that boy who molested me screwed up my life. I can truly see now that I really wasn't crazy; I was just a very angry, troubled, and hurt boy.

God loves me; this I do know, and I look forward to the next world, as this one hasn't been all that hot. I don't go to church because there are so many hypocrites, but I do pray almost daily.

I wish I had some great words of inspiration for all of you foster kids out there, but I don't. Just keep on keeping on, and don't drive your car to the top of the bridge.

Wanda Frisbee

My Story...Sad, but True

I was born in 1944 in Arkansas and was just a baby when I was moved to Illinois. My mom was only 15 years old when she married and 16 when she had her first child. There were four of us kids and the whole family lived in two small rooms, in a small town. My mom fell when she was seven months pregnant with her last child and the premature baby had to have special care for awhile, which caused huge medical bills. The financially stressful situation created more and more stress in the family and our home became a battleground between two drunks. I can remember a lot of drinking, hitting, and fighting. One time my dad even cut my mom's eyeball with a knife. I remember it getting so bad that I hid under the kitchen table because I didn't feel safe. I never felt safe there in that home. I always felt like I had to shield myself from the violence. This is when "wall number one" went up around me.

I don't exactly remember when, but sometime when I was between the ages of 5-7 my mom took off, writing a letter to my dad explaining that "we were better off with him because he made better money." My oldest sister, who was ten years old at the time, took on the "mommy" role at that point and cared for me. My dad continued drinking heavily, leaving us unsupervised while he was gone working and drinking.

One day while my dad was gone, somebody, probably a neighbor, called the state Child Welfare Services and turned our family in and we were taken away from our home. I have a very vivid memory of that day. We were taken to the Children's Home of Rockford, Illinois, and I was *so* scared. I just wanted my mom. We were all separated there and I used to talk with my brothers through the door that separated our rooms. I thought I had to be strong for my brothers. I was so hurt and numb that I don't even know how long I was there, but I think it was about one year. There is hardly a word to describe how I felt, but I guess the closest I can come to is to say I was so traumatized. It marks you for life. One day my mom came to visit us at Rockford and told us she wanted all of us kids to stay together and she told me, "make sure you look after your brothers," and she told my older sister to look after all of us. To this day my sister feels guilty.

One day while was talking with my brother through the door, I found out my older sister and younger brother were taken to ISSCS (Illinois Soldiers and Sailors Children School) in Normal, Illinois. I can still remember the social worker, who I called "Mr. Baldie," coming in and informing me that he had found a "nice foster home" for me, and me asking him, "Why are you splitting us up? Why can't I go with them?"

So, when I was about 9 years old, I went to a foster home. They were well-to-do Jewish people and we were the "hired hands" on their dairy farm. She was a slapper, a real hell on wheels, an older woman going through the change of life. He tried sexually abusing me, coming in my dark bedroom and patting me through the bed covers. While I was there I never heard any words of appreciation or got any hugs. This foster home was an experiment in terror. It was like a work camp. I was there about two years, and then when I was about 11 years old, my mom got us all back together for a little over a year. I was "deliriously happy" to be back with my mom. She had remarried and we moved to Texas with her and my step-dad, who had his own trucking company. Things took a turn for the worse, though, when my mom was diagnosed with cancer and due to the high cost of medical bills, by step-dad lost his business, and then it was the same old scenario as before, except this time there wasn't all the fighting; he was just gone all the time and there was never enough food to eat. My step-dad also tried patting me on the bed covers at nighttime and I would run out of bed, go into the bathroom, and lock the door so he couldn't get me.

My older sister had married when she was 16 years old and when my mom became real sick, she knew she was dying, so she sent us back to Illinois to live with her sister (my aunt) until she could get us into ISSCS (Illinois Soldiers and Sailors Children School). She rationalized her decision by telling us that she and our dad never had much of an education and she wanted better for her children and thought we could get a good education at ISSCS. This didn't make the hurt go away, but it did make me understand her little better and what made her do it.

Photo of me in front of ISSCS cottage

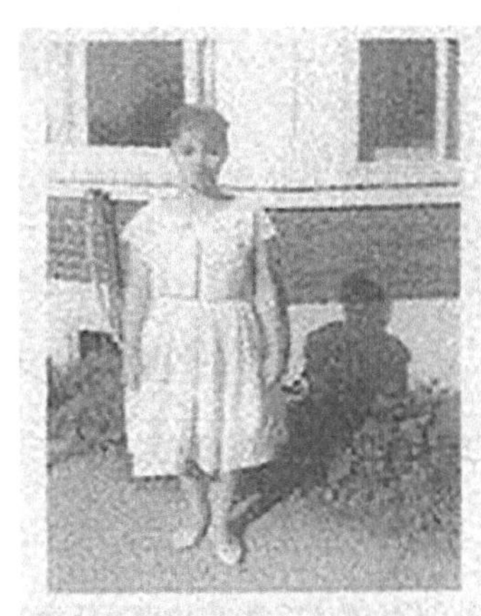

In 1958, when I was 13 years old, I went to ISSCS. I ran away two times while I was there---once after my mom's death and again after my grandma died. I think I just wanted to escape from myself, from my painful feelings. I felt so angry, hurt, and abandoned, but who in the world are you going to talk to about it? I just couldn't suppress my anger and hurt anymore, so I ran away. My dad came to visit me one time while I was there, but he never had a lot to say; he was just floundering about and still drinking heavily. When I was about 16 years old, I asked my dad why he didn't get us back, and his reply was, "I tried to move heaven and earth to get you all back, but your mom would stop it each time she found out." He said her attitude was, "I don't want the kids, but I don't want you to have them either."

ISSCS was a "step-up" from my past homes I'd lived in, even though it was very regimented, like a military school. I needed the structure and stability it gave me. But I still hurt inside. When I seen a psychiatrist there, the psychiatrist told me he could help me and I said, "Unless you can bring my mom back from the dead and make us a family again, I don't think you can help me." I am thankful for ISSCS, but I needed compassion, which they didn't give me there. All they told me was to "be grateful." Crying would have been a luxury there. I left ISSCS to visit with my aunt one summer and since I was 18 years old and of age to leave, I never went back there. The staff tried to get me to return, but I refused. I left ISSCS very scared, not knowing what to do, but I still wanted to leave.

After my dad died of alcoholism (cirrhosis of the liver), I found a letter in his possessions, and I cried when I read it. I was so angry and hurt because I thought my in-laws would take care of us. I felt so abandoned by everybody. I found out that the foster home I was in got in trouble. The social worker was getting a kickback when he put kids in homes where they were worked.

I hated God for a long time. I blamed my parents, then I prayed to God to make us all a family again, and then I blamed God because it never happened. I was very judgmental at one time, not trusting anybody, but I eventually realized that there truly are people who care; you just have to learn to trust again and to love again. There are better days ahead. The hurt, loneliness, and rejection don't last forever. You never forget, but there comes a point in your life when you can put it behind you. I feel my experience made me a stronger person and a better parent to my children.

My sister told me about a story I wrote in 2nd grade about a sofa we had, that she remembered the sofa being ugly and full of big holes, but I wrote about it being beautiful, soft, and cozy. I had to look for the beauty. Everyone tells me that I don't look at life realistically, and I say, "What the heck for? I've had my fill of ugly in my childhood; I would rather look for the beauty in life."

William Cass

Luckier Than Most

I was born in 1922, the oldest of three children. My mother died when I was just 8 years old, and when I was about 9, my dad remarried, but the marriage only lasted about a year. My dad moved us to Flint, Michigan, where he had found a job, but since he was gone working so much, we were left unsupervised most of the time, so my dad decided it would be best to put us in a home for children, the Whaley Home, where we lived for three or four months. Memories of that time are very vague in my mind, except that I know I didn't like the place. By this time I was about 11 years old, my brother Bob was 9, and my sister Cecil was 7.

My dad eventually moved us back to Chicago to live with an aunt and uncle, but that didn't work out very well either, so he started contemplating another home for us. He had heard about the Illinois Soldiers and Sailors Children's School around this time, and even though he knew he would have to sign us over to the state of Illinois, that we would become wards of the state, he decided that it would be better for us. We would at least be well taken care of, which wasn't happening prior to this time.

After a court session on December 5, 1933, we were all taken to ISSCS in Normal, Illinois. I was 11 years old and in sixth grade at the time and up until then I had been in many schools, so now at least I would have stability. The first five to six weeks were hard for me at ISSCS, especially the first week, when I was put in a receiving cottage all alone to be checked for communicable diseases. No one can imagine how I felt being separated from my dad and not knowing what was to come, but you can visualize it. I cried a lot. I cried the whole first week because I felt so all alone, in isolation in the receiving cottage. It's hard to find yourself all alone in the world without parents. I felt like I was just yanked out of society and put in jail, but once I was taken out of the receiving cottage and put in a cottage with other boys, I didn't feel so alone and even began to like the home.

At this time there were approximately 700 boys and girls in the home, so I definitely wasn't alone. Of course I missed my dad, but he did visit me some, so I didn't feel completely abandoned by him. Considering the fact that my dad had lived a very chaotic and hobo-like existence from the ages of 13-28, I think he did the best he could under the circumstances. My aunt and uncle visited me more often than my dad because they lived closer. I recall them taking me to the zoo and bringing me a bushel of pears from their farm. Christmas was a happy time, even though I only got a few gifts. I had no real complaints with ISSCS I was well fed, clothed, educated, and had recreational activities, such as going to the movies, listening to radio programs, playing on the playground trapeze, playing baseball and football, roller skating, sledding, and swimming. Although the boys had their share of fights and arguments, most of the time we got along, if for no other reason than to avoid punishment, which might involve doing squats, duck-waddling, laying on the basement floor with our nose to a crack, restriction, and missing meals. If a boy became extremely rebellious he was fostered out to a farm as a farm hand. Life at ISSCS was very regimented, but I looked at it as being stabilizing for me. We all had chores to do, which included vegetable gardening in the summer.

My sister left ISSCS after her 8th grade graduation to live in a foster home because there wasn't enough room on girl's row to house all of the older girls, but I remained there through high school. Right after graduation, I went to live in a foster home in Springfield, Illinois for one year while I attended Illinois Business College. I had mixed feelings about leaving ISSCS because high school was one of the most enjoyable periods of my life, but there were several other boys from ISSCS who went there with me, so I didn't leave everyone behind, and the foster parents were real nice (I called them uncle Tilden and aunt Susie). I was given a clothing allowance and $10 a month spending allowance, which although doesn't seem like much now, was a big increase over what I had previously, which was less than $50 for the total time spent at ISSCS. I bought a bicycle with some of this saved cash and rode it all over town in the summer of 1940 and I also rode it to college. While I was a student at IBC, I would meet my uncle Bud Scheffler and ride out to a farm where I had cousins. Over the years the Scheffler family and the foster family took the place of my parents, which I am grateful for. Not everybody is that lucky.

I was placed at my first job as a timekeeper and stock clerk at an electrical company and was thrilled to get my first pay check. I was on my own from this point on, but I roomed with a good friend of mine from ISSCS. I felt prepared to be on my own; I was comfortable and confident. After about 21/2 years of working as a timekeeper, I was given an accountant position, and then I joined the Navy when I was 20 years old. I was in the Navy for four years, got back out for four years, then went back in for four years (I was in the Reserves), becoming an instructor for yoeman.

After I got out of the Navy in 1953, I became involved in church and worked myself up in the ministry, eventually traveling around as an evangelist. Looking back, I realize that something from the church services I attended at ISSCS influenced my decision to be involved in the ministry, even though I never made a spiritual commitment during my seven years at ISSCS. I moved around a lot, and I married three times and have four children. I had to divorce my first wife due to her infidelity, and my second wife died. As I write this, I am 88 years old and am still living with my third wife.

I realize that children these days have it a lot worse than I did. I was fortunate to be put in ISSCS and given opportunities. Times have changed, though, and there aren't as many children's homes available, leaving most children forced to be put in foster homes. My prayer for these children today from broken homes is that they find happy foster homes with loving people who care for them, so that they can have a successful future. They deserve that.

Anonymous

No Family

I decided to share some emails I sent to Carol Lucas instead of writing an actual story, as it reveals my innermost feelings better. She had saved them. When you read them you might understand why I am anonymous. Here they are:

Hi, I wanted to write when I first got your email and then the computer erased my entire message and I just went to bed. Fatigue is a big aspect of my life with the kids by myself. I haven't had the time to write since. My isolation is painful and difficult, more so because I DO have kids alone, not because I DON'T have kids. Before I had kids I had time and space to express myself and my journey through my emotions, and I was only materially responsible for me. The isolation had little material impact compared to my situation now. With kids, the material circumstances, the impact of poverty, is very, very related to not having any family at all. In the political system of Canada if you don't have family and you have kids or are a single parent, you need some relatives. So it's had a very painful impact on my kids. We live in severe poverty, and when something happens there is no one's couch to sleep on if homeless. Once I had to be hospitalized and my son had to go into foster care because there was no family to take care of him. Even that I had to advocate for because there was no abuse. They wouldn't take him initially; they couldn't actually comprehend that there was really no family at all. If I have no food, there is no relative, whether we get along or not; they don't exist in my life, to get milk or anything else from, no co-signors, nothing. Every single thing, and the single things are accumulated by a trillion after becoming a parent, is done and experienced completely alone. There is no security in my life. No child care, no support, no fallback when things go wrong. Even when I am sick the kids have missed school because there is no one else to take them to school. Unless I pay for help no one exists in our lives. The loneliness without having personal space since I have no child care, is worse, as I cannot do anything by myself; I cannot even work hours I would otherwise work, due to child care, and even if I want to talk to someone about a show, or TV program or just an idea, there's just no one to call. People I've met are busy with their families, even the ones where there is abuse or other problems in their families, and they are unavailable outside designated times when I see them at a specific meeting, for example. In Toronto people's lines between friends (?) and family are very, very distinct. And people get scared off, too, by my reality and the impact of this family isolation on my life. I think it scares them to consider these types of realities.

Hi, I am so glad to hear from you. You are the first person outside of two therapists I have had who actually did not get scared off or freaked out by both the fact and the impact of my not having any family in my life. That's why I was so happy when I found your site. I had spent years of entering different internet searches trying to find information on others in this situation. I only found a few articles from England about the likelihood of homelessness, as well as depression from isolation, etc. when there is significant family loss. The loneliness is overwhelming. I sometimes find myself calling my ex (to him I am not an ex, but a mistake equivalent to a one-night stand, after almost ten years of what I thought was together), who stated and demonstratively dislikes me and never loved me, just to hear another voice when I have something to share. Like two days ago, I got a call back for a job interview, the first job I've applied for since I started job hunting since things changed with my ex and I, and it was so exciting and encouraging, and I wanted to share my joy with someone. A day later I discovered ways I could reenter school, even at the Graduate level, and I also wanted to share this. I called him and told him. He was completely invalidating and demeaning, and in the middle of his response, I remembered this is the reality with him. And I knew before I called him, but I just wanted a voice on the other end of the line to share it with. Because I've known him for more than a decade, he's the only one who has know me over a period of time, as I have no contact with anyone from my childhood or anything, so without anyone else there over time, and no pictures from my childhood or anything, he's the closest thing to someone to reflect me having any history and my development as an adult, and that one person unfortunately is someone like him. So I refrain from calling more and more, but then I'm sitting at home alone, watching the phone, watching the computer, and knowing there's no one there at all. The desolation and isolation is overwhelming. I wish sometimes I could numb it out. Just numb it out. Like I said, I've never been able to share this with a non-professional, so it's coming out in huge waves in my email to you. I hope that's ok. It's so nice to just have the experience validated. Usually people ask, "What do you mean there's no family?" And they keep going down the family options---"What about a cousin, and aunt, an uncle, etc." Or asking "Do I mean I have family, but I don't get along with them?" It's a very hard concept for people to consider. It's too scary. And then of course the final realization of what I mean, and that if there's no family it's likely due to something very severe. I know I somehow have to resolve both the reality of my childhood, and the degree of abuse and neglect, and the consequential isolation now as an adult. I just don't know where to begin. I've resolved so many other experiences of my life, but that part remains. I think the isolation now is a reminder, a daily and loud reminder, of the absolute abandonment of myself as a human being from those who were the ones expected to care for me. And though I am learning to love myself, I still seem unworthy to all others to love as well. Thank you, Thank you, Thank you, for being an ear. It's a small break in the midst of this heavy silence and pain. And a tremendous gift that I think I'm just responding to like a bottle of pop that's overflowing just after being opened. Thank you.

Not much has changed on my end. I'm still single, still living in poverty, raising two kids who both have disabilities---same stuff. I have no pragmatic structure to fall back on without family, and without a husband, in a culture where kinship definitions are very limited, by blood alone, and sometimes not even that. Most other non-western cultures are not like that. I don't have much positive to say. I've been hoping to find a life partner, open myself up to that recently since my separation years ago, but that's turning out to be a challenge. Most people are very superficial (it could be the city I'm in); they don't want to connect deeper. My world views tend to be very out of sync with north American popular culture, additively so because I have multiple cultures in my background, so I'm still in culture shock, permanent culture shock (laugh…not funny actually; it's painful and isolating). I'm still here; live, as my kids need me. I just hoped to satisfy other aspects to me than motherhood, but it's impossible to do in poverty and isolation (no child care, etc.). I moved just outside Toronto for affordable housing, but everything else is more expensive, there aren't any free events for kids, or anyone, and I need a car. Anyway, I won't go on. I wish I had something wonderful to tell you. I can only speak my actual experience. I hope you're doing well. I think, I know, FACT is much needed. It'll help many people know in an actual way that at least they're not alone in their experience, even if pragmatically they're alone. Take care, and thanks so much for remembering me, and writing. I often think that I could live my life and pass away and no one but my kids will remember I even existed.

Cynthia Stephens

The Long Way Home

My name is Cynthia and I am a former foster child. I am a survivor to say the least! I was removed from my single parent at the age of 4 and stayed in foster care until I was 18, after the death of my sister, who was 16 months younger than me. I don't think people believe children that age know what's going on around them, but I am here to tell you we do. Maybe we don't know all of it in details but it's affecting us. I have some memories burned into my very soul. I remember my sister's funeral. I remember asking why she had on lipstick and I was shushed. I never got an answer, but now I know of course.

My youngest brother was malnutritioned by this time, so something needed to be done. Something was done all right. The adults in our lives had failed so we were taken. I remember so vividly sitting in a car in the front of our three room apartment with this strange woman I didn't know. My mom was getting out of the car and we were still in there. I wanted to get out and go with my mom and my brother held me back. I remember screaming and looking at my mother as if to say "get me outta here," but she just stood there crying. I remember sitting in the driveway of another house and we were allowed to get out, but my other two brothers stayed in the second car and didn't get out. I asked my brother why and he said they were not staying, and I started to run towards the car and my brother caught me, and again I started screaming and crying, calling for them. I could see their tear streaked faces. My eldest brother was put with us two younger kids and the other two were taken some place else. I didn't see them again for a very long time. When I did, I didn't remember there faces. I was in this home for 8 years.

Eventually I noticed I didn't fit the mold of the other children. I only had a momma and she wasn't really my momma. Where was my momma? Five years later she came back, but she had not changed so we could go back with her. She soon disappeared again.

My first foster mother was an elderly woman and at age 75 she became disabled and could not care for us. I was 10 by this time so I took care of her, bathing her and cleaning her up after she potted like a baby, until she passed away. I cooked and cleaned and looked after my little brother as best as a 10 year old could do. My mother… well she was no where to be found.

Before I tell you more, I have to let you know so you can understand the story. The next home was with some relatives. We knew them; they were familiar people in our lives. We were with them often. Anyway, I turned 13 and went away for summer vacation to my great aunt's house in the country as I had done when I was in the previous home.

Well when I came back, so did a lie! My world started spinning and it was spinning downward…fast! Well as you know, teenagers lie; they never tell the truth, especially 'those foster kids.' This is what was in the mind of the caring adults in my life. I was not a liar and no one had ever known me to lie, so why now? Well, the plot thickens, and I won't go into details; it would take too long, but my dear, for reasons I can't speak of, I was taken out of this home.

I was on my way to another home in less than a year, and without my brother. We were all we had in common. The foster mother in this home sat me down and specifically said to me, "DON'T GO NEAR MY HUSBAND!" Now why would she say that? The lies had gone with me. I don't remember seeing the lie, but it must have sneaked into my suitcase, because that was all I had, a suitcase.

This home was like going from riches to rags. It looked like it had once been a gas station. The concrete slab was still in the front. The front of the house was screened in, but it was make shift, put together by a self proclaimed builder. The back was the same, screened in by this same builder. There were three other foster kids there and one biological child. At this junction I had became Cinderella to the third power. Whatever I said was a lie straight from hell. So I stopped talking about anything. The hatred inside of me began to build. It got so strong that I became consumed with it. I had almost forgotten I had a little brother out there. I could not go see him, nor could I call him. I was far removed from anyone and everything I knew. This is where I became a real, in your face, foster kid. It wasn't as prevalent before, though I knew. But now, each time I was introduced, I was introduced as 'my foster child,' Cynthia. Before, I was always introduced as Anthony's sister by his father, Anthony being my youngest brother. It used to make me cry, so it stopped. But then I was just 'Cynthia,' not my daughter. So it still didn't give me a sense of belonging. As a foster child, you really don't belong anywhere. People are just getting paid to keep you in their house. I say 'house' because they never felt like a home. My youngest brother's father finally called me his baby girl on his death bed when I was in my mid-thirties, and I can not explain in words the emotional uproar that caused. I finally belonged to someone! Writing this just brings those same emotions to surface again. School had always been hard for me, but now I didn't care. I just went to keep from staying home. I slept in class all the time, everyday. I was a loner; I would not connect with anyone. I had a couple of girls I would allow myself to be in there company with, but I really didn't fit. I put on a happy face when I needed to so I wouldn't be questioned. At the house I would laugh until I cried. Every time. I became a hysterical laugher. It worked. No one every asked me why I was crying. So I was hidden. I would write notes to myself and then tear them up. I stayed in this home for 5 years. It was not an easy 5 years. In this house I experienced jealousy, envy, mental abuse, some physical abuse. I was beaten over the head with the bible. Remember, everything I said was a lie, so I had to read this Bible verse everyday about liars. I tried to commit suicide twice while I was here, and failed. After I turned 18 I left. I was smart enough to secure another place for myself to stay, at least until I finished high school.

I moved in with my biological father's sister. I stayed quiet, did chores, and went to school. I was still sleeping in class. This was yet another school for me to adapt to and I refused to. I did not want to conform anymore. I was tired. So I did what I needed to do. One of my cousins took me under her wing....at least so I thought. Wherever you saw her, you saw me. I was starting to feel like someone actually cared. Wrong!!!!! When I graduated high school, no one showed up for my graduation. I was alone in my celebration. Only God knows how I finished! When summer was over, I was dropped off at college and left, never to hear from anyone again.

That did it. That sent me over the edge. I realized that no one cared and no one would ever care and I could not trust anyone with my feeling ever again in life. I was always let down. There was no more room for hope. So after two years of trying to be a college student, I hit the streets. I didn't care what happened to me. Who was I going to make proud of me? I was spiraling deeper into the rabbit hole and did not know how, or even want, for that matter, to get out. I did whatever I wanted to do and did not care what anyone thought of it. I carried hatred around with me like a cloak for a very, very, very long time. I am going to end my story right here, but let me tell you, the strong arm of God pulled me out, and today I am a mother, grandmother, business woman, and author on a small scale. I still have emotional hurdles but I take it one day at a time.

Mandy

Still Needy

I have intentions of completing my own book, an autobiography/novel, but having come across the FACT website and becoming friends with Carol Lucas, decided to share my story in this book. Perhaps sharing my story will help relieve my writer's block, enabling me to eventually complete my book. It isn't easy to share such painful memories, but for the benefit of myself and others, I will. Galatians 6:2 in the Bible says: "Bear one another's burdens, and so fulfill the law of Christ." I like to believe that by former foster children sharing our experience, strength, and hope with each other we are doing this.

I was in the foster care system twice as a child---the first time at the age of 16, during the time my mother had been sent to a psychiatric hospital, and the second time at the age of 13, when I was kicked out onto the street on a cold winter's night just before Christmas. This was the last time I lived with my mother.

The years in between the two foster care experiences were painful and humiliating as I came to terms with mother's mental demise, starvation for up to 3-4 days at a time, bullying, unlawful beatings with blunt objects that drew blood from head wounds, scratches on necks, fractured limbs, and being chucked down flights of stairs, passing out at school, and experiencing further bullying due to being generally dirty, thin, and not looked after. I was also harboring a genetic medical condition which accelerated the speed of my decline without the right medical help. Having to walk miles to school in this condition, with holes at the bottom of my shoes so large that my shoes were a mere cover for the top of my feet, I was walking on the bare ground feeling every pebble, flex, and stone. I decided that charging out after school was the best way to avoid being home to face the explosion of violence and trauma, so I would visit friends' homes and hope to God that their parents would offer me food, and if not, I stole it, or 20 pence if I could find it, to buy biscuits.

I was placed with a lady who had no interest in children, but only what she could gain from the system in making her home the best kept home on the street. The rest, really, is the story of either Annie or Cinderella. We (me and the other foster kids) were made modern day slaves to keep her house pristine clean, under the ever watchful, critical eye of our carer, making sure every surface was highly polished and all the chores in the house were completed. Cleaning came before our homework or exam revisions. Since we were foster children we were blamed a lot, and had an awful lot of emotional baggage dumped on us. We were accused, publically humiliated, and sentenced heavily for minor things.

There were repeated incidents and reminders that we arrived with black bin liners, and we would be put out the gate if we put a foot wrong. We lived in fear of doing or saying the wrong thing. Our wrong doings became public knowledge within our foster carer's circle of friends, who would mock us in front of us and behind our backs; even personal things that mattered only to a developing 13 year old girl became public knowledge. We were jeered at and regarded as second class citizens. Everything we did wrong was mocked and criticized in front of strangers. It later turned out that this carer was more sinister than I had known, which couldn't be disclosed then, but had to be alerted to the authorities in the future.

I left under a depressive cloud on a dark night after I was told that my foster carer's 18 year old stone body builder son-in-law should have thumped me in the face after I offered to speak with him when I noticed something was wrong. I was so ashamed to be a foster child through my school years. It was my best kept secret until I was made to feel the size of an ant when I was forced against my wishes to appear in the newspaper, smiling happily with my foster mother to publicize the achievements of her as a carer, which won me a MBF award from HRH and gained front page press coverage. She played 'happy families' with me in the public eye as she usually did, and there I was answering questions from school colleagues, having to explain why I had been on the front page picture of a popular national newspaper. Her award was given in error and was so far from the truth. We knew this was a major oversight.

Through my late teenage years and as an adult I endlessly tried to fit into the glove of my own family that really wasn't interested in helping my mother. They sat by and watched her suffer with two children, and paid no visits to her in the mental institution or to us as fostered children.

I tried desperately to be included, and wanting the sense of belonging to my own family was very strong. I bought them gifts with my grant money as I studied hard to be a student, and I kept up visits, but it was not reciprocated. So I realized I had no place to belong.

My friends became my family. They all had a drive to be better, so naturally we all pursued a career through education and studied hard at degree level. I continued on to achieve my Masters degree. The importance of acceptance and being in a fold was a really big thing. The safest way for me to have someone next to me who cared was to always be in a relationship. I was never single from the ages of 14-21. I was exposed too early to relationships (although school age relationships were not real relationships, just simple teeny bopper boy loves girl high school stuff), yet my interest in boys was merely out of the need to be loved and cared about. Believe it or not, throughout this period I developed a faith in God, and although not perfect, and constantly falling away, I made a firm decision to allow Christ into my life and to walk with Jesus at the age of 21.

With Jesus Christ in my life I didn't need men to feel loved, and I felt warmth and healing from my church family. I later married and began a family of my own. My faith has been keeping me through all the moments I feel I will fold when I think back to the time of all my graduations. They were attended by friends and major hospital admissions due to my illness were looked after by friends. Advice about important future decisions were inspired because I had friends close by; inspiration and hopes for the future were shared with friends. When friends weren't there and I knew I needed a family, those were the coldest moments to face as an ex foster child. Those moments met with desperation, depression, abandonment, feelings of helplessness, rejection, a wasted life, and suicide, and actively trying to end my life.

As an adult who has been fostered:

* I find that others will override my motherly decisions if my decisions do not match theirs. Since I wasn't tenderly raised, my views on how I raise my children are not equally respected.

* People wonder why I rarely speak of my family or why I suddenly speak about a brother I had never mentioned before.

* The constant need to have a healthy balance of my in-laws and my own family who are absent in my life leaves me with no other option but to call help or prayer lines for comfort.

* Being the bate of snubbing by others, as they often think I have no mother or father or family to back me up, makes me an easy target for someone to mistreat

* I am extremely overly sensitive to being mistreated so unfairly.

* Where I live, being fostered is seen as a taboo word and people automatically assume 'what on earth could I have done to be placed in foster care.' There is *still* limited understanding in some communities, where people do not see that perfectly well behaved kids can and do end up in the care of social services due to their home circumstances.

In the past I have battled with insecurity and low self-esteem, but my faith has helped me to feel valued. In the face of it all, by God's grace I know I have triumphed through some very difficult moments. I am proud of who I am and proud to know I have overcome so many obstacles.

Through my marriage and my faith I have found some peace, but there is *still* that void. As great and wonderful as moving on with life can be, life *still* brings its ups and downs. Even at this age I find myself still looking for that someone who would take me under their wing, *still* in need of that shoulder to cry on, and when the going gets tough I *still* need a mother, and even find myself searching for a mother figure to be at the end of the phone when life has its way with me. I *still* need a caring, unbiased blood related hand in my life that will not take sides. I *still* need that person who can lovingly share the joy of my kids with them as their own. My faith has kept me through these moments of despair and the scars of the past. I know somehow I will feel completed. That is something I still pray for, and eagerly await.

I Was, I Am, a Foster Child

A dysfunctional family is shunned upon,
So the court steps in to get things done.
Our family grew up in different towns;
Siblings not knowing where
The others could be found.
Life in a "home" is not the greatest,
Dysfunction still remains prevalent.
To be made fun of and ridiculed really hurts,
Self-esteem hits the bottom and pride is non-existent.
So what is a foster child to do?
Don't give up, somehow find the way,
Let your Spirit take a stand within your life today.
Sometimes defiance and definitely loss of pride,
Is not the answer to heal your heart inside.
I found by writing my feelings out,
I was able to learn what I am about.
Past situations never go away,
They seem to haunt my soul every day.
The journey I am on is never ending,
I must guard my soul with all my strength.
If I lose myself to others, they win not I,
Relating to the Lord's journey helps when I cry.
When a child grows up with nothing,
Pain is welcome to own.
Releasing the pain seems to mean I will return to nothing,
Yet as long as I carry the pain, in this cage I will remain.
Tiny steps of courage lead me back to life again,
I have learned to open my palms to the sun.
Warmth of God's love penetrates the acid rain,
In giving to another, love blossoms from my heart.
I have learned I am God's child, chosen, in life to remain.
This effort has been my journey most of my life,
Now I hold my head high as I walk by your side.
I have learned to reach out my hand in love and in trust,
In doing so, I have discovered there are many of us.

©Patricia Kenyon 2013

Part Two

Documents for FACT Support Group

Fostered Adult Children Together

On the Bridge to Healing

Stepping Forward

One Stepping Stone at a Time

Our Mission

FACT is an alliance of adults who as children lived in foster care. We seek support and mutual understanding of our unique problems in coping with life and learning how to find our place in the world. We are self-supporting, and believing in spiritual principles, but unaffiliated with any religion. Our hope and purpose, we believe, is that by gathering together we will end our isolation and give each other courage, strength and hope in recovering from our unique issues. The mission of FACT is to help former foster children walk a new path that will build a bridge to healing.

Our Unique Issues

Many of us have found that as former foster children we have several characteristics in common. Having been separated from our biological parents, we developed many emotional problems that have complicated our relationships with other people. We have trouble trusting others; therefore we find it extremely difficult to bond with people. Much of this is due to the fact that we were moved around so often from home to home. This instability causes other emotional difficulties.

As adults many of us have become isolated individuals who are terrified of intimacy. We feel very different and alone. For many of us this leads to an unhealthy sense of self-sufficiency and independence. We adopt the attitude that we don't need others because of fear, due to our childhood experiences, which taught us that we could not depend on other people. Because many of our dependency needs were not met as children, we also tend to go to the other extreme and become overly dependent adults. Many former foster children suffer from the turmoil of either desperately wanting relationships and doing anything to hold on to them, or being too independent out of fear of emotional investment and possible rejection.

As former foster children we never developed a strong sense that we belonged anywhere, that we had a home. Many of us live unsettled lives as a result of this instability. We want to feel as if we fit in somewhere, but have a hard time feeling comfortable anywhere. We tend to alternate between the extreme of being terrified of change and feeling as if we must have change. Many of us compulsively seek change in order to survive the past trauma of having had the foundation of our lives repeatedly ripped out from beneath us at a moment's notice.

Our experiences as foster children left us with an overall sense of insecurity about ourselves and the world around us. We feel alienated in our own world, a world that is rightfully ours, but from which we feel separated. As former foster children we feel the stigma of that label and have much shame.

Foster children have suffered many losses during their childhood and therefore have serious grieving issues. Many foster children have problems with depression, largely because of our unresolved grieving issues.

Due to the trauma and instability in our lives, many foster children are prone to having an Adult Attachment Disorder, Adult Separation Anxiety Disorder and/or Post Traumatic Stress Disorder.

A good book to read about relationships is WHY YOU DO THE THINGS YOU DO by DR. TIM CLINTON and DR. GARY SIBCY.

Our Collective Experience

There are currently about 500,000 children in the foster care system in the U.S. and 88,000 in Canada.

Many former foster children:

- Have problems with stability because we were moved so many times, usually from town to town and sometimes from state to state

- As adults change vocations on average every six months and change types of vocations far more often than the general population

- Work at low-paying minimum-wage jobs

- Don't get high-school diplomas but obtain GED certificates five to ten years later

- Report cases of sexual abuse, usually by relatives and friends of the foster parents

- Report cases of physical and emotional abuse

- Suffer from low self-esteem and confidence, especially between the ages of eighteen and twenty-eight

- Have stress disorders that appear around twenty-eight years of age

- Often have poor social interactions; friendships, even long-term ones, are usually on and off due to instability, moving around a lot, changing vocations and psychological stress

- Have difficulty bonding with other people

- Have emotional turmoil with personal relationships

- Question their parenting abilities

- Have trouble managing their finances and budgeting their money

- Haven't had solid role models and therefore lack a good understanding of social roles and social expectations

- Struggle with guilt and shame because we feel as if we must be bad people in order for our parents and foster parents to have abused, neglected, and/or rejected us

- Suffer from Adult Attachment Disorder

- Suffer from Adult Separation Anxiety Disorder

- Suffer from Post-Traumatic Stress Disorder (PTSD) and feel frozen in the past, afraid to move forward and strive for a better life

- Have problems with depression, largely because of our unresolved grieving issues

- Are homeless (currently at least 25% of the homeless population are former foster children)

- Are at least 30% more prone to alcohol and substance abuse than the general population

- Are inmates in our prison system (at least two out of three according to conservative estimates)

- Are 50% more likely to have a history of domestic violence than the overall population

- As heads of households have already lost at least one child to foster care

- Are four times more likely to be sexually abused than children in the general population

If you are a former foster child you could benefit from reading the document on Post Traumatic Stress Disorder and Trauma and Recovery, Adult Attachment Disorder, and Adult Separation Anxiety Disorder. You could also read the FACT document, which elaborates on statistics concerning former foster children.

The Ten Stepping Stones Healing

The mission of FACT is to help former foster children walk a new path that will build a bridge to healing. The **First Stepping Stone** on this path is to recognize we have been injured from our foster care experience, that we are powerless over our past and our lives are unmanageable. The **Second Stepping Stone** is to come to realize we can not heal alone, that only a Power greater than ourselves could restore order, hope, and sanity to our lives. The **Third Stepping Stone** is to make a decision to turn our lives over to the care of God as we understand Him. The **Fourth Stepping Stone** is to make a searching and fearless emotional inventory of our foster care experience to discover the nature of the damage. The **Fifth Stepping Stone** is to share this inventory with God and another human being. The **Sixth Stepping Stone** is to work through our anger, hurt, and pain. The **Seventh Stepping Stone** is to become aware of how our injuries hurt others and accept responsibility for our responses to the trauma we suffered. The **Eighth Stepping Stone** is to continue to take personal inventory and become willing to let go of our resentments. The **Ninth Stepping Stone** is to seek through prayer and meditation to improve our relationship with God was we understand Him, praying only for knowledge of His will for us and the power to carry that out. The **Tenth Stepping Stone** is to have a spiritual awakening as a result of these Stepping Stones, to reach out to other former foster children, and practice these principles in our lives.

The Ten Stepping Stones

The **First Stepping Stone** is to recognize that we have been **injured from our foster care experience, that we are powerless over** our past and our lives are unmanageable. It is stated "**We** recognize that **we** have been injured from our foster care experience that **we** are powerless over **our** past and **our** lives are unmanageable. Notice the word '**we**' is mentioned three times and the word '**our**' twice. This is important. '**We**' and '**our**' are plural, meaning we are a collective group of people. We are not alone. This is a very important point, since foster children often feel so isolated and alone. How comforting it is to finally realize '**we**' are not alone, that there are thousands of other former foster children who have had the same similar or exact experiences as '**we**' have. It is called **Fostered Adult Children Together** for a reason---'**we**' Fostered Adult Children are '**Together.**'

Now that '**we**' has been established, I want to elaborate on the first part of the First Stepping Stone, which states "We recognize we have been injured from our foster care experience." In order to do this, we must first acknowledge that we were in foster care. Some people believe that the only kind of foster care is when you are a state ward and live in a state-funded foster home, but there are actually different forms of foster care. There is relative foster care, when a child is cared for by an aunt and/or uncle, grandparents, or even an older sibling, sometimes not even being paid by the state for their fostering. There are group homes, where many children are being cared for. There are children homes, where children live in cottages according to age and gender and are cared for by cottage parents. And there are orphanages. To be 'fostered' means 'to be cared for,' so anytime a child is being cared for by anyone other than his or her natural parents, he or she is being fostered. Obviously, if we don't believe we were a foster child, we won't believe we need any healing, so it is important that we recognize that we were foster children, as it is what lays the foundation for us to walk across the 'bridge to healing.'

Now that the fact that we were foster children has been established, I want to elaborate on recognizing that we have been injured from our foster care experience. Many former foster children, especially those whose circumstances were severe, will probably have no doubt that they were injured by their foster care experience, but others, whose circumstances weren't as severe, may question that they have been hurt. And then for some there may be denial, regardless of the severity. Sometimes our foster care experience is just too painful to deal with, so we deny or minimize the hurt. We might say, "Well, I wasn't really a foster child because I was with my aunt and uncle," or "I wasn't really affected by foster care, as I was only in there one year," or "I know I was injured, but it could have been much worse." There are all kinds of different scenarios of foster care and there is always somebody out there who had it worse or better than us, but it isn't good to compare too much with others, as it prevents us from looking at our own issues, working through them, and healing. In order to heal, we need to come out of denial and look at the truth, as that is what will set us free. If there is any doubt in your mind that you were affected by foster care, I suggest you look at *Our Collective Experience* or *FACT* in the literature, as they state things that former foster children have in common, such as homelessness, poverty, lack of education, relationship struggles, *PTSD (Post Traumatic Stress Disorder), AAD (Adult Attachment Disorder), ASAD (Adult Separation Anxiety Disorder),* sexual abuse issues, etc. Have you ever experienced any of these things? Are you experiencing any of these things now? It should become clear to us after reading the lists whether or not we were injured.

If we can see that we have been injured, we should be able to recognize whether or not we are powerless over our pasts and our lives are unmanageable, which is the last part of the First Stepping Stone. It should be fairly easy to recognize that we are powerless over our past, as we didn't have the power as children to change anything about our foster care experience, and we are powerless to change anything about it now. But the one thing we can change is our attitude about it, by using these Ten Stepping Stones as a guide. And as for our lives being unmanageable, it is easy to see if we are homeless, but other things creating unmanageability might not be so easy to recognize. Many former foster children are so used to experiencing bad things that they don't realize how bad they really have it. When you are used to poverty, you might not realize how poverty stricken you are, or how much better you could have it. A BIG issue for foster children is a lack of self-worth and self-esteem. In order to have self-esteem we need to have a sense of self-worth, a fundamental sense that we are worth something, that we are worth loving and caring for, not just by others, but more importantly, by ourselves. It is harder to have reciprocal love when we don't love ourselves first. Many foster children have been so love deprived that they don't feel worthy of anything good, but in reality, we are all children of a loving Father and we are all worthy of His love and blessings.

ALL foster children have been traumatized to some degree, whether we fully realize it or not. Many former foster children suffer from *PTSD (Post Traumatic Stress Disorder)*. In fact, according to research, foster children suffer from *PTSD* twice as much as war veterans! When you take into consideration that we were taken out of traumatic situations and often put in to more traumatic situations, it shouldn't come as any surprise that so many of suffer from *PTSD*.

Another big issue for former foster children is relationship struggles, which is discussed in '*Our Unique Issues*,' and which could be classified as *AAD (Adult Attachment Disorder)*. Most of us either cling to people for dear life, even when they aren't good for us, or go to the other extreme, becoming super independent, believing we don't need anybody. Often we vacillate between the two extremes. Our fears of abandonment are such that we are very clingy and needy, or we're so afraid of needing anybody that we don't depend on anybody. Underneath this is a hurt child who desperately wants to be loved and cared for.

And then there is *ASAD (Adult Separation Anxiety Disorder)*, which many former foster children also have. Do you get separation anxiety when you are away from your loved ones or worry excessively about their welfare, for fear of losing them? It is not uncommon for former foster children to have terrifying fears of abandonment, and is it any wonder why? Being taken away from parents, no matter how neglectful, abusive, or poverty stricken they might have been, is still very traumatic for a child; in fact, it is the worst thing that a child can experience, and we foster children experienced it. Our whole worlds turned upside down when we entered foster care and some of us, depending on our age, might have thought we wouldn't survive without our parents, that we would die. This is very traumatic for children.

Sexual abuse is another big issue for former foster children, and unfortunately a very common one. There is a lot of shame associated with sexual abuse and therefore it is not an easy topic to address, but when we face it we will have less shame about it and feel freer. Sometimes the abuse has been suppressed or repressed because it was so traumatic, but the unconscious remembers and the memory gets stored in our body. People who have been physically abused by being beaten can also react this way.

We could have many problems due to our foster care experience, but because our lives have always been at least somewhat unmanageable, we might not recognize how unmanageable they really are. If you are in denial about how unmanageable your life is as a result of being in foster care, a good suggestion is to observe other people and families for a comparison. Although there is no such thing as a perfectly functional person or family, most have not experienced the trauma that former foster children have. Admission of this will end up being a firm foundation upon which our lives will be happy and purposeful. Only through a complete realization about our powerlessness over the past are we able to take our first step toward liberation and move on to the Second Stepping Stone.

The **Second Stepping Stone** is to come to realize we can not heal alone, that only a Power greater than ourselves could restore order, hope, and sanity to our lives.

The first part of this Stepping Stone is 'to come to realize we can not heal alone,' which we obviously have done at least to some degree by coming to FACT. Probably the main reason we were drawn to FACT was a desire to end our isolation, which is a huge step, one that will help us to ease our loneliness, shame, and pain and walk the bridge to healing. Together we realize we don't have to carry the burden of our past alone, that there are others out there who have experienced the same things we have and understand our pain. What a wonderful and comforting feeling it is to finally realize this. The FACT itself states this: Fostered Adult Children 'TOGETHER.'

The second part of this Stepping Stone says 'that only a Power greater than ourselves could restore order, hope, and sanity to our lives.' Nobody is telling us who or what this "Higher Power' is, only that we need to rely on something greater than ourselves. Some of us won't believe in God, others can't, and others who do believe in God don't have the faith that He or She will perform this miracle of restoring order, hope, and sanity in their life. Take it easy, relax, nobody is demanding or dictating that you believe anything. All of these Ten Stepping Stones are only suggestions and guidelines. For some former foster children their 'higher power' might just be the people in FACT and for others it might be what religion calls 'God.' This simple, but wise saying is enlightening: "I sought my God, but He eluded me, I sought my soul but my soul I could not see, I sought my brother and found all three." I believe what this is saying is that God is in everyone and we are all connected to each other through Him. By former foster children gathering together, we are giving God a chance to speak through us for the purpose of each other's healing. Many people might cross the threshold by making the FACT group their higher power and then once across, their faith might broaden and deepen.

We have already recognized in the 1st Stepping Stone that we have been injured from our foster care experience and for most former foster children it will probably be clear that their lives before and during foster care did not have much, if any, order, hope, or sanity. This is not to say that we are insane, only that the circumstances of our lives were. If we were taken out of disorderly homes and possibly put in an even more disorderly homes or homes, it should be clear to us that there wasn't much order or sanity in our lives as children. For most of us we felt like our lives were tossed around in the wind. As for hope, many of us had very little, if any, depending on the severity of our circumstances. For many foster children, their lives are like roller coaster rides---they get their hopes up only to have them dashed again, until they lose all hope.

Now that we recognize the hopeless instability we had as foster children, how do restore order, sanity, and hope? The word 'restore' implies we once had these things and often we didn't, so how can we restore something we never had? Again, I suggest you observe other people and families who are at least somewhat stable, 'functional' if you will, and you should begin to see what you lost. The word 'lost' also implies you had it at one time, and maybe you did to some degree, but even if you didn't have any stability, you deserved it as much as any other child does and didn't have it, therefore, it is a loss. It may bring great sadness and grief to realize how bad our childhoods were, but it is important to see this, otherwise we won't make the connection between our lives as children and our lives as adults, which might still be unstable.

As I suggested in the 1st Stepping Stone for your validation of being injured, if there are doubts as to how our pasts as foster children have affected our adult lives, read 'Our Collective experience.' If you are homeless, incarcerated, or addicted to drugs and/or alcohol, it shouldn't be hard to see how unstable your life is, but for others whose circumstances aren't that severe, it might be more difficult to recognize. Do you have problems with stability, always moving around from place to place, and/or job to job? Do you have relationship problems? I suggest you read *'Our Unique Issues,'* which discusses this, the documents on *AAD (Adult Attachment Disorder)* and *ASAD (Adult Separation Anxiety Disorder).* Do you suffer from depression and anxiety? These are symptoms of *PTSD,* which is very common with former foster children due to the trauma we suffered.

Once we begin to accept how we have been affected by foster care, and that we need a Higher Power to help us heal, we can move on to the 3rd Stepping Stone.

The **Third Stepping Stone** is to turn our lives over to the care of God as we understand Him.

In the 2nd Stepping Stone we came to realize that only a Power greater than ourselves could help us heal and now we are hopefully ready to take this a step further to the 3rd Stepping Stone.

First of all, let me emphatically express this: FACT IS NOT RELIGIOUS! It is spiritual, based on 'God as we understand Him.' It is stated this way for a good reason. This allows each person to approach their Higher Power in the manner in which he or she is comfortable with. Most people are very turned off by a wrathful God who sends his people to hell for being bad. We grew up feeling like we were defective, that we were 'bad,' and God knows we have already been through hell, so the last thing we need is to be God- fearing! We need to be God-loving. God is love, period. And He does care for us foster children, just as much as He cares for any of His children.

For some former foster children, particularly those who have been physically and/or sexually abused, and many of us were, the idea of God as a father might be very uncomfortable, especially if we were abused by a father, foster father, or any male. This is particularly damaging if it was done by a clergyman or somebody in a church that we looked up to. If the concept of you being a child of a Heavenly Father is too overwhelming for you in the beginning, then just remember that it is 'God as we understand Him,' or 'Her,' if you are uncomfortable with Him. I only use the word 'Him' as a general term, but God is ultimately Him and/or Her. The point is to be comfortable with your understanding of God. There is no hammer hitting you over the head saying, "You must believe!" In reality nobody can make us believe anything about God anyway; we can only believe as much as we can believe according to where we are spiritually.

Most former foster children suffer from low self-esteem and may find it difficult to fathom the idea of anybody 'caring' for them, but if we can begin to grasp the idea that we are worth loving, the idea of God caring for us should bring us comfort.

As foster children we felt we had no control over our lives, and as a result may feel the need to be in control as adults, but the reality is that we can only control our lives to a certain degree. The best and most certain way to be in control of our lives is by letting God care for us and guide us. He will never steer us in the wrong direction and He will always take care of us. What a huge blessing it is to finally realize that although we were abandoned as children, God will NEVER EVER abandon us!

If you can't make a decision to utterly and completely surrender your life over to the care of God, at least becoming willing. Really, the only key is willingness. All we need is the key and a decision to open the door, and once unlocked by willingness the door almost opens by itself. All is required is a mustard seed of faith. God will do the rest. The spiritual document at the end of the book should bring you hope, and hope is really what this 3rd Stepping Stone is all about. And remember that humility brings strength out of weakness. We all want assurance that God's grace can do for us what we cannot do for ourselves. God bless you all!

Now that we have become willing to surrender our lives over to the care of God, as we understand Him, we should be ready to go on to the 4th Stepping Stone.

The **Fourth Stepping Stone** is to make a fearless emotional inventory of our foster care experience to discover the nature of the damage.

Now that we have become willing to turn our lives over to the care of God as we understand Him, we are now ready to walk to the 4th Stepping Stone, which involves taking a fearless and honest inventory of our past in foster care, so that we can uncover the damage that was done to us. This won't be an easy thing for most of us to do. It can be quite painful, but if we really want to heal from our past, we must be willing to do this. We need to be real to heal and the only way out of our past is to face it. We need to go backward to move forward. Honesty, open mindedness and willingness are the essentials needed for seeking help from God for healing from our past.

It is very important that we are fearless about this, which should be easier since we now have a loving concept of God. Hopefully through that we now have come to realize that we are children of a loving Father, or for those who are uncomfortable with that concept, at least worthy human beings. Being fearless and honest is really the key to this Stepping Stone. It may seem difficult at first, but once we begin looking at our past for what it truly was, we should begin to feel freer. There is no freedom in lies or half-truths, only truth. The old saying, "The truth will set you free" is true. We need to do a fearless inventory in order to have faith for our daily living.

As for the 'nature' of the damage, this is related to the 1st Stepping Stone and recognizing that we have been injured, only now we are not only recognizing we have been injured, we are looking at how the injuries affected us.

Doing this emotional inventory is of course, emotional, and you will need emotional support more than ever during this time. For those of you who are in therapy, and a lot of former foster children are, you are no doubt doing your personal inventory there, but those of you who aren't, the FACT meetings and other former foster children should be a good source of emotional support for you.

It isn't absolutely necessary, but if you like journaling, you could do a written inventory. It might be a good idea to write down all of your losses and then write down how you think each loss has affected you. There is something about seeing your life on paper that makes it more real, and it can be very therapeutic and healing to write down your thoughts and feelings. The former foster children who shared their stories in the FACT book were basically doing the 4th Stepping Stone without even realizing it, and many of them told me they had a sense of relief after doing it. For some of them, it was the first time they had ever even told anyone about their past, let alone write about it, so it was like having a huge burden lifted off their shoulders. Most importantly, they felt validated, which is SO important for former foster children, who have pretty much felt invisible and unimportant all their lives. And even though we are talking and/or writing about very painful issues, things that gave us a low sense of self-esteem and self-worth, we should begin to have a better sense of being worthy human beings after doing this.

One thing I want to emphasize though is that if you become emotionally overwhelmed, set it aside for a bit, until you feel calmer. Former foster children have been traumatized enough, so the last thing we need is to become traumatized by our trauma! Many of us have poor boundaries, essentially meaning we don't know how to take care of ourselves, but we need to learn that we are worth taking care of in every way, including emotionally. Be gentle with yourself.

So as for the nature of the damage, think about your injuries and how you were affected by them. If you were shuffled around from home to home a foster child, do you long for stability, but still move around a lot? Are you afraid of attaching yourself to any one person, place, or thing? If your education suffered as a result of your foster care experience, how has that affected you as an adult? Do you wish you could get a better education, but have such fears of failure due to your low self-esteem that you are afraid to even try? Are your fears of abandonment such that you are stuck in a bad relationship or afraid to be in one at all? Are you afraid to make friends for fear of losing them? *'Our Unique Issues'* discusses our relationship issues. Has past sexual abuse affected your sexual relationships, making you either afraid of sex or going to the other extreme of acting out sexually? Do you have an eating disorder, being either overweight or anorectic? Do we suffer from PTSD? These are all examples of ways we might have been damaged. If we feel stuck in the past, but are afraid to move forward, this Stepping Stone should be at least the beginning of healing. Now we should be ready to move on to the 5th Stepping Stone, one that is crucial for our healing.

The **Fifth Stepping Stone** is to share this inventory with God and another human being.

The 4th and 5th Stepping Stones are really tied together and we can't do this Stepping Stone until we have completed the previous one.

As I have already mentioned while discussing the 4th Stepping Stone, we could already be doing an inventory with a therapist or somebody in FACT, or a clergyman, or friend, but if you aren't, you need to find somebody you are comfortable sharing your past with. It isn't enough to just write your past down on paper and then just let it sit, because there is not enough release this way. As it is stated, we need to share our inventory with God and another human being.

As for God, by now you should have a comfortable and comforting concept of God enough to realize He loves you and knows how much you have been hurt, but expressing these 'injuries' to God will help build a trust in your relationship with Him. He knows how much pain you have been in and how much anger and resentment you might have about your past, but loves you not just in spite of it, but because of it. Doesn't that bring you some comfort? It should. We want to do a fearless inventory, not a fearful one. Sharing our inventory with God should not only give us a sense of comfort, but it should draw us closer to God and help us to trust Him more.

It is also important to share your inventory with another human being. Although we are all children of God and ultimately our self-worth is found through Him, our human connection through Him is really what validates us, especially when we are connecting with other former foster children who understand our hurt and pain so well. Solitary self-appraisal won't be enough. Only by discussing ourselves with God and another human being, withholding nothing, will we begin to feel good about ourselves. We might try to do this with just God, believing He knows everything about us anyway, and it doesn't seem as scary as facing another human being, but until we actually sit down and speak aloud about ourselves, we won't completely clean house. Being honest with another person confirms that we have been honest with ourselves and God. Another important point is that what comes to us alone could get garbled by our own rationalization and wishful thinking. The sharing with another person is that there could be more objectiveness, whereby we can get good counsel. It is very freeing to let our damned up emotions come out. We should feel more tranquil. Many people will feel the presence of God as they never had before. It is quite likely that we will feel more connected with God and man, not feeling so isolated anymore. The terrible burden of our pasts will fall off of our shoulders and we will find rest.

If you are involved in a FACT group, this is a good place to share your inventory, either with an individual or the group at large, whatever you are comfortable with. The important thing is to be comfortable, and trust the person or persons you are sharing with, as you are really baring your soul in this Stepping Stone. It is important that you trust the person to be confidential. And as for sharing at a FACT group, "What is said there should stay there."

Now that you have done the 4th and 5th Stepping Stones, it is now time to move on to the 6th Stepping Stone, which is tied closely to these.

The **Sixth Stepping Stone** is to work through our anger, hurt, and pain.

Now that we have done the emotional inventory and shared it with God and another human being, it is time to work through our anger, hurt, and pain, which will be more emotional yet. But there is no way to truly heal without doing this. When we have emotional baggage we are carrying around, we can't really put it down until we can acknowledge our anger, hurt, and pain about the past, and work through our feelings.

For some foster children the hurt could be so deep that the emotional pain might feel overwhelming. Again, if you are in therapy or attending FACT meetings, or possible both, these are good places to vent your feelings and the get the emotional support you that you will need more than ever now.

There is a lot of ways to work through our anger, hurt, and pain, and some are mentioned in *'Healing Suggestions,'* such as punching pillows, throwing rocks outside or kicking rocks while you are walking, yelling in your car, or talking to an empty chair. Writing your feelings of anger down on paper is also a good idea, but it doesn't really release the anger physically like other ways. Allowing yourself to cry when you need to will help, and not only is it a healthy way to release emotions, but it also has a tranquilizing effect. Exercising or doing anything physical is a healthy outlet for emotions, as it releases bottled up energy, including emotional energy.

We suffered many losses as foster children and therefore have serious grieving issues. Unresolved grief can lead to a multitude of problems, including depression and even suicidal tendencies, and as mentioned in 'Our Collective Experience' and 'FACT,' we are prone to these, so it is very crucial that we allow ourselves to grieve, as it will help heal us. As former foster children, many of us remain stuck in the depression, but we aren't aware that we have so much anger, hurt, and pain. In order to begin grief work, we need to recognize what we have lost, which we should have done in our inventory. As I already mentioned, it might be beneficial to make a list of all the things you feel you lost as a foster child in order to get in touch with your feelings about them.

Since much of our depression is repressed or suppressed anger, working through anger in constructive ways will help alleviate it. Venting our anger with safe people will be both validating and releasing at the same time. It is important that we express our emotions and accept the confusion that they might generate. As we work through our grief, we will probably begin to discover deep underlying sadness over all of the losses we suffered as foster children. Many unshed tears will likely accompany this sadness and we should allow ourselves to cry when we need to. I know I talked about crying before, but this can't be stressed enough, how healing crying can be.

Be gentle with yourself. Nurture your inner child a lot while you are working through intense grief, as your hurt inner child will be especially vulnerable at such times. And remember this: only the 1st Stepping Stone, where we come to realize our powerlessness over our past, can be done with absolute perfection. The remaining 9 Stepping Stones are perfect ideals, goals to look toward, and a way of measuring our progress. It would be highly beneficial to read *Working Through Our Anger and Pain---Healing Rage*, as it will bring even further insight about anger and rage.

The last thing I want to say about this Stepping Stone is that we will probably never be completely healed from our past. We will probably always have some hurt over our past, but as we do this emotional work, the deep wounds we had before will begin to close up until all that remains are the scars, and although scars aren't pretty, we can live with them.

A good book to read while working through our anger, hurt, and pain, is **Healing Rage** by Ruth King.

Now that we have done the emotional work, we are now ready for the 7th Stepping Stone.

The **Seventh Stepping Stone** is to become aware of how our injuries hurt others and accept responsibility for our responses to the trauma we suffered.

This Stepping Stone can be a particularly difficult one to do, as we are opening up old emotional wounds, and there might be a strong temptation to attempt to sidestep it altogether, but in order for us to truly begin healing, we need to look at how our past might have influenced us to hurt others, either unintentionally or intentionally.

To become 'aware' of how our injuries hurt others, the first thing we need to do is acknowledge how we were injured, which should already be clarified by doing the 1st, 4th, and 5th Stepping Stones. And again, if there are any doubts about how you were injured, read *Our Collective Experience or FACT*.

It should be easy for most of to recognize how we were hurt by others, but recognizing how those hurts might have caused us to hurt others might not be so easy; after all, as foster children WE were the victims! It would be easy to have the tendency to resentfully focus on all the wrongs done to us as a way to escape looking at the wrongs we have done to others and to use another person's misbehavior as an excuse to forget our own. The prospect of facing, or even writing or calling people can be overwhelming.

Sometimes we can't make restitution at all, and sometimes we shouldn't, but we should make an accurate survey of our past as it has affected others. And even if somebody we harmed doesn't think they were harmed, we harm ourselves emotionally and spiritually because it continues to live in our unconscious. 'Harm' could be called 'the result of instincts in collision, which causes physical, mental, emotional, or spiritual damage to people.' While it is a fact that we were indeed victims as children, in order for us to grow and have happier lives, we shouldn't remain victims of our past. And while it is true that we should look back at our past, it is only for the purpose of moving forward.

If you are incarcerated you might be able to make the connection from the past to the present and recognize how much harm you have caused, but many former foster children won't be that aware. If we have doubts about this, I suggest we write down the ways we were injured and then after thinking about it honestly, write down how we think we might have injured others. Did we turn to alcohol and/or drugs as a way to cope? If so, while under the influence, did we commit robbery or do immoral things like be unfaithful to our husband, wife, boyfriend, or girlfriend? Were we dishonest some way in our job? If we are a parent, do we abuse our children, verbally, emotionally, or physically? Many times parents don't intend to harm their children; it just happens automatically, especially when they are under a lot of stress. Being a parent can be stressful under any circumstances, but when a person with such strong emotional issues as we foster children have, it can be compounded. Have we abandoned our children, either emotionally or physically? Some people are so afraid of parenting they just run from the responsibility. Do we owe back child support? Sometimes people will go to the other extreme and try to live through their children, which can be hurtful also because it makes the child feel suffocated and doesn't allow him or her to be their authentic self. It shouldn't come as any surprise that parenting can be an issue for us; after all, we didn't have the best role models for parents when we were children. Most people tend to pass on what was given to them and former foster children are no exception to the rule. But it is also true that if we are aware of how we have been affected by our past, we will go out of our way not to repeat it.

Accepting responsibility for our responses to the trauma we suffered doesn't mean we have to bend over backward to make amends to everyone we have harmed, but it does mean we 'acknowledge' and 'accept responsibility' for our responses. We should avoid harsh judgments of ourselves as well as others, not exaggerating our faults or theirs. We shouldn't wallow in self-remorse when making amends, but we should be forthright, sincere, and giving. We should be ready to accept the full consequence of our past actions, taking responsibility for others, and especially our own, well-being. We should have a quiet objective outlook. This will be the beginning of the end of our isolation from God and our fellowman. The purpose of this Stepping Stone isn't to make us feel 'bad.' This is implied by saying 'responses to the trauma we suffered.' The reason we hurt others is because we were hurt. ***We aren't bad people trying to be good;*** **we *are hurt people trying to heal.***

Now that we have taken responsibility for our actions, it is time to put that in action in the 8ᵗʰ Stepping Stone.

The **Eighth Stepping Stone** is to continue to take personal inventory and become willing to let go of our resentments.

In the 4th Stepping Stone we took an inventory of our past, in the 5th Stepping Stone we shared it, in the 6th Stepping Stone we worked through our anger, hurt, and pain, in the 7th Stepping Stone we took responsibility for our responses to that pain, and now what we are ultimately doing in the 8th Stepping Stone is continuing this on a daily basis, so we can be free from the 'monkey on our backs.'

As former foster children, keeping the past behind us is not always an easy thing to do; in fact, it can be quite difficult, especially when things come up that are always reminding us of our past. Maybe we are having relationship struggles, maybe we are having a difficult time parenting, maybe we are struggling to maintain sobriety, or maybe overall we just aren't doing very well and can't seem to have enough self-worth to take care of ourselves, or enough self-esteem and confidence to do the things we really want to do, such as pursue a better job or education. We are never going to perfectly get over our past; it will always be a part of us, but we hope to get beyond it. By continuing to take personal inventory, we are continually healing. Remember, we are striving for progression, not perfection.

Our inventory should be become a regular part of our everyday life that will help us with the ups and downs of life and keep us in balance. We should be willing to admit when we have done a wrong and be equally willing to forgive others who have wronged us. We begin to have true tolerance when we see that we are all emotionally ill to some degree and are often wrong. We are all human. Pray for those who harm us, even being kind and courteous, or going out of our way to understand and help them. We should show justice and mercy. If we are having trouble doing this, we should pause and quietly say, 'Not my will, but Thine, be done.' We should try to treat others as we would want to be treated. The old Golden Rule goes a long way and will bring us peace and joy. When taking a daily inventory we should strive for gratitude for our blessings, however small we might think they are, and a willingness to strive for better things tomorrow. We should search our hearts fearlessly and humbly, thanking God for all our blessings so we can sleep in good conscience.

The second part of this Stepping Stone says to 'become willing to let go of our resentments.' Notice that is says 'willing.' It doesn't say we must, or we have to, or that it is mandatory. It simply says 'willing.' It is important to tread lightly with the topic of resentments, as giving them up can be very difficult, and can even seem impossible at times, but we should at least be willing to try, and the more willing we become, the easier it should come.

Many of us former foster children have a lot of anger and resentment about our pasts, and understandably so, but as long as we are resentful about it, our past is controlling us and the whole point in doing these Stepping Stones is to help us walk across the Bridge to Healing that will ultimately give us a better sense of control in our lives. We want to walk across this Bridge to Healing into a brighter future and we can never do that with the monkey of our past on our back all the time. Resentment means to continually feel anger about something, and it eats away at you constantly. The Alcoholics Anonymous Big Book says that 'resentment is the number one offender of alcoholics' and causes more alcoholics to drink than anything else. For those of you who have or had alcohol and/or drug addictions (and it is common with former foster children), and who possibly are involved in AA or NA, you should already be aware of the danger of resentments. For those of you who aren't though, resentment is still the number one offender. Not only is it bad for us emotionally and physically, but most importantly, it is bad for us spiritually, and our spiritual condition is really the key to healing.

Having worked through our anger, hurt, and pain, we might have already given up some of our resentment, and we might even have at least a glimmer of forgiveness, which is very healing. But let me make this very clear: forgiveness is something we do for ourselves, not for those we are forgiving. And forgiving somebody doesn't mean we have to have a relationship with them; it just means we are willing to give up our resentment toward them so WE can be free. In the 4th Statement of Beliefs it says 'We believe we can be reconciled with those who injured us.' Some people who read that may interpret that as restoring us to a relationship, but that isn't necessarily true. What it is really saying is that we can be reconciled within ourselves toward those who hurt us. The 5th Statement of Beliefs says 'We believe releasing those who injured us leads to healing,' which is really what the 7th Stepping Stone is saying. By releasing them, we are letting go of their power over us, which leads to our own healing.

I know is easier said than done, but we need to be willing to do this in order for *US* to heal.

The **Ninth Stepping Stone** is to seek through prayer and meditation to improve our relationship with God, as we understand Him, praying only for knowledge of His will for us and the power to carry that out.

This Stepping Stone is a continuance of the 3rd Stepping Stone, when we turned our lives over to the care of God, as we understand Him, but it goes further, to seek through prayer and meditation for the purpose of getting closer to God, praying for guidance in our daily lives, seeking knowledge of His will for us and the power to carry that out.

Since we all have our own personal relationship with God, we also have our own personal ways of seeking through meditation and prayer to improve it. There is no wrong or right way to do this. The important thing is to be comfortable in our approach, and most important is what is in our hearts. God hears our hearts, whether we are silent with Him or sing, shout, or even get angry at Him. And yes, we can get angry at God! He understands very well our anger, hurt, and pain from the past and He understands all the emotional struggles we have. He even understands our reluctance to trust Him enough to surrender our lives to Him.

There is no such thing as perfectly doing this, and sometimes we might take two steps back from God and then take a step forward to Him again, but the important thing is to 'seek.' We are seeking in this 9th Stepping Stone, maybe not absolutely finding anything, but the more we seek, we will find. Again, all we need is a mustard seed of faith and it will grow.

When we pray, we are talking to God; when we are meditating, we are listening to Him. We may feel like we are just talking to thin air sometimes, but just do it anyway. He hears us anyway, whether we think

He has or not. Prayer is the rising of the heart and mind to God, which includes meditation. Prayer is a petition to God. As for meditating, we should just try to be quiet, if only for a few minutes. We probably won't hear God's voice, but we might have an intuitive thought about something, or just an overall calmer feeling. Prayer and meditation is as essential as air and sunshine. We deprive our minds and emotions of vital support when we don't pray and meditate. Our soul needs it. We all need God's light, His strength, and grace. It is a foundation for life. One of the greatest benefits of prayer and meditation is the sense of belonging we get. We don't view the world as being so hostile. We don't feel like we are just lost and frightened and floundering about without a purpose. When we begin to see a glimpse of God's will in our lives and see truth, justice, and love as real things, we aren't so disturbed by the evil around us, even the evil from our pasts. We believe that God lovingly and protectively watches over all of His children. We begin to really feel that all will be well when we are in a relationship with God. Meditation and prayer is a big step toward God, and the most important one we will ever take. God is the best source of emotional stability we can ever have. He can give us the inner strength and peace we so need.

There are many ways to pray and meditate. Meditation has no boundaries. It is an individual venture, but the intent is always the same---to improve our conscious contact and our relationship with God 'as we understand Him.' It deepens our connectedness with God and ourselves. It will help give us love, grace, and wisdom and will help balance us emotionally. We might do it formally in a church or at a prayer group, or we might pray and meditate by reading inspirational books. There are many prayer and meditation books available that can give us hope, inspiration, and deep insights about life.

What we are doing is seeking to improve our relationship with God. Improve implies imperfection, not perfection. Try to remember, progress, not perfection. God is patient with us, as we should be with ourselves. And remember, if our Higher Power has restored some hope, order, and sanity to our lives, and has enabled us to live with some serenity, then He is worth knowing.

The **Tenth Stepping Stone** is to have a spiritual awakening as a result of these Stepping Stones, to reach out to other former foster children, and use these principles in our lives.

After having done the previous nine Stepping Stones, we should come to some sort of spiritual awakening. Although it is possible to have a sudden spiritual awakening, most people experience it slowly over a period of time. Many people feel as though they have found an inner resource, which they conceive as a Power greater than themselves. Religious people might call it "God consciousness," but whatever we choose to call it, most people believe the awareness of a Power greater than them is the essence of spiritual experience. We may begin to have more spiritual qualities, such as patience, tolerance, unselfishness, peace of mind, honesty, and above all else, love, and although we made ourselves ready to receive it, it is a free gift, one that we are now ready to share with others.

Honesty, open mindedness, and willingness are the essentials needed for seeking help from God for healing from our past.

Reaching out to other former foster children is the key to the end of our isolation. And by reaching out to others we don't feel so imprisoned by our past. When we reach out to others, we not only help them; we help ourselves. Their load becomes lighter and so does ours. There is something about being with kindred folks that make us feel more connected, with each other, and with God. This saying says it all: ***"I sought my God, but my God eluded me; I sought my soul, but my soul I could not see; I sought my brother and found all three."***

The last part of this stepping stone says to 'use these principles in our lives,' which means all of the Ten Stepping Stones. We will never do all this perfectly, and as I said before, 'progress, not perfection.' Don't be too hard on yourself when find yourself falling back into the past somehow. The past is a part of us and will always be there, but by the Grace of God and each other, 'together' we can walk the Bridge to Healing.

The Ten Traditions

1. Personal healing depends upon FACT unity. We are fostered adult children TOGETHER. FACT leaders should be guided in the spirit of service, for they are only trusted servants of the whole; they do not govern. Our common welfare should always be our number one priority.
2. The ultimate authority for our FACT group purpose is a loving God 'as we understand Him,' who may express Himself in our group conscience.
3. FACT is for ALL former foster children. The only requirement for FACT membership is a desire to heal from our past as foster children; therefore, we should never refuse any former foster child who has a desire for healing. Hence our members should include ALL who wish to do so. Also, FACT is never dependent upon conformity or money. Any two or three former foster children who gather together for the purpose of healing may call themselves a FACT group, providing they have no other affiliation as a group.
4. Except in matters that affect other FACT groups or FACT as a whole, each group should be autonomous. Regarding its own affairs, the only authority each FACT group should be responsible to is its own conscience. But other neighboring FACT groups should be consulted when their welfare is of concern due to another group's plans. Common welfare is paramount; therefore, no individual or group should ever do anything that could greatly affect FACT as a whole without consulting with Carol Lucas, the founder of FACT at <u>carolannlucas@hotmail.com</u> or in the event of her death, whoever she has been appointed to take her place.
5. The primary purpose of each FACT group is to carry the message of hope and healing to other former foster children. First and foremost, we are Fostered Adult Children Together and we should never let anything distract us from that.

6. FACT groups should never be a business, lending, financing, or endorsing the FACT name to any related facility or outside enterprise. We should not allow problems of money, property, and prestige to divert us from our primary purpose. A FACT group should not bind itself to anyone. Although a FACT group may cooperate with anyone, never so far as actual or even implied endorsement or affiliation. Also, FACT should forever be non-professional, never counseling former foster children for hire or fees, or paying people to do the 10th Stepping Stone. Reaching out to other former foster children should always be a matter of the heart, not of monetary value.

7. FACT is self-supporting through its own contributions.

8. FACT should never be too organized, with each group having the least possible organization. The best way to avoid problems is by rotating leadership, which promotes universal respect and allows each person to feel useful and part of the whole.

9. A FACT group or member should never publically voice any opinions or views on controversial issues, especially those pertaining to politics or sectarian religion. FACT does not oppose anyone. This may be difficult for some to do since so many former foster children were hurt by the foster care system, but we need to strive to be neutral. But if a public figure, such as a professional working in the foster care system approaches us, we are free to speak.

10. Personal anonymity should be a choice, but not a necessity. If someone chooses to be anonymous, it should be respected. This is a good reminder that we should always place principles before personalities and have a genuine humility, to always be thankful for our blessings from the Father of us all. All former foster children who attend FACT meetings should respect this.

Goals of Recovery

As former foster children, we believe there are certain goals we need to pursue in order to secure a better future. These goals are:

Make better decisions in our lives by becoming aware of how the past affects our decisions today

Become more patient and tolerant, especially with ourselves

Learn to love ourselves in a more wholesome and healthy way

Gain better self-worth and self-esteem

Cut the cords of shame that binds us by realizing that the abuses of the past are not our fault

Improve the quality of our life and our standard of living

Enhance the quality of our social and intimate relationships

Be able to reach out to others who feel lost or abandoned

Improve our relationship with God, as we understand Him

Realize that our Heavenly Father will NEVER abandon us

It is our hope that as we endeavor to reach these goals, we will begin to cast our own shadow rather than live in it.

Healing Suggestions

These are suggestions that could be helpful on your path to healing:

JOURNALING: Keep a private journal and when you feel the need to vent feelings or get a perspective on a troubling issue in your life, just begin writing and you will be able to make more sense out of whatever is troubling you.

WRITING LETTERS: Write letters to people in your past who you feel harmed you. This is an excellent way to constructively deal with anger. You can burn the letter after you've done if you wish.

INVENTORY: Do a thorough inventory of your past, including the people who harmed you, how you were affected by it, and how you may have retaliated. Share this inventory with someone you trust, such as a good friend, a therapist, or a priest or minister.

THERAPY: Seek additional help in therapy if you feel you need it. It is a good way to get new insights about yourself.

EXCHANGE PHONE NUMBERS: It is important to have people who you feel comfortable with when things come up from day to day for which you need support.

SELF-WORTH AFFIRMATIONS: This can be very beneficial for your self-esteem. As you begin to declare some positive things about yourself, you may begin to believe them. Here are a few suggestions for self-affirmations:

I am a good person with a good heart.
I am worthy of all the blessings I receive.
I am an attractive person.
I am worthy to be loved.

I am a loving person.
I am safe.
I deserve to have boundaries.

PRAYING: When we pray we are talking to our Higher Power. When we begin to see our prayers answered, it increases our faith and also our self-esteem, as we begin to feel worthy of God's blessings.

MEDITATING: Meditating is listening to our Higher Power, which has a calming effect and builds a closer relationship with God, however we understand Him to be. Listening to meditation tapes is also very relaxing.

NURTURE YOUR INNER CHILD: It is very important to nurture your inner child, as our inner child was wounded when we were little and suffered much trauma. Our inner child was neglected years ago and we need to give him or her recognition, validation, and love. Here are ways to nurture your inner child:

Hug a teddy bear when you feel insecure.
Tell your inner child you love him/her and will never abandon him/her.
Take a warm bubble bath.
Give your inner child a pet to love, such as a dog or cat.
Go for a walk and enjoy nature.
Be silly and laugh. Watch a funny movie or act goofy.
It is a good way to lighten up and not be so serious.
Take it easy. Be gentle with yourself. Nurture yourself.
Sit in the sun and read a good book.
Have a hobby, such as gardening.

SEEK SUPPORT FOR SEXUAL ABUSE: If you were sexually abused, we encourage you to seek additional help for this, either in FACT with someone else who was sexually abused, in a sexual abuse support group, or with a qualified sexual abuse counselor.

WORK THROUGH EMOTIONS: As we begin to feel our feelings that many times have been buried, we need to find ways that will be helpful in venting them. One of our strongest emotions is anger and many of us will have a tremendous amount of it about the unfair circumstances of our past and the people who harmed us. It is very important to work through our anger and we need to have healthy ways to do this. Working through anger can be a bridge to healing and can even lead us to the beginnings of forgiveness. Here are some constructive ways to work through anger:

Punching pillows
Throwing rocks outside or kicking rocks while you are walking
Yelling in your car
Talking to an empty chair and pretending it is whoever hurt you
Writing your anger down on paper
Crying---Allow yourself to cry when you need to. Not only is it a healthy way to release emotions, but it also has a tranquilizing effect.
Exercising---Doing anything physical, especially running or walking---Exercise releases bottled up energy and will raise your endorphin level, which has a calming, yet uplifting effect.
Be grateful---Make a gratitude list of all the things for which you can be grateful. Try to see your cup as half full instead of half empty. This helps a person feel happier.
Become more health-conscious---More and more evidence suggests that nutrition affects our mental and emotional states, so learning proper nutritional habits is essential in maintaining a healthy body, mind and spirit.
Reading---Read recovery books. Two good ones are *Trauma and Recovery* and *Healing Rage*

GRIEVING: As foster children we suffered many losses and therefore have serious grieving issues. Unresolved grief can lead to a multitude of problems, including depression and even suicidal tendencies. It is crucial that we allow ourselves to grieve because this will help us to heal. As former foster children, many of us remain stuck in the depression, but aren't aware that of the anger and hurt behind it. In order to begin grief work, we need to recognize what we have lost. It could be helpful to make a list of all of your losses and then write down how you think each loss has affected you, emotionally and otherwise. Since much of our depression is repressed or suppressed anger, working through anger in constructive ways will help alleviate it. Venting our anger with safe people will also be beneficial and will be both validating and releasing at the same time. It is important that we express our emotions and accept the confusion that these emotions generate. Emotions can be uncomfortable, but they won't kill us. An additional place besides FACT to work through grief could be a grief group or with a qualified therapist. As we work through our grief, we will begin to discover deep underlying sadness over all of the losses we suffered as fostered children. Many unshed tears will probably accompany this sadness and we should allow ourselves to cry when we need to. Nurture your inner child a lot when you are working through intense grief, as your inner child will be especially vulnerable at such times.

Here is a list of self-help books that could be helpful in your healing process:

BOUNDARIES---by Dr. Henry Cloud and Dr. John Townsend
HEALING RAGE---by Ruth King, M.A.
HEALING THE SHAME THAT BINDS YOU---by John Bradshaw
LETTING GO OF SHAME---by Ronald Potter and Patricia Potter-Efron
SELF-PARENTING---by Dr. John K. Pollard
THE COURAGE TO HEAL---by Ellen Bass and Laura Davis
THE ROAD LESS TRAVELED---by Scott Peck
THE SURVIVOR PERSONALITY---by Al Siebert
TRAUMA AND RECOVERY---by Judith Herman
WHY YOU DO THE THINGS YOU DO---by Dr. Tim Clinton and Dr. Gary Sibcy

Here are some resources for former foster youth:

www.fc2success.org/knowledge-center/groups-and-support/
www.thruproject.org
www.fosterclub.com
www.thenewfostercare.com
www.unitedfriends.org
www.ifoster.org
www.healthchoice.pa.gov/formerfosteryouth
www.michigan.gov/fyit
www.fostercarealumni.org
www.fosteringsuccessmichigan.com

SELF-HELP SUPPORT GROUPS: There are various self-help support groups available that could help in recovery from various issues. If you are an alcoholic and/or drug addict you can attend Alcoholics Anonymous or Narcotics Anonymous. There is also Al-Anon for people who are affected by alcoholics and/or drug addicts in their lives, and there is Adult Children of Alcoholics for people who came from alcoholic homes. There are many addictions that people have and there are support groups for all of them--- Overeaters Anonymous, Gamblers Anonymous, and support groups for Sex Addiction. There is also Codependents Anonymous and support groups for Grief. And last, but not least, there is FACT. For anyone interested in forming FACT meetings, here are some useful ideas for getting started:

The first thing you need to do is find other former foster children who are interested in attending FACT meetings. You could do this by completing the provided FACT flyer with information about your desire to hear from those interested in attending FACT and posting these flyers in supermarkets, community centers, foster-care agencies, libraries, supermarkets, community centers, schools, churches, other support groups, and your local self-help clearinghouse. It's also good to advertise by word of mouth.

Once you have a few people interested, you could begin meeting in someone's home. As membership increases the members may decide to hold meetings in a more public location. Consider contacting your local churches, community centers, counseling centers, hospitals, college campuses, and foster-care agencies.

After the meeting location has been determined, you can use the provided FACT flyer by completing it with information about your agreed upon meeting time, location, and contact numbers, then post these flyers in the various places previously mentioned.

Another good way to advertise is with free public broadcasting, which is available through many local television channels, cable companies, and radio stations. Just contact them to find out the exact procedure required. You can also advertise by completing the provided FACT press release with your meeting information and sending copies to your local newspapers.

You're on your way!

If you need any further assistance please contact Carol Lucas at carolannlucas@hotmail.com

FACT Meeting Format

Hello everyone and welcome to FACT. We would especially like to welcome any newcomers. If you feel comfortable telling us your name, please do so. We would like to acknowledge you and encourage you to keep coming back.

MISSION STATEMENT

OUR MISSION

FACT is an alliance of adults who as children were separated from their parents and lived in foster care. We seek support and mutual understanding of our unique problems in coping with life and learning how to find our place in the world. There are no dues or fees for membership. The only requirement for attendance at a FACT meeting is a desire to heal from our past by sharing our experience, strength and hope. FACT is not a replacement for individual counseling and strongly encourages people to seek additional help if necessary. If everyone is comfortable doing so, we'd like to hold hands and say a short FACT prayer.

As we unite, no longer is there a sense of isolation. By reaching out to one another, we hope to find strength in recovering from our unique issues as former fostered and abandoned children, for the purpose of moving into a brighter future.

(Ask one person to read HEALING)

HEALING

The mission of FACT is to help former foster children walk a new path that will build a bridge to healing. The **First Stepping Stone** on this path is to recognize we have been injured from our foster care experience, that we are powerless over our past and our lives are unmanageable. The **Second Stepping Stone** is to come to realize we can not heal alone, that only a Power greater than ourselves could restore order, hope, and sanity to our lives. The **Third Stepping Stone** is to make a decision to turn our lives over to the care of God as we understand Him. The **Fourth Stepping Stone** is to make a searching and fearless emotional inventory of our foster care experience to discover the nature of the damage. The **Fifth Stepping Stone** is to share this inventory with God and another human being. The **Sixth Stepping Stone** is to work through our anger, hurt, and pain. The **Seventh Stepping Stone** is to become aware of how our injuries hurt others and accept responsibility for our responses to the trauma we suffered. The **Eighth Stepping Stone** is to continue to take personal inventory and become willing to let go of our resentments. The **Ninth Stepping Stone** is to seek through prayer and meditation to improve our relationship with God as we understand Him, praying only for knowledge of His will for us and the power to carry that out. The **Tenth Stepping Stone** is to have a spiritual awakening as a result of these stepping stones and to reach out to other former foster children and practice these principles in our lives.

(Ask one person to read STATEMENT OF BELIEFS)

STATEMENT OF BELIEFS

WE BELIEVE there is hope, through God as we understand Him.

WE BELIEVE and accept that we are powerless over the circumstances of our past.

WE BELIEVE in healing from our childhood injuries.

WE BELIEVE we begin to heal by facing our anger toward people who injured us.

WE BELIEVE releasing those who injured us leads to healing.

WE BELIEVE we have a rightful place in the family of man.

WE BELIEVE we are neither slaves of the past nor masters of the future.

WE BELIEVE our isolation ends when we share our pain.

WE BELIEVE that in finding others who are lost we find ourselves.

WE BELIEVE there is purpose with God.

Each Stepping Stone on this bridge to healing is an integral part of the healing process. It is our hope that as we work through these stepping stones we can come to embrace all of these beliefs.

(Ask one person to read GOALS OF RECOVERY)

GOALS OF RECOVERY

As former foster children, we believe there are certain goals we need to pursue in order to secure a better future. These goals are:

> Make better decisions in our lives by becoming aware of how the past affects our decisions today
> Become more patient and tolerant, especially with ourselves
> Learn to love ourselves in a more wholesome and healthy way
> Gain better self-worth and self-esteem
> 5. Cut the cords of shame that binds us by realizing that the abuses of the past are not our fault
> Improve the quality of our life and our standard of living
> Enhance the quality of our social and intimate relationships
> Be able to reach out to others who feel lost or abandoned
> Improve our relationship with God, as we understand Him
> Realize that our Heavenly Father will NEVER abandon us

It is our hope that as we endeavor to reach these goals, we will begin to cast our own shadow rather than live in it.

Are there any announcements concerning FACT?

On the tables are list of FACT discussion issues that relate to the 10 Stepping Stones. In each meeting we will focus on one particular Stepping Stone and discuss Related Issues, Goals of Recovery, and Statement of Beliefs.

The **Stepping Stone** that will be discussed tonight is __________.

Since FACT is a new support group, things may not be perfected yet. We want everyone here to feel a part of FACT and we encourage anyone who might have any new ideas for FACT to share them with us after the meeting. We value your input and respect your opinions.

As stated in the group rules, there is no cross-talking allowed during the meeting. If you desire feedback from someone, wait until the meeting is finished. It is also crucial that what we discuss in these meetings remain confidential. We also ask that you be considerate of how much time you spend talking so that everyone has a chance to share.

There are refreshments on the counter for everyone. Feel free to help yourself. The meeting will last 1 and ½ hours. At the end of the meeting, all who are comfortable doing so will hold hands and say the Serenity Prayer. Enjoy you meeting.

ENDING PRAYER FOR FACT MEETINGS

SERENITY PRAYER

God grant me the…Serenity to accept the things I can not change
Courage to change the things I can, and the
Wisdom to know the difference
Patience for the things that take time
Appreciation for all that we have, and
Tolerance for those with different struggles
Freedom to live beyond the limitations of our past ways, the
Ability to feel your love for us and our love for each other and the
Strength to get up and try again even when we feel it is hopeless.

Group Rules

FACT is a self-help support group, not a reference agency or resource center, but we do not discourage individual members from assisting others.

FACT is for anyone who is a former foster child.

No alcohol or drugs are allowed in FACT meetings. We will not turn away those who are currently abusing drugs or alcohol, but because your addiction can only interfere with your recover from FACT issues, we strongly recommend you seek additional help for your addiction.

Each person should be allowed (but not required) to speak.

No one should get up to leave while a FACT meeting is in progress unless it is an emergency.

We are free to express our emotions as long as it isn't done violently.

No feedback or cross-talking is allowed during FACT meetings. If feedback is desired, wait until the meeting is over.

Do not have side communication; it is discourteous to whoever is talking.

No hugging or touching is allowed unless it is desired.

If someone is crying, don't offer the person a tissue or pat the person on the back (this could suggest to them that they shouldn't be crying, which is non-validating and could interfere with their emotional healing).

Never ridicule someone for his or her feelings. Be validating towards other people's pain.

We listen and express our feelings. We do not prescribe, diagnose, judge, or give advice. We offer suggestions if they are sought.

What we share is confidential and we have a right to remain anonymous if we so choose.

We each share responsibility for making the group work. We have no group leader.

FACT meetings will be limited to 1 and ½ hours.

10 Stepping Stones
And The Bridge To Healing

1. We recognize we have been injured from our foster care experience, that we are powerless over our past and our lives are unmanageable.
2. Come to realize we can not heal alone, that only a Power greater than ourselves could restore order, hope, and sanity to our lives.
3. Make a decision to turn our lives over to the care of God as we understand Him.
4. Make a searching and fearless emotional inventory of our foster care experience to discover the nature of the damage.
5. Share this inventory with God and another human being.
6. Work through our anger, hurt, and pain.
7. Become aware of how our injuries hurt others and accept responsibility for our responses to the trauma we suffered.
8. Continue to take personal inventory and become willing to let go of our resentments.
9. Seek through prayer and meditation to improve our relationship with God as we understand Him, praying only for knowledge of His will for us and the power to carry that out.
10. Having had a spiritual awakening as result of these Stepping Stones, we reach out to other former foster children and practice these principles in our lives.

Each Stepping Stone on this bridge to healing is an integral part of the healing process. In each meeting we will focus on one particular Stepping Stone and discuss related issues.

RELATED DISCUSSION ISSUES

1. Isolation and loneliness
2. Loss and grief
3. Anger
4. Sense of failure
5. Abandonment
6. Poor social interaction
7. Poor parenting skills
8. Instability (moving a lot)
9. Vocational problems
10. Educational problems
11. Sexual abuse
12. Self-esteem
13. Stress disorders
14. Financial problems
15. Guilt
16. Independence versus dependence
17. Sense of being failed by the foster-care system
18. Alcohol and substance abuse problems
19. How to break the cycle of foster care
20. Difficulty with emotions
21. Trust
22. Shame
23. Depression
24. Difficulty believing in and/or trusting God
25. Domestic problems
26. Criminal behavior

Statement Of Beliefs

WE BELIEVE there is hope, through God as we understand Him.

WE BELIEVE and accept that we are powerless over the circumstances of our past.

WE BELIEVE in healing from our childhood injuries.

WE BELIEVE we begin to heal by facing our anger toward people who injured us.

WE BELIEVE releasing those who injured us leads to healing.

WE BELIEVE we have a rightful place in the family of man.

WE BELIEVE we are neither slaves of the past nor masters of the future.

WE BELIEVE our isolation ends when we share our pain.

WE BELIEVE that in finding others who are lost we find ourselves.

WE BELIEVE there is purpose with God.

We are the lost and abandoned children of this world. We do not wish to come before the bar of man as yet another voice clamoring for rights. We make no claim in any earthly court for our birthrights which have been taken. We come from many lands and speak many languages, but our stories are remarkably the same. Our journeys have been through the darkest streets of the soul you can imagine. Often there was little light, neither from man who injured us, nor from God who seemed to stand by in divine indifference to our suffering. The petitions of our hearts fell on what seemed the deaf ears of a callous universe that had cast us away. For us the ties of blood and family were severed. For us, home was no longer a present place of safety and a loving refuge, but rather a hoped for destination we might find some day. Like so many tiny boats adrift on the ocean, we have looked long for the lighthouse of our homeland.

Where once we lived in the hope and expectation of rights conferred by man, rights which we have learned are only promises to be kept or broken according to earthly whims and the arbitrary exercise of power, we who have been lost in that maelstrom now claim the inexhaustible grace and love of a Higher Power, our loving Creator, the Source of all goodness Whom by many names we call God. Where once we sought the right not to be deprived of a family and wandered in the hazards of this world in search of a home, we now find a safe haven in the fellowship of the Spirit. Where once we felt abandoned and had lost all trust, now we walk in harmony with each other in the assurance of safety. Where once our rights to love and affection were taken, they are now restored in and by God. Where once we were deprived of earthly food, we are now sustained by Spirit in the promise that all gifts we have need of will be provided. Where once we could not speak in defense of ourselves, our voice in Truth now speaks for us. Where once we lived in the exile of a hardened heart, now we are joined in grace to others. Where once we sought emancipation from the bondage of man, now we claim the right to heal in the lasting peace of kinship with God.